Friedemann Kainer | René Repasi (eds.)

Trade Relations after Brexit

HART
PUBLISHING

Nomos

The Deutsche Nationalbibliothek lists this publication in the Deutsche Nationalbibliografie; detailed bibliographic data are available on the Internet at http://dnb.d-nb.de

ISBN: HB (Nomos)   978-3-8487-5133-4
        ePDF (Nomos)   978-3-8452-9334-9

British Library Cataloguing-in-Publication Data
A catalogue record for this book is available from the British Library.

ISBN: HB (Hart)   978-1-5099-2551-3

Library of Congress Cataloging-in-Publication Data
Kainer, Friedemann / Repasi, René
Trade Relations after Brexit
Friedemann Kainer / René Repasi (eds.)
415 pp.
Includes bibliographic references and index.

ISBN   978-3-8487-5133-4 (Print)
        978-3-8452-9334-9 (ePDF)

1st Edition 2019
© Nomos Verlagsgesellschaft, Baden-Baden, Germany 2019. Printed and bound in Germany.

Table of Contents

Trade Relations after Brexit: An Introduction

Friedemann Kainer & René Repasi

The trade relations between the EU and the UK are intense. The economies of both are deeply interwoven. In 2017 the EU accounted for 44% of the UK exports and 53% of the imports.[1] The UK had in 2017 an overall trade deficit with the EU of around 78 billion Euro. Whilst the number dropped in the last decades in relation to exports from 54.6% in 1999 to 44% in 2017, the number in relation to imports remained stable with 56% in 1999. These numbers make clear that any changes to the legal framework defining the trade relations between the EU and the UK will have a significant impact on trade relations that are meaningful for the UK.

As it stands today, trade relations between the EU and the UK will have to be completely rearranged. This is the result of the referendum of 23 June 2016, which was initiated at the suggestion of then Prime Minister David Cameron and paved the way for the UK's withdrawal from the EU with a 51.9% 'leave' result. Although the referendum was only advisory in nature and does not bind Parliament, Theresa May, who took the office of Prime Minister soon after the resignation of David Cameron, was determined to deliver 'Brexit' and to fulfil the will of the people as expressed by the majority in the referendum vote. Following the vote, there was no debate about the promises made by withdrawal campaign, which was by no means completely committed to the truth. This is astonishing because key elements of the leave campaign were declared untrue already days after the referendum took place. Nor were the nations of the United Kingdom given a say. The latter particularly affects the Good Friday Agreement, which has constitutional status in Britain and ensures peace in Northern Ireland.

Even if the result of the referendum has not been and is not questioned, it only gives an indication of the direction of the political path that the UK has to take: it has to leave the European Union. Important questions as to what kind of 'Brexit' should take place were not addressed by the referendum. The will of the people voiced therefore that the UK should leave the

---

1 These and the following numbers are taken from *House of Commons*, Statistics on EU-UK trade, Briefing Paper, No. 7851, 11 January 2019.

EU, but the future shape of political and economic cooperation remained completely unclear and is still extremely controversial today. Key issues, such as the consequences of a withdrawal for the fragile balance of communities in Northern Ireland, were scarcely touched on in the referendum campaigns and even less publicly discussed.

The actual design of the UK's withdrawal lay with politicians framed by the two-stage withdrawal procedure under Article 50 of the EU-Treaty. The withdrawal clause was by no means an integral part of the original Treaty of Rome, which was concluded for an indefinite period of time. It originated textually from the 'Convention on the Preparation of a Constitution for the European Union' and was put into force unchanged by the Lisbon Treaty in 2009. The provision allows each Member State to initiate a withdrawal procedure by means of a unilateral declaration. The withdrawal procedure consists essentially of two periods. The first step is to negotiate a withdrawal treaty within a period of two years, which sets out the details of the withdrawal by taking into account the framework for the future relationship between the withdrawing Member State and the EU. While the withdrawal treaty therefore essentially contains transitional provisions and rules dealing with enduring legacy issues stemming from the period of membership, the withdrawing State and the EU only negotiate their future relationship after the withdrawal has come into force – on the basis of a policy document negotiated and agreed upon in the first stage, which sets out the prospective framework of the future relationship.

In the particular case of the withdrawal of the UK from the EU, the issue of a future external border between the EU and the UK on the Irish island became particularly pertinent. In order to prevent any revival of the Northern Irish conflict, a hard border on the Irish island with physical border controls had to be avoided by all means. Hence, the UK had to accept a so-called 'backstop' solution that was designed to prevent a controlled customs border in Northern Ireland. This highly controversial 'backstop' led to the withdrawal agreement failing in the House of Commons in three votes. At the time of writing and shortly after the announcement of Theresa May's resignation as Prime Minister, it is unlikely that the withdrawal agreement will find a majority in Parliament.

Irrespective of whether or not it is still possible to ratify and to subsequently implement a withdrawal agreement and irrespective of whether there will be a 'hard Brexit' or a variation of the withdrawal agreement, it remains a permanent task for both the EU and the UK to provide a stable and lasting basis for trade and future political relations between them. It can be considered certain that, in the event the current version of the withdrawal agreement will be ratified, the envisaged transition period of 21 months (as planned until 31 December 2020) will not suffice for the negotiation and ratification of an agreement covering the future relationship between the EU and the UK; on the contrary, the negotiations are unlikely to last any shorter than in the case of CETA, for example. This is supported by the UK's antagonistic claim to largely regain sovereignty on the one hand and to continue frictionless trade on the other, despite the current approximation of laws between the EU and the UK in a 45-year history of joint integration.

This book discusses the negotiation process for a future agreement between the EU and the UK. It deals with specific reference questions in order to present solutions and arguments for the negotiations. What could be the basis for a free trade agreement? What international precedents could the agreement be based on? What concrete problems will arise and how could they be tackled? What solutions are available to combine the conflicting ends of free trade and sovereignty?

Against the backdrop of these overarching questions, the book is divided into three parts, dealing with, first, the current state of affairs, second, the principle foundations, on which any legal framework of the future relationship will be based, and, third, specific trade-related issues that will have to be addressed by a future trade agreement between the EU and the UK.

The first part gives attention to the current state of affairs. Here *Elmar Brok,* being a member of the European Parliament's Brexit Steering Group, and *Anne Liekenbrock* develop the basic lines of the EU 27's negotiating position, drawing on the (pre)history of the European Union, the goals of the British Brexit movement, the negotiating goals of the UK Government and the EU's response and strategy. In particular, it outlines the course of negotiations to date within the framework of the withdrawal agreement. *Patrick Minford* as a member of the 'Brexit' supporting group 'Economists for Free Trade' contrasts this with the view of the 'Leave' campaign. To this end, he sets out a very different story of the European integration from the perspective of the UK, an organisation that is transforming itself from an economic community into a political union and taking over more and more power and control. In the editors' opinion, the understanding of this position is essential for a successful negotiation strategy. Unless a moderate political camp prevails in Westminster, this narrative and the *Minford* idea of untying economic chains will stand in the way of closer ties between the UK and the EU. The economic promises of a 'Brexit' as hard as possible may be highly exaggerated, but they are part of the 'Brexit' movement. *Jürgen Matthes* counters this economic minority position with a series of arguments that put the idea of a 'Global Britain' into perspective and draws a rather gloomy overall economic picture of Britain as a result of its withdrawal from the EU. *Matthes* also discusses the – relatively manageable – economic consequences of Brexit for Germany and the EU. This perspective is of great importance for the negotiation process because it allocates the negotiating powers in accordance with the economic interests that are at stake. Depending on which economic view prevails on the part of the British negotiation team, a harder or softer negotiating line may be expected. Recent economic estimates by the British Government itself point in the second direction.

The second part of the book turns to the foundations for the future trade relationship between the EU and the UK. *Christoph Herrmann* looks at the WTO. Trading under the conditions defined by WTO law is the absolute fallback framework for the trade relations between the EU and the UK since both are fully-fledged members of the WTO. In this context he refers to the issue of schedules of concessions and tariff rate quotas that are currently held by the EU for both. 'Brexit', so *Herrmann*, will require a renewal or revision of these schedules and their notification to the WTO, which will trigger lengthy and cumbersome negotiations with the other WTO members as changes to the EU schedules due to 'Brexit' must be considered as changes to the value of concessions. Due to the generally pragmatic approach pursued in the WTO and by its members issues that have to be addressed at the level of WTO law will most likely be solved after 'Brexit' so that the WTO will form a minimum framework within which the EU and the UK will be able to trade with each other. Any further step towards more integrated markets between the UK and the EU will require a tailor-made free trade agreement. *René Repasi* doubts, however, that any free trade agreement between the EU and the UK can uphold the level of market integration as it currently stands under the conditions of EU membership. He explains that the instrument of a traditional international law agreement does not allow for far-reaching mutual recognition obligations as such agreements cannot provide for the necessary mechanisms to avoid a run to the bottom in terms of standards. This inability is due to the fact that only autonomous institutions with own decision-making powers that are sufficiently democratically legitimatised can provide for such mechanisms. The mere *ex ante* ratification and possible *ex post* approval of decisions taken by Treaty bodies is not sufficient to legitimise such far-reaching decision-making powers. He therefore concludes that any agreement between the EU and the UK will fall short of EU membership and therefore leads to less market integration than currently under the conditions of the EU internal market. Nevertheless, it is the objective of both sides to make the future economic objectives as ambitious as possible, in particular, in order to ensure the free movement of goods and services and, in particular, not to jeopardise the supply chains necessary for the economy based on the division of labour.

On this basis, *Friedemann Kainer* examines the need for a far-reaching alignment of standards between the EU and the UK. He develops the thesis that ambitious market access rights, as provided for in the EU by the fundamental freedoms, are only compatible with the EU competition principle if both parties guarantee a level playing field and thus avoid competition distorting regulatory cost difference. In his view, the scope of this regulatory alignment must go beyond the directly affected product standards and also include general standards in areas such as the environment, social affairs and labour, etc. *Kainer* proposes to make sector-specific market access dependent on a sufficient alignment of standards in future and takes the EEA as a model in this respect. A newly created international authority is to be responsible for the necessary administration. He also shows that such an approach is consistent with the more general objective of avoiding incentives ("cherry-picking") to leave the European Union.

The third part of the book looks at specific issues that a future trade agreement between the EU and the UK has to address given the UK's current fully-fledged integration in the EU's internal market. *Armin Cuyvers* speaks about free movement of goods post-Brexit and looks at the triangle of conflicting objectives in the shape of 'sovereignty', 'trade' and the 'Northern-Irish peace'. He makes clear that all proposals that are currently discussed fall short of realising all three objectives. Finding an optimal solution that keeps the Irish border open for goods in terms of customs and regulatory alignment, that takes sovereignty seriously and avoids the divisibility of the four freedoms requires both the UK and the EU to reconsider their fundamental policy objectives. If not, he predicts that any solution that is found will harm the free movement of goods. *Gavin Barrett* turns thereafter to the freedom of services. He places the freedom of services in its political context in the sense that providing cross-border services requires cross-border free movement of natural persons, who provide services – something that the UK excludes. Furthermore, leniency on the part of the EU with regard to the future regime on free movement of services would set incentives for future disintegration of the EU as it could show to other EU-sceptic countries that they can get the benefits of the internal market without the institutions that protect it. After having analysed the various policy documents and proposals for a future trade arrangement on services he concludes that everything currently proposed falls short of what a fully-fledged EU membership can offer. That is especially true in the area of services where a deeper liberalisation is much more difficult to achieve than in the area of tariffs and when you are within a bloc of countries than outside of it. The special case of financial services, which is discussed by *Wolf-Georg Ringe*, constitutes a showcase in this regard. This is the only economic area, in which the UK has a trade surplus with the EU. Having an open access to the internal market is therefore in the interest of both the UK and the EU. Yet, having the recent financial crisis in mind, the dangers linked to low protection standards and supervision are deeply enrooted in the minds of policymakers. The common interest of both the UK and the EU in an open market access will, however, prevail according to *Ringe* so that he expects a legally robust solution for the free movement of financial services that protects vital economic interests of business located on both sides of the Channel.

After having discussed the product freedoms, *Menelaos Markakis* looks at the free movement rights of persons. Since the rights of Union citizens in the UK and of UK citizens in the EU are one of the core issues related to the withdrawal of the UK from the EU, his contribution deals with both the draft withdrawal agreement and a future mobility framework. Whilst the withdrawal agreement deals with the legacy issues by a continuation of the existing EU legal regime transposed into articles of the withdrawal agreement, the situation looks more complicated with regard to a future framework of mobility. Outlines for such framework reflects the promise made by 'Brexit' to put an end to the free movement of persons. The policy documents are rather vague and seem to be open for a strictly work-related free movement. His contribution concludes with an outlook on the legal situation of persons in the event of a 'no-deal Brexit' that contains only one certainty, which is an unbearable uncertainty for the persons concerned.

Florian Wagner-von Papp's contribution deals with the question of how cooperation in competition policy between the EU and the UK can be organised in the future. Naturally, the main question here is whether it will be more likely to be characterised by approximation or whether the UK could go its own way in the areas of antitrust law, merger control or state aid control. Based on the economic expediency of the greatest possible level playing field, *Wagner-von Papp* examines the changes currently planned in the UK. The greater freedom resulting from the withdrawal from the EU could lead to deviations, in particular in the field of supervision of state aid. The author shows how important standards especially in the area of state aid are by taking a closer look at the provisions foreseen by the so-called 'backstop' in the Protocol on Ireland and Northern Ireland of the draft Withdrawal Agreement. From a procedural perspective, *Wagner-von Papp* discusses future cooperation between the EU and UK competition authorities. He considers further membership of the Competition and Markets Authority (CMA) in the ECN unlikely. The contribution finds further implications of Brexit in the context of private enforcement (in particular by being no longer bound by decisions of EU competition authorities) as well as in the necessity of transitional rules for ongoing proceedings, which are addressed in the Withdrawal Agreement, but which would be missing in the case of a no-deal Brexit.

Another field of particular importance for the future trade relations between the UK and the EU is public procurement. *Albert Sanchez-Graells* presents some thoughts on the EU-UK procurement-based trade relations after 'Brexit'. In his view, public procurement is a major tool to dismantle non-tariff barriers to trade in public markets, to foster administrative cooperation as a trade-facilitation strategy, and to boost the enforceability of a rules-based system. A future trade agreement between the EU and the UK should accordingly include rules on public procurement that aim at realising precisely these objectives. In achieving this effort *Sanchez-Graells* identifies two obstacles: the adjustment of current commitments under the WTO agreement on government procurement (GPA) and the current position of the UK to reject the CJEU's jurisdiction on the interpretation of EU law. Once these issues are solved in a satisfying manner, a public procurement chapter in a free trade agreement between the EU and the UK can be successful.

In his concluding contribution, *Peter-Christian Müller-Graff* discusses possible scenarios in the future relations between the EU and the UK with regard to the legal protection of trade-related rights. As the experience of over 60 years of the Treaty of Rome has shown, it is precisely the subjective legal character of the fundamental freedoms and their legal enforcement by the Member States' courts and – above all – the European Court of Justice that has made internal market law effective. The author deals with possible scenarios (no agreement, common rules for trade relations, scenario for establishing rules for judicial protection) and elaborates on models for the most effective protection of market-constituting interests. These can range from autonomous legal protection by courts of both sides to the attribution of legal protection to the courts of one side (the ECJ). There are also clear limits indicated, as can be seen, for example, with regard to the case of a 'Common Dispute Resolution Model', from the most recent Singapore opinion and the 'Achmea' ruling of the ECJ. The contribution concludes with three recommendations for the ongoing negotiations with the EU: to immunise the values and objectives of the Union against any relativising interests of the UK; to prevent a proliferation of bilateral treaties that might contribute to a weakening of legal protection; and to keep the possibility for a potential return of the UK to the EU in the future open.

This edited volume emerged from a conference that was jointly organised by the Mannheim Centre for Competition and Innovation (MaCCI) and the European Research Centre for Economic and Financial Governance (EURO-CEFG) of the Universities of Leiden, Delft and Rotterdam, which took place on 25 and 26 January 2018 in Mannheim. The conference was entitled 'Trade Relations after Brexit: Impetus for the Negotiation Process' and was financially generously supported by both centres. The contributions to the volume were for the most part presentations held at this conference. The contributions for this edited volume were all submitted before the expiry of the original negotiation period for a withdrawal agreement, which was 29 March 2019. They therefore reflect the state of the negotiations between the EU and the UK and within the UK of before this date. Still more than two and a half years after the referendum vote on the withdrawal of the UK from the EU it is unclear, in which direction the relationship between the EU and the UK will head. Even remaining a member of the EU is not yet off the table. Provided some sort of 'Brexit' will happen, the legal arrangement of this withdrawal remains a mammoth task for a whole generation of lawyers. Howsoever a 'Brexit' may look like or take place, it is clear that both the EU and the UK being geographically so closely located will have to find a legally sustainable way to frame their future trade relationship. This edited volume wants to present its contribution to perform this task.

Part 1 State of Affairs

Brexit – The Negotiation Position of the EU 27

Elmar Brok & Anne Liekenbrock

The European Union (EU) has always stood for political integration through economic integration and has ensured peace and prosperity on the European Continent. Of course, taking this for granted seems rather foolish as history would suggest something different. The Napoleonic wars had just ended in 1815, just 4 years before Queen Victoria was born. Queen Victoria and her ambitious husband Albert shared the same ideas and ideals and wanted to create alliances across Europe that would bring peace to the divided continent.

Political alliances of the time were as much borne out by blood as by institutions and treaties. Queen Victoria and her husband married off their children into other royal and noble families across Europe. Very successfully too, she ended up with 40 grandchildren and 88 great-grandchildren, who were widely spread throughout the major and minor monarchies of Europe – earning her the moniker of "the grandmother of Europe".

Striving towards peace in Europe had little to do with general broad-mindedness, but rather to stabilise Great Britain's claim to power and to build a dynasty that would stretch across Europe. Britain's imperial century saw its territories and peoples expand to cover almost a quarter of the world's population. Building the greatest empire the world has ever seen, was neither completed in a day, nor was it won without the use of weapons or violence. To the contrary, securing the British Empire turned out to be a bloody business.

Sadly, Queen Victoria's dream of a peaceful Europe was shattered by human nature. The catastrophic wars of the 20th century could not be stopped – despite the existing family bonds. In the era of imperialism, countries such as France, Austria and Germany engaged in political, economic and territorial power games that proved both irresistible and fatal. When in 1914 Kaiser Wilhelm II of Germany's, King George V of England's and Tsar Nicholas II of Russia's countries were on the verge of entering World War I, the family bond (they were cousins), childhood memories and a previously close relationship could not stop the start of the war. The famous 'Willy–Nicky' correspondence between Wilhelm and Nicholas (both grandsons of Queen Victoria) just before the outbreak of the First

World War trace the sentiments of the time quite well. The early telegrams were very friendly, leaning heavily on the family bond: *"[...] to try and avoid such a calamity as a European war I beg you in the name of our old friendship to do what you can to stop your allies from going too far. Nicky"*,[1] Inevitably, however, they become harsher and more distant over time, as the prospect of war grows ever closer: *"Immediate affirmative clear and unmistakable answer from your government is the only way to avoid endless misery. Until I have received this answer alas, I am unable to discuss the subject of your telegram. As a matter of fact I must request you to immediately order your troops on no account to commit the slightest act of trespassing over our frontiers. Willy."*[2] The same day this telegram was sent, Germany declared war on Russia.

Through the lens of European history, we can safely say that the European Union is a success story. It has brought not only peace, welfare and prosperity to the continent and has made all nations draw closer together in partnership – not only economically but also culturally. From the model of single, small and medium-sized States to a union that is not only economically strong but has also managed to reinforce itself politically in a globally more and more intertwined world.

Every country that is part of the European Union brings its own ~~bit of~~ culture and history to the table, but ultimately, we all share the same basic values: human dignity, freedom, democracy, equality, rule of law and human rights. These values constitute the basis of the European way of life. *"If Europe were once united in the sharing of its common inheritance there would be no limit to the happiness, prosperity and glory [...]."*[3] Winston Churchill's quote is as apt today as the day it was uttered. Not only have we managed to keep peace, but we have steadily built a common European identity. This does not mean that we have to give up our national identities, that we cannot be proud of them too. It is an addition to what we already have. It enriches us and broadens our view and possibilities. There is no need to be either German or European, either English or European. We can be both! We can listen to Italian opera and British pop music, like French wine and British ale. We should be proud of this achievement.

---

1 Neiberg, The World War I Reader (2007), "Telegram One: Tsar to Kaiser, July 29, 1914", page: 46.
2 Neiberg, The World War I Reader (2007), "Telegram Ten: Kaiser to Tsar, August 1, 1914", page: 49.
3 Winston Churchill, Speech delivered at the University of Zurich, 19 September 1946. https://rm.coe.int/16806981f3.

Make the UK great again?

In her (in)famous *Mansion House* speech in March 2018, Theresa May presented her vision for the UK's relationship with the EU after Brexit. The Prime Minister made a stand on what kind of a country the UK wants to be once it leaves the EU: *"[...] a modern, open, outward-looking, tolerant, European democracy. A nation of pioneers, innovators, explorers and creators. A country that celebrates our history and diversity, confident of our place in the world [...]."*[4] Where is the dividing line from the EU itself? There are many who would happily substitute this as the vision for our continent as a whole. So why did the UK and its citizens decide to leave? Was it to become more modern, more open and more outward-looking than the EU? Arguably three themes stood out during the campaign: sovereignty, migration and money.

The UK's loss of sovereignty

First, there was the question about the loss of sovereignty of the UK under the EU's umbrella. Boris Johnson complained about *"a slow and invisible process of legal colonisation, as the EU infiltrates just about every area of public policy"*[5] and made this the central tenet why he wanted to leave the EU. There may be good reason why this line of argument was so enticing. Robert Armstrong, the chief leader writer of the Financial Times (FT), made a convincing (and very funny) argument in August that distaste for being told what to do is the true essence of the British character.[6]

But here, we will repeat the challenge of Poland's former Foreign Minister – Radek Sikorski to British "leavers", who asked what is the first thing you wish the UK Government to do that the EU is preventing you from doing? Nobody has yet been able to answer this challenge. Either, it can be done under existing EU laws, or has nothing to do with the EU.

There is no denying that the EU today is a different beast to the one that was brought to life as the European Economic Community (EEC) in 1958.

---

4 Theresa May, speech at the Mansion House https://www.gov.uk/government/speec hes/pm-speech-on-our-future-economic-partnership-with-the-european-union, all sources last accessed on 07.12.2018.

5 B. Johnson, 'Does the EU impact on UK sovereignty?', BBC, https://www.bbc.com/ news/uk-politics-eu-referendum-35630757 (23.02.2016).

6 Armstrong, 'Why Stubbornness is the Secret to Britishness', Financial Times, https:/ /www.ft.com/content/0c454858-9408-11e8-b67b-b8205561c3fe (01.08.2018).

While the EEC focused on intertwining European countries on an econo-mical level in order to avoid yet another war on the continent, the EU has been given new responsibilities by Member States for many different areas of policy reaching from human rights to climate action and trade[7]. Howe-ver, there are also limitations to the EU's influence on its Member States. It has never tried to change the constitutional structure of its Member States or align languages, cultures and traditions.

Klaus Welle, Secretary General of the European Parliament, stated in a speech in 2016 that *"[...] Political minorities, religious minorities, ethnic mino-rities. We are an assembly of minorities."*[8] The EU's model of sovereignty re-flects its general notion of pluralism. With the distribution of power be-tween the European Commission (EC), the European Council (Council) and the European Parliament (EP) the EU's countries are represented by their governments but additionally via the bridge function via the direct election of the EP every five years. This adds a vertical power to the hori-zontal power the EU carries via the EC.

The merits of the EU's involvement in the myriad of different realms that come under its command may be debatable. However, one thing that should not be denied is the careful justification the EU applies to getting involved in any of these areas. One of the most common turns of phrase in EU-speak is "subsidiarity" – the notion, in essence, that if it can be done by the Member States it should be and the EU should keep its nose out of whatever it might be.

We should also not forget that the UK is part of the EU, not a disinter-ested observer. Since the UK joined the EU in 1973, it has been shaping and creating the EU we live in today. The UK was part of every decision to extend the EU's competences and every legislation process. For those in the Brussels bubble, the efficiency and influence of the UK's civil servants in 'UKRep' have long been the envy of other countries. Michael Gove's *idea "[...] our membership of the EU prevents us being able to change huge swa-thes of law and stops us being able to choose who makes critical decisions which*

---

7 https://europa.eu/european-union/topics_en.
8 Welle, 'Europe and Sovereignty: Realities, Limits and Projects', Egmont Royal Insti-tute for International Relations, http://www.europarl.europa.eu/the-secretary-gener al/en/%E2%80%9Ceurope-and-sovereignty-realities-limits-and-projects%E2%80%9 D.

affect all our lives"[9] gives a false impression of reality. The UK has on an average voted 95% with the rest of the European Council.[10]

"TAKE control" was one of the slogans of the pro-Brexiteers – it almost felt as if they were not part of the EU's club but merely the victim of the EU's dastardly plans. The discussion about sovereignty feels nostalgic, dowdy. Like the parallel pitch for sovereignty in today's United States, it feels like a movement looking for inspiration in the past, not the future. Not make the UK great but make the UK great *again*. Whereas all other EU member States have understood that they cannot survive in a globalised world, with new economic and geopolitical challenges, the UK wants to go back to a model of nation States that seems obsolete. As the Danish Finance Minister, Kristian Jepsen, puts it: *"There are two kinds of European nations. There are small nations and there are countries that have not yet realized they are small nations".*[11]

Unsurprisingly, some people wonder if the UK is still hanging on to former times, when the UK was an imperialistic global power. A time when the narrow strip of water separating the UK from the rest of the continent took on an outsized importance and the UK's view was seen to be determinedly out to the rest of the world, rather than towards its immediate neighbours. The machinations of Victoria and Albert indicate that the reality was rather less simplistic but the tried and trusted narrative claims that geographic isolation gave the UK the possibility to keep its distance from European politics – a luxury the rest of the continental countries were unable to afford. Whatever the true nuances of the UK's former geopolitics, there's likely to be more than a grain of truth in the idea that the UK traditionally had more space to make its own decisions, rather than having to listen to others and to compromise. This is of course more difficult as a member of the EU. The EU's *raison d'être* is based on consensus, political and economic collaboration and the shared idea to strive in a globalised world with many new challenges, which states on their own will hardly be able to deal with.

---

9 Gove, 'EU referendum: Michael Gove explains why Britain should leave the EU', Telegraph, https://www.telegraph.co.uk/news/newstopics/eureferendum/12166634 5/European-referendum-Michael-Gove-explains-why-Britain-should-leave-the-EU. html (20.02.2016).

10 UK in a Changing Europe Fellows and Full Fact team, 'EU facts behind the claims: UK influence', Fullfact, https://fullfact.org/europe/eu-facts-behind-claims-u k-influence/ (25.04.2016).

11 Jepsen, conference 'Road to Brexit', Politico, https://www.politico.eu/article/kristia n-jensen-brits-angry-at-danes-small-nation-jibe/ (13.06.2017).

So what does "TAKE control" mean? When Europhobic populists call for 'sovereignty', they mean 'supreme authority'. Hence, nothing higher than their own national authority, freedom to do what they want. This, rather simplistic, idea of sovereignty would postulate, that the actions of countries are not influenced by the actions and ideas of other countries. An idea that we can discard rather quickly in the 21st century, where the interdependencies between States in all kinds of areas are undeniable. The UK has in the past decades decided to block the idea of a common EU defence policy. The UK's "NATO first" attitude came in the way of the EU's proposed defence cooperation. For example, the idea of an EU operational headquarter independent from that of the NATO. Despite this, the EU Member States cooperation in many areas connected to the EU's defence policy has continuously increased in the past decades. In 2009 the EU passed a directive requiring member States to publish defence tenders and contracts the same way as other public procurement projects recarried out in the EU. The only country that really opened up its procurement to suppliers from other EU member States was the UK. Also, the UK has continuously driven the Commission's efforts to improve the EU's defence market and make it more competitive, as the EU's national defence budgets are often spent inefficiently.

The protection of the territory in today's world depends more and more on cooperation. This is the same for a number of other issues such as global warming, terrorism or the safeguarding of our energy supply. In addition, economic issues do not stop at the frontiers of our States. Spillover effects such as the financial crisis in 2009 are not a national matter but are better dealt with together.

Another question that arises when talking about the UK's sovereignty is the UK's memberships in NATO, the European Convention on Human Rights and the UN, among others. Here the UK is obliged to defend their allies in case of war, to uphold fundamental rights of its citizens and cooperate on economic, social, cultural and humanitarian issues. So, is the answer to leave such organisations, conventions and treaties? Or are those in favour of such 'sovereignty' comfortable with such inconsistencies?

The Brexiteers "TAKE control" slogan gave the illusion that supreme authority is still possible in the 21st century. The fact that so many people seem to have agreed with this idea perhaps shows that the UK never fully managed to arrive in the EU in the first place, having failed to understand what they were signing up for.

Migration

One of the lowest moments during the Brexit campaign was when the words *"Breaking Point – The EU has failed us all"* were placed on a poster featuring refugees crossing the border between Croatia and Slovenia – most likely fleeing from war. Nigel Farage, the leader of the right-wing populist UK Independence Party (UKIP), wanted to make a bold statement and show his voters how endangered their homeland was by the invasion of the masses of refugees from the European mainland – sad for him, that he ran out of refugees at the UK's own borders.

Secondly, the refugee crisis was a simple peg for those in favour of the UK leaving the EU to hang their hats on. Change in society is always cause for concern as it comes with uncertainties. So sadly, the campaign by Vote Leave, based on wrong facts and designed to scare the people was and still is successful. Michael Gove, Justice Secretary, "warned" the public in an article, published by *The Times* in April 2016: *"Because we cannot control our borders – and because our deal sadly does nothing to change this fact – public services such as the NHS will face an unquantifiable strain as millions more become EU citizens,"* he wrote. *"There is a direct and serious threat to our public services, standard of living and ability to maintain social solidarity if we accept continued EU membership,"* he added.

The reality is that the UK has largely been a bystander as the masses of people that had to flee their countries in 2015 knocked on Europe's doors. Once more, it fell back on that thin strip of water. As a non-Schengen country, it was easy for them to control their borders and select whom they would let into the UK and, more importantly, whom not. While Germany accepted 712 235 refugees in 2016 and Italy 128 850, the UK only accepted 34 780.[12]

---

12 Eurostat, 'Asylum and first time asylum applicants by citizenship, age and sex Annual aggregated data', http://appsso.eurostat.ec.europa.eu/nui/show.do?query=BO OKMARK_DS057066_QID_5C5B0FBF_UID_3F171EB0&layout=TIM E ,C,X,0;GEO,L,Y,0;CITI-ZEN,L,Z,0;SEX,L,Z,1;AGE,L,Z,2;ASYL_APP,L,Z,3;UNIT,L,Z,4;INDICA-TORS,C,Z,5;&zSelection=DS057066CITIZEN,EXT_EU28;DS057066U-NIT,PER;DS057066ASYL_APP,NASY_APP;DS057066INDICA-TORS,OBS_FLAG;DS057066-SEX,T;DS057066AGE,Y_LT18;&rankName1=UNIT_1_2_1_2&rankName2=AGE_1_2_1_2&rankName3=CITIZEN_1_2_1_2&rankName4=INDICA-TORS_1_2_1_2&rankName5=ASY-LAPP_1_2_1_2&rankName6=SEX_1_2_1_2&rankName7=TIME_1_0_0_0&rank Name8=GEO_1_2_0_1&sortC=ASC_1_FIRST&rStp=&cStp=&rDCh=&cD-

When in March 2016 the EU and Turkey reached an agreement in order to stop the flow of irregular migration via Turkey to Europe it helped control an unprecedented migration crisis in Europe. The number of refugees from Syria reduced significantly in only one year, from 1 322 845 in 2015 to only 712 235 in 2017. To put those numbers into perspective, in 2015 Turkey received approximately 1.2 million and in 2017 almost 3.6 million refugees only from Syria. However successful this deal was for the EU, it has been criticised by human rights groups as well as European politicians. Until today, it has not provided the wanted improvement for the refugees itself – and that despite high payments of the EU to Turkey.

When Mr. Gove claims that the UK will face a future migration 'free-for-all' unless it leaves the European Union, one has to wonder where he thinks all of those people will come from. The "Vote Leave" campaign claimed that the UK population could increase by 5.2 million by 2030[13]. They base this on the assumption that Turkey, Albania, Montenegro, Serbia and Macedonia would join the EU by 2020 and that their citizens receive the automatic right to live in the UK.[14] The possibility that any of these countries will enter the EU in the next years is practically zero. It's not just a case of the accession criteria but also politics. It is safe to say that Mr. Gove's warning was *"much ado about nothing"*[15].

Sadly, it has become tough-sell politically in recent years to make the case in favour of immigration. Wild claims that the *"migrant crisis will cost £20 BN"* or *"migrant mothers cost NHS £103 BN"* published by the *Daily Express* tabloid predict a dark economic future for the UK if more migrants are allowed in. Academic studies that look at the actual impact migration has on the labour market, economic growth and the overall costs for the government associated with net migration tend to take a less pessimistic view.

In Europe, labour markets have strongly benefited from migrants, who accounted for 70% of the increase in the workforce in Europe over the past

---

Ch=&rDM=true&cDM=true&footnes=false&empty=false&wai=false&time_mode=ROLLING&time_most_recent=false&cfo=%23%23%23%2C%23%23%23.%23%23%23&lang=en.

13 Gove, 'Soviet-style control freaks are a threat to our independence', The Times, https://www.thetimes.co.uk/article/soviet-style-control-freaks-will-worsen-migration-free-for-all-m3rfb6vmb (25.04.2016).

14 Gove, 'Gove: EU immigrant influx will make NHS unsustainable by 2030', The Guardian, https://www.theguardian.com/politics/2016/may/20/eu-immigrant-influx-michael-gove-nhs-unsustainable.

15 William Shakespeare, *Much ado about nothing* (1600).

ten years. Looking at the UK in 2017, nearly one in two recent migrants was in the highest educational category compared to only one in three UK born. Migrants arrive with skills that contribute to our labour market. After the recession in 2008, employment growth has been impressive across the UK and as well the UK as the EU citizens have benefitted. Of course, this is an easy equation to make. The more people there are, the more goods and services are required overall. This translates directly into jobs as those goods and services need to be produced or offered. EU migrants to the UK are often younger than the average UK worker, better educated and enjoy the same or even higher employment rates than natives, hence contributing to the UK's GDP. The claim migrants weigh heavily on our welfare systems does not hold true either. A survey from 2018 shows that there were 1.07 million unemployed UK born people, but only 266 000 unemployed non-UK born people. As a group, immigrants contribute more in taxes and social contributions than they receive in benefits.[16]

Far from the truth, the slogans offering scapegoats for societal shortcomings were well received by the population and deepened the fear many people had grown once the migration crisis had started. There was a degree of exceptionalism in the UK's media coverage of migration, which often did not coincide with the truth but impacted public opinion on migration and border control. Cardiff University published a study on press coverage across Europe and stated *"[...] the right-wing press in the United Kingdom expressed a hostility towards refugees and migrants which was unique."*[17] In 2015, the UK received approximately 60 asylum applications per 100 000 UK citizens. The EU-wide average is 260 applications per 100 000 citizens[18].

It is sad to say but the country that claims to be a 'modern, open, outward-looking, tolerant, European democracy', has decided to leave the EU partly due to the promise to reduce immigration to the UK, backed up by false, or at the very least misleading, data and promises.

---

16 Secretary General of the OECD, 'Is migration good for the economy?', Migration policy Debate, https://www.oecd.org/migration/OECD%20Migration%20Policy%20Debates%20Numero%202.pdf.

17 Berry/Garcia-Blanco/Moore, 'Press Coverage of the Refugee and Migrant Crisis in the EU: A Content Analysis of Five European Countries', Cardiff School of Journalism, Media and Cultural Studies, http://www.unhcr.org/56bb369c9.html.

18 Eurostat, 'Asylum quarterly report', https://ec.europa.eu/eurostat/statistics-explained/index.php/Asylum_quarterly_report (20.09.2018).

EU, the Bottomless Money Pit

Being part of a club means that you have to pay a membership fee. In exchange, you are entitled to receive the benefits. However, the UK's contribution to the EU's budget has been a thorn in the Brexiteer's side for many years and they were not shy to distort reality to make their point. Right-leaning newspapers such as the *The Sun, Daily Mail, Telegraph* and *Daily Express* repeatedly featured that being part of the EU means, *"giving £20 billion a year or £350 million a week to Brussels"*[19].

These sums are not difficult to unpick. The same forces that idolised the UK's rebate as the symbol of Thatcher's European legacy conveniently forgot about it when it came to determining the UK's bill. *"I want my money back"* became *"what money"*?[20] The exact calculation of the 'correction' for the UK's relatively large net contributions is complex and varies by year but as a rule of thumb it reduces the UK's contribution by a quarter. Taking this into account the UK made an estimated gross contribution of £13.0 billion in 2017. In addition, Vote Leave ignored the money that the EU redistributes to the UK (public sector receipts) for different areas such as agricultural, social, economic development and competitiveness programmes. In 2017, for example, the UK received £4.1 billion of public sector funding from the EU. Taking all those factors into account, the UK's net contribution and receipts to the EU in 2017 was an estimated £8.9 billion. This number is not fixed, as gross contributions as well as receipts vary every year. However, between 2011 and 2015, the years just before the referendum, the average net contribution of the UK was £8.5 billion, not even half of what Vote Leave claimed.

Studies by the CBI have shown "for every £1 we put in the EU, we get £10 from the EU back"[21]. What the EU provides is a focus for local authorities, businesses, and the central authorities to fund needed projects that otherwise would not have been done.

---

19 M. Elliott on behalf of Vote Leave, 'Cost of the EU – Let's spend our money on our priorities', http://www.voteleavetakecontrol.org/briefing_cost.html (01.10.2018).

20 Margaret Thatcher, Speech to European Parliament, Debates of the European Parliament No.2-346, session pp 41-68, 1986/87.

21 CBI, 'CBI Literature review of the impact of EU membership on the UK economy' http://www.cbi.org.uk/business-issues/brexit-and-eu-negotiations/eu-business-facts/cbi-literature-review-of-the-impact-of-eu-membership-on-the-uk-economy-pdf /.

Yes, it is still a big number. Nevertheless, when dealing with big numbers it is useful to provide some context. While the EU funds a number of important programmes, budget is not the first tool that springs to mind when one considers the EU's powers. It does not control the big power-houses of public sector spending, such as health, education, social security and defence. Mapping the amount the UK Government spends on the EU to the total public sector spend helps provide some much-needed perspective. The UK's own Office for National Statistics calculates the EU as a little over 1% of the total government budget. Moreover, if you jump from the big picture to the cost for individual citizens, the bill is roughly £140 a year.[22] For some the net spend of the UK might be the killer blow but – at the risk of seeming out of touch – others are scratching their heads as to why this had such a central role in the debate.

Undeterred by the criticism of the figures during and after the campaign, Boris Johnson has doubled-down. In an interview in the *Guardian* in January 2018, he stated *"there was an error on the side of the bus. We grossly underestimated the sum over which we would be able to take back control"*. It's difficult to be any more generous than to view this as straight out of the 'alternative facts' playbook.

Beyond the budget discussion, the other side of the economic argument presents the EU as a millstone around the UK economy's neck – holding it back from its natural status as a paragon of dynamic growth and innovation. Lacking any further explanation, in 2016 Johnson stated that the *"EU is a graveyard of low growth"*. Again, looking at numbers the picture looks very different and shows that the UK has profited strongly from being part of the EU. Since the UK joined the EU in 1973, the per capita GDP of the UK economy grew by 103%, higher than Germany's 99% and comfortably outpacing France's 74%.[23] The reverse argument could be made that the fact the UK has grown so well – and is outpacing its neighbors – demonstrates the 'drag' effect rather than the UK's successful exploitation of the growth conditions afforded by the EU. That the UK is the smart pupil in the class, if you will, being held back by a learning environment focused on her less-gifted classmates. But if that was the case, one would expect that the UK would be outperformed by other developed nations not fettered by the EU's constraints. With 97% growth, however, the US was also

---

22 Office for National Statistics, 'The UK contribution to EU budget', https://www.o ns.gov.uk/economy/governmentpublicsectorandtaxes/publicsectorfinance/articles/ theukcontributiontotheeubudget/2017-10-31 (31.10.2017).

23 Hendry/Farmer/Roser, 'How did the UK economy do since joining the EU?', letter to 'The Times', https://www.inet.ox.ac.uk/news/Brexit (06.06.2016).

outperformed by the UK over the same period. Or maybe a better comparison is with itself. Harking back to the 'glory days' of the Empire once more, however, sees a rather sluggish growth rate of 0.9% per capita from 1872 – 1914, as opposed to the rather brisk 2.1% since EU membership. In addition to strong economic growth, the Institute for New Economic Thinking shows that the fruits of this growth have been fairly evenly spread, at least in comparison to the US. The median income in the UK has grown by 79% since 1974, in contrast to 16% in the US.[24]

The reasons why the UK voted in favor of Brexit – or at least the arguments positioned by the Vote Leave campaign – are perplexing for many in the corridors of the EU. At face value, the claims seem almost too easy to debunk. Why were the UK's populace taken in? When the practicalities of organizing Brexit subside – along with some of the emotions – perhaps there will be time to reflect and learn lessons. It might not be the specific claims of the campaign that are important but a deeper and more rudimentary sense that the Brexiteers tapped into. A lack of trust in an establishment that gave us the global financial crisis and subsequent great recession; an unease in how culture is evolving or a common identity and community that is neither as strong or deep as was believed. Nevertheless, it is sad to think that pride in 60 years of peace and prosperity took second billing to squabbles over who decides what, closing the door on outsiders and transactional costs.

The UK's Take in the Negotiation and the EU's Dilemma

Even now, more than two years after Theresa May triggered Article 50 of the Lisbon Treaty, the UK is still heavily divided on the question of leaving the EU. Although the EU Council agreed to extend the negotiation period, the clock is still ticking ominously and relentlessly and a decision will have to be made inevitably.

The Prime Minister said in June 2016 *"Brexit means Brexit"*[25]. Even at that early stage, the phrase seemed to indicate that the energies were as likely to be expended on herding cats in Westminster as on negotiating with EU partners. It attempted to placate those on the right-wing of her party –

---

24 Hendry/Farmer/Roser, 'How did the UK economy do since joining the EU?', letter to 'The Times', https://www.inet.ox.ac.uk/news/Brexit (06.06.2016).
25 Theresa May, speech in front of the Houses of Parliament https://www.independe nt.co.uk/news/uk/politics/theresa-may-brexit-means-brexit-conservative-leadership -no-attempt-remain-inside-eu-leave-europe-a7130596.html (11.07.2016).

and perhaps in the media – by hinting that the vote would be respected and was not to be rerun under any circumstances and that the UK's exit would not be on paper only – that there would be differences in substance in the UK's institutional relationship with the EU. At the same time, in order not to immediately expose the factions in her government, the phrase was delightfully non-committal. In academic terms, it is a tautology – it adds nothing to the common ground.[26] Unsurprisingly, perhaps, the EU had to wait a long time before it received an answer as to what the UK wanted once it had left the EU.

The UK's Red Lines

The UK was quicker, however, to let the EU know what it *didn't* want rather than providing a coherent strategy that would allow for structured negotiations. They laid out their **red lines** right after the decision of exiting the EU. All in all that is a bit light on detail as a negotiation strategy and, as it turned out, proved inconsistent as they had to loosen them the longer negotiations went on.

"*We will take back control of our laws and bring an end to the jurisdiction of the European Court of Justice (CJEU),*"[27] May said. It seemed clear, that the CJEU's jurisdiction for the UK would end the day the UK had exited the EU. UK courts would have supremacy and the UK would regain the sovereignty it had dreamed of. The UK was also very clear about leaving the single market and the customs union of the EU. The UK wanted to be able to do its own trade deals and negotiate tariffs with third countries rather than being tied to those the EU had negotiated. Of course, negotiating trade deals take several years and officially – as still being a member of the EU – the UK is not allowed to start negotiations until it has left the EU. A big political song and dance was made of the money, of course, as May stated that the payments to the EU would be over after Brexit. Boris Johnson, who is never short of one-liners, said that the EU could "*go whistle*" over its "*extortionate demands*"[28].

---

26 Neutral Footing, 'Brexit means Brexit' https://neutralfooting.wordpress.com/brexit-means-brexit/ (03.10.2018).
27 Theresa May, speech to the Lancaster House, https://www.gov.uk/government/speeches/the-governments-negotiating-objectives-for-exiting-the-eu-pm-speech (17.01.2017).
28 Boris Johnson to the House of Commons, https://www.bbc.com/news/uk-politics-40571123 (11.07.2018).

But while the EU has made the negotiations a priority, mainly also to protect its citizens living in the UK, it almost seemed as if the Brits were so shattered by their own decision to leave the EU, that they did not quite know how to move forward.

Of course, it is debatable if it is wise to have a referendum making a decision on such a scale as the future of a nation. Especially since the information provided to people were left to mainly populist politicians, rather than having neutral information from a reliable source. However, there were no impact assessments made before the referendum, as well as no plans for the future in case it would come to this decision. It caught the UK as red-handed as the rest of the EU when the people voted to leave.

The EU had made it clear that negotiations could only start once Article 50 of the Treaty of the European Union (TEU) was triggered, setting into motion the two years deadline for negotiation. However, rushing into it was a political statement and had little to do with the UK Government's preparedness.[29] When Theresa May over hastily triggered Article 50 barely nine months after the referendum in March 2017, the dimension of what was going to come was not yet entirely clear.

The time pressure was on, but valuable time was wasted for the lack of a negotiating position of the UK. Long delays and waste in resources -with it the dwindling chance of reaching an agreement before the deadline.

Then May's decision for a snap election in June 2017, suspending Parliament for weeks to allow for campaigning. Believing to leave her with more negotiating power, Prime Minister May campaigned explicitly on a Brexit platform. It left her with little success. The result removed the narrow Tory majority in the House of Commons from the 2015 election. As a result, the Tories needed to enter a confidence and supply arrangement with the Democratic Unionist Party (DUP) from Northern Ireland, which was not always going to be without its hitches. May promised the DUP to ensure the same deal for Northern Ireland as for the rest of the UK.

Since 2016 May has regularly been declared dead in the water but is struggling on – often with little trust or sympathy of her own political party. It is certainly an impossible task to please everyone as positions of Brexit are so divided in the UK. At this point in time it is much easier for Brexiteer Tory MPs to distance themselves from the Brexit negotiations and the possible deal that might be agreed, than to be tainted by the compromise

---

29 C. Cooper, 'UK screwed in Brexit negotiations, says EU ambassador', Politico, https://www.politico.eu/article/ivan-rogers-brexit-uk-screwed-in-brexit-negotiation s-says-ex-ambassador/ (25.10.2017).

or the failure of the negotiations. It is rather an invidious task May took on.

Michel Barnier stated in his first interview since Article 50 was triggered *"Next week, it will be three months after the sending of the Article 50 letter ... I can't negotiate with myself."* Even months after Article 50 TEU had been triggered, there was still little clarity what the UK's negotiation position was. Guesswork was strongly required, as most information about how the UK wanted to move forward was given through Mrs. May's speeches. However, speeches cannot replace position papers or well-prepared negotiators. Throughout the negotiations in 2017 many EU officials started wondering if the ill-preparedness on the UK's side was maybe just a bluff? As it turned out it was not, there was no genius plan brewing on the UK's side to ensure an orderly Brexit.

For the EU it was much easier to come up with a detailed negotiation position. While having a member leave the EU was new ground, the EC has existing powers, processes and experience to negotiate third country deals – from bilateral trade agreements to the full integration of accession to the EU. Task force 50, the Commission's negotiation team led by Michel Barnier, started their work and prepared the options that were left after the red lines by the UK were considered. Of course, the body of European law (known as the acquis) comes with limitations for a future deal that need to be respected. The outcome was simple: the future relationship could be done in the form of a Free Trade Agreement (FTA), as the EU has with Canada or Japan. This was not the Brexit the UK had dreamed about, however, as the economic implications for the country would be huge. The question is whether the people were aware of the consequences Brexit was going to have on their country and their life.

Slow Progress

The EU communicated its ground rules from very early on and has been consistent in their implementation throughout the negotiations.

Main points were: the UK cannot cherry-pick its favorite parts of the EU rulebook, the CJEU must oversee and enforce any transitional deal, EU citizens will not pay for the British Brexit bill — the UK must pay the EU costs that *"arise directly from its withdrawal"*[30], the final deal cannot include a trade-off between trade and security cooperation, no EU agencies in London after Brexit, the UK must adhere to EU environmental and tax-evasion rules for close cooperation after Brexit and the right order of negotiations must be respected [the withdrawal agreement (also often referred to as divorce agreement) comes before any trade agreement].[31]

To ensure basic guidelines and to make the following negotiations easier, the EU wanted three complicated issues to be discussed before the negotiations of the future agreement could start, namely, citizens' rights, UK's financial settlement and the issue of the border between the Republic of Ireland and Northern Ireland (UK).

The EU's main aim was to provide certainty to EU citizens living in the UK, and UK citizens living in the EU, that their rights enjoyed under EU law will be maintained. The critical point for Brexiteers was the oversight by the CJEU. The EU however wanted the CJEU to stand as a guardian for citizens' rights. A compromise was found in late 2017, as the UK has agreed that its national courts will take the CJEU's case law into account so the EU can keep indirect influence via the CJEU. Additionally, the EC and an independent national authority in the UK will monitor the implementation of citizens' rights to ensure correct implementation.

A sore, and on both sides very political topic was the financial settlement of the UK to the EU. Whereas the UK had originally stated it would not pay any money to the EU, a compromise was found. The UK will pay its share in the current EU budget, which runs out in 2020. But due to the nature of the EU budget and other long-term commitments the UK has in the EU (for example, the pensions of UK officials in the EU), some of the payments will need to be paid long after 2020 – which the UK has also agreed to. The EU has never come up with a final number as real payments

---

30 European Parliament resolution of 5 April 2017 on negotiations with the United Kingdom following its notification that it intends to withdraw from the European Union (2017/2593(RSP)), P8_TA(2017)0102, Para. 19, http://www.epgencms .europarl.europa.eu/cmsdata/upload/b9a0c645-21c2-4117-b933-04689cf7cb46/Eur opean_Parliament_Resolution_5_April.pdf (05.04.2017).
31 European Parliament resolution of 5 April 2017 on negotiations with the United Kingdom following its notification that it intends to withdraw from the European Union (2017/2593(RSP)) P8_TA(2017)0102
Para. 13-15, http://www.epgencms.europarl.europa.eu/cmsdata/upload/b9a0c645-21c2-4117-b933-04689cf7cb46/European_Parliament_Resolution_5_April.pdf (05.04.2017).

are not predictable. Experts predict it up to €40 – 45 billion in total over the next decades.[32]

However, one unsolved topic remains until today: the Irish peace settlement (Good Friday Agreement), which cannot be jeopardized. The EU and the Republic of Ireland stated early on that a hard border had to be avoided to anticipate a newly burgeoning conflict on the island. The only realistic way to ensure no hardening of the border means that Northern Ireland's regulations stay close to the EU's. Even now, this is May's biggest dilemma. Her Northern Irish allies, the DUP, protest against creating a new 'division' within the UK. Additionally, Scotland and Wales said they then wanted the same conditions as Northern Ireland. This is an (almost) impossible trick to pull off.

To find a workable solution the EU proposed a backstop solution. It will apply *unless and until* another solution is found; hence, it is an insurance policy for both sides that will most likely never be applied.

The EU's proposal was to leave the border between Ireland and Northern Ireland open with Northern Ireland having access to single market for goods – with all its consequences, such as EU tariffs and rules of origins, applying.[33] Custom checks would have to take place between the EU (including Northern Ireland) and the UK. The already existing checks in Belfast and Dublin would be used and its scope simply extended. The UK did not agree to this proposal as the UK does not want to accept a different customs regime, a border, within the United Kingdom, not even as a backstop.

Instead, in early July 2018, with the long-awaited Chequers Plan (the UK's vision for the Brexit scenario), the UK proposed a free trade area for goods between the UK and the EU. Meaning, the UK would be part of the single market for goods only.The Chequers Plan also proposed that the UK would apply its own tariffs and an independent trade policy for goods intended for consumption in the UK. To sum it up, the UK would still seek to strike its own trade deals around the world, even though it would be bound by EU rules and regulations.

---

32 Theresa May, speech to the House of Commons, https://hansard.parliament.uk/C ommons/2017-12-11/debates/965E301041F64353A2CC2F5A6C31495F/BrexitNeg otiations?highlight=%22%C2%A3%2039%22#contribution-1DCE63EC-EC22-433 0-8169-3FBEED63560D (11.12.2017).

33 Draft agreement on the withdrawal of the UK of Great Britain and Northern Ireland from the EU and the European Atomic Energy Community, Protocol on Ireland/Northern Ireland, 108-117, https://ec.europa.eu/commission/sites/beta-politi cal/files/draft_agreement_coloured.pdf (19.03.2018).

Of course, this proposal could not be agreed to by the EU as it compromises the integrity of the single market. The Chequers Plan ignores three of the EU's four freedoms, which seek to guarantee the free movement of goods, capital, services, and labour and is a fundamental part of the EU. According to the UK's proposal, the UK would also not recognise the CJEU's jurisdiction, which is the EU's ultimate legal authority on rules the UK proposes to harmonise.

On 20 July Barnier gave a clear direction of how the EU would respond to the Chequers Plan by stating *"there are some elements [of the white paper] which do seem to contradict the guidelines of the EU council, the heads of government and State, namely the indivisibility of the four freedoms and the integrity of the single market."*[34]

Sadly for Mrs. May, resistance also came from within her own government and there was a wave of resignations, including Foreign Secretary Boris Johnson, Brexit Secretary David Davis and Parliamentary Undersecretary at the Department for Exiting the European Union Steve Baker. Boris Johnson said: *"It occurs to me that the authors of the Chequers proposal risk prosecution under the 14th-century statute of praemunire, which says that no foreign court or government shall have jurisdiction in this country."*[35]The Prime Minister's Chequers Plan was seen as a betrayal by many Brexiteers.

At the conference in Salzburg in late September 2018 the UK seemed surprised by the moment of truth on the Chequers Paper. Donald Tusk, President of the European Council, made it very clear that the Chequers proposals for dealing with the Irish border and trade relations after Brexit must be *"reworked and further negotiated: everybody shared the view that while there are positive elements in the Chequers proposal, the suggested framework for economic cooperation will not work, not least because it risks undermining the single market."*[36]

Just a few days prior to the conference May had stated *"I believe we will get a good deal. We will bring that back from the EU negotiations and put that*

---

34 Boffey/Rankin, 'Barnier dismisses Theresa May's Brexit white paper demands', The Guardian, https://www.theguardian.com/politics/2018/jul/20/france-minister-nath alie-loiseau-brexit-concessions-theresa-may-commons (20.07.2018).

35 See Bienkov, 'Boris Johnson says Theresa May could be prosecuted for her Chequers Brexit plan', UK Business Insider, http://uk.businessinsider.com/boris-johnso n-says-theresa-may-could-be-prosecuted-for-her-brexit-chequers-plan-2018-10?r=US &IR=T (02.10.2018).

36 See Blenkinsop/Psaledakis/Strupczewski, 'EU leaders comments on Brexit at informal summit in Austria', Reuters, https://www.reuters.com/article/us-eu-summit-hi ghlights/eu-leaders-comments-on-brexit-at-informal-summit-in-austria-idUSKCN1 M00VT (20.09.2018).

to Parliament. I think that the alternative to that will be not having a deal."[37] It's difficult to say whether Mrs. May's optimism that the Chequers proposal would sail through Salzburg with barely a ripple was borne out of domestic posturing or the illusion that the hard-fought battle of the internal negotiation meant the fight was already won before it had really begun.

Eventually, however, the UK proposed their own version of the backstop solution, which would keep the whole of the UK aligned with the EU customs union. That the proposal actually allows for less independence than the one offered by the EU, affecting the whole UK rather than Northern Ireland alone, points to the importance of territorial integrity in the UK debate – and keeping May's DUP allies on the side. While the EU accepted the proposal, back in the UK Parliament it went on to become a lightning rod for discontent and division.

The backstop was part of the Withdrawal Agreement, which the EU and the UK Government agreed on in mid-November 2018. The big issues of how the UK can leave the EU were outlined in nearly 600 pages followed by a roadmap of 20 pages, outlining the future relationship between the EU and Britain.

In Brussels it was clear to all that the deal was the only one available that respected the UK's red lines, but back in the UK it came under criticism from all sides of the political spectrum. Opposition Labour Party leader Jeremy Corbyn said in the House of Commons "*it represents the worst of all worlds*"[38]. After a fraught period of threats and promises in an attempt to buy party loyalty, the deal was finally voted down on 15 January in the heaviest parliamentary defeat of any UK Prime Minister in the democratic era.

Two weeks later, the UK Parliament had a chance to vote on what they wanted May to do instead in a series of amendments to her statement on the defeat of her Brexit Bill. The result was hardly illuminating. MPs voted against amendments to debate and vote on alternative approaches, to give themselves an option to call for the deadline to be extended or to change tack and support a customs union and stronger alignment with the single market. Amendments calling for a second referendum never made it to the table. The two amendments that were (very narrowly) supported stated

---

37 Sabbagh/Weaver/O'Carrol, 'Brexit: May's 'Chequers or no deal' warning angers Tory right', The Guardian, https://www.theguardian.com/politics/2018/sep/17/onl y-alternative-chequers-no-deal-theresa-may-bbc-brexit (17.09.2018).

38 https://www.theguardian.com/commentisfree/2018/dec/06/jeremy-corbyn-general -election-brexit-labour-theresa-may.

that the UK would not leave the EU without a deal (conveniently side-stepping that this would be the default option in less than two months) and that May should go back to Brussels to renegotiate the backstop.

Why is the backstop so controversial? After all, the instincts of both sides will be to strike a 'partnership agreement' (i.e. trade deal) to replace it – possibly before the backstop has even become a reality. Opting not to strike an agreement would be politically and economically disadvantageous for both the UK and the EU. Given the proposed 2 to maximum 4 years of transition phase, where the UK would stay in the single market, the backstop would most likely never be enforced. However, both sides have always been clear that going back to a hard border is no option and must be avoided under all circumstances. And the backstop is the insurance for that. This is a priority for the EU, and expecting a solution to the border based on non-existent technology, allowing the UK to unilaterally pull out of the backstop or limiting it to a fixed time period, are not palatable options.

It may be a relatively small group in Parliament that genuinely believe that the backstop is the main issue – fearing the UK would be locked into the backstop on a permanent basis or that it may offer the UK less leverage in the trade negotiations. For many others, the backstop debate is a chimera. For a group of hardline Brexiteers, one suspects that if it wasn't the backstop it would be something else. They will be the only ones cheering if the UK free-falls out of the EU on 29 March. For hopeful remainers, the backstop isn't the real issue – at best it's a means to engineer their real goal or a second referendum. For the Labour leadership, the prize isn't even Brexit-related – it's a chance in a general election and taking power. Whether any new concessions on the backstop (if they are even possible) would be enough to win over a majority in Parliament, remains to be seen.

The EU is, yet again, waiting for a proposal from London. The UK government remains in a deadlock situation and has so far not made any new proposals that would help solve the situation. The fear of a non-deal scenario is as big as two months ago. While the UK seems lost in their internal political struggle the EU can merely watch and hope for the best. It is not the EU's task to solve the UK internal disputes.

Mrs May's domestic troubles have done little to sway the EU's position. Mr Barnier made it very clear on where the EU 27 stands in saying that "*the Withdrawal Agreement and Political Declaration agreed by all 27 Leaders and the United Kingdom Government (...) remains the best and only deal possible"*[39].

The EU has to be clear from the very start that it wants to avoid a no deal scenario, but not by compromising what it stands for. It is clear that a no deal scenario would have a negative impact on the EU and the UK, politically, economically and for the future of our relationship. However, we need to be clear that it would hit the UK much harder than it would hit the EU. Even at this late stage the EU is ready to work with the UK negotiators to find a solution but it will not be made at any cost. Major concessions are unlikely to be made solely to appease a UK Parliament that seems uncertain what it stands for. In the worst-case scenario of a no deal the EU will end up with a black eye, while the UK is likely to be flat out on the canvas.

The Economic Implications of Brexit

Leaving the EU is proving to be more difficult than the British expected. Intertwined in many areas, politically and economically, the process of unwinding from the EU comes at a high price. This is not because the EU wishes to punish the UK – as so many Brexiteers have repeatedly stated[40]- but due to the nature of the affair. Negotiations uncovered how interlaced and therefore complicated it is going to become to separate the UK from the EU. While UK and EU are both being affected by Brexit, especially in case of a no deal scenario, the economic implications for the UK are most likely going to be huge.

Currently, approximately 45% of UK exports are to the EU 27, 10% to Germany alone. Vice versa, 7% of EU 27 exports are to the UK, making up 53% of all UK imports. Of course, currently there are no tariffs on trade as the UK is part of the EU. This is due to change with Brexit as goods that are imported from a third country will pay the EU's common external tariff [World Trade Organisation (WTO) rules apply] unless there is a free trade agreement between the EU and the third country.

The important British industrial verticals have value chains that are highly integrated with Europe. The chemical, leather, textile and clothing, petroleum and electro industries are particularly reliant on EU export. In

---

39 http://europa.eu/rapid/press-release_SPEECH-19-789_en.htm.
40 Hunt/Wheeler, 'Brexit: All you need to know about the UK leaving the EU', BBC News, https://www.bbc.com/news/uk-politics-32810887 (27.09.2018).

2011, the UK exported approximately 60% of its produced leather and chemical products to the EU 27. In textile and clothing industry it was almost
50% and vehicle manufacturing was around 29%.[41] Certain territories are
especially vulnerable. For example, 60% of goods (not services) produced
in Wales are exported into the EU 27, 59% from the North East. While tariff rates differ between goods the average for leather is 4.1%, for chemicals
4.5%, for textile 6.5% clothing 11.5% and for electrical and non-electrical
machinery between 1.9 and 2.8%.[42]

For the UK the EU is the largest trading partner and there is no denial
in that any form of Brexit will harm the UK's economy. Contrary to Mr
David Davis belief that *"you don't need a piece of paper with numbers on it to
have an economic assessment"*[43], the EU 27 has been pointing this out from
the very start of the negotiations and has voiced its concerns about the economic impact Brexit will have. There is no better way than describing the
UK's denial of the situation then hard line Brexiteers promptly delivered
by stating, that they would simply trade with Australia and Canada. This is
not a promise for a very bright future, as they account for a paltry 3% of
current UK exports combined.[44]

Undeniably, there will be negative implications for the EU economy,
too. Supply chains will undoubtedly be interrupted in the short term
which may mean the end of the "just in time" method of production in
the UK. But the EU has a big advantage: its size and market integration.
The EU 27 will continue to be the biggest trading bloc in the world. That
makes it an attractive target for both domestic and foreign companies looking to take up the slack. The UK remains a wealthy and reasonably-sized
market and in the short term it will also benefit from regulatory alignment
with the EU. A component designed for the EU market, for example,
should in theory be saleable in the UK. Regulatory divergence over time,
however, is likely to impact scalability – an anathema for modern global
go-to-market models and supply chains.

---

41 Wells/Skuse, 'Trade in goods, country -by-commodity experimental data: 2011 to
    2016', https://www.ons.gov.uk/economy/nationalaccounts/balanceofpayments/arti
    cles/tradeingoodscountrybycommodityexperimentaldata2011to2016/2018-04-16
    (16.04.2018).
42 WTO, ITC, UNCTAD, 'WTO World Tariff Profiles 2017', https://www.wto.org/eng
    lish/res_e/booksp_e/tariff_profiles17_e.pdf, p.82 (31.05.2017).
43 Bienkov, 'David Davis admits he has not calculated the huge costs of a no-deal
    Brexit', http://uk.businessinsider.com/david-davis-admits-he-has-not-calculated-cost
    -of-a-no-deal-brexit-2017-3?r=UK&IR=T (15.03.2017).
44 Fox, 'Brexit Britain looks to Commonwealth 2.0', https://www.euractiv.com/sectio
    n/uk-europe/news/brexit-britain-looks-to-commonwealth-2-0/ (06.04.2018).

This has not gone unrecognized by companies, banks and investors. On the contrary, the first ramifications are already visible. The European Central Bank (ECB), for example, states that 20 banks have already applied for a license in the Euro area, and 30 more have asked how to relocate their business. Additionally, several foreign banks have already announced that Frankfurt in Germany or Dublin in Ireland will be their permanent headquarter instead of London. Ernst and Young (EY) has added, that in June 2018, of 222 large banks, insurers, asset managers and other financial services companies more than a third are thinking or have confirmed that they are moving operations and staff to the EU. One quarter has confirmed at least one relocation destination. There are around 1.1 million direct jobs associated with the financial services in the UK, mostly in or just outside London. How many of those will be affected is not predictable at this point.[45]

According to the Chartered Institute of Procurement and Supply (CIPS), 14% of European firms with a presence in the UK have already started the process of moving their offices or storage facilities into the EU 27 and to relocate their supply chains. Other big companies such as Jaguar Land Rover, Ford, BMW or Airbus have already announced that they would move from the UK in case of a bad or a no deal scenario. Panasonic announced in August 2018 that it would move its European headquarters from the UK to Amsterdam.[46]

A study by the OECD from 2016 compares the difference GDP scenarios of the UK remaining and exiting the EU. In case a transition phase is applied until the end of 2020, hence EU and UK will be able to make a deal, the GDP will have dropped around 3.3%. Long-term predictions of the UK leaving the EU vary from a loss of optimistic 2.7% to pessimistic 7.7% GDP in the UK by 2030. Different channels of capital, immigration and lower technical progress would be the cause for those economic impacts. In particular, labour productivity would be held back by a drop in foreign direct investment and a smaller pool of skills (reduced migration

---

45 MacAskill/Jessop/Cohn, 'Exclusive: 10.000 UK finance jobs affected in Brexit's first wave – Reuters survey', Reuters, https://www.reuters.com/article/us-britain-eu-jobs-exclusive/exclusive-10000-uk-finance-jobs-affected-in-brexits-first-wave-reuters-survey-idUSKCN1BT1EU (18.09.2017).

46 Topham, 'Toyota says hard Brexit would halt UK plant as BMW warns over Mini', The Guardian, https://www.theguardian.com/business/2018/oct/02/toyota-hard-brexit-uk-plant-bmw-mini-jaguar-land-rover (02.10.2018).

into UK).[47] The OECD's recommendation is abandonedly clear: "In contrast, continued UK membership in the European Union and further reforms of the Single Market would enhance living standards on both sides of the Channel."[48]

Predictions for a hard Brexit are much worse and the drop would come much more sudden with the day the UK leaves the EU in March 2019, as no transition phase would give us the time to prepare. A lot of areas will be affected but one of the hardest hit will be transport. As not being part of the EU the UK will lose its right to fly into the air space in the EU or land on our airports. Lorries, cars and ships will be stuck at custom checks that are not prepared for the load that is going to come. It is predicted that in the first days and weeks only a small amount of today's trade will be able to cross the border from and to the UK.[49]

Undeniably, the EU 27 will also experience a loss in its GDP after Brexit- mainly due to uncertainties about the future of Europe. It is a misnomer to think the EU would stay clean from economic fallout. However, the loss will be much lower in comparison and due to more flexibility of the EU's market, recover much faster (less than 1% by 2020). With an estimated loss of 10% at best but down to 20% in a worst-case scenario, long-term trading scenarios for the UK made by the OECD do not look promising either.

That companies are taking decisions before the UK has officially left the EU is a symptom of the uncertainties about the aftermath of Brexit and the real consequences it has for both sides – the EU and the UK. Having passed the deadline of 29th March 2019 by almost two months, it is still not certain that there will be a deal. The one the EU and the UK Government have agreed on has still not been confirmed by the House of Commons and we are therefore still no step closer to finding a solution for the time after the UK has left the EU.

Most companies do not have any assurance on what is going to happen and do not have time to wait. In essence, they are preparing for a no deal scenario. After the initial shock – or for those with a more optimistic bent,

---

47 Kierzenkowski/Pain/Rusticelli/Zwart, 'The economic consequences of Brexit: A taxing decision OECD Economic Policy Paper', http://www.oecd.org/eco/the-econ omic-consequences-of-brexit-a-taxing-decision.htm, (27.04.2016), p. 5.

48 Kierzenkowski/Pain/Rusticelli/Zwart, 'The economic consequences of Brexit: A taxing decision OECD Economic Policy Paper', http://www.oecd.org/eco/the-econ omic-consequences-of-brexit-a-taxing-decision.htm (27.04.2016), p. 5.

49 Owen/Shepheard/Stojanovic, 'Implementing Brexit: Customs', Institute for Government, https://www.politico.eu/wp-content/uploads/2017/09/IfG_Brexit_custo ms.pdf (09.2017).

teething problems – the real implications of Brexit are likely to play out gently but inexorably over a much longer timescale. There's likely to be enough wiggle room for both sides to dispute cause and effect. In the sober world of economists and statisticians, however, it's unlikely that many will paint a rosy picture.

Resume

Looking at the Brexit scenario from an outside perspective tells us that there will be no winners. We can merely try to minimize the losses on both sides – and how heavy they will be depends on how the negotiations turn out. Predicting the future is an impossible task – as the outcome of the 2016 Brexit referendum demonstrated. We can only guess what the future will bring and hope that the UK will come to its senses and leave the EU with a deal that allows for a transition phase and a future partnership.

Looking at the facts, it's clear that a no deal scenario should be avoided as the economic ramifications would be terrible. The UK would feel the brunt but the EU would suffer too. In November 2017 the Bank of England stated that *"Britain crashing out of the European Union without a deal could trigger a deep and damaging recession with worse consequences for the UK economy than the 2008 financial crisis"*[50]. They predict GDP to fall by as much as 8% in a year and unemployment to rise to 7.5%.

Arron Banks, a major bankroller of the campaign to leave the EU, reflected on the referendum by saying "Brexit was a war. We won." The use of militaristic language touches on something true for many leavers. The vote to leave was in many ways a gut reaction, a rose-tinted desire to 'take back control', a nostalgia for the glory days of imperial power, national sovereignty and close-knit and unchanging communities. An emotional appeal with which those who supported the EU failed to compete. The UK has been the victim of mismanagement of expectations and it was just the right time. After the 2008 financial crisis and its economic fallout and the refugee crisis in 2015, people were easier to convince. Historically, populists have always been more successful in times of uncertainty – and play on the fear of the other and the supposed disconnect of the elite from the concerns of the common man. As successful as the Brexiteers might have

---

50 https://www.theguardian.com/business/2018/nov/28/bank-of-england-says-no-deal
-brexit-would-be-worse-than-2008-crisis.

been to convince the UK to make this step into unknown territory, it only just be a matter of time until the first negative impacts become obvious.

For the EU it was certainly a shock when the UK decided to leave, but the EU 27 looked into the future and went on with daily business. *"I will miss my British friends but I am not going to cry like a child, climb up a tree with my toys and not come down."*[51] With this, the European Commissioner for Transport, Violeta Bulc, might have just hit the nail on the head. The EU 27 will continue to stand for democracy, peace and prosperity and make the life of its 447 million inhabitants as progressive, free and safe as possible.

After the negotiations are finalised, the reality remains that we will still be neighbours. But the ties that bind us together will be that little bit looser – and the extent to which we synchronise our movements remains to be seen. As the UK moves forward into unknown territory, we can only hope that they, and we, are able to adopt the attitude of Queen Victoria: *"we will not have failure – only success and learning".*

51 Heath, 'Politico Brussels Playbook: EU birth certificate – Trump tones it down – Europe's military HQ', https://www.politico.eu/newsletter/brussels-playbook/politico-brussels-playbook-eu-birth-certificate-trump-tones-it-down-europes-military-hq / (03.01.2017).

Understanding the UK negotiating position on Brexit

Patrick Minford

Any account of British concerns that led to Brexit must begin with the way in which the EU's decision-making functions.

Since the advent of the Single Market, EU decisions have largely been taken by Qualified Majority Voting (QMV) instead of unanimity. This has meant that the UK, which has been unable to assemble a blocking minority, has been unable to stop a wide variety of measures to which it has been opposed. 'Subsidiarity', once suggested as a principle for decisions, has turned out to be an empty word. In practice a blocking minority has not existed; and in this respect other countries have also found themselves in the UK's position. With progress towards a 'Federal Union' having become a mantra for the EU's future official plans, these problems of the lack of UK Voice threatened to spread from the existing areas of economics – trade policy, regulation and immigration – to wider areas covering foreign policy, defence and internal justice. It became apparent to more and more British citizens that they were losing democratic control over their laws, institutions and practices. This was the most powerful general motivator of Brexit.

I. Un peu d'histoire

The history by which this situation occurred is instructive. During the 1980s the Thatcher government was enthusiastic about membership of the EU, seeing it as promoting competition, market integration, free trade and free market policies generally. Because of this enthusiasm, the government promoted strongly the idea of the EU Single Market as an instrument for furthering these free market objectives, with mutual recognition of differing regulative approaches at its centre. M. Delors, then the Commission President, was grateful for this promotion and used it to persuade others in the EU to accept the Single Market (SM), with its commitment to QMV. However, once it was incorporated in the EU Treaties, M. Delors announced several new initiatives. The first was for a new Social Policy to be implemented via the Single Market. The second was a drive for uniform regulation in goods as far as possible, leaving mutual recognition for areas such as some services where uniform standards would be impracticable. The third was a push for European Monetary Union and the Euro, with accompanying macroeconomic controls to support it.

These initiatives were regarded by the Thatcher government as a betrayal of the objectives they had backed in the Single Market proposal. Since that time both government and public opinion in the UK has soured towards the EU.

Matters however came to a head because of the massive immigration into the UK from Eastern Europe, permitted under the SM migration freedom. The Blair government in 1997 contributed to the problem by deciding against a 7-year moratorium which was available and adopted by most other countries. A further factor was the UK's non-contributory welfare system, under which any UK citizen is entitled unconditionally to a wide range of tax credits and tax-funded benefits, such as housing benefits, free health care and free education. Because immigrating citizens from the rest of the EU are entitled by law to the same rights as UK citizens – indeed under EU law they are all EU citizens with common rights – they could not be denied this UK taxpayer support. Three million immigrants from Eastern Europe are now in the UK, enjoying these rights. While skilled immigrants contribute amounts in taxes that generally exceed these benefits, unskilled workers (about a third of the total) do not; for them we calculate that there is approximately a 20% UK taxpayer wage subsidy. Furthermore these workers drive down unskilled wages for UK unskilled workers – an estimate for the Bank of England found that every 10% rise in immigrant unskilled workers there would be a 2% drop in UK unskilled wages. To make matters worse politically, these costs are highly localised in the poorer areas where unskilled immigrants settle: it is the poor residents of these areas who lose through worse health care and education, higher house prices, and lower wages[1].

Into this explosive mixture intruded the financial crisis and the resulting UK 'austerity' programme. The result was the quick growth of UKIP, to a situation where it was getting some 16% of the national votes, with the Conservatives haemorrhaging support for it. Thus was born David Cameron's promise of a referendum: he hoped it would spike the UKIP attack and yet not be lost to Brexit.

---

[1] See Ashton/MacKinnon/Minford, 'The economics of unskilled immigration' (2016), available: http://www.economistsforfreetrade.com/the-economics-of-unskilled-immigration/.

However, his plan went awry, largely because the situation in the UK was not understood elsewhere in the EU. Had it been, and meaningful concessions been offered to Mr. Cameron, the government might have won the referendum. But none were and so the government fought the Brexit case without any solution to offer to the problems I have sketched out above. It was forced to fight on the platform of the 'economic disruption' from Brexit, which as we know failed.

Some now believe that the situation is still salvageable for Remain, through a second referendum. However, there is no precedent in the UK for overturning a referendum, when promised by Parliament to be binding as it was on this occasion. Public opinion is also strongly against another referendum: people regard the necessity to be involved in these decisions as burdensome, indeed complained initially vociferously about the first referendum but later realising its national importance, decided to buckle down and take a lot of personal trouble to decide. A long campaign, virtually six months in length, with massive spending on both sides, was endured; but the idea of a repetition 'until you get the answer right' is dismissed as insulting and totally unjustified. Instead according to the opinion polls there has been since the referendum a large majority for the government 'getting on with Brexit'.[2]

Plainly if the economy were to collapse as the Remain side claimed before the referendum the state of public opinion might change radically. Remainers forecast a recession in the second half of 2016 followed by low growth well below 1% in 2017. This has proved wrong. Growth has continued, even on early ONS estimates that will probably be revised upwards, at close to 2%; the economy is currently at very full employment, with unemployment around 4% and wages starting to grow somewhat faster under tight labour market conditions. Plainly without Brexit employment could not have been any fuller; and of course it is far too early for Brexit to have any effect on productivity. So Brexit cannot have had any effect on the level of output. What it has done via the large Brexit devaluation is shifting demand away from consumption towards net exports, improving a bad current account deficit that was running at 7% of GDP, but is now down to 3.4%.

In sum, the current political situation is volatile, with the main debate today is on whether there should be a 'hard' or a 'soft' Brexit. I now turn to

---

2 Roberts/Curtis, 'Forget 52 %. The rise of the "Re-Leavers" mean the pro-Brexit electorate is 68 %' (2017), available: https://yougov.co.uk/news/2017/05/12/forget-52-rise-re-leavers-mean-pro-brexit-electora/.

this issue. At the time of writing, Parliament has repeatedly rejected the proposed Withdrawal Agreement and there is no consensus within it on a way forward. My analysis here is on what agreement will eventually be possible with the EU, **in the long term**, satisfying constraints on both sides. I assume in all this that there will not be a second referendum- there ia a large majority against this in Parliament-and that the UK will leave the EU at some point; the polls are clear that UK majority public opinion is in favour of ‚getting Brexit done'. Plainly short-term disagreements may well persist for some time to come. Brexit is not an event but an evolving process.Thus any Agreement in the short term will in the long term need to be superseded by a sustainable agreement that rflects the economic interests on both sides that I am about to discuss.

II. What sort of Brexit?

This debate immediately runs up against a problem: 'soft' is not Brexit at all. So it contradicts the referendum and is on the face of it impossible. 'Hard' or 'Clean' Brexit means that the UK leaves the Single Market and the Customs Union, and controls migration; it will also pursue Free Trade Agreements (FTAs) with the rest of the world. This was supposed to be Government policy. However the Conservative Party has now been plunged into confusion by Mrs. May's 'Chequers proposals', which lie at the extreme 'soft' end of the Brexit spectrum. They envisage the adoption of the EU Single Market rulebook on goods, together with social and environmental regulation; in practice close to the existing Single Market regulative set-up. This and the proposed Customs Arrangement also makes FTAs with the rest of the world impossible on standards and difficult even for tariffs. As the proposals cut across EU Single Market rules on migration and financial contributions to 'rule upkeep', further UK concessions on these points appear inevitable.

The economic effects of Brexit

The arguments now focus on the long-term effects of Brexit over the next decade and a half. HM Treasury forecast long-term trade disaster with a 7% fall in GDP if the UK left under WTO rules with no EU trade deal. But more recent work shows this is wrong.

The Treasury (and a number of sympathetic other organisations including the LSE trade group, NIESR, OECD and the IMF) used data correlations between trade agreements, trade, FDI and productivity[3] instead of using a Computable General Equilibrium model whose behaviour is based on causal economic theory. These correlations were defended on the grounds that they reflected the role of 'gravity' (i.e. closeness and size affect trade); but plainly correlations do not imply causation and a CGE approach must be used which may have more or less 'gravity effects' in it. In recent work the Civil Service has produced a joint approach based on a large CGE model along the lines of the GTAP model built at Purdue University, Indiana, and widely used by governments and international institutions to assess trade agreements; in using this model the Civil Service has simply abandoned the methods of the Treasury and its allies. In Cardiff we have built a smaller and simpler CGE model, in both a 'gravity' and a 'classical' version, for testing whether it can match the UK facts; we find that the gravity version is rejected and the classical fits those facts[4]. However, most telling is that whichever CGE version one uses, Brexit generates similarly strong trade gains.

Besides this original failure of methodology, the wide range of groups finding that the Brexit trade regime damages the UK have all (including a few such as PWC that used a CGE model) made unfavourable and, as we will see indefensible, policy assumptions about Brexit. The latest Civil Service work based on the GTAP-style CGE model is no exception.

Its Cross-Whitehall Report, which has now been repeatedly leaked to the media and in the summary form of some two dozen PowerPoint slides can be accessed on the House of Commons website[5], assumes that except under the status quo large-scale barriers due to both divergent standards and border hold-ups will emerge between the EU and the UK. It also assumes that we will be unable to reduce trade barriers against other countries much via our proposed FTAs around the world, estimating the gains at only 0.3-0.6% of GDP. Even taking the higher figure this is small indeed. With these assumptions the economy takes a panning, and of course with

---

3 HM Treasury, 'HM Treasury analysis: the long-term economic impact of EU membership and the alternatives' (2016).
4 Minford/Xu, 'Classical or Gravity? Which Trade Model Best Matches the UK Facts?' (2018) 29 OER, 579.
5 Civil Service, EU Exit Analysis: A Cross Whitehall Briefing (2018), available: https:/ /www.parliament.uk/documents/commons-committees/Exiting-the-European-Uni on/17-19/Cross-Whitehall-briefing/EU-Exit-Analysis-Cross-Whitehall-Briefing.pdf.

it virtually all individual sectors as well, including the government and its revenues.

These assumptions are however totally baffling. Standards in the EU and the UK are currently the same and so for either side to maintain, they were suddenly incompatible after Brexit would be illegal under WTO rules which outlaw discrimination against foreign suppliers. As standards alter in the future exporters on both sides will adapt in the normal way exporters do all over the world, so again there would be no incompatibility. Furthermore, border hold-ups are also proscribed by WTO rules which mandate a seamless border.

Finally, there is huge scope for our FTAs to reduce the EU trade barriers we inherit: these average 20% on both food and manufactures according to both our own and other research. We know[6] that abolishing these via FTAs with the rest of the world would gain us no less than 4% of GDP according to the GTAP model.

The Table below summarises the situation for Canada+ and the WTO option under both the assumptions of this Cross-Whitehall Report and also our own work for Economists for Free Trade (EFT).

Table: Trade Effects under Brexit Scenarios According To GTAP-type Model used by Whitehall

A: Whitehall Assumptions   B: EFT Assumptions

Trade Barriers expressed as % Tariff Equivalent; Effect on GDP shown as % of GDP in italics

	Canada+	WTO	Canada+	WTO
Tariffs	-	4.5	-	4.5
Effect on GDP	-	*-1.0*	-	*-1.0*
New Standards	16.2	20.3	-	-
Effect on GDP	*-3.6*	*-4.5*	-	-
New Customs	5.8	5.8	-	-
Effect on GDP	*-1.3*	*-1.3*	-	-
Total Tariff Equivalent (%)	22.0	30.6	-	4.5
Total Effect on GDP (% of GDP)	*-4.9*	*-6.8*	-	*-1.0*

6 Ciuriak, D./Jingliang/Ciuriak, N./Dadkhah/Lysenko/Narayanan, 'The Trade-Related Impact of a UK Exit from the EU Single Market' (2015), available: http://ssrn.co m/abstract=2620718.

FTAs with rest of world
Effect on GDP (% of GDP)   +(0.3-)0.6   +4.0
All Trade Effects on GDP
(% of GDP)   -4.3   -6.2   +4.0   +3.0

Hence, the Civil Service findings using a GTAP-style model come about using some deeply pessimistic and indefensible assumptions. When reasonable assumptions are put into the GTAP model, it generates good growth from the free trade scenarios of Canada+ or the WTO option. Indeed, the GTAP has examined many such policies over the years, including Australia's extensive and comparable liberalisation of trade in the past thirty years where it found a gain in GDP of 5.4%[7].

In our own Cardiff trade model we estimate that the net gains to GDP would be rather larger than this in the case of the WTO option: this brings us more gains than Canada+ because Brexit comes earlier, the budget contribution falls away, and the tariff revenues redound to the UK Treasury's benefit – details of this are discussed in the next section.

On top of such trade policy gains we estimate from our Cardiff modelling that there will be gains from pursuing a degree of UK deregulation compared with highly intrusive EU directives under the SM. Then there are the gains from controlling unskilled migration; and finally the return of our budgetary EU contribution. Together with trade our work[8] suggests this will add 0.5% per annum to growth over the next fifteen years – around 7% in total to GDP. Consumer prices fall 8% and the living standards of low income households rise 15%.

III. UK negotiations with the EU: possible long term outcomes

We now turn to the question of the likely outcome of the UK negotiations with the EU. We consider in turn three possibilities: a Soft Brexit, No (Trade) Deal and Canada-plus. We will proceed in the manner of Sherlock Holmes, first noting the impossible and then after eliminating the impossible seeing what is left. We will see that neither a Soft Brexit nor a No

---

7 Australian Department of Foreign Affairs and Trade, 'Australian Trade Liberalisation: Analysis of Trade Impacts' (2017), available: https://dfat.gov.au/about-us/publications/trade-investment/Documents/cie-report-trade-liberalisation.pdf.

8 Minford, 'From Project Fear to Project Prosperity, an Introduction' (2017), available: https://www.economistsforfreetrade.com/wp-content/uploads/2017/08/From-Project-Fear-to-Project-Prosperity-An-Introduction-15-Aug-17-2.pdf.

Deal are possible, the first because it is unacceptable to the UK, the second because it is unacceptable to the EU. This, we will argue, leaves only Canada-plus as the acceptable option.

A. EU trade negotiations: the outcome from a full Brexit compared with a Soft Brexit

First consider the gains the UK can expect from leaving the EU's Customs Union and Single Market. The EU's protectionism of food and manufactures raises prices for all those products by an average of 20% over the best available prices in the developed world; it could be much more than that compared with the best available in the developing world, especially China.[9] Eliminating this protection by setting our own tariffs against major world exporters of these products at zero via Free Trade Agreements would give a big gain from the resulting free trade: calculations indicate that by just eliminating half of these barriers consumer prices would fall 8% and GDP be 4% larger.[10]

The EU's Single Market entails EU regulation across the whole of the UK's economic life – production methods, labour relations, energy market and financial markets – even though only 12 per cent of our GDP is involved in selling to the EU. The rest of the economy sells either in the UK or in the rest of the world. By leaving the Single Market the UK can in time recalibrate that regulation to suit the UK economy, with gains estimated at around 2 per cent of GDP.[11] The firms in the 12 per cent who sell to the EU would simply need to meet EU product standards, nothing else. Immigration can be controlled, especially of the unskilled where the UK is obliged under EU free movement within the Single Market to give a 20 per cent wage subsidy to EU immigrants through tax credits (net of taxes paid), housing benefits, and benefits in kind such as education and the NHS (see

---

9 Minford/Gupta/Le/Mahambre/Xu, *Should Britain leave the EU? An economic analysis of a troubled relationship*, (2nd Edition, 2015), chapter 4; for direct estimates of non-tariff barriers consistent with these calculations: Berden/Francois/Tamminen/Thelle/Wymenga, *Non-Tariff Measures in EU-US Trade and Investment: An Economic Analysis*, 13 et seq.
10 Minford, 'From Project Fear to Project Prosperity, an Introduction' (2017), available: https://www.economistsforfreetrade.com/wp-content/uploads/2017/08/From-Project-Fear-to-Project-Prosperity-An-Introduction-15-Aug-17-2.pdf.
11 Minford/Gupta/Le/Mahambre/Xu, *Should Britain leave the EU? An economic analysis of a troubled relationship*, (2nd Edition, 2015), chapter 2.

Ashton et al., 2016, for details). This would give another gain which is particularly significant for poorer households whose wages are also depressed by this subsidised competition. These households in fact benefit on the calculations by around a 15 per cent rise in living standards from the trade and immigration changes.

Any UK trade deal with the EU needs to leave these gains from a 'clean' Brexit intact. This is an economic must as well as politically necessary to honour the referendum result. Moreover, for any government at the latter stage of a Parliament, it should be a key part of a strategy to boost the economy and demonstrate the future gains to be had from policies that optimistically build on Brexit.[12]

It follows that any agreement with the EU must include such a clean Brexit – otherwise the UK will lose these enormous potential gains. A Soft Brexit denies them to the UK. It is therefore unacceptable to the UK. This unfortunately rules out Mrs. May's Chequers Proposals, which have proved extremely unpopular in the UK.

B. What if there was no Trade Deal with the EU?

Here it is important to use a proper trade model. The classical model passes the test of matching the facts of UK trade, while the gravity model is rejected.[13] Accordingly we will use the classical model.

Under no deal, but one where the UK pursues its planned policy outside the Single Market and Customs Union, of creating free trade by signing agreements with the non-EU world, the key effect is to lower UK prices of food and manufactures and create competition inside the UK economy with these new prices. Plainly with an EU free trade deal with no reciprocal tariffs and other trade barriers, EU goods would also arrive free of any duty or other hindrance in the UK and would also compete with these world prices; we can assume that in order to preserve their sales their prices would fall in line; otherwise they would lose all their sales, which we assume they continue, in order to contribute to their overheads.

For UK producers selling in the EU home competition would force their EU prices to equality with world prices: where one UK producer to

---

12 Minford, 'A Budget for Brexit- Economic Report' (2017), available: https://www.ec onomistsforfreetrade.com/

13 Minford/Xu, 'Classical or Gravity? Which Trade Model Best Matches the UK Facts?' (2018) 29 OER, 579.

get more others would divert output to their market, driving prices into line.

Suppose instead there was no deal and this consisted of existing tariffs being levied mutually by both sides (this in fact is the most likely scenario since non-tariff barriers would be discriminatory, given all export products on both sides satisfy product standards and can be assumed to continue to do so by virtue of industries' own self-interest). Then the logic of the competition set out in the previous paragraph would force both EU exporters to charge world prices in the UK market, and UK exporters to charge world prices in the EU market. The implication is that any tariffs placed by the UK on EU exporters would have to be absorbed by those exporters; while any tariff placed by the EU on UK exporters would have to be absorbed by EU importers. Hence the tariffs on both sides would be paid by the EU, the UK tariffs by EU exporters to the UK Treasury, the EU tariffs by EU importers; of course the EU would receive its tariff revenue from its own consumers, making its overall loss equal to the UK tariff revenue – estimated at approximately £13 billion.[14]

On top of this the no deal outcome would mean that there would be no UK financial settlement and no transition period. The EU would be short of some £28 billion over the rest of its budgetary septennial to 2020 (with the UK paying two years' contributions at about £14 billion a year); it would also lose the long term contribution to net liabilities, reported to be worth another £10 billion or so. Also because its customs union with the UK would stop immediately, it would lose two years worth of the terms of trade gain its producers make on its balance of trade surplus with the UK – estimated at around £18 billion a year: so two years worth of that would be another £36 billion one-off loss. Some have suggested that the EU Commission would, on a narrow view, welcome receiving the tariff revenue on UK exports, even though this would be being paid for by EU consumers; however this is estimated at a mere £5 billion per year,[15] less than half the loss of the UK contribution. It does not alter the grim picture of no trade deal for the EU.

From the UK viewpoint paying no financial settlement would be a gain, avoiding the need to pay some £38 billion. So with no transition period,

---

14 Protts, 'Potential post-Brexit tariff costs for EU-UK trade' (2016), available: http://www.civitas.org.uk/reports_articles/potential-post-brexit-tariff-costs-for-eu-uk-trade/.

15 Protts, 'Potential post-Brexit tariff costs for EU-UK trade' (2016), available: http://www.civitas.org.uk/reports_articles/potential-post-brexit-tariff-costs-for-eu-uk-trade/.

free trade, own regulation and own border-control would come two years earlier, bringing forward that long-term gain at roughly 6 per cent of GDP excluding the budgetary transfer, that would amount to some 12 per cent of GDP; assuming that it would otherwise arrive in 2030, bringing it forward to 2028, when discounted at 3 per cent a year, means it would be worth around an extra one-off gain of 9 per cent of GDP, around £180 billion. It would also gain that tariff revenue paid by the EU producers to the UK Treasury, of £13 billion p.a.; which again, discounted, would be worth some £433 billion.

It would seem that overall the breakdown of talks would be positive for the UK to the tune of a one-off gain of £38 billion on the EU budget, plus £180 billion from bringing forward the non-budgetary Brexit gains, plus £433 billion from EU tariff revenue, some £651 billion in all. For the EU it would mean a one-off loss of £38 billion in financial settlement, plus another one-off loss of £36 billion in terms of trade gain, plus the permanent loss due to paying UK tariff revenue of some £13 billion a year which at a 3 per cent discount rate would be equivalent to a one-off loss of £433 billion. So plus £651 billion for the UK versus minus £507 billion for the EU: it could not be more open and shut who least wants a breakdown. For the UK a breakdown would be a short-term nuisance but a substantial economic gain; for the EU it is both a short-term nuisance and a substantial economic loss.

It follows therefore for this No Deal scenario that the EU could not tolerate it – it is simply too damaging.

C. Canada-plus: the only possible negotiated outcome

By 'Canada' we mean a simple zero reciprocal tariff agreement on goods. Since the UK's product standards are already aligned and since it is to be assumed that rational UK exporters would continue to keep them aligned on their exports to the EU, there can be no 'non-tariff barriers' either way. As we mentioned above, it would be illegal under WTO rules for either the UK or the EU to deny entry to the other's goods on grounds of standards, while also border procedures must be seamless. On this basis there would be 'Full Access' to the Single Market. Combined with UK free trade agreements around the world this would ensure that all goods from anywhere reach UK consumers at the most competitive available prices- giving the trade gains of a clean Brexit. Because the UK would be free to regulate its economy as it wished it would also obtain its regulative gains, and also control its borders.

When we turn to services, we can describe Canada-plus as this goods agreement plus mutual recognition of service provision. In other words as now UK service providers to the EU and EU ones to the UK would each be free to ply their trade as now.

There continues to be some pressure for the continuation of the Single Market in financial services in order to retain 'passporting rights' in some form. The Chancellor has tried to accommodate this by indicating that financial services must be part of a final trade deal 'with some sort of enhanced equivalence regime', which will replace existing passporting arrangements[16]. In principle, whilst this is a desirable outcome, so long as it is implemented in a way that avoids the UK becoming a rule-taker, economically the City will continue to thrive as the world's leading financial centre, deal or no deal. It has been shown that there are various ways to conduct business with EU 27 customers from the UK with minimal moves of infrastructure to the EU 27 after Brexit.[17] Indeed there is no actual necessity for the City to be part of the Single Market. And whilst having an 'enhanced equivalence' deal would be preferable this is not absolutely essential either. The sector would also flourish if the UK were its own financial centre, having led the way in framing and shaping much of the international rulebook for financial services.

As the world's leading financial centre, the City sells in all the major markets of the world without receiving any EU protection. In fact what the EU does and increasingly seeks to oblige its EU Member States to do is to put in place a variety of controls for City services, mainly through national regulations of who may sell what in their countries; all that 'passporting' does is to reduce some of the national barriers between Member States, making retailing within the EU a bit easier. The estimates suggest only around 9 per cent of City business is even in theory affected by passporting.[18] In practice with most firms the passport is principally used for wholesale business and barriers remain in the retail markets. Firms doing retail business inside EU countries typically use local subsidiaries anyway as 'work-arounds' for national regulations.

---

16 https://www.bloomberg.com/news/articles/2018-01-25/hammond-says-he-s-very-ha ppy-with-where-pound-is-at-the-moment.

17 Reynolds, 'The Art of No Deal: how best to navigate Brexit for financial services' (2017).

18 Economists for Brexit, 'A brief on the City after Brexit: written evidence to the International Trade Committee, December 2016' (2016), available: https://www.eco nomistsforfreetrade.com/wpcontent/uploads/

The City will gain from Brexit through the UK reclaiming financial regulation from the EU; and it will expand as free trade brings down its key input prices, especially land, i.e. rent as an input cost. It would of course be helpful in the EU trade deal if the EU were to agree to broad-based 'equivalence' under which both sides recognise each other's financial standards as adhering to international overarching principles established by the world's regulatory bodies.[19] This would bring great benefits to the EU in keeping financial markets free within Europe. The EU needs the City which is a significant provider of many financial services.

Should the EU refuse this type of deal and in effect behave in a protectionist self-damaging way, the City would be no worse off in the longer term. Our economic model suggests the logic of world market competition will be followed: the City will divert its trade to other world markets, getting the same world prices there as it did before in its EU trade. This simply follows from the logic of world market competition: the EU by restricting its demands for UK financial products in favour of its home producers does not reduce total world demand for these products nor change world supply, so while the UK sells less in the EU, it replaces EU supply in the rest of the world and world prices are the same. Plainly a sensible equivalence deal is preferable as it avoids the short run costs of such 'trade diversion'; but these are small and quickly got over. To avoid these rather trivial costs by staying in the Single Market would lose the UK's large and permanent gains from controlling its regulations and its borders described above. I am not including such routine things as airline agreements, tourism or visa arrangements in this 'deal'; these are matters of simple co-operation which need to be concluded for ordinary people all over our continent to carry on their lives. Mostly these agreements are concluded within international bodies (such as IATA in the case of airlines). Some such as visas involve bilateral action by governments. In some cases (such as hotel provision) firms simply need to adopt country standards in shaping their products.

What we notice from this analysis is that the EU gains from access to UK service provision, especially the City. In general the EU Commission has pushed for freer trade in services consistently, attempting to reduce national protection of services not always successfully. On a variety of indicators the UK erects few barriers to foreign service provision already. The EU would not wish to erect barriers on top of those already in place from EU

---

19 Reynolds, 'A Template for enhanced equivalence: creating a lasting relationship for financial services between the EU and the UK' (2017).

27 national governments. It follows that the EU will gain from continuing the existing situation in services, while the UK will be content to carry on as now. This gives us the 'plus' in Canada-plus.

IV. Conclusions: the post-Brexit world will be a better world

Out of this Canada-plus agreement will come a Brexit that will promote economic gains not merely for the UK but also internationally. The UK will sign FTAs around the world – with countries including US, China, South Korea, Australia, and New Zealand. These FTAs will cause a drop in world protection and lead to a general search among participating countries for better world trade relations.

The UK and the EU will continue to have open capital markets as now, benefiting from free flows of capital including Foreign Direct Investment.

The UK will regulate pragmatically in areas that are important for its future growth, especially for new technologies, such as biotechnology in food and medicine. It will create a good environment for its vital financial industries. It will look again at regulation in the area of energy policy and climate change, and seek a less costly approach.

In immigration the UK will move to a skills-based policy, which is even-handed between immigrants from all over the world.

As a result of faster growth there will be a Brexit dividend for the UK public finances, which we estimate at £60 bn p.a. by 2025. This can be used to deliver tax cuts and meet public spending priorities, ending 'austerity'. Lower income households will benefit particularly.

The EU will gain too. It will have on its doorstep a country pursuing free market policies. Its loss of one-fifth of its protected market in food and manufactures will force its producers to become more productive.

It will lose 11% of its budget: so it will need to make cuts in subsidy programmes and find a way of raising new general taxation that can buy off vested interests without giving protection, the EU's internal curse.

With exit now seen to be a viable alternative, resistance to centralisation will increase across the EU; this will strengthen the EU as an institution, permitting more regulatory competition and devolution of power.

Brexit will therefore strengthen free markets not just in the UK but also the EU and the rest of the world. It will inaugurate an important supply-side revolution.

Bibliography

Ashton, P., MacKinnon, N. & Minford, P. (2016) 'The economics of unskilled immigration', (London) http://www.economistsforfreetrade.com/the-economics-of-unskilled-immigration/

Australian Department of Foreign Affairs and Trade (2017), Australian Trade Liberalisation: Analysis of Trade Impacts, https://dfat.gov.au/about-us/publications/trade-investment/Documents/cie-report-trade-liberalisation.pdf

Berden, K., Francois, J., Tamminen, S., Thelle, M., & Wymenga, P. (20009) 'Non-Tariff Measures in EU-US Trade and Investment: An Economic Analysis', Final report, Ecorys; cited in Breinlich et al (2016) [Table of ntbs on p 123.]

Breinlich, H., Dhingra, S, Ottaviano, G., Sampson, T., Van Reenen, J. & Wadsworth, J. (2016) 'BREXIT 2016: Policy analysis from the Centre for Economic Performance', (London, 2016), pp154.

Ciuriak, D. & Jingliang X., with Ciuriak, N., Dadkhah, A, Lysenko, D. and Badri Narayanan G. (2015) 'The Trade-related Impact of a UK Exit from the EU Single Market' - a Research Report prepared for Open Europe by Ciuriak Consulting, (2015) http://ssrn.com/abstract=2620718

Civil Service (2018) EU Exit Analysis: A Cross Whitehall Briefing, https://www.parliament.uk/documents/commons-committees/Exiting-the-European-Union/17-19/Cross-Whitehall-briefing/EU-Exit-Analysis-Cross-Whitehall-Briefing.pdf

Economists for Brexit, 'A brief on the City after Brexit: written evidence to the International Trade Committee, December 2016' (2016) https://www.economistsforfreetrade.com/wpcontent/uploads/2017/08/ABriefontheCityAfterBrexit-WrittenEvidencetoIntlTradeCom....pdf

HM Treasury (2016) 'HM Treasury analysis: the long-term economic impact of EU membership and the alternatives', Ref: ISBN 978-1-4741-3089-9, PU1908, Cm 9250PDF, 8.97MB, 206 pages (2016)

Minford, P., with Gupta, Le V., Mahambare, V. and Xu, Y. (2015) 'Should Britain leave the EU? An economic analysis of a troubled relationship, second edition, December 2015', pp. 197, (Cheltenham, 2015)

Minford, P. and Xu, Y. (2017) 'Classical or gravity: which model best matches the UK facts?' forthcoming *Open Economies Review*, (2017), https://link.springer.com/content/pdf/10.1007%2Fs11079-017-9470-z.pdf

Minford, P., (2017a) 'From Project Fear to Project Prosperity, an Introduction', https://www.economistsforfreetrade.com/wp-content/uploads/2017/08/From-Project-Fear-to-Project-Prosperity-An-Introduction-15-Aug-17-2.pdf

Minford, P., (2017b) on behalf of Economists for Free Trade, 'A Budget for Brexit-Economic Report', https://www.economistsforfreetrade.com/wp-content/uploads/2017/11/EFT-Budget-for-Brexit-14.11.17.pdf

Protts, J., (2016) 'Potential post-Brexit tariff costs for EU-UK trade' Briefing note: October 2016, Civitas, (2016), http://www.civitas.org.uk/reports_articles/potential-post-brexit-tariff-costs-for-eu-uk-trade/

Reynolds, B., (2017a) *A Template for enhanced equivalence: creating a lasting relationship for financial services between the EU and the UK*, (London, 2017a)

Reynolds, B., (2017b) *The Art of No Deal: how best to navigate Brexit for financial services*, (London, 2017b)

Economic Implications of leaving the EU for the United Kingdom

Jürgen Matthes

A. Introduction

The withdrawal of the United Kingdom (UK) from the EU (Brexit) will be the first significant event that EU integration goes into reverse. The decision for Brexit has been mainly motivated by the political objective to "take back control"[1], especially to control immigration from the EU and to quit the jurisdiction of the Court of Justice of the European Union (CJEU). However, also economic considerations have played a role. Some proponents of Brexit have even argued that other economic benefits (achieved e.g. by means of deregulation that the EU currently prevents) could outweigh the economic costs of disintegration which are claimed to be only small for the UK.[2]

Moreover, it was alleged before the Brexit referendum on 23 June 2016 that the UK could expect a soft Brexit with only a rather limited reduction of economic integration. Influential Brexit proponents expected that remaining EU countries (particularly Germany and German business organisations) would strongly lobby for such an outcome, because the EU 27 countries overall (including Germany in particular) have a significant surplus in merchandise trade with the UK that would be endangered by a hard Brexit. However, judging from the current negotiating positions of the EU 27 (and Germany) this seems to have been a miscalculation. Instead, the EU 27 (and Germany) put great effort in preventing a kind of Brexit that could be regarded as not establishing a proper balance of rights and obligations, or in other words, that could allow the UK a strategy of "cherry picking" on EU trade preferences. While it still has to be seen whether this negotiating position will prevail, the EU position held up

---

1 May, 'The government's negotiating objectives for exiting the EU: PM speech' (2017).
2 Congdon, *How much does the European Union cost Britain?*, (2014); Minford/Gupta/Le/Mahambare/Xu, *Should Britain leave the EU? An Economic Analysis of a Troubled Relationship* (2nd edition, 2016).

rather firmly in the negotiations about the UK's withdrawal. This is likely to be also due to the fact that in bilateral trade negotiations the relative strength of negotiating positions is generally determined by the relative size of the two markets (and less by the trade balance). As the UK is the much smaller market and is much more reliant for its exports to the EU 27 market than vice versa, the EU 27's negotiation position appears to be considerably stronger.[3] In fact, the EU 27 only exported 5.6 percent of its merchandise exports to the UK in 2017, while the UK's export share to the EU 27 amounted to 47.9 percent.

Apart from these political considerations, the question arises what mainstream economists have to say about the economic effects of Brexit. This article provides an overview of important studies based on a meta-study published shortly before the referendum.[4] This overview is completed by portraying important studies published afterwards. A focus is laid on qualitatively assessing the reliability of the state-of-the-art trade models to predict the economic impact of Brexit. The analysis will centre on the long-term economic effects of Brexit on the UK. However, some sketchy analysis will also be provided on short-term effects for the UK and on economic consequences of Brexit for the EU and Germany.

B. Long-term implications for the UK

The long-term effects of Brexit for the UK depend on the future economic partnership agreement which will determine how severe the economic disintegration will be between the UK and the EU. As this is still an open question, the economic consequences can currently only be analysed with economic models by regarding different scenarios.

This chapter provides a quantitative overview of the results that important studies have produced (Chapter B I) and, in a second step, qualitatively evaluates mainstream economic models (Chapter B II). Moreover, an assessment is provided, how realistic it is that the benefits of Brexit for the UK are realised – i.e. deregulation, new free trade agreements (FTAs) and an end to EU contributions (Chapter B III).

---

3 Matthes/Busch, 'What next after Brexit? Considerations regarding the future relationship between the EU and the UK', IW-Report 16 (2016); Matthes, 'Brexit: Was kommt auf die deutschen Unternehmen zu?', IW-Report 8 (2018).

4 Busch/Matthes, 'Brexit – The Economic Impact A Meta Analysis', IW-Report 10 (2016).

I. Quantifying the economic costs of disintegration and Brexit

1. Early studies

Before the referendum, some Brexit proponents alleged that Brexit would benefit the UK in economic terms, while Remain Campaigners warned about considerable economic damage. Such diverging forecasts call for sound economic research to clarify the net effects of Brexit. In fact, already before the referendum, many analyses attempted to quantify the longer term economic effects of Brexit (or of EU membership) for the UK. The results range from significant advantages to marked losses. At one extreme, it is estimated that the UK would be about 11.5 percent of GDP worse off because of EU membership and would thus benefit from Brexit to this degree.[5] The other extreme is covered by studies that estimate the possible benefits of the UK's EU membership to be in the range of 20 percent (GDP per capita) and more.[6] The UK would lose a sizeable amount of these benefits in case of Brexit. Results in the range of up to 30 percentage points are very dissatisfactory and call for a deeper comparative analysis.

Busch and Matthes[7], on whom this section extensively draws, survey the economic impact studies that were published until April 2016. They distinguish between theory-based forward looking (ex ante) studies (many but not all of which based on own models) and backward looking (ex post) studies. Overall, their comparison shows that the diverging results can be explained by significantly different methods and assumptions as well as a varying coverage of effects:

- On the negative side, in case of Brexit there will be losses due to reduced trade integration with the EU. These disadvantages will be augmented by future losses from foregone new EU trade agreements and from foregone reductions of non-tariff barriers in the internal market.
- On the positive side, fiscal savings due to the (partial) elimination of EU contributions are possible. In addition, lower economic distortions

---

5 Congdon, *How much does the European Union cost Britain?*, (2014), 25.

6 Henrekson/J. Torstensson/R. Torstensson, 'Growth Effects of European Integration' (1997) 41 European Economic Review, 1537–1557; Badinger, 'Growth Effects of Economic Integration: Evidence from the EU Member States' (2005) 141 Review of World Economics, 50–78. Campos/Coricelli/Moretti, *Deep Integration and Economic Growth: Counterfactual Evidence from Europe* (2015).

7 Busch/Matthes, 'Brexit – The Economic Impact. A Meta-Analysis', IW-Report 10 (2016); Busch/Matthes, 'Brexit: The Economic Impact – A Survey' (2016) 2 Cesifo Forum, 37–44.

could be effected because the UK can conclude new FTAs in order to lower external trade barriers that are relatively high for agricultural goods, a limited number of manufactured goods and in large areas or services. It could also withdraw from the common agricultural policy with its strong focus on various farming subsidies. Moreover, in case burdensome and overreaching EU regulations are changed, compliance costs can be reduced and markets could potentially made more flexible.

Busch and Matthes[8] document in their survey that nearly all studies that can be considered relatively reliable and comprehensive[9] come to the conclusion that the disadvantages of Brexit from lower economic integration outweigh the economic advantages. This is a result of most pertinent ex ante economic models employed by the respective authors. However, the size of net costs is considered to be only moderate by the studies published until April 2016, implying a reduction in the level of GDP in the lower one-digit range in the long term (10 to 15 years). This result appears to indicate that the economic effects of Brexit are manageable. Thus, the Brexiteers could easily portray the decision to leave the EU to be mainly a political decision to take back sovereignty and regain self-determination.

---

8 Busch/Matthes, 'Brexit – The Economic Impact – A Meta-Analysis', IW-Report 10 (2016).
9 See e.g. Ottaviano/Pessoa/Sampson/van Reenen, 'The costs and benefits of leaving the EU', CFS Working Paper 472 (2014); Ottaviano/Pessoa/Sampson/van Reenen, 'Brexit or Fixit? The Trade and Welfare effects of Leaving the European Union' CEP Policy Analysis, (2014), http://cep.lse.ac.uk/pubs/download/pa016.pdf [2016-3-8]; Booth/Howarth/Persson/Ruparel/Swidlicki, 'What if ...? The consequences, challenges and opportunities facing Britain outside the EU', Open Europe Report 3 (2015); Aichele/Felbermayr, *Kosten und Nutzen eines Austritts des Vereinigten Königreichs aus der Europäischen Union* (2015); Dhingra/Ottaviano/Sampson/van Reenen, 'The consequences of Brexit for UK trade and living standards' for CEP (2016) for CGE trade models and PwC, Leaving the EU: Implications for the UK economy (2016) and Oxford Economics, Assessing the economic implications of Brexit, Executive Summary (2016) for general CGE macroeconomic models. A dissenting view by Economists for Brexit who estimate positive net effects of Brexit (also based on a CGE model) is thoroughly criticised by Sampson, Economists for Brexit: A Critique (2016), Brexit Paper 6.

2. Qualification of the early studies

However, Busch and Matthes[10] elaborate on the fact that the methods applied in the above depicted ex ante studies fail to cover all relevant channels by which economic integration raises the level of welfare (for more details see Chapter B II). This is due to the fact, that there is no universally accepted ex ante method for model-based estimation available to integrate all of these positive effects of economic integration in a comprehensive way.

Moreover, they point out that according to ex post studies, theoretical ex ante trade models (such as CGE models) tend to significantly underestimate trade effects of free trade agreements.[11] Analyses of the impact of NAFTA (North American Free Trade Agreement) show, for instance, that the underestimation bias can be substantial: a static Computed General Equilibrium (CGE) model predicted an increase of Mexico's exports (imports) relative to GDP amounting to 51 (34) percent during the period from 1988 to 1999.[12] Ex post analysis shows though that the relative increase in exports (imports) during that period was substantially larger with about 140 (50) percent[13].

A relatively new strand of the literature argues that traditional gravity models – the workhorse for ex post analysis of trade agreements – also tend to underestimate trade outcomes[14]. A more modern gravity approach finds

10 Busch/Matthes, 'Brexit – The Economic Impact – A Meta-Analysis', IW-Report 10 (2016).

11 Rosa/Gilbert, 'Predicting Trade Expansion under FTAs and Multilateral Agreements', Peterson Institute for International Economics Working Paper 05-13 (2005); Baier/Bergstrand/Egger/McLaughlin, 'Do Economic Integration Agreements Actually Work? Issues in Understanding the Causes and Consequences of the Growth of Regionalism' (2008) 31, 4 The World Economy, 461–497. Pelkmans/Lejour/Schrefler/Mustilli/Timini, 'The Impact of TTIP: The underlying economic model and comparisons', CEPS Special Report 93 (2014).

12 Brown/Deardorff/Stern, 'A North American Free trade Agreement: Analytical issues and Computational Assessment' (1992) 15 The World Economy, 11–30.

13 Kehoe, 'An Evaluation of the Performance of Applied General Equilibrium Models of the Impact of NAFTA' in Federal Reserve Bank of Minneapolis (ed.), *Research Department Staff Report 320* (2003).

14 Baier/Bergstrand, 'Do free trade agreements actually increase members' international trade?' (2007) 71 Journal of International Economics, 72-95. Egger/Larch/Staub/Winkelmann, 'The Trade Effects of Endogenous Preferential Trade Agreements' (2011) 3 American Economic Journal: Economic Policy, 113–143.

significantly larger results. For example, Baier et al.[15] estimate that membership of the EU (and of its institutional predecessors) has raised trade between members by 100 to 125 percent over a 15-year period alone.

Thus, the question arises whether Brexit could cause significantly higher economic damage to the UK. Looking at the results of several strands of ex post studies, this notion cannot be easily rejected. In fact, Busch and Matthes[16] describe three strands of backward looking studies that attempt to quantify income or growth effects in a more encompassing (but necessarily only implicit) way:

- Using recent forecasts for the negative effects of Brexit on bilateral trade between the UK and the EU, the induced income decline can be quantified in a tentative way. Based on a general **trade-income relationship** calculated by recent thorough studies, three studies estimate that UK incomes could possibly decline by around 10 percent or more in a more pessimistic scenario.[17] An important shortcoming of these attempts lies in the fact that the trade-income relationship could not be tailored specifically to the UK.
- Several studies employ **regression analyses**.[18] Even though the results differ in their details, these studies identify sizeable effects of EU membership on the level of GDP in the long term – mostly in the range of 20 percent or more. However, some uncertainties remain, as the results are in part not completely robust and as growth regressions are notoriously difficult to make watertight.

---

15 Baier/Bergstrand/Egger/McLaughlin, 'Do Economic Integration Agreements Actually Work? Issues in Understanding the Causes and Consequences of the Growth of Regionalism' (2008) 31, 4 The World Economy, 461–497.

16 Busch/Matthes, 'Brexit – The Economic Impact – A Meta-Analysis', IW-Report 10 (2016); Busch/Matthes, 'Brexit: The Economic Impact – A Survey' (2016) 2 Cesifo Forum, 37–44.

17 Ottaviano/Pessoa/Sampson/Reenen, 'The costs and benefits of leaving the EU' (2014), CFS Working Paper 472 (2014); Ottaviano/Pessoa/Sampson/van Reenen, 'Brexit or Fixit? The Trade and Welfare effects of Leaving the European Union' (2014b), CEP Policy Analysis, http://cep.lse.ac.uk/pubs/download/pa016.pdf (2016-3-8). Aichele/Felbermayr, *Kosten und Nutzen eines Austritts des Vereinigten Königreichs aus der Europäischen Union* (2015).

18 Henrekson/J. Torstensson/R. Torstensson, 'Growth Effects of European Integration' (1997) 41 European Economic Review, 1537–1557; Badinger, 'Growth Effects of Economic Integration: Evidence from the EU Member States' (2005) 141 Review of World Economics, 50–78. Cuaresma/Ritzberger-Grünwald/Silgoner, 'Growth, Convergence and EU Membership' (2008) 40 Applied Economics, 643–656.

- Campos et al.[19] apply a relatively new **Synthetic Counterfactual Method** (SCM) which was developed by Abadie and Gardeazabal.[20] Mimicking the approach of clinical studies, the authors construct an artificial synthetic control group by selecting countries with similar economic performance to the UK during a longer time *before* EU accession in 1973 (pre-treatment period). The effect of EU membership (treatment) can be deduced from the difference between the economic outcome for the UK and that for the control group. Campos et al.[21] estimate that in the long run (between EU accession of the UK up to 2008), real GDP per capita in the UK is nearly 24 percent higher than in the synthetic control group. However, this result is not very robust. Focusing on the findings of various robustness checks on productivity increases over a ten year horizon, the respective results lie in the higher single digit range (up to 10 percent). This is still a substantial result, particularly when taking into consideration that benefits might increase further over time.

Figure 1 provides an overview of the approach used by Busch and Matthes[22] to question the notion that long-term economic net costs of Brexit lie only in the lower single digit range. In summary, the authors warn that – in a more pessimistic Brexit scenario – the risk of GDP losses

---

19 Campos/Coricelli/Moretti, 'Economic Growth and Political Integration: Estimating the Benefits from Membership in the European Union Using the Synthetic Counterfactuals Method', IZA Discussion Paper 8162 (2014). Campos/Coricelli/ Moretti, *Deep Integration and Economic Growth: Counterfactual Evidence from Europe* (2015).

20 Abadie/Gardeazabal, 'The Economic Costs of Conflict: A Case Study of the Basque Country' (2003) 93 American Economic Review, 113–132.

21 Campos/Coricelli/Moretti, *Deep Integration and Economic Growth: Counterfactual Evidence from Europe*, (2015).

22 Busch/Matthes, 'Brexit – The Economic Impact – A Meta-Analysis', IW-Report 10 (2016).

to the UK in the broad range of 10 percent or more cannot be ruled out in the long run. This study was also quoted by HM Government[23].

Figure 1: Approach Busch and Matthes

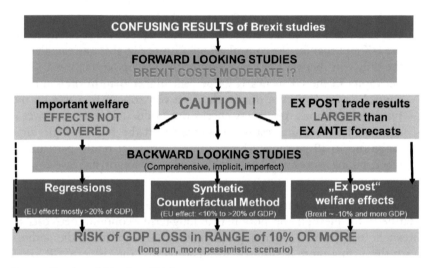

Source: Busch and Matthes, 2016b

---

23 HM Government, HM Treasury analysis, The immediate economic impact of leaving the EU (2016), https://www.gov.uk/government/uploads/system/uploads/attachment_data/file/524967/hm_treasury_analysis_the_immediate_economic_impact_of_leaving_the_eu_web.pdf (2016-9-9).

3. Newer studies

Several studies were published after April 2016 but before the Brexit referendum.[24] Busch and Matthes[25] provide an overview of these studies that include some important effects which these authors criticise to be left out by former studies, particularly a reduction of productivity due to lower trade and foreign direct investment (FDI). The newer studies do so, however, by applying a modular approach. They use a renowned macroeconomic model (NIGEM) that is per se hardly suited for trade policy analyses. Therefore, the respective authors use results from the economic literature and separate estimations, e.g. to determine the effect of Brexit on trade and to calculate the impact of this trade effect on productivity. Strikingly, these studies estimate that the long-term net economic costs of Brexit (in a pessimistic scenario) could lie in the upper single digit range, up to 9.5 percent of GDP in one study.[26]

Several additional studies were published after the Brexit referendum.[27] Depending on the methodology used, nearly all authors come to comparable results as portrayed above.[28]

---

24 HM Government, Treasury analysis, The long-term economic impact of EU membership and the alternatives (2016), https://www.gov.uk/government/publications /hm-treasury-analysis-the-long-term-economic-impact-of-eu-membership-and-theal ternatives (2016-9-9). Kierzenkowski et al., The Economic Consequences of Brexit: A Taxing Decision, (2016) OECD Economic Policy Paper 16, http://www.oecd.org /eco/the-economic-consequences-of-brexit-a-taxing-decision.htm (2016-9-9); Ebell/ Warren, 'The Long Term Economic Impact of Leaving the EU (2016) 236 National Institute Economic Review, 121–138; Ebell/Hurst/Warren, 'Modelling the long-run economic impact of leaving the European Union', 462 NIESR Discussion Paper (2016);Busch/Matthes, Ökonomische Konsequenzen eines Austritts aus der EU am Beispiel des Brexits, IW-Analysen 112 (2016).

25 Busch/Matthes, Ökonomische Konsequenzen eines Austritts aus der EU am Beispiel des Brexits, IW-Analysen 112 (2016).

26 HM Government, Treasury Analysis, The long-term economic impact of EU membership and the alternatives (2016), https://www.gov.uk/government/publica tions/hm-treasury-analysis-the-long-term-economic-impact-of-eu-membership-and-thealternatives (2016-9-9).

27 For an overview of important ones see House of Commons, 'EU Exit Analysis, Cross Whitehall Briefing' (2018), https://www.parliament.uk/documents/commo ns-committees/Exiting-the-European-Union/17-19/Cross-Whitehall-briefing/EU-E xit-Analysis-Cross-Whitehall-Briefing.pdf.

28 This is not the case for studies by Economists for Free Trade (2018 – including Bootle et al. (Alternative Brexit Economic Analysis, https://www.economistsforfre etrade.com/wp-content/uploads/2018/03/Alternative-Brexit-Economic-Analysis-Fi nal-2-Mar-18.pdf (February 2018)) who estimate a positive net effect of Brexit in

II. Qualitative analysis – Additional positive effects of economic integration

Busch and Matthes[29] summarise the substantial but scattered evidence available on individual additional effects of trade or economic integration on welfare and growth, many of which have been shown by sound empirical research to substantially improve welfare and/or growth. The same is true for additional positive non-trade effects of economic integration. These positive effects are partly lost to a country leaving the EU. However, many of these additional effects are not covered by the ex ante trade models portrayed above.[30]

1. Additional static trade effects

The above-mentioned static ex ante models mostly rely on the theoretical framework of perfectly competitive markets[31] where prices merely cover costs and no durable profits exist. However, in reality markets are often not perfectly competitive and in particular firms that differentiate their goods can charge prices above their own costs (mark-up pricing). Higher international competition can lead to lower mark-ups to the benefit of consumers. Thus, the reliance on perfect competition excludes important benefits of economic integration which are particularly relevant for trade between industrialised countries. In fact, higher international competition indeed de-

---

case of implementing unilateral free trade towards the rest of the world (apart from the EU) and in case of broad-based domestic deregulation. However, Smith (Smith/Alasdair, Written evidence submitted (ETP0004) to the UK Parliament – International Trade Committee and Treasury Committee Oral evidence: The economic effects of trade policy, HC 931i, (ETP0004), http://data.parliament.uk/writt enevidence/committeeevidence.svc/evidencedocument/international-trade-commi ttee/the-economic-effects-of-trade-policy/written/83106.pdf (24 April 2018)) points out in detail that this result is obtained by relying on implausible assumptions.

29 Busch/Matthes, 'Brexit: The Economic Impact – A Survey' (2016) CESifo-Forum, 37–44.
30 For a categorisation of studies issued before the referendum according to the effects covered (or not), see Busch/Matthes, 'Brexit: The Economic Impact – A Survey' (2016) CESifo-Forum, 37. This subchapter draws closely on Busch/Matthes, 'Brexit: The Economic Impact – A Survey' (2016) CESifo-Forum, 37.
31 E.g. Ottaviano, 'European Integration and the Gains from Trade', CFS Working Paper 470 (2014); Booth/Howarth/Persson/Ruparel/Swidlicki, 'What if ...? The consequences, challenges and opportunities facing Britain outside the EU', Open Europe Report 3 (2015).

creases markups and raises efficiency in firms, as has been empirically proven.[32] This in turn lowers prices and raises real incomes of consumers.

Additional positive static effects are also relevant (Figure 2):

- Lower prices also result from economies of scale when firms can serve larger markets via exporting and can spread fixed costs over a larger production volume.[33]
- The price dampening effect of open markets has been clearly demonstrated.[34]
- International trade increases product variety which also tends to raise consumer welfare. This important feature of international trade rests on thorough theoretical insights.[35] Empirically, it has been shown for the US that the significant increase in imported product varieties over the last decades has raised consumer welfare by around 3 percent of GDP.[36] Similar evidence also exists particularly for smaller European countries.[37]
- Firms are heterogeneous in reality but not in the economic models employed in the mainstream studies. With heterogeneous firms, import

---

32 Tybout, 'Plant- and Firm-Level Evidence on 'New' Trade Theories' in E. Kwan Choi (ed), *Handbook of International Economics* (2001), 388–415; Feenstra, 'Measuring the gains from trade under monopolistic competition' (2010) 43, 1 Canadian Journal of Economics, 1–28. Feenstra, 'Restoring the Product Variety and Pro-Competitiveness Gains from Trade with Heterogeneous Firms and Bounded Productivity', NBER Working Paper 19833 (2014). Feenstra/Weinstein, 'Globalization, Markups, and the U.S. Price Level', NBER Working Paper 15749 (2010). For evidence on EU countries see Chen/Imbs/ Scott, 'The dynamics of trade and competition' (2009) 77, 1 Journal of International Economics, 50–62.

33 Krugman, 'Increasing Returns, Monopolistic Competition and International Trade' (1979) 9, 4 Journal of International Economics, 469–479.

34 E.g. Erixon, 'Globalization, earnings and consumer prices: taking stock of the benefits from global economic integration', ECIPE Policy Briefs 05 (2008).

35 Krugman, 'Scale Economies, Product Differentiation, and the Pattern of Trade' (1980) 70, 5 American Economic Review, 950–959; Feenstra, 'Measuring the gains from trade under monopolistic competition' (2010) 43, 1 Canadian Journal of Economics, 1–28; Feenstra, *Product variety and the Gains from International Trade* (2010).

36 Broda/Weinstein, 'Globalization and the Gains from Variety' (2006) 121, 2 The Quarterly Journal of Economics, 541–585. See also Feenstra/Kee, 'Export variety and country productivity: estimating the monopolistic competition model with endogenous productivity' (2008) 74, 2 Journal of International Economics, 500–518.

37 Mohler/Seitz, 'The gains from variety in the European Union' (2012) 148, 3 Review of World Economics, 475–500.

competition as well as export opportunities tends to lead to a reallocation of resources (within and among sectors). This reallocation takes
place from less productive firms (which shrink or close down) towards
more productive firms (that can expand). This effect raises the productive efficiency of an economy, as has been shown by various studies.[38]

Figure 2: Selected static effects of trade on welfare levels

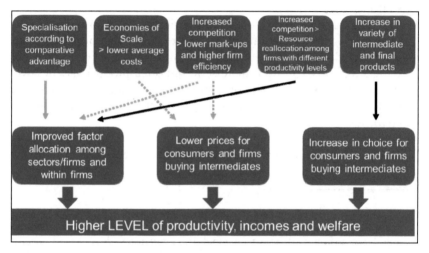

Green arrow: effect covered in most ex ante CGE and NQTM trade models (not in
non-trade CGE models for UK).

Dotted green arrow: effect covered in at least one, but only few ex ante models; these
models only cover selected effects.

Black arrow: effect not covered in ex ante models.

Source: own design

---

38 Tybout, 'Plant- and Firm-Level Evidence on 'New' Trade Theories' in E. Kwan
Choi (ed),*Handbook of International Economics* (2001), 388–415; Feenstra, 'Measuring the gains from trade under monopolistic competition' (2010) 43, 1 Canadian
Journal of Economics, 1–28; Feenstra, *Product variety and the Gains from International Trade* (2010); Melitz/Redding, 'Missing Gains from Trade?' in American Economic Review (2014) Vol. 104 No. 5, 317–32. Edmond/Midrigan/Xu, 'Competition, markups, and the gains from international trade', NBER Working Paper
18041 (2012). for the EU see Corcos/Del Gatto/ Mion/ Ottaviano, 'Productivity
and Firm Selection: Quantifying the 'New' Gains from Trade' (2012) 122, 561 The
Economic Journal, 754–798.

2. Additional dynamic trade effects

Potentially even more important is that the above-mentioned ex ante models mostly lack dynamic effects which induce higher economic growth on a long-term or even permanent basis. The mainstream studies usually estimate a one-off change of the level of GDP (or of living standards) in the medium term by comparing two alternative scenarios for the future. In this respect, they are called (comparative) static. However, sound theoretical deliberations support the notion that additional (dynamic) effects on economic growth are generated by freer trade and by more economic integration.

Various channels come to play in this respect (Figure 3):

- Higher incomes generated by the static effects raise capital returns and thus provide incentives for more investment which increases the capital stock and generates higher economic growth. The capital accumulation induced by lower trade barriers (Baldwin/Seghezza, 2008) might not only be transitory [until the new (static) production level in the medium term is achieved]. It can also be dynamic when a self-reinforcing effect is set in motion that induces a more permanent dynamic effect on economic growth. Wacziarg (2001) as well as Wacziarg and Welch (2008) underline the relevance of capital accumulation as an important channel for the overall positive effect of trade on growth. Based on an analysis of a large country sample for the period 1950 to 1998, Wacziarg and Welch (2008) found that countries which have liberalised their trade regimes experienced about 1.5 percentage points higher annual economic growth rates and 1.5 to 2.0 percentage points higher annual investment rates than before liberalisation.
- The incentive and ability to invest in research and development (R&D) is raised as firms see more opportunities to increase export revenues and profitability when tariffs in foreign markets are lowered and better access to these markets becomes available (Bustos, 2011; Aw et al., 2011). Upgraded technologies and more innovations tend to raise economic growth and thus to have dynamic effects.
- Higher competition due to trade liberalisation also raises the incentives of firms to invest in R&D and to become more efficient and productive. The link between competition and more R&D efforts can be empirically supported (Bloom et al., 2011; Impullitti/Licandro, 2013). Moreover, several studies have shown that more international competition (particularly from lower wage countries) and higher productivity

growth go hand in hand (for the US see Bernard et al., 2006; Auer/ Fischer, 2008; for several EU countries see Chen et al., 2009).

- A positive dynamic effect on productivity growth and thus on economic growth can also result from higher competition via so-called selection effects that imply a reallocation of resources among firms in a sector (Bernard et al., 2006; Bloom et al., 2011; Impullitti/Licandro, 2013; Sampson, 2013). The least efficient firms tend to exit the market due to higher competitive pressures and more efficient firms with higher capacities for innovation and productivity growth tends to grow and absorb more resources. Moreover, the most productive and innovative firms tend to choose to become exporters (self-selection) and they expand with the new exporting opportunities (e.g. Aw et al., 2011). Therefore, a dynamic growth-enhancing reallocation of resources is set in motion towards firms with higher productivity growth and more innovative power.

- The effects of competition, higher innovation incentives and selection effects work in parallel and should thus be seen in combination. In fact, a few studies have attempted to quantify these combined effects: For example, Impullitti and Licandro (2013) estimate in a model simulation fitted to US data that these combined growth enhancing dynamic effects contribute around 60 percent to total welfare gains, if trade costs are reduced from 13 percent of import value to zero. Bloom et al. (2011) calculate for a panel of up to half a million firms across twelve European countries that between 2000 to 2007 increased competition from China alone accounts for around 15 percent of total European technology upgrading. These results should be taken with caution and only as a broad indication, as they rely on the specifications of the respective models.

- Dynamic effects on economic growth can theoretically also be caused by technology spillovers and learning effects that are induced by trade (Grossman/Helpman, 1991). Imported goods contain technological knowhow that can be decoded by the domestic firms, as has been shown empirically particularly for imported intermediate goods (Keller, 1999; 2002; Altomonte et al., 2013). Similarly, exporters can learn from technologies in the world market and can also gain experience and become more productive after entry to export markets (Albornoz et al., 2012; Loecker, 2013). Overall, technological transmission was found to be a relevant channel and to contribute about 20 percent to the positive effect of trade liberalisation on economic growth which was identified by Wacziarg (2001) in a study for 57 countries spanning the period from 1950 to 1989.

Figure 3: Selected dynamic trade effects on economic growth

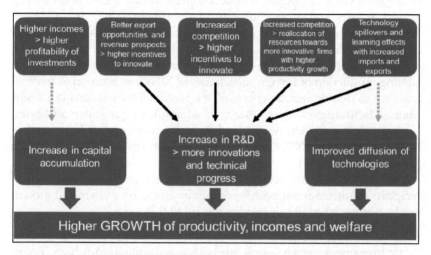

Dotted green arrow: effect covered in at least one, but only few ex ante models; these models only cover selected effects.

Black arrow: effect not covered in ex ante models.

Source: own design

3. Additional non-trade effects of economic integration

The above-mentioned deliberations apply solely to effects of trade on welfare. However, the Single Market relies on the four freedoms. In order to provide a comprehensive picture of possible economic effects of Brexit, the welfare effects of the free movement of capital and of labour also need to be considered. Figure 4 provides an overview of selected channels in this respect and focuses on the relevance of inward FDI. The following section provides some illustrative highlights on these effects.

Generally, mobility of production factors allows for a better allocation of resource internationally that enhances welfare. This is true for capital (Jäger-Ambrożewicz/Matthes, 2012) and – despite the political sensitivity of the migration issue – basically also pertains to labour mobility (Giovanni et al., 2012; Aichele/Felbermayr, 2015; Wadsworth, 2015). Regarding capital, for example, investors can better diversify their portfolio to optimise the return-risk relationship.

On the enterprise side, if domestic manufacturing firms and service providers are free to choose their locations internationally they can optimise global value chains and production networks by means of offshoring as well as sales and production abroad (Markusen, 2002). In particular, British providers of financial and business services take advantage of this opportunity. Empirically, the inclusion of the activities of multinational companies (MNCs) is highly relevant in terms of economic welfare. Including production of foreign subsidiaries of MNCs in addition to trade effects, up to double welfare effects of international transactions can result (Ramondo/Rodriguez-Clare, 2013). In addition, in particular offshoring has been shown to increase productivity, competitiveness and also welfare in general (OECD, 2007; Grossman/Rossi-Hansberg, 2008; Matthes, 2008; Melitz/Redding, 2014).

Inward FDI is particularly important for the UK as the largest European recipient country. Several positive economic effects on welfare and growth can be distinguished in this respect: Inward FDI can

- increase the domestic capital stock, if it does not substitute for domestic investment, which is only likely if capital utilisation is high (Booth et al., 2015);
- raise competitive pressures so that the incentives of domestic firms increase to become more productive and innovative;
- lead to spillovers of technology and knowledge from foreign to domestic firms. As a result, diffusion of technical progress is enhanced and best practices in management are spread (MacDuffie/Helper, 1997; Baldwin et al., 2005); and
- overall, Pain and Young (2004) provide evidence that an increase in the level of the inward FDI stock raises the level of technical progress.

Figure 4: Selected effects on non-trade integration

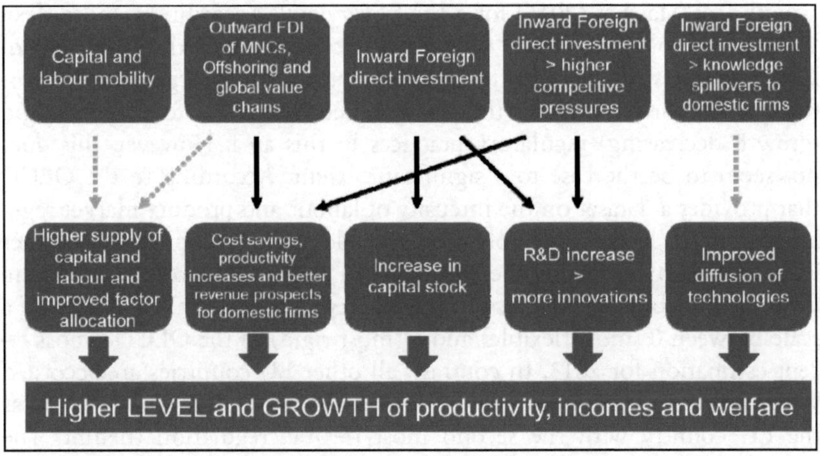

Dotted green arrow: effect covered in at least one, but only few ex ante models; these models only cover selected effects.

Black arrow: effect not covered in ex ante models.

Source: own design

III. *Relevance of positive effects resulting from Brexit*

Not all mainstream ex ante studies include all the potential *positive* benefits of Brexit that were mentioned above, i.e. the abolishing costly and restrictive EU regulations, concluding new liberal FTAs, leaving the EU's Common Agricultural Policy, and eliminating contributions to the EU. Thus, it is important to provide a qualitative assessment of the extent to which these benefits are likely to materialise. In fact, the claim that Brexit would lead to positive net effects for the UK relies on the assumption of exploiting these potentials to a large degree (Busch/Matthes, 2016a; Emerson et al., 2017).

1. *What scope for deregulation?*

A key question is in how far EU regulation leads to economic costs in the UK. In this respect, a differentiation between different kinds of regulations is useful.

To begin with, an extensive literature demonstrates a close relationship between the **regulation of labour and product markets** and economic growth [see Matthes (2015) for a brief overview]. Accordingly, more flexible markets go hand in hand with higher economic growth (in the case of labour markets this pertains to employment protection legislation). Thus, the question arises whether the UK is forced by the EU to adapt to rigid (growth decreasing) regulatory practices in this area. However, this does not seem to be the case to a significant extent. According to the OECD that provides a dataset on the intensity of labour and product market regulation, the UK has considerably more flexible markets than nearly all other EU countries. Concerning the protection of permanent workers against individual and collective dismissals, the UK regulation is ranked at 1.59 on a scale between 0 (most flexible) and 6 (most rigid) in the OECD's most recent estimation for 2013. In contrast, all other EU countries are accorded values above 2. Also in product market regulation, OECD ranks the UK as the EU country with the second most flexible regulation (behind The Netherlands). Thus, the EU does not appear to prevent the UK from choosing rather flexible markets to a considerable extent.

Concerning **product specific regulation and standards**, the UK does not appear to have a large incentive to deviate from EU standards (Matthes/Busch, 2016; Matthes, 2018b) because this would create costly non-tariff trade barriers for UK companies when accessing the EU market which is by far their most important export destination. In case of different standards, UK products would have to be adapted to EU standards to be allowed to be sold in the EU and additional testing and certification procedures could be needed. Both requirements would imply higher production costs and would lessen the price competitiveness of UK products in the EU market. Therefore, UK businesses are actively lobbying for identical or at least very similar product specific regulations and standards. And also the UK Government has already indicated that it intends to maintain closely aligned regulations and standards in this respect (May, 2018).

With regard to EU-driven **regulations of production processes**, criticism were brought forward before the referendum that the EU approach was seen as excessive and costly in a variety of regulatory areas (Open Europe, 2015). Examples with the highest cost burden were found in environmental regulation (e.g. on climate change and renewable energy) and in labour market regulation (e.g. regulation of working time or of agency workers). From this perspective, the UK would have incentives to change certain EU induced regulations. It is questionable, yet, whether this would be done with the intention to lower the protection of workers, of consumers or of the environment, because this is likely to be rather unpopular with the electorate. Notwithstanding this consideration, there might be less costly regulatory approaches to achieve the same or very similar outcomes which the UK Government could choose instead of an EU-based approach. However, the EU is very anxious that the UK could engage in a cost dumping strategy in product markets. Thus, the EU negotiation guidelines condition a future free trade agreement with the UK on maintaining a *"level playing field"* and to *"encompass safeguards against unfair competitive advantages through, inter alia, tax, social, environmental and regulatory measures and practices"* (European Council, 2018). This also applies to tax competition and State aid. As the EU is in a strong negotiation position, the EU's restrictive approach could hamper the regulatory freedom of the British Government that strives for an ambitious future FTA. In a possibly related reaction to this situation, Theresa May (2018) has stated in her Mansion House Speech on 2 March 2018: *"…in other areas like workers' rights or the environment, the EU should be confident that we will not engage in a race to the bottom in the standards and protections we set."*

In summary, it is thus an open question, in how far the economic benefits of deregulation are likely to materialise eventually.

2. What potential for "Global Britain" and new FTAs with third countries?

The UK Government maintains that large opportunities and economic gains are possible by concluding new FTAs with third countries and by thus going for a vision of "Global Britain" (May, 2018). However, also this potential can be qualified.

After Brexit, the UK will lose the trade preferences in accessing third country markets that the EU has negotiated for all Member States – at least after the end of the envisaged transition period, if not already during this time (Burchard, 2018). The decisive question concerns the quality of the new FTAs the UK will be able to negotiate with each of these third countries. To begin with, this will take a longer time period, because FTA negotiations are rather time consuming. What is more, the UK appears to have a weaker negotiating position than the EU had – for several main reasons:

- The UK can only offer a much smaller market than the EU. As trade negotiations are driven by reciprocity considerations, the trade preferences that the UK can obtain in third markets might be of a lower quality compared to the current status.
- The British Government will be in the position of a demandeur as it needs to substitute the loss of market access to many third markets due

to Brexit, while the third countries might feel less pressure to replace the worsened access only to the UK.

- This would all the more be true, if the UK did not worsen the access for third markets to the British economy before a new FTA is concluded (and after the transition period, during which the UK has to provide third countries with the same trade preferences in accessing the British market which the EU has conceded). If the UK found itself in a state where it has lost trade preferences to third countries, but was not prepared to raise trade barriers against these countries during the negotiation phase, there would hardly be any leverage for the British Government.

- Finally, the UK Government has announced to turn to a more liberal trade policy so that the third countries might have to offer less in reciprocal exchange compared to negotiations with a government with a protectionist stance.

However, the UK might offer a larger degree of access to its market compared to the current status by lowering tariff protection particularly in agriculture, but also in more highly protected manufacturing sectors such as passenger cars. However, it remains to be seen whether the UK Government would be able to withstand foreseeable political resistance from protected industries. The same is true for agricultural policy. While Brexit offers the opportunity to leave the EU's inefficient CAP, it remains an open question if UK Government will be able to significantly cut subsidies for British farmers.

Finally, even if the UK were successful in negotiating new FTAs with third countries, it cannot "defy gravity" (Springford/Lowe, 2018). This means that the economic benefits of these new FTAs are likely to be smaller than the economic costs of losing access to the EU market (in a harder Brexit scenario), because the EU is by far the largest trading partner of the UK and is also very close geographically. Trade relations are more intense, the nearer and the larger a partner is, which explains the analogy to gravity.

3. No more contributions to the EU?

The proponents of Brexit often argue that the UK, being a net payer into the EU budget, would no longer have to contribute and could thus use the saved net amount to finance domestic purposes, such as the British National Health Service. There will indeed be relevant savings, but it is unlikely that the full net contribution is available. In her milestone speech on 17

February 2017, Theresa May announced that the UK will no longer pay "vast sums" into the EU budget (May, 2017). In particular, the British Government is prepared to contribute to certain EU programmes.

Moreover, speculations are possible that the UK could offer to pay certain amounts in order secure preferential market access to the EU's market, if trade preferences go beyond a traditional FTA. A parallel could be drawn mainly to Norway, but also to Switzerland that also contributes to the EU (Matthes/Busch, 2016).

C. Short-term implications for the UK

While long-term implications of Brexit are notoriously difficult to estimate because of scenario dependence and model uncertainty, the calculation of short-term effects is somewhat more reliable, as it can be based on ex post data or short-term forecasts.

The UK's exit from the European Union will take place after 29 March 2019. Thus, the economic effects of economic disintegration will only materialise afterwards. Short-term economic effects of Brexit in the meantime are mainly due to anticipating decisions of economic actors.

I. Limited impact of Brexit in 2016

Several studies had forecasted that the uncertainty created by a pro-Brexit outcome of the referendum would lead to an immediate downturn in the British economy (e.g. HM Government, 2016a; Kierzenkowski et al., 2016; PwC, 2016). However, in the second half of 2016 the growth momentum in the UK prevailed and real Gross Domestic Product (GDP) in 2016 increased by 1.9 percent year-on-year. Contrary to expectations, most economic sentiment indicators dropped only temporarily, so that uncertainty effects were limited to a slight decline in private investment (see below). They were countered, before all, by a more expansionary monetary policy of the Bank of England, a strong labour market and buoyant household consumption, and by a certain gain in export competitiveness due to a lower external value of the British currency.

The devaluation of the British pound was one of the most obvious immediate economic effects of the Brexit decision. Following the EU referendum, the pound sterling depreciated by more than 10 percent against the euro. Before the referendum, the British pound was quoted at around 1.30

euros. But even this level was already lower than in the fall of 2015, when the pound was still worth 1.40 euros. At the end of 2015, speculation increased that the EU referendum could take place in the spring of 2016, rather than by the end of 2017. The June 2016 date was finally announced by Prime Minister David Cameron on 20 February 2016. In this phase between November 2015 and February 2016, the exchange rate slid to the pre-referendum level of around 1.30 euros. In 2017, the value of the pound sterling fluctuated within a wider range around 1.15 euros. Compared to the 1.30 euros before the referendum, this translates into a devaluation in a broader band around 12 percent, compared to the 1.40 euros in autumn 2015, the depreciation amounts to around 18 percent.

II. *Losses in real income in 2017 due to pound devaluation*

The effect of this devaluation almost developed in textbook fashion in the British economy in 2017, via inflation, real wage declines and lower private consumption, as the following analysis shows (based on Matthes, 2018a).

While the pound depreciation made British exports cheaper on the world market, it rendered British imports more expensive. Reinforced by the fact, that the UK imports much more than it exports, this import price increase had a significant (albeit delayed) impact on domestic consumer prices. In 2015, the UK inflation rate (according to the Eurostat Harmonised Consumer Price Index) still fluctuated around 0 percent. But after the end of 2015, it rose almost continuously. It reached 3 percent in September 2017 and broadly remained at this level until early 2018. The pound devaluation is likely to have contributed significantly to this increase in inflation.

Figure 5: UK: Effect of the pound sterling devaluation on real wages and private consumption

Pound sterling in euros; other items: percentage change between values for fourth quarter of respective years compared to the same quarter in the previous year (yoy)

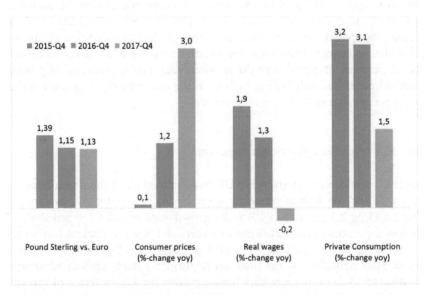

Real wages: average weekly earnings, (total and regular real pay), annual growth rates, whole economy, seasonally adjusted; pound exchange rate, consumer prices, real wages: quarterly average of monthly values.

Sources: ONS; Eurostat; German Economic Institute

The significantly higher price increase reduced real incomes in the UK. This can be illustrated by the development of nominal and real wages. Total pay (including bonus payments) in nominal terms increased by 2.5 percent year-on-year in the fourth quarter of 2017, according to the Office for National Statistics. The nominal wage increase was thus the same as in the fourth quarter of 2016 and even higher than in the fourth quarter of 2015 (2 percent, Figure 5). But with inflation soaring, real wages in the UK did not rise further as before, but actually fell slightly. In fact, in the fourth quarter of 2017, the year-on-year decline was –0.2 percent. In May 2017, the real wage loss had even reached –0.6 percent year-on-year. Compared to previous years, this is a marked change. Real wages had increased in the fourth quarter of 2016 compared to the previous year by 1.3 percent and in 2015 (Q4) by 1.9 percent. While the increase in the inflation rate will only be temporary, the negative effect on the level of real wages will prevail. In this respect, British employees already had to suffer a negative permanent effect from Brexit.

On top of this, also domestic private household consumption lost momentum and contributed to a lower rate of economic growth, because the fall in real wages reduced the purchasing power of private households. As a result, the growth rate of private consumption declined significantly. In real terms, consumer spending in the fourth quarter of 2017 increased by only 1.5 percent compared with the previous year. This growth rate of private consumption was only half as high as in the two previous years, when the increase amounted 3 percent respectively.

III. Slower economic growth and investment

Overall, economic growth in the UK has declined since the Brexit referendum. While the British economy grew by an impressive 3.1 percent in 2014 and by 2.3 percent in 2015, the growth rate of real GDP fell slightly below 2 percent in the following two years and is set to decline further to about 1.5 percent and less from 2018 to 2020 according to current forecasts. Strikingly, the UK has thus lost its formerly stable growth advantage compared to the Euro area that has overtaken the UK in terms of growth momentum since 2017 (Figure 6): While real GDP in the Euro area grew by between 1.3 and 1.7 percent in the period 2014 to 2016, economic growth in the Euro area accelerated to 2.5 percent in 2017 and was forecasted by the OECD in June 2018 to reach more than 2 percent in 2018 and 2019.

Figure 6: Economic growth in the UK and the euro area since 2010

Percentage change of real GDP

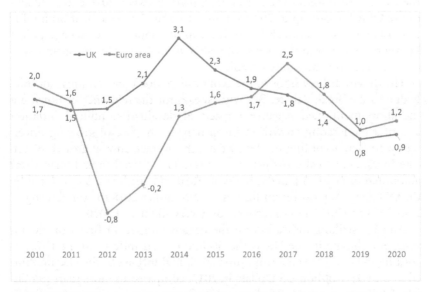

2019 and 2020: Forecast of the OECD March 2019 Economic Outlook update.

Source: OECD

The growth decline in the UK is also highly relevant from a domestic British perspective. This can be illustrated by the medium term growth forecasts of the UK's Office for Budget Responsibility (OBR) that are presented biannually for the budget speeches of the British Chancellor of the Exchequer. In the following, the OBR's economic outlook after the Brexit referendum is compared to that of autumn 2015 – i.e. before the debate about Brexit gained momentum. This comparison highlights that the British Government has continually corrected its growth forecasts downwardly (for more details see Matthes et al., 2017).

In November 2015, the OBR forecasted relatively dynamic real economic growth of between 2.3 and 2.5 percent per year for the years 2016 to 2020. As a matter of fact, however, real GDP grew by only 1.9 percent in 2016, 1.8 percent in 2017 and only 1.4 percent in 2018. In its March 2019 report, the OBR forecasted an even lower growth rates of 1.2 percent for 2019, and 1.4 percent for 2020. These downward revisions are significant in a medium term perspective. This can be shown by cumulating the projected GDP growth rates and thus calculating the growth over the entire period from 2016 to 2020. In November 2015, the OBR anticipated cumulative real GDP growth of 12.6 percent over that period. In March 2019, the cumulated result of the economic growth between 2016 and 2018 and of the OBR forecast up to 2020 amounts to only 7-9 percent. If both OBR forecasts are taken seriously, there is a gap of about 4.7 percentage points between the two resulting levels of real GDP in 2020. This prospective decline in economic output is sizeable.

The downward revisions of the economic outlook are certainly not solely due to the Brexit debate. But what speaks for the relevance of Brexit are the above-mentioned negative impacts of devaluation-induced inflation and of a moderating growth in investment in the face of growing uncertainty. In fact, according to OECD data, the average annual growth of private investment (real gross private non-residential fixed capital formation) amounted to nearly 5 percent between 2010 and 2015, but is forecasted by the OECD in its most recent forecast of November 2018 to even fall slightly in 2018 and 2019 and to recovery only very slightly in 2020.

Another striking indication for the negative impact of Brexit on the investment climate in the UK is the decline in FDI inflows to the UK. According to UNCTAD data from June 2018, FDI inflows to the UK amounted to only 15.1 billion US Dollars in 2017, compared to more than 196 billion US Dollars in 2016. While the 2016 figure appears to be extraordinarily high, a comparison to a medium term average also indicates the declining attractiveness of the UK as an international investment destination. In fact, the average FDI inflows between 2010 and 2016 amounted to nearly 66 billion US Dollars annually (2010-2015: 44 billion US Dollars). In this time span, but also in the longer term comparison of 2000-2016, the UK used to be the top FDI destination in the EU 28. Currently, this is no longer the case. In 2017, more FDI flowed to the Netherlands ($58 bn.), France ($50 bn.), Germany ($35 bn.), Ireland ($ 29 bn.), Spain ($ 19 bn.), Italy ($ 17 bn.) and Sweden ($ 15.3 bn.).

D. Economic implications for Germany and the EU

The main focus of this article lies on the economic impact of Brexit on the UK. However, some brief and sketchy analysis of the economic consequences for the EU and Germany will be provided in the following section. Generally speaking, the most important determinants for the economic effects (apart from the Brexit scenario) are the existing degree of trade integration with the UK, the negative impact of Brexit on UK demand for

EU exports and the extent of the exchange rate change of the British pound – with a pound devaluation implying a loss of price competitiveness of EU exports in the UK (and a gain for domestic consumers due to cheaper imports from the UK).

While the EU 27 exported 5.6 percent of its merchandise goods exports to the UK in 2017, for Germany this share amounted to 6.6 percent. This renders the UK the fifth largest merchandise trading partner for the German economy. Moreover, the German merchandise trade surplus with the UK accounted for 19 percent of the overall German merchandise trade surplus. Taking into account cross-border value chains (and the extent to which local production is directly or indirectly exposed by trade connections via other countries to Brexit), Germany is the second most exposed EU country behind Ireland (Chen et al., 2017). At first sight, these facts seem to indicate that Brexit could be rather detrimental to the German economy. Therefore, Germany is chosen as an illustrative example.

I. Long-term implications

However, while the available empirical evidence on the impact of Brexit on Germany is very scarce, the few existing studies indicate that the negative effects are likely to remain rather limited. This is the result of one kind of the above-mentioned forward-looking trade models (Chapter B). Accordingly, even the impact of a hard Brexit (WTO scenario with tariffs and with ambitious UK FTAs with the USA, Canada, Japan) would lower the level of real GDP in Germany by only 0.24 percent in the long term (Felbermayr et al., 2017). Another earlier model approach by the ifo Institute comes to qualitatively similar conclusions (Aichele/Felbermayr, 2015). While these models are susceptible to the above-mentioned criticism and might thus underestimate the economic consequences (Chapter B II), even an assumed doubling or trebling of these effects would result in only a minor overall impact in the long term.

Another qualitative result is important: The UK is estimated to be considerably more negatively affected by Brexit than Germany. This result also holds up for the EU 27 in total and for most individual EU Member States – with only a few exceptions such as Ireland, Luxembourg and Malta

(Emerson et al., 2017; Felbermayr et al., 2017).[39] This relative statement is rather independent of the criticism of the trade models that can be brought forward.

The contradicting evidence to the above impression that Germany could also be severely affected by Brexit can be largely explained by the following arguments: The UK is only one of Germany's many trading partners of moderate relevance; Brexit will not lead to a complete stop of trade relations; some former German exports to the UK can be diverted to other countries; some former German imports from the UK will be replaced by domestic German production; and the EU is a larger trading partner for the UK than vice versa.

II. Short-term implications

Even though the above-mentioned qualitative results appear to be broadly reliable, more precise quantitative results depend on the Brexit scenario and eventually rough estimations remain. Again, in the short term, Brexit effects can be quantified with less uncertainty. Apart from the certain decline in economic growth in the UK (and thus in demand for EU exports), the devaluation of the British pound after the referendum is the main economic Brexit effect to date (Chapter C).

Kolev et al. (2016) calculate the impact of the pound depreciation on German trade with the UK and on Germany's economic output by means of a cointegration analysis (Johansen, 1988). Thus, based on historical data the relevant long-term effects can be identified. The study reveals the following results (for details see Kolev et al., 2016):

- A coefficient of –0.62 was calculated for the exchange rate responsiveness of German exports of goods and services to the UK. On this basis, a depreciation of the pound by 10 percent against the euro is accompanied by a reduction in German exports to the UK by some 6 percent (ceteris paribus).
- For the responsiveness of German UK exports to economic growth in the UK, the coefficient lies at 1.78. Thus, a decline in the UK's GDP by about 1 percentage point is associated with a decline in German exports to the UK by around 1.8 percent (ceteris paribus).

---

39 For a comparative survey of studies on the impact of Brexit on the EU-27 see Emerson et al., *An Assessment of the Economic Impact of Brexit on the EU27, Study by CEPS for the European Parliament* (2017).

- The effect of the depreciation of the pound on Germany's imports from the UK is smaller, but still negative. The coefficient lies at –0.35, implying that a 10 percent depreciation of the British pound is accompanied by a decline in Germany's imports by 3.5 percent. This negative effect contradicts the prevalent textbook hypothesis that a depreciation of a partner country's currency tends to have a positive impact on the home economy's imports. In Germany's case, this is likely to be due to the strong link to the UK in terms of intermediate input and the high share of imported intermediate inputs used in German exports.
- The analysis of impulse response functions shows that a shock coming from the exchange rate or from GDP of the UK would have a lasting impact on Germany's exports and that this long-term effect would already set in after two or three quarters.

Taken together, what does this mean for German trade with the UK and German GDP in the second half of 2016 (after the Brexit referendum)? When taking into account that (despite expectations to the contrary) economic growth in the UK remained relatively robust at 1.9 percent, only the pound depreciation of 10 to 15 percent after the referendum is of major relevance. According to the above-mentioned elasticities, German exports to the UK should have fallen by about 6 to 9 percent by the end of 2016 – in fact somewhat less than that when bearing in mind that the effects take two to three quarters to materialise. As a matter of fact, according to official trade data German merchandise exports fell by 7.2 percent in the second half of 2016 compared to the second half of 2015. In 2017, the short-term devaluation effect was hardly relevant any longer and economic growth remained at slightly below 2 percent in 2017. As a result, German merchandise exports to the UK remained broadly stable in 2017.

The pound devaluation's effect on German exports and imports can be estimated to have reduced Germany's economic output by about one-fourth of a percentage point in the second half of 2016. In other words, economic growth in Germany would have been higher in 2016 without Brexit by approximately this amount. However, including the Brexit effect, German real GDP still grew by 1.9 percent. Based on strong domestic demand and a buoyant labour market, the German economy managed to weather the first Brexit storm without really feeling the chill. However, the uncertainty about a possible No-Deal-Brexit since autumn 2018 might have contributed to the cooling-off of the German economy since mid 2018.

E. Bibliography

Abadie, Alberto/Gardeazabal, Javier, 'The Economic Costs of Conflict: A Case Study of the Basque' Country (2003) 93, 1 American Economic Review, 113–132.

Aichele, Rahel/Felbermayr, Gabriel, *Kosten und Nutzen eines Austritts des Vereinigten Königreichs aus der Europäischen Union* (Munich April 2015).

Albornoz, Facundo/Calvo Pardo, Héctor F./Corcos, Gregory/Ornelas, Emanuel, 'Sequential exporting' (2012) 88, 1 Journal of International Economics, 17–31.

Altomonte, Carlo/Aquilante, Tommaso/Békés, Gábor/Ottaviano, Gianmarco I. P., 'Internationalization and innovation of firms: evidence and policy' (2013) 76 Economic policy: a European forum, 663–700

Auer, Raphael/Fischer, Andreas M., 'The Effect of Trade with Low-Income Countries on U.S. Industry' (2008) CEPR Discussion Paper Series 6819.

Aw, Bee Yan/Roberts, Mark J./Yi Xu, Daniel, 'R&D Investment, Exporting, and Productivity Dynamics' (2011) American Economic Review 101, 4, 1312–1344.

Badinger, Harald, 'Growth Effects of Economic Integration: Evidence from the EU Member States' (2005) 141 Review of World Economics, 50–78.

Baier, Scott L./Bergstrand, Jeffrey H., 'Do free trade agreements actually increase members' international trade?' (2007) 71, 1 Journal of International Economics, 72–95.

Baier, Scott L./Bergstrand, Jeffrey H./Egger, Peter/McLaughlin, Patrick A., 'Do Economic Integration Agreements Actually Work? Issues in Understanding the Causes and Consequences of the Growth of Regionalism' (2008) 31, 4 The World Economy, 461–497.

Baldwin, Richard/Seghezza, Elena, 'Testing for Trade-Induced InvestmentLed Growth' (2008) 61, 2–3 Economia Internazionale/International Economics, 507–537.

Baldwin, Richard/Braconier, Hernik/Forslid, Rikard, 'Multinationals, Endogenous Growth, and Technological Spillovers: Theory and Evidence' (2005) 15, 5 Review of International Economics, 945–963.

Bernard, Andrew B./Jensen, J. Bradford/Schott, Peter K., 'Trade Costs, Firms and Productivity' (2006) 53 Journal of Monetary Economics, 917–937.

Bloom, Nicholas/Draca, Mirko/Van Reenen, John, 'Trade Induced Technical Change? The Impact of Chinese Imports on Innovation, IT and Productivity', (2011) NBER Working Papers 16717.

Booth, Stephen et al., *What if…? The consequences, challenges and opportunities facing Britain outside the EU*, Open Europe Report 3(London 2015).

Bootle et al., Alternative Brexit Economic Analysis, (February 2018) https://www.ec onomistsforfreetrade.com/wp-content/uploads/2018/03/Alternative-Brexit-Econo mic-Analysis-Final-2-Mar-18.pdf

Broda, Christian/Weinstein, David E., 'Globalization and the Gains from Variety' (2006) 121, 2 The Quarterly Journal of Economics, 541–585.

Brown, Drusilla K./Deardorff, Alan V./Stern, Robert M., 'A North American Free Trade Agreement: Analytical Issues and Computational Assessment' (1992) 15, 1 The World Economy, 11–30.

Burchard, Hans von der, EU trade partners demand concessions for Brexit transition rollover. During a transition period, the UK must abide by EU trade agreements but has no guarantee that third countries will do the same, Article for Politico, (5 February 2018) https://www.politico.eu/article/eu-trade-partners-obje ct-to-brexit-transition-roll-over/

Busch, Berthold/Matthes, Jürgen, 'Brexit – The Economic Impact – A Meta-Analysis', IW-Report 10 (Cologne 2016a).

Busch, Berthold/Matthes, Jürgen,'Brexit: The Economic Impact – A Survey' (2016b) 2 CESifo-Forum, 37–44.

Busch, Berthold/Matthes, Jürgen, 2016c, *Ökonomische Konsequenzen eines Austritts aus der EU am Beispiel des Brexits*, IW-Analysen 112 (Cologne 2016c).

Bustos, Paula, 'Trade Liberalization, Exports and Technology Upgrading: Evidence on the impact of MERCOSUR on Argentinian Firms' (2011) 101, 1 American Economic Review, 304–340.

Campos, Nauro F./Coricelli, Fabrizio/Moretti, Luigi, 'Economic Growth and Political Integration: Estimating the Benefits from Membership in the European Union Using the Synthetic Counterfactuals Method', IZA Discussion paper 8162 (Bonn 2014)

Campos, Nauro F./Coricelli, Fabrizio/Moretti, Luigi, *Deep Integration and Economic Growth: Counterfactual Evidence from Europe*, mimeo (Brunel University 2015)

Chen, Natalie/Imbs, Jean/Scott, Andrew, 'The dynamics of trade and competition' (2009) 77, 1 Journal of International Economics, 50–62.

Chen, Wen et al., The continental divide? Economic exposure to Brexit in regions and countries on both sides of The Channel, Papers in Regional Science, Open Access, (2017) https://onlinelibrary.wiley.com/doi/full/10.1111/pirs.12334.

Congdon, Tim, *How much does the European Union cost Britain?* (UKIP, Dagenham 2014).

Corcos, Gregory/Del Gatto, Massimo/Mion, Giordano/Ottaviano, Gianmarco I. P., 'Productivity and Firm Selection: Quantifying the 'New' Gains from Trade' (2012) 122, 561 The Economic Journal, 754–798.

Crespo Cuaresma, Jesus/Ritzberger-Grünwald, Doris/Silgoner, Maria Antoinette, 'Growth, Convergence and EU Membership' (2008) 40, 5 Applied Economics, 643–656.

Dhingra, Swati/Ottaviano, Gianmarco/Sampson, Thomas/Reenen, John van, The consequences of Brexit for UK trade and living standards, CEP, (2016) http://cep. lse.ac.uk/pubs/download/brexit02.pdf [2016-3-22].

Ebell, Monique/Warren, James,'The Long Term Economic Impact of Leaving the EU' (2016) 236 National Institute Economic Review, 121–138.

Ebell, Monique/Hurst, Ian/Warren, James, 'Modelling the long-run economic impact of leaving the European Union', NIESR Discussion Paper 462 (London 2016).

Economists for Free Trade, What if we can't agree? Why a world trade deal exit from the EU will be best for the UK, (June 2018) https://www.economistsforfreetrade.com/wp-content/uploads/2018/06/Why-a-World-Trade-Deal-exit-from-the-EU-m ay-be-best-for-the-UK-Final-15.06.18.pdf

Edmond, Chris/Midrigan, Virgiliu/Xu, Daniel Y., 'Competition, markups, and the gains from international trade', NBER Working Paper 18041 (Cambridge, MA 2012).

Egger, Peter/Larch, Mario/Staub, Kevin E./Winkelmann, Rainer, 'The Trade Effects of Endogenous Preferential Trade Agreements' (2011) 3, 3 American Economic Journal: Economic Policy, 113–143.

Emerson et al., *An Assessment of the Economic Impact of Brexit on the EU27, Study by CEPS for the European Parliament* (Brussels 2017).

Erixon, Frederik, 'Globalization, earnings and consumer prices: taking stock of the benefits from global economic integration', ECIPE Policy Briefs 05 (Brussels 2008).

European Council, European Council (Art. 50) guidelines following the United Kingdom's notification under Article 50 TEU, (2018) http://www.consilium.eur opa.eu/en/press/press-releases/2017/04/29/euco-brexit-guidelines/.

Feenstra, Robert C., 'Measuring the gains from trade under monopolistic competition' (2010a) 43, 1 Canadian Journal of Economics, 1–28.

Feenstra, Robert C., *Product variety and the Gains from International Trade* (Cambridge, MA 2010b).

Feenstra, Robert C., 'Restoring the Product Variety and Pro-Competitiveness Gains from Trade with Heterogeneous Firms and Bounded Productivity', NBER Working Paper 19833 (Cambridge, MA 2014).

Feenstra, Robert C./Kee, Hiau Looi, 'Export variety and country productivity: estimating the monopolistic competition model with endogenous productivity' (2008) 74, 2 Journal of International Economics, 500–518.

Feenstra, Robert C./Weinstein, David E., 'Globalization, Markups, and the U.S. Price Level', NBER Working Paper 15749 (Cambridge MA 2010).

Felbermayr, Gabriel et al., *Ökonomische Effekte eines Brexit auf die deutsche und europäische Wirtschaft*, Studie im Auftrag des Bundesministeriums für Wirtschaft und Energie (BMWi), ifo Studie (Munich 2017).

Giovanni, Julian di/Levchenko, Andrei/Ortega, Francesc, 'A Global View of Cross-Border Migration', CReAM Discussion Paper Series 18/12 (London 2012).

Grossman, Gene M./Helpman, Elhanan, *Innovation and Growth in the Global Economy* (Cambridge, MA 1991).

Grossman, Gene M./Rossi-Hansberg, Esteban, 'Trading Tasks: A Simple Theory of Off-Shoring' (2008) 98, 5 American Economic Review, 1978– 1997.

Henrekson, Magnus/Torstensson, Johan/Torstensson, Rasha, 'Growth Effects of European Integration' (1997) 41 European Economic Review, 1537–1557.

HM Government, HM Treasury analysis. The immediate economic impact of leaving the EU, (2016a) https://www.gov.uk/government/uploads/system/uploads/att achment_data/file/524967/hm_treasury_analysis_the_immediate_economic_im pact_ of_leaving_the_eu_web.pdf [2016-9-9].

HM Government, Treasury analysis. The long-term economic impact of EU membership and the alternatives, (2016b) https://www.gov.uk/government/publicati o n s/ hm-treasury-analysis-the-long-term-economic-impact-of-eu-membership-and-thealternatives [2016-9-9].

House of Commons, EU Exit Analysis, Cross Whitehall Briefing, (2018) https://ww w.parliament.uk/documents/commons-committees/Exiting-the-European-Union /17-19/Cross-Whitehall-briefing/EU-Exit-Analysis-Cross-Whitehall-Briefing.pdf.

Impullitti, Giammario/Licandro, Omar, 'Trade, firm selection, and innovation: the competition channel', University of Nottingham, School of Economics (ed.), Discussion Papers 13/04 (2013).

Jäger-Ambrożewicz, Manfred/Matthes, Jürgen, ,Finanzmarkt – Beschleuniger oder Bremse des Wachstums?', in Institut der deutschen Wirtschaft Köln (Ed.), *Wirtschaftswachstum?! – Warum wir wachsen sollten und warum wir wachsen können*, IW-Studien (Cologne 2012), 173–188.

Johansen, S., *Likelihood-Based Inference in Cointegrated Vector Autoregressive Models*, Oxford University Press (Oxford 1988).

Kehoe, Thimoty J.,'An Evaluation of the Performance of Applied General Equilibrium Models of the Impact of NAFTA', in Federal Reserve Bank of Minneapolis (ed.), Research Department Staff Report 320 (2003).

Keller, Wolfgang, 'How Trade Patterns and Technology Flows Affect Productivity Growth', NBER Working Papers 6990 (1999).

Keller, Wolfgang, 'Trade and the Transmission of Technology' (2002) 7, 1 Journal of Economic Growth, 5–24.

Kierzenkowski, Rafal et al., The Economic Consequences of Brexit. A Taxing Decision, OECD Economic Policy Paper 16, (2016) http://www.oecd.org/eco/the-eco nomic-consequences-of-brexit-a-taxing-decision.htm [2016-9-9].

Kolev, Galina/Matthes, Jürgen/Busch, Berthold, Brexit impacts on Germany?, IW-Kurzbericht 71 (Cologne 2016)

Krugman, Paul, 'Increasing Returns, Monopolistic Competition and International Trade' (1979) 9, 4 Journal of International Economics, 469–479.

Krugman, Paul, 'Scale Economies, Product Differentiation, and the Pattern of Trade' (1980) 70, 5 American Economic Review, 950–959.

Loecker, Jan de, 'Detecting Learning by Exporting' (2013) 5, 3 American Economic Journal: Microeconomics, 1–21.

MacDuffie, John Paul/Helper, Susan, 'Creating Lean Suppliers: Diffusing Lean Production Through the Supply Chain' (1997) 39, 4 California Management Review, 118-151.

Markusen, James R., *Multinational firms and the theory of international trade*, (Cambridge,MA 2002).

Matthes, Jürgen, 'Globalisierung – Ursache zunehmender Lohnungleichheit', in IW Köln (ed.), *Die Zukunft der Arbeit in Deutschland – Megatrends, Reformbedarf und Handlungsoptionen* (Cologne 2008), 31–64.

Matthes, Jürgen, 'Krisenländer: Relevanz von Strukturreformen für Wachstum und Währungsraum' (2015) 92, 2 Wirtschaftsdienst, 106-113.

Matthes, Jürgen, 'Wachstumskosten des Brexit', IW-Kurzbericht 81 (Cologne 2017).

Matthes, Jürgen, 'Brexit führt zu Schwäche bei Reallöhnen und Konsum', IW-Kurzbericht 18 (Cologne 2018a).

Matthes, Jürgen, 'Brexit: Was kommt auf die deutschen Unternehmen zu?', IW-Report 8 (Cologne 2018b).

Matthes, Jürgen/Busch, Berthold, 'What next after Brexit? Considerations regarding the future relationship between the EU and the UK', IW-Report 16 (Cologne 2016).

Matthes, Jürgen/Busch, Berthold/Kolev, Galina, 'Auswirkungen des Brexit auf das UK und Deutschland' (2017) 1 List-Forum, 35–55.

May, Theresa, 'The government's negotiating objectives for exiting the EU: PM Speech' (17 January 2017).

May, Theresa, 'PM speech on our future economic partnership with the European Union', (2 March 2018) https://www.gov.uk/government/speeches/ pm-speech-on-our-future-economic-partnership-with-the-european-union [2018-3-2].

Melitz, Marc J./Redding, Stephen J., 'Heterogeneous Firms and Trade' (2012) NBER Working Paper 18652 (Cambridge, MA 2012).

Melitz, Marc J./Redding, Stephen J., 2014, Missing Gains from Trade?, in: American Economic Review, Vol. 104, No. 5, pp. 317–321.

Minford, P./Gupta, S./Le, V./Mahambare, V./Xu, Y., *Should Britain Leave the EU? An Economic Analysis of a Troubled Relationship*, (2nd edition, IEA 2016).

Mohler, Lukas/Seitz, Michael, 'The gains from variety in the European Union' (2012) 148, 3 Review of World Economics, 475–500.

OECD – Organisation for Economic Co-operation and Development, *Offshoring and Employment: Trends and Impacts* (Paris 2007).

Open Europe, Top 100 EU rules cost Britain GBP 33.3bn, 16 March, (2015) http://openeurope.org.uk/intelligence/britain-and-the-eu/top-100-eu-rules-cost-britain33-3bn/ [2016-3-8].

Ottaviano, Gianmarco I. P., European Integration and the Gains from Trade, (2014c) CFS Working Paper 470.

Ottaviano, Gianmarco/Pessoa, João Paulo/Sampson, Thomas/Reenen, John van, 'The costs and benefits of leaving the EU', CFS Working Paper 472 (Frankfurt am Main 2014a).

Ottaviano, Gianmarco et al., Brexit or Fixit? The Trade and Welfare Effects of Leaving the European Union, CEP Policy Analysis, (May 2014b) http://cep.lse.ac.uk/pubs/download/pa016.pdf [2016-3-8].

Oxford Economics, *Assessing the economic implications of Brexit, Executive Summary* (London 2016).

Pain, Nigel/Young, Garry, *The macroeconomic impact of UK withdrawal from the EU*, National Institute of Economic and Social Research (London 2004).

Pelkmans, Jacques/Lejour, Arjan/Schrefler, Lorna/Mustilli, Federica/Timini, Jacopo, 'The Impact of TTIP: The underlying economic model and comparisons', CEPS Special Report 93 (Brussels 2014).

PwC (for CBI), Leaving the EU: Implications for the UK economy, (2016) http://ne ws.cbi.org.uk/news/leaving-eu-would-cause-a-serious-shock-to-uk-economynew-p wc-analysis/leaving-the-eu-implications-for-the-uk-economy/ [2016-3-22].

Ramondo, Natalia/Rodriguez-Clare, Andres, 'Trade, Multinational Production, and the Gains from Openness' (2013) 121, 2 Journal of Political Economy, 273–322.

Rosa, Dean A. de/Gilbert, John P., 'Predicting Trade Expansion under FTAs and Multilateral Agreements, Peterson Institute for International Economics', Working Paper 05-13 (2005).

Sampson, Thomas, 'Dynamic Selection and the New Gains from Trade with Heterogeneous Firms', FIW Working Paper Series 122 (2013).

Sampson, Thomas, 'Economists for Brexit: A Critique, Centre for Economic Performance', London School of Economics, Brexit Paper 6 (London 2016).

Smith, Alasdair, Written evidence submitted (ETP0004) to the UK Parliament –International Trade Committee and Treasury Committee Oral evidence: The economic effects of trade policy, HC 931i, (ETP0004), (24 April 2018) http://data.pa rliament.uk/writtenevidence/committeeevidence.svc/evidencedocument/interna tional-trade-committee/the-economic-effects-of-trade-policy/written/83106.pdf

Springford, John/Lowe, Sam, Britain's services firms can't defy gravity, alas, Centre for European Reform, CER-Insight, (5 February 2018) https://www.cer.eu/sites/d efault/files/insight_JS_SL_5.2.18.pdf.

Tybout, James R., 'Plant- and Firm-Level Evidence on 'New' Trade Theories', in Handbook of International Economics, 388–415 (2001).

Wacziarg, Romain, 'Measuring the Dynamic Gains from Trade' (2001) 15, 3 World Bank Economic Review, 393–425.

Wacziarg, Romain/Welch, Karen Horn, 'Trade Liberalization and Growth: New Evidence' (2008) 22, 2 World Bank Economic Review, 187–231.

Wadsworth, Jonathan,'Immigration and the UK Labour Market', Centre for Economic Performance Election Analysis 1 (London 2015).

Part 2 Foundations of a future relationship between the EU and the UK

Brexit, WTO and EU Trade Policy

Prof. Dr. Christoph Herrmann, LL.M. [*]

The notified withdrawal of the United Kingdom (UK) from the EU (Brexit) raises numerous legal questions in various fields of law. The disentanglement of the UK from the EU's Common Commercial Policy (CCP) and the related parallel membership in the World Trade Organization (WTO) are particularly complex in that regard.
The present contribution gives an overview of pertinent problems and provides some first tentative solutions.

A. Introduction

Since the referendum on the UK leaving the EU (Brexit) more than two years ago the framework and structure of the Brexit negotiation process has become apparent.[1] The UK notified its intention to withdraw from the EU under the Treaty on European Union (TEU) Art. 50(2) on 29 March 2017.[2] On 28 February 2018, the Draft Withdrawal Agreement was first published.[3] An updated version from 19 March 2018 indicates that the UK formally intends to leave the EU as of 29 March 2019, but will remain within the single market and customs union during a transition period, which is scheduled to last until 31 December 2020.[4] Meanwhile, there is also an in-

---

[*] The author is holder of the Chair for Constitutional and Administrative Law, European Law, European and International Economic Law at the University of Passau. An earlier German version of this article was published in EuZW 2017, 961.

1 See the documents available at the EU Commission's website <https://ec.europa.eu/commission/brexit-negotiations_en>; for the ones by HM Government see <www.gov.uk/government/collections/article-50-and-negotiations-with-the-eu>; *Peers*, 'Guide to the Brexit Negotiations' (*EU Law Analysis*, 4 April 2017) <http://eulawanalysis.blogspot.de/2017/04/> accessed 7 February 2018.

2 Letter of the British Prime Minister May to the European Council President Donald Tusk, available at: https://www.gov.uk/government/uploads/system/uploads/attachment_data/file/604079/Prime_Ministers_letter_to_European_Council_President_Donald_Tusk.pdf.

3 Draft Withdrawal Agreement of 28 February, available at: https://ec.europa.eu/commission/sites/beta-political/files/draft_withdrawal_agreement.pdf.

4 Art. 121 of the Draft Agreement on the withdrawal of the United Kingdom of Great Britain and Northern Ireland from the European Union and the European

dication of the future trade relations envisaged by the UK. On 8 December 2017, the EU and UK negotiators issued a Joint Report, which allowed the European Council on 15 December 2017 to give green light "to move to the second phase related to (inter alia) the framework for the future relationship".[5] Accordingly, the UK intends the conclusion of "a wide reaching, bold and ambitious free trade agreement and will seek a mutually beneficial new customs agreement with the EU".[6] This plan was reiterated and fine-tuned in a July 2018 White Paper[7], but the practicalities of the envisaged FTA-run-like-a-customs-union remain dubious and have been rejected by the EU 27 side already.

As of September 2018, it also remained uncertain whether an agreement on the future relations could be reached by year's end and whether the withdrawal agreement could be concluded. Under the draft withdrawal agreement, the UK would go through a transition period during which it would largely remain a de facto EU Member State, yet without any voting rights in the institutions.

In the following, the implications of Brexit on one of the essential areas of EU law is to be examined: the Common Commercial Policy (CCP) based on the Customs Union. Regaining sovereignty in the field of trade policy seems to be of crucial importance for the political evaluation of Brexit in the UK.[8] Yet, in particular the WTO law implications are obviously only understood in parts.[9] The subsequent observations apply at least for the time after the envisaged transition phase. During the transition, the

---

Atomic Energy Community, 19 March 2018, available at: https://ec.europa.eu/com mission/sites/beta-political/files/draft_agreement_coloured.pdf.

5 European Council Guidelines of 15 December 2017, para 1.

6 UK White Paper of 17 January 2017, Principle 8. See also European Council Guidelines of 29 April 2017, para 19.

7 See HM Government, 'The Future Relationship between the United Kingdom and the European Union' (July 2018) <https://www.gov.uk/government/publications/th e-future-relationship-between-the-united-kingdom-and-the-european-union>.

8 *Trommer*, 'Post-Brexit Trade Policy Autonomy as Pyrrhic Victory: Being a Middle Power in a Contested Trade Regime' (2017) 14 Globalizations 810.

9 For an in-depth analysis, see the contributions in *Hillman/Horlick* (eds), *Legal Aspects of Brexit* (Institute of International Economic Law 2017); cf. *Baetens*, "No Deal is Better than a Bad Deal"? The Fallacy of the WTO Fall-Back Option as a Post-Brexit Safety Net, (2018) 55 Common Market Law Review 133; *Herrmann*, Brexit and the WTO: challenges and solutions for the United Kingdom (and the European Union), in: ECB (ed.), Shaping a new legal order for Europe: a tale of crises and opportunities, 2017, 165; *Lux/Pickett*, 'The Brexit: Implications for the WTO, Free Trade Models and Customs Procedures' (2017) 12 Global Trade and Customs Journal 92; *Kim/Kuelzow/Strong*, 'The US Response to Brexit: Implications for Inter-

current legal situation in the WTO (and in relation to other CCP aspects) would – arguably – remain unchanged at large (and the intricacies of the possible transition are beyond the scope of this contribution, as are the legal problems raised by the possible backstop solution for Northern Ireland).

B. Trade policy background for the Brexit process

The CCP is among the oldest and most highly integrated EU policy fields. It falls within the exclusive competence of the EU [Treaty on the Functioning of the European Union (TFEU) Article 3(1)(e)], comprising trade in goods, services, commercial aspects of intellectual property rights, and foreign direct investment [Articles 206, 207(1) TFEU]. Instrumentally, the CCP comprises the conclusion of bilateral, plurilateral and multilateral trade agreements (contractual trade policy) as well as secondary legislation regulating cross-border trade on the basis of international treaty obligations (autonomous trade policy), covering in particular import, export, and trade defence instruments – as well as the inextricably tied set of regulations in the field of customs and tariffs, although the latter is legally based on the EU Treaty provisions on customs union.

This overarching structure determines trade relations between the EU and third countries, thereby building the "external window of the Single European Market". National Member State competences in this area are exclusively confined to the enforcement of directly applicable EU regulations, legal protection in this regard, as well as trade of military weapons and foreign portfolio investments.[10] As a result, EU Member States do not have relevant statutory law at their disposal, which would regulate, for instance, applicable rates of custom duty, import quotas, or even anti-dump-

---

national Trade Rights and Obligations Under the WTO System' (*Trade Lab*, 2 July 2017) <https://tradelab.legal.io/guide/5958bf1c28d5ea0202000000/The+US+Response+to+Brexit+Implications+for+International+Trade+Rights+and+Obligations+Under+the+WTO+System> accessed 7 February 2018; *Messenger*, Membership of the World Trade Organization in *Dougan* (ed.), The UK after Brexit – Legal and Policy Challenges, 2018, 225; *Molinuevo*, 'Brexit: Trade Governance and Legal Implications for Third Countries' (2018) 52 Journal of World Trade 599.

10 For an overall view, see *Niestedt* in *Krenzler and others* (eds), Europäisches Außenwirtschafts- und Zollrecht (loose-leaf commentary, 9th ed, May 2017) Intro 10. For details see: *Boysen*, 'Das System des Europäischen Außenwirtschaftsrechts' (§ 9) in *von Arnauld* (ed), Europäische Außenbeziehungen, Enzyklopädie des Europarechts, vol 10 (2011).

ing duties. Currently, this also holds true for a post-Brexit UK that, in the first place, will have to create its own respective legal framework according to British national law or, alternatively, will have to provide reference to the EU external economic law.[11]

C. Brexit and WTO law

I. Starting point: Parallel membership of EU and EU Member States in the WTO

First of all, the applicable international economic law regime for the UK's future trade relations with the EU and third States may be questioned. The fundamental pillar of EU trade policy is the membership in the World Trade Organization (WTO), which – with its 164 members – provides a nearly universal framework governing international trade relations. Substantially, WTO law largely falls within the exclusive EU competence derived from Article 207 TFEU. WTO law therefore binds the EU and the Member States on the basis of Article 216(2) TFEU. However, the EU Member States – despite the lack of any WTO-relevant powers – continue to be formal WTO members in parallel to the EU. Opinion 1/94 formed the basis for of the WTO agreement's conclusion as a mixed agreement. Here, the ECJ decided that the competence for the conclusion of the WTO agreement (which forms a package deal) was shared between the EU and the Member States.[12]

---

11 The UK is in the process of adopting a Trade Bill (Bill 122). The Taxation (Cross-Border Trade) Bill („Customs Bill") (Bill 128) received Royal Assent on 13 September 2018. Together, they provide for the external trade framework of the UK post Brexit. cf. *Cremona*, UK Trade Policy, in Dougan (ed.), 'The UK after Brexit – Legal and Policy Challenges', 2018, 247; *Henig*, Assessing UK Trade Policy Readiness, ECIPE Policy Brief 4/2018.

12 For a full study of the legal aspects of parallel membership in the WTO see *Herrmann/Streinz*, 'Die EU als Mitglied der WTO' (§ 11) in *von Arnauld* (ed), Europäische Außenbeziehungen, Enzyklopädie des Europarechts, vol 10 (2011).

II. WTO membership of the UK after Brexit

1. Formal membership status

It is uncontroversial that Brexit will not alter the UK's formal status as an "original member" of the WTO. The UK was founding party to the GATT 1947 and is one of the founding members of the WTO established in 1995.[13] Hence, the UK will also be subject to WTO law in the future – not only towards third countries, but also towards the EU itself. While WTO law is neither applicable to the relations between the EU and its Member States nor to the one between individual Member States,[14] it will be applicable between the UK and the EU 27 after the day of withdrawal. The "WTO option" is therefore not an option but an inevitable consequence of Brexit. Any future trade agreement between the UK and the EU 27 may encompass far-reaching liberalisation beyond the WTO framework (so-called "WTO-plus" approach). Yet, such an agreement must fully comply with the WTO requirements for regional economic integration – specifically Art. XXIV GATT and Art. V GATS (see below E.).

The UK's formal status as WTO member is thus undisputed. The same can, however, not be said about the scope and substance of the UK's WTO law commitments after Brexit. It is crucial to emphasize that WTO law rests on two different pillars: multilateral and plurilateral agreements basically generating the same legal obligations for all WTO members (multilateral)[15] or signatory parties (plurilateral)[16] on the one hand, and all the other requirements of membership resulting from the individual schedules of concessions by each single member, on the other hand. The latter particularly concerns the areas of tariffs and tariff rate quotas, agricultural subsidies and market access for services. An additional specific issue relates to the field of trade defence instruments.

---

13 As far as could be determined this is the unanimous view in literature: see only *Mishra*, 'A Post Brexit UK in the WTO: The UK's New GATT Tariff Schedule' in *Hillman/Horlick* (eds), *Legal Aspects of Brexit* (Institute of International Economic Law 2017) 9 (10).

14 As an exception, WTO law can be invoked by Member States against the Union or against each other on behalf of their respective overseas territories to which the Treaties do not apply. An example of this unusual situation is provided by the case European Union – Measures on Atlanto-Scandian Herring, WT/DS496 where the complaint was brought by Denmark, on behalf of the Faroe Islands. The case was settled in August 2014, WT/DS469/3, G/L/1058/Add.1.

15 Art. II:2 WTO Agreement.

16 Art. II:3 WTO Agreement.

2. Scope of legal obligations

WTO law is in principle a so-called single undertaking, i.e. all multilateral agreements are binding for all WTO members. Consequently, the UK's formal membership status necessarily ensures the legally binding effect of the multilateral agreements of Annexes 1, 2 and 3, in particular because the EC had concluded the WTO Agreement as a mixed agreement at the time which implies that the agreement was also signed and ratified by the UK. A recourse to the legal concept of State succession – directly or by analogy –, as occasionally propagated,[17] is neither necessary nor persuasive in the special case of Brexit.

Yet, the WTO legal framework has not been static over the past 23 years. On 23 January 2017, for example, an amendment of the Agreement on Trade-Related Aspects of Intellectual Property (TRIPS)[18] entered into force, which has been ratified by the EU alone. The EU's instrument of ratification indicates that the amendment also binds the Member States *as a matter of EU law* [former Treaty establishing the European Community (TEC) Art. 300(7)]; however, it was not (additionally) concluded nor ratified by any of the Member States.[19] The period for acceptance by WTO members, which have so far remained inactive, will expire by 31 December 2019, subject to possible future extensions, so that the UK may be able to accept the TRIPS amendment unilaterally.[20] The case is similar for the Agreement on Trade Facilitation (ATF),[21] which was concluded as an "EU-only" agreement without mentioning the Member States' obligation to be

---

17 See especially *Bartels*, 'Understanding the UK's position in the WTO after Brexit (Part II – The consequences)' (*International Centre for Trade and Sustainable Development (ICTSD)*, 26 September 2016) <www.ictsd.org/opinion/understanding-the-uk-0> accessed 7 February 2018; *Mishra*, 'A Post Brexit UK in the WTO: The UK's New GATT Tariff Schedule' (n 12) 9, 11; for a different view see *Kim and others*, 'The US Response to Brexit: Implications for International Trade Rights and Obligations Under the WTO System' (fn 9).

18 Decision WT/L/641 of 6 December 2005 of the WTO General Council, entered into force on 23 January 2017.

19 See Instrument of Acceptance by the European Community, of the Protocol amending the Agreement on Trade-Related Aspects of Intellectual Property Rights (TRIPS), of 19 November 2007.

20 General Council decision WT/L/1024 of 30 November 2017. The UK may have to ask the EU for permission to conclude the TRIPS amendment during the transition period (Art. 124 Draft Withdrawal Agreement of 19 March 2018).

21 General Council decision of 28 November 2014, WT/L/940, Protocol amending the Marrakesh Agreement establishing the World Trade Organization, insertion of the Agreement on Trade Facilitation into Annex 1A of the WTO Agreement.

bound under Union law [now Art. 216(2) TFEU]. However, a footnote to the Protocol amending the WTO Agreement, which refers to the calculation of the necessary quorum, can be read as an indication of the instrument being binding also on the EU's Member States under WTO rules.[22] Another possible option would be a later unilateral adoption by the UK, since no time limit was set in this case. Conversely, the recently decided amendment of the Trade Policy Review Mechanism (TPRM)[23] is – on the basis of Article X:8 WTO Agreement – binding on all WTO members anyway, so that no further ratification is required.

More problematic is the question of the UK's signatory status concerning the plurilateral Government Procurement Agreement (GPA). The agreement was signed in 1994 by the EU as well as its Member States, but was ratified by the EU alone. An amended version of the GPA, which entered into force in April 2014, was accepted and ratified solely by the EU.[24] Principally, a unilateral formal signature and ratification of the GPA by other WTO members is not provided for in the GPA, as the requirements for acceptance – particularly the institutional scope of GPA commitments – have to be negotiated with the other GPA contracting parties (see Article XXII GPA). Yet, the respective annexes of the GPA for the EU contain an extensive list of UK public bodies.[25] Regardless, it was questionable whether the UK would choose a unilateral approach towards the GPA and whether other signatories would accept this without demanding renegotiations aiming at more extensive market access.[26] On 27 February 2019, the parties to the GPA finally gave their approval to the UK's accession to the pact, in its own right, once it leaves the EU.[27] The draft Trade Bill – in its Part 1 – explicitly grants the UK Government the power to join the GPA.

---

22 cf. WT/Let/1090 re. WLI/100 of 16 October 2015.

23 See <www.wto.org/english/news_e/news17_e/tpr_26jul17_e.htm> and the related proposal WT/TPR/399 of 10 July 2017.

24 See WTO (ed), *Status of WTO Legal Instruments* (2015) 124 and 127.

25 *Bartels*, 'Understanding the UK's position in the WTO after Brexit (Part II – The consequences)' (fn 16).

26 See *Kim* and others, 'The US Response to Brexit: Implications for International Trade Rights and Obligations Under the WTO System' (n 9) under "Procurement"; *Lumley*, 'The United Kingdom's Public Procurement Regime in a Post-Brexit Landscape' in *Hillman/Horlick* (eds), *Legal Aspects of Brexit* (Institute of International Economic Law 2017) 101, 110.

27 See <www.wto.org/english/news_e/news19_e/gpro_27feb19_e.htm>.

3. Schedules of Concessions; Tariff Rate Quotas (TRQ)

According to Article XI:1 WTO Agreement, original membership in the WTO required the annexing of Schedules of Concessions and Commitments to the GATT as well as to the GATS for the respective member. At present, the schedules that "relate" to the UK are the ones of the EU (to the GATT 1994) or of the EU and its Member States (to the GATS). These schedules form an integral part of each of the agreements (see Art. II:7 GATT; Art. XX:3 GATS). How this situation is going to be dealt with after Brexit is central to the debate on the feasibility of the "WTO option". Reference is often made to the pragmatic approach chosen in similar cases, namely Rhodesia/Nyasaland and the dissolution of Czechoslovakia, the treatment of independence of former colonies, and the law of state succession and its prevailing principles.[28] Yet, none of these situations are fully comparable to Brexit.

The EU Schedules of Concessions are currently also binding on the UK and a claim could be brought against the UK before the WTO dispute settlement bodies for their violation. As consequence of Brexit, however, the UK will have to present its own schedules, which it plans to generate by replicating the EU schedules as far as possible.[29] This process may work out relatively smoothly with regard to the usual ad valorem tariffs. It will, however, cause problems for specific and compound duties because of the necessary currency conversion and, in particular, in context of the 99 EU Tariff Rate Quotas (TRQs). The latter allow for import of certain goods at favourable rates – predominantly for agricultural products (86) – up to a certain amount (*in quota*), while for exceeding amounts (*out of quota*) high, partly prohibitively high duties apply. This raises the question of how to split up the TRQs between the EU 27 and the UK as well as how to regulate future trade between the two partners: Up until today, trade with the respective goods is subject to Single Market rules, i.e. duty-free, quota-free, and therefore outside the TRQ system. Assuming that the EU and the UK cannot agree on the conclusion of a comprehensive free trade agreement, a partly massive – increase of TRQs would be necessary to also accommodate hitherto intra-EU trade relations. Specific issues are raised by the fact that

---

28 *Bartels*, 'Understanding the UK's position in the WTO after Brexit (Part II – The consequences)' (n 16); *Kim and others*, 'The US Response to Brexit: Implications for International Trade Rights and Obligations Under the WTO System' (n 9) under "Tariffs".

29 *Braithwaite*, Ensuring a smooth transition in the WTO as we leave the EU, 23.1.2017, https://blogs.fco.gov.uk.

the EU TRQs often date back to the foundation of the WTO (1994), so that, for instance, later WTO members often do not have any share in terms of country allocated TRQs.[30] The Commission – in May 2018 – has published a proposal for a regulation that would allow the apportionment of the TRQs as well as for a mandate authorising the Commission to negotiate new TRQs in the WTO.[31]

Generally, Brexit requires the renewal or revision of the schedules and their notification to the WTO. The procedure that has to be applied under WTO rules is currently uncertain. For purely formal changes a so-called rectification suffices. Although such rectification has to be certified by the WTO to be legally binding, negotiations about compensations are not required. Provided, however, that the value of concessions changes, one speaks of a so-called modification, which – according to Article XXVIII GATT – requires negotiations with the respective main supply countries or those WTO members proving a special trade interest in the good in question.[32] It is to be expected that a great number of WTO members will consider the Brexit-related schedule revisions to be modifications, as not only currency conversions in case of specific duties and TRQ splits, but also the loss of access to the EU Single Market with its principle of free circulation (Article 29 TFEU) will be interpreted as changes to the value of concessions. The resulting negotiations are usually lengthy and cumbersome. For instance, the revised schedules of concessions following the 2004 EU enlargement were only certified in December 2016, thus after twelve years. This already addresses the next problem, which results from the fact that the EU currently has only certified schedules based on EU 25 at its disposal, whereas the schedule offers taking into account the enlargements of 2007 and 2013 are secret.[33] At least, this intricate situation is eased due to the – controversial – dispute settlement practice according to which certification of schedules by the WTO is not considered a requirement for their

---

30 For a comprehensive account see *Downes*, 'The Post-Brexit Management of EU Agricultural Tariff Rate Quotas', (2017) 51 Journal of World Trade, 741; *Henig*, The UK's First International Trade Negotiation – Agriculture at the WTO, ECIPE Policy Brief 7/2018.

31 See COM(2018) 312 final.

32 The procedural details are laid down in GATT, Procedures for Modification and Rectification of Schedules of Tariff Concessions, Decision of 26 March 1980, L/4962 and GATT Doc. C/113 of 5 November 1980, Procedures for Negotiations under Article XXVIII.

33 See *Kim and others*, 'The US Response to Brexit: Implications for International Trade Rights and Obligations Under the WTO System' (n 9) under "Tariffs".

application.[34] However, this does not imply that WTO members could not take action against the conduct of the EU 27 and the UK under the WTO dispute settlement system (in accordance with Article XXIII GATT) when they see their trade advantages at stake because of the changes made.

4. Agricultural subsidies

A similar, albeit less serious issue compared to the TRQs is raised by the upper limits to trade distorting internal subsidies for agricultural products to the amount of 72.4 billion euros contained in the EU Schedule of Concessions (cf. Art. 3.1 Agreement on Agriculture[35]). This capping amount (so-called AMS) has to be split between the EU 27 and the UK, which will not cause all too many difficulties, as only 8% of the Union's total AMS are currently used within the Common Agricultural Policy (CAP).[36] Since the WTO ministerial conference in Nairobi in 2015, export subsidies in the area of agriculture are completely prohibited for developed-country members anyway, so that in this connection no transitional issues arise.[37]

5. Market access for services

The separation of the obligations of the EU 27 and the UK in the area of service trade is equally practicable. These obligations result from currently five EU Schedules of Commitments covering the main commitments,[38] exceptions from MFN,[39] commitments relating to mode 4 (movement of nat-

---

34 See European Union – Measures Affecting Tariff Concessions on Certain Poultry Meat Products, Panel Report, WT/DS492/R, adopted 19 April 2017, para. 7.550 and fn. 750.

35 OJ 1994 L 336/22.

36 See *Kim and others*, 'The US Response to Brexit: Implications for International Trade Rights and Obligations Under the WTO System' (n 9) under "Agriculture"; *Matthews*, 'WTO dimensions of a UK "Brexit" and agricultural trade' (*CAP Reform blog*, 5 January 2016) <http://capreform.eu/wto-dimensions-of-a-uk-brexit-and-agricultural-trade/> accessed 7 February 2018; *Swinbank*, 'World Trade Rules and the Policy Options for British Agriculture Post-Brexit' (*UKTPO Briefing Paper*, 7 January 2017) <https://www.sussex.ac.uk/webteam/gateway/file.php?name=briefing-paper-7-final.pdf&site=18> accessed 7 February 2018.

37 Ministerial Decision of 19 December 2015, WT/MIN(15)/45, para. 6.

38 WTO Document GATS/SC/31, 15 April 1994.

39 WTO Document GATS/EL/31, 15 April 1994.

ural persons),[40] telecommunication services,[41] and financial services.[42] Yet, except the annexes on telecommunication and financial services, the schedules only apply to the EU 12. With regard to telecommunication and financial services EU 15 schedules apply, as they were negotiated after the EU accession of Austria, Finland and Sweden.

A common element of these schedules is their explicit designation as schedules of the *EU and its Member States*. Moreover, they describe the scope of obligations – aside from certain universal commitments – of the individual Member States, especially with regard to their relevant limitations and conditions. Nevertheless, the UK will have to present its own schedules separated from the current EU ones (which will then also find application to the EU 27). In turn, this will (have to) lead to negotiations about compensatory adjustments according to Article XXI GATS and the *Procedures for the implementation of Article XXI of the General Agreement on Trade in Services (GATS)*[43], since Brexit significantly reduces the value of concessions of the EU 27/UK. For instance, WTO members in the EU enjoy freedom of settlement in the area of financial services (mode 3), combined with *EU Passporting* resulting into freedom to provide correspondence services [i.e. market access in terms of mode 4 according to Article I:2 (c) GATS], which seems unlikely to be maintained after Brexit.[44]

6. Dispute settlement mechanism

A highly specific problem concerns the question of the effect of WTO Dispute Settlement Body decisions, which either granted the EU authorization to withdraw concessions vis-à-vis a respondent WTO member govern-

---

40 WTO Document GATS/SC/31/Suppl.2, 28 July 1995.
41 WTO Document GATS/SC/31/Suppl.3, 11 April 1997.
42 WTO Document GATS/SC/31/Suppl.4/Rev. 1 of 18 November 1999.
43 WTO Document S/L/80, 29 October 1999.
44 See the exemplary discussion of *Yin*, 'Envisaging a Post-Brexit Financial Services Sector under the GATS Framework – A Case Study of Euro Clearing' in *Hillman/Horlick* (eds), *Legal Aspects of Brexit* (Institute of International Economic Law 2017) 230ff. See also *Evenett*, 'Resilient Soft Law? Lessons from the US-EU TTIP negotiations on Financial Services Regulations', (2017) 22 European Foreign Affairs Review 37, *Delimatis*, 'The Evolution of the EU External Trade Policy in Services – CETA, TTIP, and TiSA after Brexit', Journal of International Economic Law 2017, 1 or *Wymeersch*, 'Some Aspects of the Impact of Brexit in the Field of Financial Services', in *Busch and others (eds.)*, Capital Markets Union in Europe, OUP 2018, Chapter 5.

ment – or vice versa [Articles 22.2-22.9 Dispute Settlement Understanding (DSU)]. A case-by-case analysis will show if and to what extent the UK, i.e. UK statutes and practice, were decisive for the respective proceedings or to what extent UK trade with the respective third country impacted the scope of withdrawn concessions. Such an individual case study is of particular importance with regard to mutually agreed solutions to disputes (Articles 3.3-3.6 DSU).

7. *Trade defence measures*

Finally, attention has to be paid to the field of trade defence measures. On the one hand, the EU cannot simply continue to apply anti-dumping or anti-subsidy duties in cases, where the industry quorum in favour of an investigation or the determination of the relevant prices or material injury to "domestic industries" did take into account UK industries.[45] On the other hand, it seems impossible that, after Brexit, the UK will be able to further apply trade defence instruments (TDIs) of any kind autonomously, since, as an independent WTO member, it would not fulfil the necessary requirements – neither in formal nor in substantive terms.[46] However, the UK has already launched a process of transition of existing EU measures as well as the foundation of a Trade Remedy Authority.[47]

D. *Other EU trade agreements*

Apart from WTO law, EU trade policy is also bound by numerous international free trade agreements and customs union agreements which grant third countries customs-free market access to the EU and, vice versa, must

---

45 See *Kim and others*, 'The US Response to Brexit: Implications for International Trade Rights and Obligations Under the WTO System' (fn 9) under "Anti-dumping and Countervailing Duty Orders" with examples of relevant cases.

46 *Lux/Pickett*, 'The Brexit: Implications for the WTO, Free Trade Models and Customs Procedures' (2017) 12 Global Trade and Customs Journal 92, 102.

47 cf. HM Government, 'Trade Remedies if there's no Brexit deal' (23 August 2018) at https://www.gov.uk/government/publications/trade-remedies-if-theres-no-brexit -deal; Provisional findings of the call for evidence into UK interest in existing EU trade remedy measures (24 July 2018) at https://www.gov.uk/government/consult ations/call-for-evidence-to-identify-uk-interest-in-existing-eu-trade-remedy-measure s/provisional-findings-of-the-call-for-evidence-into-UK-interest-in-existing-EU-trad e-remedy-measures.

grant the same advantages to imported EU goods.[48] Until recently[49], these agreements were – almost without exception – concluded as the so-called mixed agreements, i.e. as agreements that list the Member States as contracting parties alongside the EU. Hence, the question arises if these agreements will be legally binding on the UK after Brexit. The overwhelmingly prevailing view rejects such continuous effects.[50] Specific problems are raised by agreements to which the UK is a signatory party, but which have not yet been finally ratified. This is the case for CETA (Comprehensive Economic and Trade Agreement between the EU and Canada), which is provisionally applied since 21 September 2017. The conditions for CETA's entry into force will have to be clarified. The UK will lose the advantages stemming from provisional application – which falls within EU exclusive competence and decision-making power – in any case after Brexit or after the end of the possible transition period at the latest.[51] Only a typical mixed agreements, to which the Member States did not become contracting parties "side by side" with the EU (the Energy Charter treaty serves as a case in point, as are the WTO agreements), will continue to apply unre-

---

48 For detailed information, see <http://ec.europa.eu/trade/policy/countries-and-regi ons/negotiations-and-agreements/>. Accordingly, the EU (latest status: September 2017) is part of three customs unions (Andorra, San Marino, Turkey), of 24 agreements in force concluding free trade components (i.e. tariff reduction), as well as of 43 concluded and currently provisionally applied agreements including free trade components.

49 In the aftermath of Opinion 2/15, the EU's trade agreements with Japan and Singapore have been (re-)designed as "EU-only" agreement; only the EU-Singapore Investment Protection Agreement will remain "mixed". See Commission, Press Release, "Trade: European Commission proposes signature and conclusion of Japan and Singapore agreements", IP/18/3325, On the splitting of trade and investment agreements see infra, note 55.

50 *Lux/Pickett*, 'The Brexit: Implications for the WTO, Free Trade Models and Customs Procedures' (2017) 12 Global Trade and Customs Journal 92, 107f; *Sosnow/ Logvin/Massicotte*, 'The Brexit Vote: Its Impact on the Canada-EU Comprehensive Economic and Trade Agreement and UK's Obligations Under Comprehensive Trade and Economic Trade Agreement' (2017) 12 Global Trade and Customs Journal 125; *Wessels*, 'Consequences of Brexit for international agreements concluded by the EU and its Member States' (2018) 55 Common Market Law Review 101.

51 *Poienaru/Savic/McCabe*, 'Brexit and the EU-Canada Comprehensive Economic and Trade Agreement: Implications for the European Union, the United Kingdom and Canada' (*Trade Lab*, 13 March 2017) <https://tradelab.legal.io/guide/58c6ed77e33a bc042b000400/Brexit+and+the+EU+Canada+Comprehensive+Economic+and+Tra de+Agreement+Implications+for+the+European+Union+the+United+Kingdom+a nd+Canada> accessed 7 February 2018.

servedly – merely modified in so far as the relationship between the UK and the EU 27 will no longer be governed by Union law.

E. Future EU 27-UK trade relations

After the Brexit referendum, the UK Government explained that it does not intend a pseudo membership – following the example set by the European Economic Area (EEA)[52] – in the EU Single Market. Likewise, it excluded a customs union due to the ensuing loss of trade policy sovereignty towards third countries. Instead, the UK envisages a deep and comprehensive free trade agreement including services obligations, repeatedly naming CETA as an example.[53] According to the sequencing of the Brexit withdrawal process at the express request of the EU, negotiations were only able to commence as of January 2018 after central issues of the withdrawal agreement were agreed upon in December 2017. Contrary to the withdrawal agreement based on Article 50 TEU, the agreement on the future trade relationship requires a separate legal basis. This can be found primarily in Article 207 TFEU since an association agreement according to Article 217 TFEU will hardly be viewed as a politically desirable option in the UK.

Following the ECJ's Opinion 2/15 on the EU-Singapore FTA of 16 May 2017[54], it should be possible to conclude an EU 27-UK FTA without "mixed" Member State ratification by the EU alone. This corresponds with recently emerged plans by the EU Commission in reaction to Opinion 2/15. Accordingly, chapters of modern EU trade agreements based on shared competence (especially in the area of investment protection) will be split from parts falling into exclusive EU competence and addressed within the scope of a separate (mixed) agreement.[55]

---

52 To the question of a continuing membership of the UK in the EEA or, respectively, its revival see *Tyne/Haugsdal*, 'In, Out or In-Between? The UK as a Contracting Party to the Agreement on the European Economic Area' [2016] European Law Review 753.

53 *Neuwahl*, 'CETA as a Potential Model for (Post-Brexit) UK-EU Relations' (2017) 22 European Foreign Affairs Review 279.

54 See Opinion of Advocate General Sharpston in Case 2/15, 16.5.2017, EU-Singapore FTA, EU:C:2017:376.

55 See *von der Burchard/Hanke*, 'Juncker's risky bid to rescue EU trade policy' (*Politico*, 12 September 2018) <https://www.politico.eu/article/juncker-trade-sotu-risky-bid-to-rescue-eu-trade-policy/> accessed 7 February 2018. On this point cf. *Gáspár-Szilágyi*, 'Opinion 2/15: Maybe it is time for the EU to conclude separate trade

An EU 27-UK free trade agreement, will have to comply with WTO law requirements for regional integration agreements (RIAs). According to Article XXIV:5 (b) and 8 (b) GATT, duties and other restrictive regulations of commerce have to be eliminated on "substantially all the trade"[56] between the EU 27 and the UK; an increase in duties or other restrictions of commerce negatively affecting trade with other WTO members is prohibited. A transitional agreement bridging the gap until the introduction of a free trade area is limited to a maximal duration of ten years. Given the depth of existing integration, both requirements should be legally and practically attainable. An increase in external duties or other restrictions towards third countries is already avoided due to the mentioned issue of tariff schedules. The rules on trade in services in a regional economic integration agreement are also only vaguely described in Article V GATS, which requires the elimination of discriminatory trade barriers (i.e. national treatment) for a "substantial sectoral coverage" according to the number of sectors, the trade volume in question, as well as the modes of supply (in terms of Article I GATS). Thereby, consideration may be given to the relationship of the agreement to a wider process of economic integration among the countries concerned. Hence, few concrete and precise details have been specified in this context. In any case, a limitation to only a small number of sectors (e.g. financial services) will hardly be sufficient with regard to the concurrent conclusion of a free trade agreement.[57]

In matters of procedure, WTO law requires an early notification of the negotiations and potential conclusion. Details are treated in the Transparency Mechanism for Regional Trade Agreements of 2006 and 2010.[58]

Predictions of the likely contents of the future EU 27-UK agreement are not reliable at this point. However, the intention of concluding a "deep and comprehensive agreement" is certainly going beyond the issue of the prohibition of customs duties.[59]

---

and investment agreements' (*European Law Blog*, 20 June 2017) <http://europeanla wblog.eu/2017/06/20/opinion-215-maybe-it-is-time-for-the-eu-to-conclude-separate -trade-and-investment-agreements/> accessed 7 February 2018.

56 See *Herrmann*/Weiß/Ohler, *Welthandelsrecht* (2nd edn, 2007), 269 ff.

57 Siehe dazu *Lydgate/Winters*, Deep and Not Comprehensive? What the WTO rules permit for a UK-EU Trade Agreement, University of Sussex Working Paper 12/2017.

58 WTO Document WT/L/671, 18 December 2016 and WTO Document WT/L/806, 16 December 2010.

59 *Holmes/Rollo/Winters*, 'Negotiating the UK's post-Brexit trade arrangements' (2016) 238 National Institute Economic Review R22; *Lux/Pickett*, 'The Brexit: Im-

In contrast, questions about the treatment of technical barriers to trade, for which EU foreign trade law offers a wide range of options, will be of more significance. It is already becoming apparent that the desired depth of the agreement will be inversely proportional to the UK's room for manoeuvre concerning technical product regulation and the like. Moreover, it is clear that any solution below the complete takeover of the EU Single Market *acquis* in the area of product and services regulation à la EEA (provided that the parties will agree to market access for this at all) will require extremely complex provisions on regulatory cooperation or mutual recognition (which only appears to be unproblematic because of the current equivalence with EU law). Such negotiations are time-consuming and the results will be measured against relevant WTO agreements (SPS and TBT). Additionally, issues of intellectual property (TRIPS-plus), public procurement (see above) and competition arise.[60] Particularly the latter is fraught with considerable problems. A continuing state aid control competence of the Commission seems politically unfeasible – and is highly atypical in the context of international trade policy.[61] Therefore, it is expected that the EU 27 and the UK will be able to agree on a prohibition of customs duties in an FTA; however, the application of trade defence instruments between the partners would likely remain possible absent a competition policy alignment.

F. *Brexit and investment protection*

Under the Treaty of Lisbon the EU has gained exclusive external competence over "foreign direct investment" (FDI) within the framework of the CCP. On this basis, the EU initiated the development of an independent EU investment protection policy. Accordingly, bilateral investment treaties (BITs) concluded by the EU Member States are now subject to Regulation (EU) No 1219/2012. Yet, after Brexit, this Regulation will not any longer apply to the UK, which will be immediately regaining full sovereignty to conclude its own BITs. The same holds true for provisions on restrictions

---

plications for the WTO, Free Trade Models and Customs Procedures' (2017) 12 Global Trade and Customs Journal 92 (103 ff).

60 With regard to the latter see also *Bechtold/Soltész*, 'Brexit: EU-Kartellrecht ohne Großbritannien', NZKart 2016, 301.

61 For a detailed analysis see House of Lords European Union Committee, "Brexit: competition and State aid", https://publications.parliament.uk/pa/ld201719/ldselect/ldeucom/67/67.pdf.

on market access for third state investors, which – despite currently still being subjected to Member State law[62] – are governed by EU law because of the transfer of powers to the EU on 1 December 2009.[63] The Commission issued a respective regulation proposal on 17 September 2017 on this basis.[64]

As consequence of Brexit, the question of the compatibility of the UK's BITs with EU Member States (so-called Intra-EU BITs), now answered by the ECJ,[65] is superfluous. These Intra-EU-BITs will turn to Extra-EU BITs of the EU 27 Member States, subject to the above-mentioned Regulation No 1219/2012.

Already today it is discussed to which extent Brexit itself, as an *investment event*, may give rise to legal actions of investors before international investment arbitration tribunals.[66] The legal basis for this could be alleged violations of the fair and equitable treatment (FET) standard or indirect expropriation. In view of the possible loss of duty-free access to the EU Single Market, the legal validity of such claims may at least not generally be rejected at the outset.[67]

---

62 For Germany cf. §§ 4(1), 5(2) AWG, §§ 55-59 AWV.
63 See *Herrmann*, 'Die Zukunft der mitgliedstaatlichen Investitionspolitik nach dem Vertrag von Lissabon', EuZW 2010, 207 (210).
64 See COM(2017) 487 final.
65 See Judgment of the Court in Case C-284/16, 6.3.2018, Achmea v Slovakia, EU:C:2018:158.
66 See *Claret de Fleurieu*, 'Brexit and Legitimate Expectations: A Case for Foreign Investors?' in *Hillman/Horlick* (eds), *Legal Aspects of Brexit* (Institute of International Economic Law 2017) 195; *Glinavos*, 'Brexit Lawsuits, But Not As You Know Them'(*Verfassungsblog*, 9 May 2018) <http://verfassungsblog.de/brexit-lawsuits-but-not-as-you-know-them/> accessed 9 February 2018; *Johnston*, 'A Violation of the Fair and Equitable Treatment Standard under Bilateral Investment Treaties as a Result of Brexit: The Example of Tata Motors' in Jennifer *Hillman/Horlick* (eds), *Legal Aspects of Brexit* (Institute of International Economic Law 2017) 218; *Ross*, 'Could Brexit trigger investment claims?' (*Global Arbitration Review*, 19 June 2017) <https://globalarbitrationreview.com/article/1143054/could-brexit-trigger-investment-claims> accessed 7 February 2018.
67 Corporate Europe Observatory, 'Brexit bonanza: Lawyers encouraging corporations to sue UK & EU member states' (25 September 2017) <https://corporateeurope.org/sites/default/files/brexit_bonanza.pdf> accessed 7 February 2018.

G. *UK's third country trade relations*

After Brexit, the UK's trade relations – as analysed above (C.) – will be shaped primarily by WTO rules. Close relations to the EU 27 will depend on the announced transitional arrangements and the planned deep and comprehensive trade agreement (see above E.). However, the UK will in all likelihood lose preferential access to markets of EU free trade partners, as well as the prospect of further free trade agreements currently negotiated or already concluded by the EU.

It is all the more important for the UK to focus on the conclusion of its own free trade agreements with third countries; however, the gain of sovereignty in this field, which the UK hopes for, will tie up significant negotiation resources and measurable results will take time.[68] This turns out to be difficult in case of partners like the US, which are, in parallel, negotiating with the Commission. Through the Council of Ministers and the Trade Policy Committee, the UK has "insider information" at its disposal and is therefore still able to influence the negotiations between the EU and the US, even though the UK itself will not be affected by the results anymore. Apart from the above-named Regulation 1219/2012 dealing with BITs, EU law only provides for the principle of loyalty [Article 4(3) TEU], which, despite of its binding character, does lack precise standards for the current situations. Moreover, the interpretation of Article 4(3) TEU may be modified in view of the notification of withdrawal by the respective Member State.[69] Against this background, in recognition of the UK's legitimate interest in leading substantial negotiations with third countries (so-called scoping has already taken place anyway[70]), it would seem appropriate to offer a solution along the lines of Regulation No 1219/2012. This would reauthorize the UK (but solely the UK) according to Art. 2(1) TFEU for the fields of law enumerated in Article 3(1)(e), 207 TFEU [possibly the same

---

68 *Lux/Pickett*, 'The Brexit: Implications for the WTO, Free Trade Models and Customs Procedures' (2017) 12 Global Trade and Customs Journal 92, 109 f; *Tietje*, 'Lost in Brexit: Rechtliche Rahmenbedingungen der Austrittsverhandlungen' (2017) 70 ifo Schnelldienst 19, 22.

69 On Brexit and the duty of sincere cooperation see *Streinz*, 'Cooperative Brexit: Giving Back Control Over Trade Policy', (2017) 15 International Journal of Constitutional Law 271 *Larik*, 'Sincere Cooperation in the Common Commercial Policy: Lisbon, a 'Joined-Up' Union, and 'Brexit'' in *Bungenberg and others (eds.)*, European Yearbook of International Economic Law 2017, 105-106.

70 See press release on a US-UK Trade Working Group for a potential future free trade agreement <https://www.gov.uk/government/news/us-uk-trade-working-group-lays-groundwork-for-potential-future-free-trade-agreement>.

applies to Articles 3(1)(a) and 31 TFEU] enabling HM Government to undertake preparatory action (also and especially within the WTO).[71] In return, the UK could relinquish the right of further participation in meetings of the competent EU organs [Foreign Affairs Council (Trade), Trade Policy Committee]. In fact, the envisaged transition period would more or less bring about such a situation.

H. Conclusion

Brexit is a legal mammoth task, which will in all likelihood concern generations of lawyers. The present contribution tried to outline the emerging problems in the field of CCP and to indicate first solutions. Thereby it (hopefully) became evident that Brexit raises complex, yet not unsolvable issues, particularly in the context of WTO law. However, due to the generally pragmatic approach pursued in the WTO, and provided that all parties involved take constructive negotiation positions, it may be possible to resolve at least the most urgent questions. Therefore, the EU 27 as well as the UK have to choose a coordinated and swift course of action.

---

71 *Cremona*, 'Negotiating Trade Deals Before Brexit?' (*Social Europe*, 25 July 2016) <www.socialeurope.eu/negotiating-trade-deals-brexit accessed 7 February 2018>; *Lux/Pickett*, 'The Brexit: Implications for the WTO, Free Trade Models and Customs Procedures' (2017) 12 Global Trade and Customs Journal 92, 109 f propose the analogous application of the Regulation. In detail see *Streinz*, 'Cooperative Brexit: Giving back control over trade policy' (2017) 15 International Journal of Constitutional Law 271.

Free Trade Agreements as a Means to Maintain and to Establish Integrated Markets

Dr. René Repasi[1]

A. The 'Brexit' Challenge in Trade: Maintaining or Establishing Integrated Markets with Means other than a Single Market

The challenge of 'Brexit' can best be identified by looking at the 'red lines' that the UK and the EU have defined for finding an agreement on their relationship with each other outside the legal and institutional framework of the EU. There is, on the one hand, the main promise made by the champions of 'Brexit': 'take back control.' The UK has to leave the EU's institutions, in which British representatives can be 'outvoted', and has to renounce the principle of supremacy of EU law and of the judgments of the Court of Justice of the EU (CJEU) interpreting EU law over UK law. It entails the UK's withdrawal from the free movement of persons as a part of the EU's internal market in order to regain control over the UK's borders. 'Take back control' came along with the pledge that an exit of the UK from the EU can be realised without sustaining damage to the British economy. Such damage was considered to be avoided by upholding the free movement of goods, services and capital between the UK and the EU without permitting the free movement of persons. In direct contrast to this stands, on the other hand, the EU's red line of 'safeguarding the integrity of the internal market'. Any frictionless access to the EU internal market for UK products or UK based market operators requires from the UK to keep its domestic territory open for goods, (natural and legal) persons, services and capital from the EU.

Both positions can be reconciled in terms of the UK's discontinued participation in the EU's institutional framework. It gets more complicated when looking at the future trade relationship between the UK and the EU. Leaving the EU means also leaving the EU's internal market. The EU's ob-

---

1 Dr. René Repasi is the Scientific Coordinator of the European Research Centre for Economic and Financial Governance (EURO-CEFG) of the Universities of Leiden, Delft and Rotterdam and Assistant Professor for European Union law at Erasmus University Rotterdam.

jective to safeguard the integrity of the internal market can therefore only be achieved by either treating the UK like any other third country – granting UK products and market operators the same access to the EU as to any other third country product or market operator – or by replicating the internal market in a bilateral manner. The latter does not correspond with the UK's goal to bring the free movement of persons, being an integral part of the EU's definition of an internal market, to an end. The first, however, is at odds with the promise of 'Brexit' to avert any damage from the British economy as a consequence of the withdrawal from the EU. At this point it is sufficient to refer to the UK Government's own long-term economic analysis from November 2018 that concluded that there is no withdrawal scenario that would not impact the UK's estimated GDP negatively compared to the estimates under the conditions of a continuous fully-fledged EU membership of the UK: 'The analysis shows that higher barriers to UK-EU trade would be expected to result in greater economic costs.'[2]

Whilst against this background, there are apparently contradictory policy goals – establishing trade in goods, services and capital with the EU with ideally no barriers or at least the lowest possible barriers between the trading partners, on the one hand, and the replication of the internal market between the EU and UK, on the other – theses contradicting goals concur in aiming at establishing (from the perspective of the UK) or maintaining (from the perspective of the EU) integrated markets with the lowest possible trade barriers between participating trading partners. The policy goals only differ in terms of the scope of trade being covered by integrated markets.

This observation reveals the legal challenge of 'Brexit' that is common to the policy goals of both the UK and the EU: To which extent can integrated markets between trading partners be established or maintained by legal means other than the 'Single Market' as defined under EU law? Or, to put it differently: What are the legal limits deriving from the nature of the instruments that are available for the UK and the EU for designing their future relationship?

In order to give an answer to these questions, an overview over the possible content of the future relationship, as it is outlined in the most recent policy documents of the EU and the UK, will be given (B.), which will

---

2 HM Government, EU Exit, Long-term economic analysis, November 2018, p. 5, available at: https://assets.publishing.service.gov.uk/government/uploads/system/up loads/attachment_data/file/759762/28_November_EU_Exit_-_Long-term_economi c_analysis.pdf.

form the subject of the subsequent analysis. This analysis consists of two parts: the identification of the type of trade cooperation the UK and the EU intend to establish (C.) and the application of the legal instruments that are available to the UK and the EU to the realisation of the identified type of trade cooperation (D.). For the first part of the analysis an analytical grid will be developed that allows for identifying various elements that define a type of trade cooperation. The identified type of trade cooperation can then be projected on the legal instruments that are available for establishing the trade cooperation. If the identified type of trade cooperation cannot be realised within the realm of a given legal instrument, the UK and the EU may either choose a different legal instrument or the intended type of cooperation must be scaled back. Such analysis of the various positions on the future relationship between the UK and the EU will show the suitability of these positions to address the 'Brexit' challenge in trade: maintaining or establishing integrated markets with means other than the 'Single Market' (E.).

B. Positions on the Future Relationship between the UK and the EU

At the time of writing it is still unclear, what shape the future relationship between the UK and the EU will take. On 22 November 2018 the UK and the EU agreed on a political declaration setting out the framework for their future relationship.[3] This declaration is part of the draft withdrawal agreement in the sense that it outlines the 'framework for [the UK's] future relationship with the Union' as required by Article 50(2) TEU. Since neither the EU nor the UK have formally ratified the withdrawal agreement at the time of writing, it is also unclear to which extent the political declaration can serve as a basis for the definition of the future relationship. But since both parties have endorsed the document at least at governmental level, it can be considered as a first consensual sketch of the future relationship. Before the approval of the political declaration, the UK Government defined its position in a white paper adopted on 12 July 2018[4] and the

---

3 Political declaration setting out the framework for the future relationship between the European Union and the United Kingdom, OJ 2019 C 66 I/185.
4 HM Government, The Future Relationship between the United Kingdom and the European Union, available under: https://assets.publishing.service.gov.uk/governm ent/uploads/system/uploads/attachment_data/file/725288/The_future_relationship _between_the_United_Kingdom_and_the_European_Union.pdf.

European Council specified the EU's position in its guidelines on the matter adopted on 23 March 2018.[5]

Common to all these documents is that certain scenarios that were discussed publicly[6] are excluded such as the EEA option, according to which the UK could first join EFTA and thereafter the EEA-Agreement, or the WTO option.[7] Although the latter is not deemed desirable by both parties, it is the default option, under whose terms the trade relationship between the EU and the UK would operate in the event of a so-called 'hostile no-deal Brexit.'[8] All these documents express their authors' preference for concluding a free trade agreement.[9]

The policy documents will form the basis for the following assessment of what type of trade cooperation the UK and the EU intend to establish, which legal instruments they contemplate making use of and whether the limits inherent to these instruments allow the realisation of the intended type of trade cooperation. Since all documents refer to the agreement as the preferred option, the currently most evolved free trade agreement of the EU (or in the words of the European Commission: 'the most ambitious trade agreement that the EU has ever concluded'),[10] which is the 'Comprehensive Economic and Trade Agreement' (CETA) with Canada,[11] will also be looked at in order to draw a realistic picture of the kind of trade cooperation that can be realised by a trade agreement.

---

5 European Council, Guidelines, EUCO XT 20001/18, available under: https://www.consilium.europa.eu/media/33458/23-euco-art50-guidelines.pdf.

6 See for an overview: Amtenbrink/Markakis/Repasi, *Legal Implications Brexit – Customs Union, Internal Market and Consumer Protection*, (Study for European Parliament, Brussels, 2017), 36 et seqq.

7 On the WTO option, see: Herrmann, 'Brexit, WTO and EU Trade Policy', in this volume.

8 A 'hostile no-deal Brexit' includes no further unilateral decisions by both the EU and the UK to mitigate the withdrawal effects. Against this stands the concept of 'managed no-deal Brexit', according to which by making use of unilateral decisions the EU and the UK pave the way for a future trade agreement despite a withdrawal of the UK from the EU without agreement.

9 Political Declaration (n. 3), No. 120 et seqq. (referring to the possibility to use the form of an Association Agreement); European Council (n. 5), No. 8; HM Government (n. 4), p. 11 (also speaking of an 'Association Agreement').

10 European Commission, Press Statement, 5 July 2016, available under: http://trade.ec.europa.eu/doclib/press/index.cfm?id=1524.

11 Comprehensive Economic and Trade Agreement (CETA) between Canada, of the one part, and the European Union and its Member States, of the other part [2017] OJ L 11/23.

C. Setting the Scene: Identifying Types of Trade Cooperation

Trade cooperation between two or more trading partners can be established in multiple ways and may take different legal forms. Different types of trade cooperation call for different legal instruments. The assessment of the suitability of a certain legal instrument requires therefore, as a first step, the identification of the type of trade cooperation that the trading partners intend to establish. This will be done by applying an analytical grid to the positions taken by the future trading partners. Based on a common goal of what a trade cooperation is, as a matter of principle, supposed to achieve (I.), an analytical grid will be developed in the following (II.). This grid will be applied to the political declaration setting out the framework for the future relationship between the UK and the EU and to CETA as the currently most comprehensive trade agreement that EU has concluded in order to compare these types of trade cooperation with each other (III.). This comparison will allow to identify areas, in which the future trade relationships intends to go beyond agreements that the EU already has concluded. Both will be compared to the membership in the EU as a type of trade cooperation, which will serve as the benchmark for the evaluation of the results of the application of the analytical grid that leads to an interim conclusion of the first step of the analysis (IV.).

I. Object Common to all Trade Cooperation: Reducing Costs Attached to Cross-Border Economic Activities

As mentioned earlier in the context of the description of the 'Brexit' challenge in trade, trade cooperation aims at reducing costs attached to the conduct of cross-border economic activities. Costs in cross-border economic activities arise as a consequence of barriers to trade and to free movement.[12] These barriers can be of a fiscal nature such as tariffs or charges having an equivalent effect as tariffs. The barriers can also be of non-fiscal nature such as quotas or non-tariff barriers. The latter encompasses regulatory and supervisory standards set by the national legal orders of the trading partners. Trade cooperation aims at lowering costs attached to the presence of fiscal trade barriers and quotas as well as to differing standards ap-

---

12 Jovanovich, *The Economics of International Integration*, (2nd edition, Edward Elgar, Cheltenham, 2015), 7.

plied to the same economic activity exercised within the territories of the trading partners.

II. Defining an Analytical Grid for Identifying Types of Trade Cooperation[13]

The following definition of the analytical grid for identifying types of trade cooperation is based on the understanding that trade cooperation is a form of international economic integration. Economic integration is here presumed to be a process and a state of affairs.[14] Whilst the 'state of affairs' refers to the absence of barriers, the 'process' element describes the course of action steered towards the abolishment of barriers. This shows that the present concept of trade cooperation is a dynamic one that can imply different types. In order to identify types of trade cooperation two or more trading partners intend to establish, the following four parameters have to be assessed. Altogether these parameters determine a type of trade cooperation:

- the intensity of trade cooperation (1.);
- the legal means to implement the trade cooperation (2.);
- the enforcement regime applicable to the trade cooperation (3.);
- the scope of the envisaged trade cooperation (4.).

1. Intensity of Trade Cooperation

The intensity of trade cooperation captures the degree to which the trading partners intend to reduce costs for economic operators that want to enter into cross-border economic activities. The options for reducing such costs range from 'minor' in the shape of a mere exchange of information about barriers to 'absolute' in the form of their complete abolition.[15] They differ in the way they affect national autonomous law-making. The more intense the trade cooperation is, the less the trading partners are free in setting up

---

13 This analytical grid was developed by the author in Amtenbrink/Markakis/Repasi, *Legal Implications Brexit – Customs Union, Internal Market and Consumer Protection*, (Study for the European Parliament, Brussels, 2017), 32 et seqq.
14 Following Balassa, *The Theory of Economic Integration*, Routledge, Abingdon, 1973, p. 1.
15 World Trade Organization (WTO), World Trade Report 2005, Exploring the links between trade, standards and the WTO, p. xxix.

or in maintaining barriers in terms of tariffs, fiscal charges or regulation applicable to products or economic operators stemming from the other trading partners. Based on the level of interference with a trading partner's autonomous law-making competence, one can distinguish the following degrees of intensity of trade cooperation:

- *Information Exchange:* The trading partners inform each other about the tariffs, charges, quotas and national regulation in place that might affect cross-border economic activities and provide for advance information on projected changes in legislation or the new introduction of rules that might affect cross-border trade between the trading partners;
- *Preferential Treatment:* The trading partners remain free in setting their own tariffs, quotas and regulatory standards. Yet, they bind themselves to unilaterally applying lower barriers to economic activities stemming from the other trading partners than to trade with third countries;
- *Mutual Recognition of Conformity Decisions:* The trading partners remain free in setting their own regulatory standards, which foreign products must observe. Yet, trading partners recognise decisions issued by authorities of the other trading partners declaring the conformity of products manufactured within the jurisdiction of this trading partner with the standards set by the trading partner, to which these products must adhere. The trading partners delegate the conformity assessment to the other trading partners and, in doing so, intend to avoid double-checks of products at the border;
- *Equivalence:* The trading partners remain free in setting their own regulatory standards, which foreign products must observe. Yet, the trading partners may decide unilaterally to recognise the regulatory standards set by other trading partners as equivalent to their home standards. As a consequence, trading partners that declared standards set by other trading partners as equivalent to their domestic ones oblige themselves to leave their borders open to products stemming from these other trading partners. Being a unilateral decision, equivalence decisions can also be revoked unilaterally;
- *Mutual Recognition of Standards:* The trading partners agree with each other to mutually recognise their regulatory standards. Products originating from the other trading partners may freely enter the national market and compete against home products that must comply with domestic law. The trading partners remain free in setting their own regulatory standards, but competition and market reactions can create pressure on the legislator to adapt its own standards to lower standards of other trading partners;

- *Full Harmonisation:* Trading partners commit themselves to set uniform rules applicable within the territories of all trading partners based on objectives commonly defined. Consequently, the trading partners lose their freedom – depending on the scope of 'full harmonisation' – to autonomously define their own tariffs, charges, quotas and regulatory standards. Full harmonisation is neutral as to the result to be achieved. It can therefore range from the mere abolition of rules applicable to the trading partners to a uniform rule that is either directly applicable in all participating countries or has to be implemented by them into national law.

2. Means to Implement Trade Cooperation

In terms of means to implement trade cooperation, trading partners may, in the first instance, exclude any legal means to realise their intention to cooperate in trade matters. In case they opt for legal means to implement their intended trade cooperation, the means that the trading partners have at their disposal can be classified into two main categories:[16] Either market operators within the trading cooperation obtain an individual right established in the trade agreement to challenge trade barriers (negative integration) or the trading partners commit themselves to set uniform rules within their national legal orders in order to even out the costs for trade between the trading partners (positive integration):

- *Negative integration:* Access to markets of the trading partners may not be precluded by (1) discriminatory and/or (2) non-discriminatory trade barriers, possibly subject to a case-by-case justification based on grounds of national policy goals;
- *Positive integration:* Access to markets of the trading partners depends on prior legislation adopted by the trading partners. Such legislation may include (1) mechanisms merely based on mutual recognition of unilaterally defined trading standards of the partners ('equivalence mechanisms') and/or (2) commonly set trading standards applicable within all trading partners.

---

16 This follows the classification first introduced by Tinbergen, *International Economic Integration,*(Elsevier, Amsterdam and Brussels, 1954), 18, 117-121 (on negative integration), 122 et seq. (on positive integration).

Both legal means are not mutually exclusive. Jointly set uniform rules (positive integration) interact, for example, with a prohibition of trade barriers (negative integration) in such a way that compliance of the trading partners with standards set by uniform rules implies a general justification of trade barriers based on these standards. In return, failed justification of trade barriers covered by the prohibition opens the scope of and the need for uniform rules.

3. Enforcement of Trade Cooperation

The effectiveness of the agreed intensity of trade cooperation and the means to implement it depends on the degree of compliance of the trading partners with the self-imposed rules. The degree of compliance is characterised by two parameters: (1) the direct effect of extranational[17] trading rules and the existence of an (2) extranational court system that ensures the uniformity in the interpretation and application of these trading rules. Direct effect refers to whether or not compliance with extranational rules can be claimed in the national court system and, by that, whether such compliance can be ensured by making use of the national rule of law of the respective trading partner. The extranational court system complements direct effect by either providing a central authority, which precludes diverging interpretation of rules having direct effect, or by opening access to (some sort of) justice for ensuring compliance with rules that don't have direct effect. The following models can be distinguished:

- *No direct effect without extranational dispute resolution mechanism:* Under this model market operators cannot claim compliance with extranational trade rules in the jurisdictions of trading partners other than their home country. They can only request from their home countries to consult with the non-compliant trading partner and are protected under the principles of consular protection. This model represents the traditional public international law approach to individual rights in international agreements;
- *No Direct effect but establishment of an extranational dispute resolution mechanism:* An extranational (mostly Treaty-based) dispute resolution

---

17 In the present contribution the term 'extranational' is used as an umbrella term for all rules whose source is to be found outside the national legal order. These sources can be international or supranational. Common to all these sources is that they are *extranational*.

mechanism compensates for the lack of direct effect. Market operators can either (1) request from their home countries to initiate proceedings against the non-compliant trading partner or (2) have direct access to the dispute resolution mechanism. Further distinctions can be made according to the binding force of the decisions rendered by the dispute resolution mechanism and to the legal consequences attached to the decision (financial compensation for damages the market operator may have sustained due to the trade barrier or disapplication of the national rules setting up the trade barrier);

- *Direct effect without extranational dispute resolution mechanism:* Market operators can invoke extranational trade rules in front of national administrations and national courts of the non-compliant trading partner. National courts are free in interpreting these rules;
- *Direct effect and establishment of an extranational court system:* Market operators can invoke extranational trade rules in front of national administrations and national courts in the non-compliant trading partner. The definitive interpretation of these rules is, however, subject to an authoritative decision of the extranational (mostly Treaty-based) court that is competent to interpret these rules in a legally binding manner.

4. Scope of Trade Cooperation

Finally, the trading partners define the scope of their trade cooperation. To begin with, the scope can be unlimited and cover all economic activities and all barriers between the trading partners. Alternatively, the trading partners can limit the scope of their trade cooperation. They can either explicitly exclude certain economic activities or certain barriers from an otherwise unlimited scope (so-called '*negative list approach*') or they can define the scope by explicitly mentioning those economic activities or barriers that they want to see covered by their cooperation (so-called '*positive list approach*').

Furthermore, trading partners can define the scope of the various elements mentioned in the previous sections (intensity of trade cooperation, means and enforcement) in a different manner. They could, for example, set an unlimited scope for 'equivalence' including a prohibition of non-discrimination ('negative integration') without direct effect but limit the scope of 'full harmonisation' with commonly set uniform rules ('positive integration') that have direct effect to a specific economic sector such as car production.

Following the literature on economic integration,[18] the scope of trade cooperation can be classified with a view to the economic activities and the barriers covered by it as follows:

- *Free Trade Area:* Tariffs, quotas and regulatory barriers in relation to trade with goods and/or services between the trading partners are covered;
- *Customs Union:* External tariff on trade with goods and/or services between the trading partners, on the one hand, and third countries, on the other, is covered;
- *Common Market:* Regulatory barriers in relation to the free movement of factors of production (labour and capital) are covered.[19]

5. *Analytical Grid*

The parameters that allow for identifying the type of trade cooperation that the trading partners intend to establish can now be translated into the following analytical grid. This grid constitutes the first step in order to visualise the degree of trade cooperation that can be achieved by trading partners.

---

18 Jovanovich, *The Economics of International Integration,* (2nd edition, Edward Elgar, Cheltenham, 2015), 8; Balassa, *The Theory of Economic Integration,* (Routledge, Abingdon, 1973), 2.

19 Further stages of economic integration mentioned by *Jovanovich* are *Economic Union* and *Total Economic Union,* which both cover goods, services, labour and capital and all kinds of trade barriers. They are to be distinguished from the 'common market' in terms of intensity as the 'economic union' includes harmonisation of regulatory standards and the 'total economic union' unified rules directly applicable within the trading partners. Since they don't differ, however, from the 'common market' in terms of scope, they are not mentioned amongst the present classification categories.

Scope	Intensity of Cooperation						Means to Implement				Enforcement				
	Information Exchange	Preferential Treatment	Mutual Recognition of Conformity Decisions	Equivalence	Mutual Recognition of Standards	Full Harmonisation	Negative Integration (discriminatory trade barriers)	Negative Integration (non-discriminatory trade barriers)	Positive Integration (mutual recognition)	Positive Integration (common standards)	Consultation Obligations	Extranational Dispute Resolution for trading partners	Extranational Dispute Resolution for Individuals	Direct Effect (without Treaty-based Court)	Direct Effect (with Treaty-based Court)
Trade in Goods															
Unlimited scope															
Limited scope															
Trade in Services															
Unlimited scope															
Limited scope															
Free Movement of Labour															
Unlimited scope															
Limited scope															
Free Movement of Capital															
Unlimited scope															
Limited scope															

Table 1. The analytical grid for identifying types of trade cooperation

The columns contain the above-mentioned parameters, including the scope of trade cooperation, the intensity of trade cooperation (ranging from information exchange to full harmonisation), the means to implement trade cooperation (ranging from prohibition of discriminations to common standards) and the compliance mechanisms (ranging from consultation obligations to direct effect with a centralised Treaty-based court system).

The rows show the different subdivisions in terms of the substantive scope of trade cooperation (trade in goods, trade in services, free movement of labour and free movement of capital), which each is broken up into the categories of 'unlimited scope', covering all sorts of trade barriers, and 'limited scope', covering only a predefined set of trade barriers. For the sake of clarification, it should be noted that the so-called 'negative list approach' is presently considered as 'unlimited' scope.

III. Applying the Analytical Grid to the 'Brexit' scenarios

1. Setting the Benchmark: Membership in the European Union

Applying the analytical grid to the membership in the European Union defines the benchmark for the assessment of the type of trade cooperation that the EU and the UK intend to achieve in the future after the withdrawal of the UK from the EU. This derives from the fact that the future trade relationship between the EU and the UK will, by definition, depart from the level of market integration that is already achieved between the UK and the remaining EU Member States under the conditions of full membership in the EU.

When applying the analytical grid to the membership in the European Union, the fundamental freedoms are classified as (1) having an unlimited scope, (2) being based on the idea of mutual recognition of standards, (3) representing negative integration in terms of a prohibition of (a) discriminatory and (b) non-discriminatory trade barriers, which (4) have direct effect and which can (a) be enforced by Member States against other Member States in front of a Treaty-based Court (Article 259 TFEU) and (b) by individuals in front of national courts that have to refer questions on the interpretation of the fundamental freedoms to a centralised Treaty-based Court (Article 267 TFEU). In terms of tariff barriers the scope is also unlimited and the abolishment of internal tariffs is covered by the category of 'full harmonisation.' Beyond tariff barriers the EU adopted harmonised rules in relation to certain economic activities and to certain regulatory standards ('limited scope')that are either directly applicable (in the case of regulations) or have to be implemented into national law (in the case of directives), which falls under the category of 'full harmonisation.' In these fields the European Commission observes the changes in the legal orders of the Member States. This categorisation applies to trade in goods in the same manner as to trade in services and to free movement of labour as to free movement of capital.

Scope	Intensity of Cooperation						Means to Implement				Enforcement				
	Information Exchange	Preferential Treatment	Mutual Recognition of Conformity Decisions	Equivalence	Mutual Recognition of Standards	Full Harmonisation	Negative Integration (discriminatory trade barriers)	Negative Integration (non-discriminatory trade barriers)	Positive Integration (mutual recognition)	Positive Integration (common standards)	Consultation Obligations	Extranational Dispute Resolution for trading partners	Extranational Dispute Resolution for Individuals	Direct Effect (without Treaty-based Court)	Direct Effect (with Treaty-based Court)
Trade in Goods															
Unlimited scope	■	■	■	■	■		■	■	■	■	■	■	■		■
Limited scope	■	■	■	■	■	■				■	■	■			■
Trade in Services															
Unlimited scope	■	■	■	■	■		■	■	■	■	■	■	■		■
Limited scope	■	■	■	■	■	■				■	■	■			■
Free Movement of Labour															
Unlimited scope	■	■	■	■	■		■	■	■	■	■	■	■		■
Limited scope	■	■	■	■	■	■				■	■	■			■
Free Movement of Capital															
Unlimited scope	■	■	■	■	■		■	■	■	■	■	■	■		■
Limited scope	■	■	■	■	■	■				■	■	■			■

Table 2. Application of the analytical grid to the membership in the European Union. The black blocks mean that a certain parameter is met.

2. Comprehensive Free Trade Agreement: The Example of CETA

The EU and Canada have given their trade relationship a broad comprehensive scope. CETA includes free trade in products, the coverage of which is defined by reference to the 'negative list approach' so that trade in products qualify for a classification as having an unlimited scope. Going beyond trade in products, CETA also contains rules on free movement of natural persons (chapter 10) and on capital (defined as 'investment') (chapter 8). Yet, the free movement of natural persons is limited to 'temporary entry and stay for business purposes' so that the scope of these rights is limited. CETA establishes therefore a free trade area with a very light version of a common market.

The intensity of trade cooperation is limited to those variants that leave the parties' autonomy to legislate untouched: information exchange, preferential treatment and mutual recognition of conformity decisions. In terms of means to implement their trade cooperation this choice is reflected by the inclusion of the only means of negative integration addressing discriminations. Market access rules aiming at non-discriminatory barriers are also present. They are, however, only applicable to pre-defined subcategories.[20] Remarkable is the legal base provided for by Chapter 11, according to which the parties are allowed to negotiate and conclude agreements on the mutual recognition of selected professional qualifications, which are considered access conditions for regulated professions. Interestingly, a Treaty body (the 'MRA Committee') adopts such agreements by means of a decision conditional upon the notification by each Party to the committee of the fulfilment of its internal requirements (Article 11.3(6) CETA). This is the only area, in which CETA makes use of positive integration through allowing a mutual recognition of standards.

In terms of compliance mechanisms CETA relies on the traditional mechanisms under international law such as the consultation obligations of the parties and a dispute settlement system for the Treaty parties (chapter 29). These traditional mechanisms are supplemented by a Treaty-based court that is accessible for individuals claiming compensation from Treaty parties for the breach of some Treaty rights in relation to services and capital (the so-called Investment Court System (ICS)) (section F of chapter 8).

---

20 See, for instance, Article 9.6 of CETA that applies only to limitations on the 'number of service suppliers', the 'total value of service transactions or assets' and the 'total number of service operations or the total quantity of service output'. Similar limitations in relation of 'investments' can be found in Article 8.4 of CETA.

Scope	Intensity of Cooperation						Means to Implement				Enforcement				
	Information Exchange	Preferential Treatment	Mutual Recognition of Conformity Decisions	Equivalence	Mutual Recognition of Standards	Full Harmonisation	Negative Integration (discriminatory trade barriers)	Negative Integration (non-discriminatory trade barriers)	Positive Integration (mutual recognition)	Positive Integration (common standards)	Consultation Obligations	Extranational Dispute Resolution for trading partners	Extranational Dispute Resolution for Individuals	Direct Effect (without Treaty-based Court)	Direct Effect (with Treaty-based Court)
Trade in Goods															
Unlimited scope	▨	▨	▨				▨	▨			▨	▨			■
Limited scope						■		■				■			
Trade in Services															
Unlimited scope	▨	▨	▨				▨	■			■	■			
Limited scope								▨	▨			▨	▨		
Free Movement of Labour															
Unlimited scope															
Limited scope	▨						▨				▨			■	
Free Movement of Capital															
Unlimited scope	▨						▨				▨	▨			
Limited scope						■		▨				▨			

Table 3. Application of the analytical grid to CETA and the membership in the EU. The black blocks mean that a certain parameter is met by the membership in the EU. The hatched block mean that a certain parameter is met by CETA.

3. The Political Declaration Setting out the Framework for the Future Relationship

In their joint political declaration setting out the framework for their future relationship the EU and the UK claimed to establish 'an ambitious, broad, deep and flexible partnership across trade and economic cooperation.'[21] In terms of scope the parties want to create a 'free trade area as well as wider sectoral cooperation where it is in the mutual interest of both Parties [...] underpinned by provisions ensuring a level playing field for open and fair competition.'[22] Their cooperation should cover trade in goods (section II of Part II) and services (sections III and IV of Part II), free movement of capital (section VI of Part II) and free movement of persons (section IX of Part II).

---

21 Political Declaration (n. 3), No. 3, p. 2.
22 Ibid., No. 17, p. 7.

Trade in goods is unlimited in scope with 'no tariffs, fees, charges or quantitative restrictions across all sectors'.[23] In terms of non-tariff barriers, the EU and the UK intend to 'promote avoidance of unnecessary barriers to trade in goods'.[24] The parties agree to recognise each other's conformity assessments. The reference to 'unnecessary barriers' insinuates that negative integration regarding both discriminatory and non-discriminatory trade barriers is the means to implement of the parties' choice. Yet, the UK declares that it 'will consider aligning with Union rules in relevant areas'.[25] This declaration can be understood as a unilateral commitment to adjust own standards to the ones set by the other trading partner (here: the EU). Translated into the analytical grid this commitment can be classified as 'equivalence' in terms of intensity with 'positive harmonisation' as a means to implement.

In relation to trade in services, the trade cooperation should have 'substantial sectoral coverage' 'building on recent Union Free Trade Agreements'. This statement is followed by a list of services that should be covered.[26] It remains unclear whether the UK and the EU would follow a 'positive list approach' or a 'negative list approach'. The wording of the declaration allows for both variants. The reference to recent EU FTAs is not providing for more clarity as CETA followed a 'negative list approach', whilst the agreement with South Korea (KOREU) adopted a 'positive list approach' for services. It is, however, more likely that the EU and the UK will opt for a 'negative list approach', given the fact that under EU law all services were covered by the internal market law. The means to implement the cooperation in relation to trade in services include, first and foremost, negative integration in the shape of 'the absence of substantially all discrimination'.[27] Beyond this, the rules on services 'should include provisions on market access and national treatment under host State rules'.[28] The fact that discriminations and market access rules are dealt with in different subsections suggests that the parties intend to establish both the prohibition of discriminatory and of non-discriminatory trade barriers. The latter, however, only in limited areas, just as it was done in CETA. The example of CETA shines also through when the parties intend to develop appropriate arrangements on professional qualifications necessary for the pursuit of

---

23 Ibid., No. 23, p. 8.
24 Ibid., No. 24, p. 9.
25 Ibid., No. 25, p. 9.
26 Ibid., No. 29 et seq., p. 10.
27 Ibid., No. 30, p. 10.
28 Ibid., No. 31, p. 11.

regulated professions. In this field a positive integration through a limited mutual recognition of professional qualifications seems imaginable. In relation to financial services the parties commit to make use of equivalence frameworks.[29]

Free movement of persons 'will be based on non-discrimination between the Union's Member States and full reciprocity.'[30] This prohibition of discriminations applies to a limited group of people (short-term visits, research, study, training, youth exchanges and business purposes).

In relation to capital, the EU and the UK briefly mention to 'include provisions to enable free movement of capital and payments [...], subject to relevant exceptions.'[31] This formulation hints at an unlimited scope with negative integration with respect to discriminatory as well as non-discriminatory barriers.

Compliance with their mutual obligations will, according to the declaration, be ensured 'through discussion and consultation.'[32] The mechanism the EU and the UK intend to establish starts with a reference of a matter of dispute to a joint committee for resolution. The joint committee may refer the dispute to an 'independent arbitration panel', which is also accessible to the parties in case the committee did not arrive at a mutually satisfactory resolution. Should the resolution involve questions of interpretation of EU law, the arbitration panel 'should' refer the question to the CJEU for a binding ruling. If after a resolution found by the arbitration panel, a party continues to fail to comply with its obligations, the other party is entitled to claim compensation or to take unilateral measures such as the suspension of obligations.[33] The political declaration is silent on the effect the agreement between the EU and the UK will have within the parties' legal orders. It also does not reveal whether individuals can claim compliance with rights foreseen by the agreement in front of an extranational dispute resolution mechanism or in front of national courts. For the purpose of applying the analytical grid to the political declaration, it will be assumed that the silence is telling to the extent that the parties exclude direct effect and direct access to a dispute resolution mechanism for individuals.

---

29 Ibid., No. 37, p. 12.
30 Ibid., No. 51, p. 15.
31 Ibid., No. 43, p. 13.
32 Ibid., No. 132, p. 33.
33 Ibid., No. 133 et seqq., p. 33.

Scope	Intensity of Cooperation										Means to Implement	Enforcement			
	Information Exchange	Preferential Treatment	Mutual Recognition of Conformity Decisions	Equivalence	Mutual Recognition of Standards	Full Harmonisation	Negative Integration (discriminatory trade barriers)	Negative Integration (non-discriminatory trade barriers)	Positive Integration (mutual recognition)	Positive Integration (common standards)	Consultation Obligations	Extranational Dispute Resolution for trading partners	Extranational Dispute Resolution for Individuals	Direct Effect (without Treaty-based Court)	Direct Effect (with Treaty-based Court)
Trade in Goods															
Unlimited scope			■						□						
Limited scope															
Trade in Services															
Unlimited scope												■	■		
Limited scope			■												
Free Movement of Labour															
Unlimited scope															
Limited scope													■		
Free Movement of Capital															
Unlimited scope									■						
Limited scope															

Table 4. Application of the analytical grid to the political declaration setting out the framework for the future relationship between the EU and the UK, CETA and the membership in the EU. The black blocks mean that a certain parameter is met by the membership in the EU, the hatched block mean that a certain parameter is met by CETA and the squares represent, which parameters are met by the political declaration.

IV. Interim Conclusion

The application of the analytical grid for identifying the type of trade co-operation that trading partners intend to establish to the EU membership as the benchmark, to CETA as the most ambitious free trade agreement concluded by the EU and to the political declaration setting out the framework for the future relationship between the EU and the UK reveals that the future relationship as sketched in the political declaration falls short of the full membership in the EU's internal market but remains at close range to CETA. It differs from CETA where the UK pledges to consider aligning with Union rules in the area of free movement of goods. It furthermore

135

does not provide for any mechanisms that will allow individuals to enforce the rules agreed under the future trade relationship.[34]

In terms of ambition, the political declaration has not yet exhausted all potential avenues in order to maximise the benefit of the future trade co-operation between the EU and the UK. Especially, elements of dynamisation such as the possibility to align each other's legal orders by means of positive integration are untapped. According to the declaration the parties intend to establish 'dialogue between the Parties at the summit, ministerial and technical level, as well as at parliamentary level'.[35] These dialogues are, however, only meant to exchange views and to make recommendations for the evolution of the future relationship between the EU and the UK. These preliminary conclusions lead to the follow-up question whether a type of trade cooperation that is more ambitious than CETA is actually achievable with the legal instruments that the EU and the UK intend to employ in order to realise their future relationship.

D. Legal Instruments for the Realisation of Trade Cooperation

This chapter will briefly outline the legal instruments that trading partners have at their disposal when realising their trade cooperation and the limits inherent to these instruments. Since the trading partners are subjects of International law with own international legal personality, the legalisation of their trade cooperation is governed by international public law. The legal instruments that are available for the trading partners are therefore taken from international public law.

I. Available Legal Instruments

The available legal instruments can be distinguished from each other according to the degree of dynamisation they allow and to the degree to which the dynamisation process is based on the will of the trading partners or on an autonomous will.

---

34 This is in contrast to the Draft Withdrawal Agreement ([2019] OJ C 66 I), which provides for 'direct effect' of the agreement rules, Article 4(1) of the DWA.

35 Political Declaration (n. 3), No. 125, p. 31.

1. Agreement

The traditional way of legalising the relationship between trading partners that are subjects of international law is the conclusion of an agreement under public international law. In doing so, the Parties agree on every matter and any changes to the Treaty require the unanimous consent by the Treaty parties in the form and following the procedure that governed the conclusion of the Treaty.

2. Delegation of Powers to Treaty Bodies

In order to make trade cooperation more flexible and to allow 'in a dynamic world [for] targeted and quick decision-making'[36] the trading partners may include into a traditional international law agreement a delegation of sovereign decision-making powers on bodies created by this agreement. Decisions by those Treaty bodies need, however, the subsequent approval of all Treaty parties in order to enter into force. In opting for this instrument, trading partners create Treaty obligations whose content is unknown *ex ante* at the time of the ratification of the original Treaty but can be specified *ex post* by decisions taken by Treaty bodies, which are composed of representatives of the governments of the trading partners. The reasons for delegating powers to Treaty bodies are 'legalization'[37] and 'de-politicization'.[38] By creating Treaty bodies and equipping them with decision-making powers, trading partners intend to deepen the legal reliability of their cooperation in a sense that they steer flexibility of their response to specific trade challenges towards a legal regime that ensures legal certainty for economic operators. At the same time, delegating powers to Treaty bodies to make decisions after a politically charged process regarding the ratification of the main Treaty allows trading partners to postpone politically delicate issues to a later moment of time.

---

36 Repasi, 'Dynamisation of international trade cooperation', (2017) 41 QIL, 73 (90).

37 Abbott/Keohane/Moravcsik/Slaughter/Snidal, 'The Concept of Legalization' (2000) 54 International Organization, 401.

38 Joerges/Neyer, 'From Intergovernmental Bargaining to Deliberative Political Processes: The Constitutionalisation of Comitology' (1997) 3 ELJ, 273call this phenomenon in relation to 'comitology' under EU law 'deliberative supranationalism', in which 'national regulators are exposed to transnational arenas scrutinising the validity of their arguments' (p. 297).

3. International Organisation

Trading partners could also choose the establishment of an international organisation entrusted with the implementation, interpretation and application of the rules the trading partners have agreed on. The trading partners can also confer decision-making powers upon an international organisation. The main difference between the delegation of powers to Treaty bodies and the delegation to an international organisation is to be found in the ability of an international organisation to autonomously make decisions. Its decisions are not subject to the subsequent approval by the Treaty parties but bind them once the decision-making procedures defined by the founding Treaty were followed. Trading partners might want to opt for the creation of an international organisation in order to achieve the effective merger of national markets into one single market, for which another institution than national ones set the rules and define the level playing field. Decisions that do not require a subsequent approval by the trading partners are taken faster and allow therefore for the highest possible degree of dynamisation of the legal order governing the cross-border economic activities.

II. Limits Inherent to the Available Legal Instruments in Establishing Different Types of Trade Cooperation

Having shown the various legal instruments available under international public law in order to realise an intended type of trade cooperation, the argument turns to the limits inherent to the respective instrument when establishing a certain type of trade cooperation.

1. Limits Inherent to Agreements

The limits inherent to the legal instrument of an agreement between the trading partners were already indicated when discussing the reasons for Treaty parties to delegate decision-making powers to Treaty bodies or international organisations. Changing agreements is a lengthy procedure so that the creation of new rules in order to react to new challenges is difficult. The more the subject of cooperation is versatile, the less the static model of an agreement is suitable for regulating this subject. Parties can then either agree to very basic rules so that unforeseen events and challenges can be dealt with by national law or settle for lengthy and detailed rules that regulate as many aspects as possible *ex ante*. Both possibilities show that an agreement is a cumbersome instrument whose limits are quickly reached once the subject of the cooperation requires some sort of flexibility and dynamisation.

2. Limits Inherent to the Delegation of Powers to Treaty Bodies

There are two limits inherent to the delegation of powers to Treaty bodies. The first refers to the degree of dynamisation that can actually be achieved by such a delegation, given that any decision taken by Treaty bodies needs a subsequent approval of the Treaty parties. The second brings the question of democratic legitimacy into the equation.[39] This issue derives from the fact that decisions taken by Treaty bodies share in the legal orders of the Treaty parties the rank of the Treaty, on which they are based. Depending on the openness of the national constitutions towards international law, their rank might be above the national constitutions or above national ordinary law.[40] This means that if national rules conflict with decisions taken by Treaty bodies, the latter trump the former. Putting it differently, rules adopted by committees of government representatives overrule rules that were adopted by national legislators. This deficiency could be compensated by a right of national legislators to decide on the approval of decisions of Treaty bodies. Yet, this is most commonly not the case in international practice and, furthermore, the approval vote amounts to a simple 'yes or no' decision whereas national legislative procedures allow for amendments of proposed legal acts. By way of contrast, one should realise that the purpose of delegating powers to Treaty bodies is to enable a cooperation of countries to decide on matters within the scope of a Treaty that were consciously left open because of the degree of precision that would be needed in order to regulate the matter or because of the controversial nature of the subject-matter. Since, in principle, such delegation of powers is allowed under both international and national constitutional law,[41] there is a cer-

---

39 More on the democratic legitimacy of the dynamisation of modern 'mega-regional' trade agreements through delegation of powers to Treaty bodies see Repasi, 'Dynamisation of international trade cooperation', (2017) 41 QIL, 73 (85-95).

40 In relation to the EU, international agreements and decision based thereon have the rank between primary law and secondary law.

41 See, for instance, CJEU, C-192/89, 20.9.1990, *Sevince*, ECR I-3461, para. 9: Article 218(9) TFEU provides in relation to associaton agreements with third countries

tain margin, within which such depoliticised decision-making, by derogation from national legislative procedures, is to be tolerated.

This line of reasoning shows that there is a trade-off between the efficiency of Treaty-based decision-making by Treaty bodies because of its depoliticising effect and the legitimacy of decisions taken by Treaty bodies. These decisions are legitimised by the delegation of powers as a part of the ratification of the Treaty, on which they are based, and by the subsequent approval by the Treaty parties in accordance with their respective internal rules.[42] The more there are obligations in an agreement whose content is unknown *ex ante* (at the moment of ratification) but left to a later decision of a Treaty body, the more there is a need for an *ex post* control of these decisions by the legislative organs of the Treaty parties.

If the scope of the agreement and of the subject-matters delegated to the decision-making of Treaty bodies is rather limited, the impact of decisions of Treaty bodies on national legislation is rather small so that the delegation of powers to Treaty bodies can be tolerated from the perspective of democratic legitimacy. Yet, if the scope of the agreement is comprehensive and the delegation of powers comprise a broad selection of topics, the democratic legitimacy of the delegation of powers becomes weak. As a consequence, the Treaty parties must decide whether they either want to limit the scope of delegated decision-making powers (taking, by that, away a lot of the efficiency gains that can be achieved in agreements with a comprehensive scope) or want to establish mechanisms that ensure enhanced legitimacy of the decisions taken by Treaty bodies. When opting for the latter, it should be borne in mind that enhanced legitimacy of decisions taken by Treaty bodies won't be achieved if only national Parliaments are more involved in the approval of decisions, but if the democratic quality of the Treaty bodies increases. Whilst there are academic points of view that champion the idea of increasing 'voice' of citizens in Treaty bodies through participation in their deliberations,[43] the experiences made with public re-

---

that the Council shall adopt a decision 'establishing the positions to be adopted on the Union's behalf in a body set up by an agreement, when that body is called upon to adopt acts having legal effects, with the exception of acts supplementing or amending the institutional framework of the agreement'. The decisions of Treaty bodies form, furthermore, 'in the same way as the Agreement itself, [...] an integral part, as from their entry into force, of the Community legal system'.

42 Repasi, 'Dynamisation of international trade cooperation', (2017) 41 QIL, 73 (86).
43 See, for instance: Dryzek, *Deliberative Democracy* (OUP, Oxford, 2000); Petman, *Participation and Democratic Theory* (CUP, Cambridge, 1970) or Quill, *Liberty after Liberalism: Civic Republicanism in a Global Age* (Palgrave, Basingstoke, 2006).

sistance against 'mega-regionals' such as CETA or TTIP show that only 'vote' for citizens in the shape of elements of formal democracy will increase the legitimacy of these bodies.[44]

In brief, a delegation of decision-making powers on Treaty bodies is limited to targeted and narrowly defined subject matters. A broader delegation of powers is not sufficiently covered by the ratification act of the Treaty creating the Treaty bodies. It requires the establishment of additional mechanisms that ensure an enhanced legitimacy of decisions taken by Treaty bodies.

For the purpose of the present argument, it is assumed that the trading partners only delegate powers without establishing additional mechanisms.

3. Limits Inherent to the Delegation of Powers to International Organisations

The limits outlined for the delegation of powers to Treaty bodies apply in the same manner to the delegation of powers to international organisations except for the limit in relation to the dynamisation of a trade cooperation that is entrusted to an international organisation. Since decisions taken by an international organisation are based on an autonomous decision-making procedure, no subsequent approval by the Treaty parties is needed. This lack of a subsequent approval of decisions amplifies, however, the issue of democratic legitimacy that has to be addressed.

III. Including the Limits of Available Legal Instruments into the Analytical Grid

The above-mentioned limits inherent to the available legal instruments show that the combination of 'full harmonisation' in terms of intensity of trade and 'positive integration' as a means to implement it, cannot be achieved by means of delegation of powers to either Treaty bodies or an international organisation without additional mechanisms that award enhanced democratic legitimacy to these decision-making bodies. Only in very exceptional cases 'full harmonisation' and 'positive integration' can be

---

44 In this sense already Peters, 'Dual Democracy' in Klabbers/Peters/Ulfstein (eds), *Constitutionalization of International law* (OUP, Oxford, 2009) 263; also Repasi, 'Dynamisation of international trade cooperation', (2017) 41 QIL, 73 (94 et seq).

realised by an agreement only. It can only occur in relation to a very narrow and precisely defined field so that the limitation of autonomous lawmaking of the Treaty parties is foreseeable for the bodies that decide on the ratification of the agreement. With this reservation, both 'full harmonisation' and 'positive integration' can be excluded as parameters of trade that can be achieved with traditional international legal instruments.

The same holds true for 'mutual recognition of standards' in terms of intensity of trade cooperation. This derives from the fact that a mutual recognition of standards is not recommendable if there is not also a legal possibility to adopt common rules in the fields covered by the obligation to mutually recognise each other's standards. Otherwise the mutual recognition of standards runs the risk of a race to the bottom, which cannot be halted by setting a uniform standard. For this reason also, there are currently no regional trade agreements that provide for a mutual recognition of standards without a further possibility to set uniform rules.[45] Consequently, mutual recognition of standards cannot be seriously realised in an agreement only. Given the high impact of mutual recognition of standards on diverging national legislation in place, a delegation of powers to either Treaty bodies or an international organisation to set uniform, legally binding standards in order to halt a race to the lowest denominator would not suffice without additional mechanisms to increase the legitimacy of these decision-making bodies.

In sum, when merging the limits of the available legal instruments for realising trade cooperation with the analytical grid for identifying the intended type of trade cooperation, one can exclude the options of 'mutual recognition of standards' and 'full harmonisation' from the available options in order to determine the intensity of trade than can be realised and 'positive integration' from the available means to realise trade cooperation. This finding is of course subject to the introduction of additional mechanisms to increase the legitimacy of decisions taken by Treaty bodies or international organisations such as the establishment of Parliamentary assemblies.

---

45 Correia de Brito/Kauffmann/Pelkmans, 'The contribution of mutual recognition to international regulatory cooperation', OECD Regulatory Policy Working Papers No. 2 (OECD Publishing, 2016), 42.

Scope	Intensity of Cooperation						Means to Implement				Enforcement				
	Information Exchange	Preferential Treatment	Mutual Recognition of Conformity Decisions	Equivalence	Mutual Recognition of Standards	Full Harmonisation	Negative Integration (discriminatory trade barriers)	Negative Integration (non-discriminatory trade barriers)	Positive Integration (mutual recognition)	Positive Integration (common standards)	Consultation Obligations	Extranational Dispute Resolution for trading partners	Extranational Dispute Resolution for Individuals	Direct Effect (without Treaty-based Court)	Direct Effect (with Treaty-based Court)
Trade in Goods															
Unlimited scope															
Limited scope															
Trade in Services															
Unlimited scope															
Limited scope															
Free Movement of Labour															
Unlimited scope															
Limited scope															
Free Movement of Capital															
Unlimited scope															
Limited scope															

Table 5. The grey highlighted columns in the analytical grid for identifying types of trade cooperation, as applied to the EU membership, CETA and the political declaration on the future relationship between the EU and the UK, visualise the parameters that cannot be achieved by a public international law agreement without additional mechanisms that ensure enhanced democratic legitimacy at the level of the agreement.

IV. Interim Conclusion

Including the limits of available legal instruments into the analytical grid provides for an explanation why the political declaration setting out the framework for the future relationship between the EU and the UK falls short of the market integration potential achieved under the conditions of EU membership and stays rather within the lines drawn by CETA. A more ambitious market integration through the use of positive integration in order to realise a mutual recognition of standards that would render border checks for regulatory purposes unnecessary or in order to set a dynamic level playing field that can easily change over time reaches the limits of what can be achieved by means of an international law agreement. Just as CETA, the political declaration mentions only very narrowly defined and specific areas, in which they can allow for mutual recognition by means of an agreement. The political declaration goes beyond CETA where the UK considers aligning with Union rules in the area of trade in goods. This alignment is, however, completely voluntary and far away from legal certainty.

The danger that lies in this orientation of the intensity of trade to the limits of what can be achieved by ordinary international law agreements is the lack of dynamisation of the trade cooperation. The lack of such dynamisation manifests itself in a twofold manner: First, it holds the parties off opting for a mutual recognition of standards as they have no possibility to prevent a harmful race to the bottom in terms of regulatory standards. In not doing so, the parties consciously fall short of the optimal reduction of costs for cross-border trade. Second, even under the prohibition of discriminations, the parties are inclined to exclude a broad range of economic activities and sectors from the scope of the agreement due to the lack of dynamisation. This follows from the fact that the equal treatment of UK products and operators with the EU ones within the EU internal market is based on the maintenance of a level-playing field between the EU and the UK.[46] Under the level-playing field rules, the regulatory standards that should remain applicable in the UK are the ones in force at the moment of the withdrawal (or, in case the withdrawal agreement will be ratified: at the moment of the expiry of the transition period). Any increase in the level of protection foreseen by EU standards will lead to a situation, in which UK operators can act under lower conditions than EU ones provided that there is no mechanism to increase the level-playing field rules with effect for the UK.[47] As a consequence both parties are inclined to exclude those economic activities and sectors from the scope of the prohibition of discriminations, where they intend to safeguard their home economies against competition of the other party based on diverging regulatory standards.

Both shortcomings will lead to a future trade agreement between the UK and the EU that will achieve a lower level of market integration than the one in the EU internal market. This difference in market integration level will cause additional costs for cross-border trade between the UK and

---

46 See, for instance, Article 6(1)(3) in conjunction with Annex 4 of the Protocol on Ireland/Northern Ireland of the Draft Withdrawal Agreement between the EU and UK.

47 Admittedly, the 'backstop' in the Draft Withdrawal Agreement provides for such a mechanism: the Joint Committee (Article 164 DWA) may adopt a decisions (Article 164(4)(f) DWA) to 'lay down higher standards' (Article 6(1)(3) of the Protocol on Ireland/Northern Ireland). Yet, the DWA is not yet ratified. The political declaration is silent as to whether such mechanism will also be foreseen in a future trade agreement.

the EU as compared to the current state of affairs. In assessing this outcome, one must bear in mind that it is a consequence of the limits inherent to the legal instrument of an ordinary international law agreement that does not provide for any substantive delegation of powers to Treaty bodies that are equipped with the necessary democratic legitimacy for such decision making.

E. *Free Trade Agreements are no Means to Maintain the Existing Level of Market Integration between the UK and the EU*

As it becomes apparent from the EU trade agreement with Canada, free trade agreements are means that are able to achieve the abolishment of discriminatory as well as non-discriminatory trade barriers between the contracting parties. They can, however, not achieve a lowering of trade barriers to zero by making use of a mutual recognition obligation of standards because of the lack of efficient mechanisms to set common minimum standards. Regulatory cooperation, as foreseen by CETA, cannot constitute such a mechanism as it does not contain legal bases for the adoption of secondary legal acts with a broad scope and as it does not possess enough democratic legitimacy for such far-reaching decisions. Going beyond the limits of regulatory cooperation between Treaty parties at the level of an agreement, even creating Treaty bodies in an agreement and entrusting them with the task of regulatory cooperation cannot achieve much more than what can be found in CETA. This conclusion is based on the observation that introducing legal bases for secondary legal acts with a broad scope, exhausts the legitimacy that can be transferred by means of an *ex ante* ratification of a Treaty and an *ex post* approval of single decisions. CETA shows therefore that a state of market integration comparable to the EU's internal market cannot be achieved by means of a trade agreement only.

This finding is far from being striking. The purpose of a free trade agreement is to mutually open up markets of the parties to the agreement. They aim, in particular, at reducing discriminatory barriers. They are meant to be another step towards market integration. Further steps towards market integration require an institutional set-up that goes beyond what can be agreed upon between parties *ex ante* in an agreement. Lowering costs linked to the presence of trade barriers necessitates an obligation of mutual recognition of standards, which itself requires a mechanism to draw a lower limit to a race to the bottom in terms of standards that is inherent to a mutual recognition obligation of standards. What is more, lowering costs to zero requires a uniform understanding of the content of both the mutual recognition obligation and of commonly set rules. In the absence of a court that ensures this uniform understanding, divergence in interpreting extranational rules in the national legal context creates costs that originally were intended to be abolished.

In brief, free trade agreements as a means to open up previously closed markets are not suitable to uphold a high level of market integration such as the one found in the EU's internal market. Their use between trading partners that were previously part of a common market cannot prevent costs attached to a market disintegration being a consequence of the withdrawal of the trading partners from the common market. At best such agreements do not contain any further reasons for disintegration than the regulatory divergence, which will develop on grounds of autonomous national decision-making.

F. Conclusions

Establishing or maintaining integrated markets between the UK and the EU requires a legal and institutional framework that goes beyond what can be realised by means of a mere agreement between the two parties or a partial and limited conferral of decision making powers upon Treaty bodies. It requires more sophisticated decision-making procedures that enjoy a higher degree of democratic legitimacy than *ex ante* ratification and *ex post* approval by the Treaty parties. Beyond what is outlined in the political declaration setting out the framework for the future relationship between the UK and the EU, in order to maintain the currently existing level of market integration between the EU and the UK, both have to address the following issues that cannot be addressed in a public international law agreement only:

(1) They have to include at Treaty level an obligation to mutually recognise each other's standards, supplemented by

(2) a mechanism that allows for setting common rules that prevent a race to the bottom in terms of standards to the effect that neither the UK nor the EU can lower the level-playing field as compared to the *acquis communautaire* at the moment of the entry into force of the agreement, but both can raise the level of protection (ideally together).

(3) They have to set up a compliance mechanisms either by way of a legal obligation in the agreement to provide for effective implementation and individual rights in national law or by way of establishing a dispute resolution mechanism at the level of the agreement that effective-

ly ensures the compliance of both the UK and the EU with their obligations under the agreement and that can be activated by individuals.

Addressing these three issues can hardly be reconciled with 'Brexit's main promise to regain formal (viz. national) control. Honouring Brexit's pledge to avoid increasing costs for Britain's economy requires, however, sharing sovereignty with the EU in order to allow for the continuation of highly integrated markets even in the area of goods, services and capital. Squaring this circle is impossible, which reflects legal reality in today's world of economic globalisation: 'control' is a relative term. Taking back formal national control comes at the expense of losing substantive but international control over keeping costs low for economic operators being established in an economy that is highly interconnected with other countries and that depends on trade. Mere free trade agreements cannot compensate for the loss in international control that results from the UK's withdrawal from the EU.

Market Access and Standards in the Future Relation between the EU and the UK

Prof. Dr. Friedemann Kainer

I. Introduction

For the future free trade agreement between the European Union and the United Kingdom, the aim should be to achieve the most iextensive trade freedoms possible. The frequently mentioned "CETA (plus)" or "Norway (plus)" solutions address the point that the withdrawal from the EU should indeed take the UK out of the political frame of the European integration but should change as little as possible the economic status quo in trading, as represented by the Union's Internal Market law. The core objective in this respect is frictionless trading. In the future, goods, services and capital (not persons) should continue to be exchanged and move freely without discrimination or hindrances between both sides. Only such continuity would prevent to jeopardise existing supply relationships, in particular 'just in time' supply chains, or the established cross-border division of labour between the British islands and the continent.

This objective, which is the clear intent of the British Government[1] and the EU[2], and has been inserted in the Political Declaration (November 2018)[3], is in conflict with the British objective inherent in the Brexit process of regaining control over its own legislation and trade policy. Even if it is often asserted by the British side that it would lower social, environmental and tax standards, for example, and that the safety of products would be

---

1 See, for example, 'The Future Relationship between the United Kingdom and the European Union' ('Chequers Proposal'), July 2018, www.gov.uk/government/publi cations, No. 1.1 ff.

2 See, European Council Guidelines for Art. 50, 23.3.2018, https://www.consilium.e uropa.eu/media/33458/23-euco-art50-guidelines.pdf.

3 Political Declaration Setting out the Framework for the Future Relationship between the European Union and the United Kingdom, 25.11.2019, https://assets.pub lishing.service.gov.uk/government/uploads/system/uploads/attachment_data/file/7 59021/25_November_Political_Declaration_setting_out_the_framework_for_the_f uture_relationship_between_the_European_Union_and_the_United_Kingdom__. pdf, No. 16 ff.

fully guaranteed at the existing level, there is an obvious danger that after the end of the transitional period the UK regulations will progressively differ from those of the EU. Otherwise, what would be the point of calling for national control over legislation to be regained? It may even be the case that a deliberate effort is being made to reduce regulatory standards in order to increase competitiveness, as has been publicly demanded for the City of London and its financial sector.

However, a progressive divergence can lead to distortions of competition and consequently to a violation of the principle of competition in the European Union. The Internal Market of the European Union is based on the guarantee of free and undistorted trade in goods and services. The jurisprudence of the European Court of Justice (hereafter: "ECJ") has extended the principle of non-discrimination established in Article 34 TFEU and 56 TFEU overtime. The ECJ developed a right to market access, beginning with the famous Dassonville Decision[4] for the free movement of goods in 1976, and extended this right to the other fundamental freedoms, namely services,[5] capital[6] and – in substance – to the freedom of persons[7]. The Court cleared the way against countless impediments to trade as a means of negative integration. But, free access to markets in the sense of the Internal Market goes beyond negative integration: it needs common or compatible standards.[8] A big part of the acquis communautaire is dedicated to this objective. The question discussed in this paper will be whether mutually compatible standards will be necessary for the future relationship between the EU and the UK, and if so, how they can be maintained. The starting point for a future relationship in the form of an international agreement could, in this respect, hardly be better, as the EU and the UK by now share common standards to a considerable degree on the basis of EU law.

In this paper, it shall first be remembered that creating mutually compatible standards, preferably in the form of harmonisation, enhances competition and benefits regulatory interests – and is necessary to maintain a level playing field and thus a condition for full market access under EU law (II). Next, different models of regulatory cooperation shall be exam-

---

4   ECJ, Case 8/74, 11.7.1974, *Dassonville*, ECLI:EU:C:1974:82.
5   ECJ, Case 33/74, 3.12.1974, *van Binsbergen*, ECLI:EU:C:1974:131; Case C-76/90, 25.7.1991, *Säger/Dennemeyer*, ECLI:EU:C:1991:331.
6   ECJ, Case 367/98, 4.6.2002, *Commission/Portugal*, ECLI:EU:C:2002:326.
7   ECJ, Case C-55/94, 30.11.1995, *Gebhard*, ECLI:EU:C:1995:411 (establishment); Case C-190/98, 27.1.2000, *Graf*, ECLI:EU:C:2000:49 (persons).
8   See M. Fox, 'Toward World Antitrust and Market Access' (1997) Vol. 91, No. 1 The American Journal of International Law, p. 5.

ined (III). These models can be used to develop concepts for a specific approach to the EU-UK future regulatory cooperation which works as a compromise between rather loose forms of regulatory cooperation in preferential trade agreements on the one hand, and the EU method on the other (IV) – thereby taking into account red lines from London as they might occur in the future negotiations, in particular to regain national regulatory sovereignty. The resulting proposals will be aggregated into a brief summary (V).

II. Mutually Compatible Standards, Trade Benefits and Regulation Objectives

In the first part of the analysis, the thesis will be put forward that common standards add to efficiency in trade (1). In some cases, standards are what make cross-border trade possible in the first place. This is, in particular, true for services (2). Finally, at least to some extent, common standards are an expression of the European Union's principle of competition, enshrined in primary law, and therefore against the background of the current development of Internal Market legislation a condition for free market access (3). From this, it can be concluded that the more comprehensive a future trade agreement and the more open its market access is to be, the greater is the need to ensure at least broadly aligned standards.

1. Common Standards and Efficiency in Trade

The understanding of the relationship between common standards and efficient trade relations has not been clarified for very long. It has only recently started to receive attention from researchers[9] and policy makers. When negotiating trade relations between the EU and ASEAN in 2004, EU trade commissioner Pascal Lamy stated his belief that "the real 21st century trade issues were standards and rules in areas such as safety, health or consumer protection", rather than tariffs or quotas.[10]

---

9 Baller, 'Trade Effects of Regional Standards Liberalization: A Heterogeneous Firms Approach' (2007) World Bank Policy Research Working Paper No. 4124, p. 11.

10 'EU and ASEAN to pave way for trade pact talks', Financial Times, 7 September 2004; quoted by Xiaoyang Chen/Mattoo, 'Regionalism in Standards: Good or Bad for Trade?' (2008) Vol. 41, Iss. 3 Canadian Journal of Economics, p. 839.

Quantitative analyses of the effects of standards on trade prove to be complex due to the large number of standards and diverging legal documents in existence.[11] Of the few empirical studies available, however, many of them found evidence that mutual standards facilitate trade,[12] always of course in combination with market access rights.[13] For example, the World Bank TBT survey[14] has looked at 689 firms in over 20 industries in 17 developing countries. 70% of these firms have reported that they face technical regulations in their export markets. EU and US regulations were generally considered the most important. In order to meet standards, firms have to invest in additional plants or equipment, one time product redesign, product redesign for each export market, additional labour for production, additional labour for testing and certification, or lay off workers instead of making these types of investment in order to keep the costs from increasing.[15]

Such costs make cross-border trade less attractive and in some cases even impossible because they impose additional costs on the exporting company and thus interfere with the level playing field and decrease competitiveness:[16] Unlike domestic competitors in the state of destination, exporting companies face regulations not only by their state of origin but also in the state of destination. This – albeit absent a discrimination – results in distortions of competition. These cannot be eliminated by market access rights based solely on the principle of equal treatment of nationals as the obligation to apply domestic standards as a manifestation of this very principle

---

11 Baller, 'Trade Effects of Regional Standards Liberalization: A Heterogeneous Firms Approach' (2007) World Bank Policy Research Working Paper No. 4124, p. 12.

12 Xiaoyang Chen/Mattoo, 'Regionalism in Standards: Good or Bad for Trade?' (2008) Vol. 41, Iss. 3, Canadian Journal of Economics, p. 865.

13 Baller, 'Trade Effects of Regional Standards Liberalization: A Heterogeneous Firms Approach' (2007) World Bank Policy Research Working Paper No. 4124, p. 26.

14 Wilson/Otsuki, 'Standards and Technical Regulations and Firms in Developing Countries: New Evidence from A World Bank Technical Barriers to Trade Survey', World Bank, June 2004, p. 2.

15 Baller, 'Trade Effects of Regional Standards Liberalization: A Heterogeneous Firms Approach' (2007) World Bank Policy Research Working Paper No. 4124, p. 11; Maskus/Otsuki/Wilson,'The cost of Compliance with Product Standards for Firms in Developing Countries: An Econometric Study' (2005) World Bank Policy Research Working Paper No. 3590, http://documents.worldbank.org/curated/en/4 41521468330948472/pdf/wps3590.pdf.

16 See M. Fox, 'Toward World and Market Access' (1997) Vol. 91, No. 1 The American Journal of International Law, p. 5.

that leads to them.[17] It is for this reason that the ECJ has defined the fundamental freedoms as prohibitions of restrictions, with the specific result of discriminations of own nationals to occur.[18]

Should the negotiations come to the conclusion that common standards were useful, two main levels of establishing mutual standards can be distinguished: Harmonisation and regulatory cooperation.

Harmonisation in general means to agree on uniform or at least approximate laws in different States. This can happen by taking international standards into account, such as the Codex Alimentarius or the standards of the International Organization for Standardization, or by regulating on an inter– or, as within the EU, supranational level.

However, harmonisation presupposes the will to establish common rules and thus common institutions and procedures. This may not be compatible with the UK's objective of regaining control over its legislation. Therefore, it may be preferable to agree on *regulatory cooperation*. Regulatory cooperation can be achieved by accepting different sets of rules as equivalent. This requires common regulatory goals in general, which may have been pursued in different ways,[19] but leading to sufficiently similar standards. Equivalence also necessitates that the implementation and enforcement of rules are equally effective,[20] for example, that the supervision of financial providers is efficient.

On the basis of a sufficient equivalence of rules, mutual recognition is possible. This refers to a concept where States agree to accept regulatory differences and allow the import of products based on the country of origin principle. A respective instrument in international trade law is the Mutual Recognition Agreement of CETA,[21] which can be concluded based on certain equivalence.

---

17 See K. Schmidt, 'The impact of mutual recognition-inbuilt limits and domestic responses to the single market' (2002) Journal of European Public Policy, p. 938.

18 ECJ, Case 332/90, 28.1.1992, *Steen/Deutsche Bundespost*, ECLI:EU:C:1992:40; Case 180/83, 28.6.1984, *Moser*, ECLI:EU:C:1984:233; Case 98/86, 18.2.1987, *Mathot*, ECLI:EU:C:1987:89.

19 Veggeland/Elvestad, *Equivalence and Mutual Recognition in Trade Arrangements*, (2004), 8.

20 Hoekman, 'Fostering Transatlantic Regulatory Cooperation and Gradual Multilateralization' (2015) Vol. 18, Iss. 3. JIEL, p. 614.

21 See below, III.2.

2. The Case for Services

In the future EU-UK relationship, special attention must be placed on the sector of services. The services sector is the most important sector of the British economy, summing up to 80% of the national GDP. The British service industry covers various areas as different as financial services, transportation, broadcasting, media services and education. Any proposal for a trade agreement which would not guarantee free trade in services would certainly not be acceptable, in particular, because the TBT-Agreement does not apply to services.[22] This makes it necessary to address the trade restricting impact of differing service standards.

In the services sector in general and for access to regulated professions in particular, the abolition of Internal Market regulations can only be balanced out to a limited extent by instruments of conventional free trade agreements. The liberalisation of services market differs in many respects from that of goods markets. First, obstacles to cross-border trade in services often lie in mere differences between national regulations[23] – such as different standards in the field of consumer protection or environmental protection; adaptation to different standards is particularly cost-intensive for companies. Secondly – and here centrally – such rules often refer not to the product itself but to the service provider.[24] Since services – in contrast to goods – are mostly of a non-physical or completely individual nature and thus tend to elude controls, quality assurance starts with the qualifications of the persons providing the service. Digital services can be traded online. This makes it especially difficult to regulate specific standards on services. Moreover, services tend to be credence products where quality is difficult to control. For example, the provision of legal services is generally reserved for professionals with a domestic qualification.[25] Such require-

---

22 See Annex 1 of the TBT-Agreement.

23 Delimatsis, *International Trade in Services and Domestic Regulations: Necessity, Transparency, and Regulatory Diversity*, (2007), 70; Overview of barriers to cross-border provision of services, cf. Hoekman/Braga, 'Protection in Trade in Services – a Survey' (1997) World Bank Policy Research Working Paper No. 174, p. 5 ff.; Pelkmans, *Contribution to Growth: The Single Market for Services. Delivering Economic Benefits for Citizens and Businesses*, https://www.europarl.europa.eu/RegData/etudes/STUD/2019/631054/IPOL_STU(2019)631054_EN.pdf, p. 22 ff.

24 Sampson/Snape, 'Identifying the Issues in Trade in Services' (1985) Vol. 8, Iss. 2, The World Economy, p. 171; Hoekman/Mavroidis, 'A Technical Barriers to Trade Agreement for Services?' (2015) EUI Working Paper RSCAS 2015/25, p. 4.

25 See Communication from the Commission to the European Parliament, COM (2017) 820, p. 17 ff.

ments of national legal systems are difficult or impossible for foreign service providers to meet, whereas national standards in relation to goods are a mere cost factor for cross-border traders. Effective liberalisation of cross-border trade in services, in particular, access to regulated professions, requires common rules, such as standards for licences and diplomas, mutual recognition and their conditions. Thirdly – and this is particularly important for controlling migration – the provision of services often requires an establishment or at least temporary access of staff at the place where the services are to be provided.[26] Immigration regulations and elementary national interests, which are particularly important in the UK because of a specific national characteristic, are thus affected: Since identity cards are unknown there as proof of identity and there are no civil registers, the British Government finds it much more difficult to control resident persons than the continental Member States of the EU. For this reason, the fear that persons admitted to cross-border services will remain illegal is more significant than elsewhere.

These considerations show the importance of common standards for the cross-border trade of services. In particular, the recognition of professional qualifications can be a condition for the effective free movement of services. For these reasons, the EU has paid particular attention to the area of services and has further deepened integration since 2014, for example through the Service Package.[27]

3. Common Standards and the EU Principle of Competition

As already outlined in the introduction, the relationship between market access rights and standards is not only utilitarian (efficiency) but also touches a constitutional principle of EU primary law. The problem of national discrimination shows that free market access does not only have positive consequences but may have an impact on the conditions of competition. This becomes most evident when considerably lower social or envi-

---

26 Delimatsis, *International Trade in Services and Domestic Regulations: Necessity, Transparency, and Regulatory Diversity*, (2007), 63 ff.; Sampson/Snape, 'Identifying the Issues in Trade in Services' (1985) Vol. 8, Iss. 2, The World Economy, p. 172.

27 See Kainer, 'Contribution to Growth. Free Movement of Services and Freedom of Establishment: Delivering Improved Rights to European Citizens and Businesses', Study for the IMCO Committee of the European Parliament, https://www.europa rl.europa.eu/RegData/etudes/STUD/2019/638394/IPOL_STU(2019)638394_EN.p df.

ronmental standards prevail in the country of origin. Under these circumstances, free market access from a third country can lead to significant distortions of competition and therefore may be incompatible with Union law. Access to the European Internal Market for a third country, such as the United Kingdom, can only be granted in coherence with the principle of competition under the Internal Market law (see a)). This requires regulatory convergence if access to the Internal Market is to be largely unrestricted (see (b)).

a) The principle of competition under the Internal Market law

The principle of competition under the Internal Market law is a European Union objective in the obligation to establish an Internal Market and to guarantee the social market economy (Article 3 para. 3 sentence 1 TEU).[28] According to Article 26 TFEU, the Internal Market comprises an area without internal borders in which the free movement of goods, persons, services and capital is guaranteed in accordance with the provisions of the Treaties. It is a system that protects competition against distortion (Protocol No. 27 on the Internal Market and Competition, Article 119 TFEU).[29] This principle of competition is more than free trade guaranteed by market access rights. It is an expression of the idea that borders and different regulatory systems are no longer relevant to competition (in perspective) and that all market-relevant barriers between the Member States are to be eliminated.[30] For this reason, the fundamental freedoms of the European Union to guarantee cross-border trade (free movement of goods, free movement of persons, freedom to provide services as well as the freedom of establishment[31]) are conceptually linked to market harmonisation. Harmonisation extends and consolidates the market access rights granted by

---

28 Šmejkal, 'Competition law and the social market economy goal of the EU' (2015) Journal of European Public Policy, p. 33.
29 Ruffert, in: Callies/Ruffert, EUV/AEUV, 5. ed. 2016, Art. 3 EUV, para. 22, 25; Pechstein, in: Streinz, EUV/AEUV, 3. ed. 2018, Art. 3 EUV, para. 7; v.Vormizeele, in: von der Groeben/Schwarze/Hatje, Europäisches Unionsrecht, 7. ed. 2015, Art. 26 AEUV, para. 28.
30 M. Schröder, in: Streinz, EUV/AEUV, 3. ed.2018, Art. 26 AEUV, para. 20; in detail Müller-Graff, *Unternehmensinvestitionen und Investitionssteuerung im Marktrecht* (1984), 280 ff.
31 Müller-Graff, in: Frankfurter Kommentar, EUV/GRC/AEUV, 2017, Art. 3 EUV, para. 32 f.

the fundamental freedoms by further reducing non-tariff barriers to trade[32] and, if necessary, also enables common standards to be established to create a level playing field.[33]

At the same time, the system of fundamental freedoms and standard setting is accompanied by competition rules to prevent private (in particular anti-trust and merger control law) and State (in particular State aid supervision and public procurement law) distortions of competition.[34] In addition, the principle of competition of legal orders applies: market participants, making use of fundamental freedoms, choose the system that seems best for them and exert pressure on the Member States to create good regulatory systems.[35] The example of company law shows that this tends to have an auto harmonising effect.[36]

In this way, comparative macroeconomic cost advantages are to be realised and welfare to be increased.[37] Altogether, the objectives of the EU In-

---

32 Müller-Graff, in: Frankfurter Kommentar, EUV/GRC/AEUV, 2017, Art. 3 EUV, para. 34; v.Vormizeele, in: von der Groeben/Schwarze/Hatje, Europäisches Unionsrecht, 7. ed. 2015, Art. 26 AEUV, para. 25.

33 Vgl. Bast, in: Grabitz/Hilf/Nettesheim, Recht der EU, 65. suppl. 2018, Art. 26 AEUV, para. 12; M. Schröder, in: Streinz, EUV/AEUV, 3. ed. 2018, Art 26 AEUV, para. 24.

34 Emmerich, in: Immenga/Mestmäcker, EU-Wettbewerbsrecht, 5. ed. 2012, Art. 101 AEUV, para. 1 ff.; Schröter, in: von der Groeben/Schwarze/Hatje, Europäisches Unionsrecht, 7. ed. 2015, Art. 101 AEUV, para. 15 ff.; Terhechte, in: Grabitz/Hilf/Nettesheim, Recht der EU, 65. suppl. 2018, Art. 3 EUV, para. 41 ff.

35 Mestmäcker/Schweitzer, *Europäisches Wettbewerbsrecht* (3. ed. 2014), § 2, para. 95 ff.; vgl. auch Tietje, in: Grabitz/Hilf/Nettesheim, Recht der EU, 65. suppl. 2018, Art. 114 AEUV, para. 114 ff. (on the relationship of competition between different systems and the approximation of laws); Mussler, *Die Wirtschaftsverfassung der Europäischen Gemeinschaft im Wandel* (1998), 68 ff. (with scepticism: 72 ff.).

36 For example, the introduction of the legal form of a limited liability company with no minimum capital requirement "UG (haftungsbeschränkt)" in Germany and of comparable company forms in other Member States was a reaction to the widespread use of the English *Limited*, *cf.* Fleischer, Internationale Trends und Reformen im Recht der geschlossenen Kapitalgesellschaft, NZG 2014, 1081 (1084 f.).

37 Müller-Graff, in: Frankfurter Kommentar, EUV/GRC/AEUV, 2017, Art. 3 EUV, para. 32, id., in: Dauses/Ludwigs, Handbuch des EU-Wirtschaftsrechts, 46. Suppl. 2019, A. I, para. 122. On the economic discussion: Molle, *The Economics of European Integration* (2006), 345 ff.; Pelkmans, *European Integration. Methods and Economic Analysis*, (3. ed. 2006), 108 f.; Thorbecke/Pagoulatos, *European economic integration*, (1975); Mayes, 'The effects of economic integration' (1978) Vol. 17 Journal of Common Market Studies, p. 3; Winters, 'Britain in Europe: a survey of quantitative trade studies' Journal of Common Market Studies 25 (1987),315 ff.

ternal Market go beyond the Ricardian model[38] insofar as an efficient allocation of production factors (e.g. through cross-border establishment) is sought through the mobility of production factors.[39]

These considerations show that competition is a constitutional principle of the EU guaranteed by primary law. The competition principle applies not only to the organisation and regulation of trade relations within the EU but also to the conclusion of trade agreements with third countries.[40]

b) Distortions of Competition due to Differences in Regulatory Costs

On the basis of the competition principle discussed above, the need for a common regulatory framework relevant to competition arises. The obligation to effectively adopt Union standards relevant to competition is indispensable for the market access of undertakings of third countries if this market access would be comparable to the rules of the Internal Market. This includes, on the one hand, secondary law based on the EU's Internal Market law competences which is per se market relevant, but also numerous other regulations, for example, in the areas of environment, energy or social policy, including labour law.

It is clear that the existence of regulation in a State not only restricts direct competitive freedoms but also imposes competitive regulatory costs on the companies concerned.[41] The relevant regulations do include product standards, but they go far beyond. For example, in steel production in the EU 99% of the regulatory costs are based on compliance with environmental and energy standards.[42]

---

38 Ricardo, *On the Principles of Political Economy and Taxation*, (1987). According to this model, free trade allows every country to focus on the production of goods in which it has a comparative cost advantage, cf. Felbermayr/Fuest/Stöhlker, 'Economic Effects of Brexit on the European Economy' (November 2017) EconPol Policy Report, 2, available at: https://www.cesifo-group.de/DocDL/EconPol_Policy_R eport_04_2017_Brexit.pdf.

39 See Kainer/Persch, 'Das Prinzip der Einheit des Binnenmarktes: Keine Rosinen für Drittstaaten', EuZW 2018, 932 (933).

40 See Kainer/Persch, 'Das Prinzip der Einheit des Binnenmarktes: Keine Rosinen für Drittstaaten', EuZW 2018, 932 (935).

41 In this context, the EU has introduced the Regulatory Fitness and Performance Programme (REFIT) to reduce excessive bureaucracy and regulatory costs., cf. Refit- Scoreboard 2017, 5.

42 See Rankin/Boffey, 'Brussels rejects Theresa May's plea to break Brexit deadlock', The Guardian, 1.10.2018, available at: https://www.theguardian.com/politics/

From the outset, it was, therefore, the policy of the European Economic Community to work towards reducing regulatory distortions of competition, as the obligation of equal payment in Article 157 (1) TFEU (Article 119 TEC) has impressively shown since 1958.[43] The principle of equal pay for equal work for men and women has been inserted into the Treaty of Rome under pressure from the French side in order to prevent competitive advantages for the German textile industry.[44] On this basic idea, the harmonisation of social and environmental standards was initially based on the Internal Market competence; both areas later received legal bases independent of the Internal Market, but without completely losing the conceptual link to the Internal Market.[45]

In addition, the pro-competitive effect of these regulations places high demands on the uniform interpretation[46] and effectiveness of their application, which must be guaranteed and which have manifested themselves in the EU in the principles of the direct application of Union law (under certain conditions including directives[47]), interpretation in conformity with

2018/oct/01/eu-brussels-rejects-plea-from-theresa-may-to-break-brexit-deadlock? CMP=Share_iOSApp_Other.

43 See Rust, in: von der Groeben/Schwarze/Hatje, Europäisches Unionsrecht, 7. ed. 2015, Art. 157 AEUV, para. 115 ff.; Rieble, 'Entgeltgleichstellung der Frau', RdA 2011, 36 (37); Franzen, *Privatrechtsangleichung durch die Europäische Gemeinschaft* (1999), 25; Langenfeld, in: Grabitz/Hilf/Nettesheim, Recht der EU, 65. suppl. 2018, Art. 157 AEUV, para. 3.

44 Rust, in: von der Groeben/Schwarze/Hatje, Europäisches Unionsrecht, 7. ed. 2015, Art. 157 AEUV, para. 115 ff.; Rieble, RdA 2011, 36 (37); Franzen, Privatrechtsangleichung durch die Europäische Gemeinschaft (1999), 25; Langenfeld, in: Grabitz/Hilf/Nettesheim, Recht der EU, 65. suppl. 2018, Art. 157 AEUV, para. 3.

45 Nettesheim, in: Grabitz/Hilf/Nettesheim, Recht der EU, 65. suppl. 2018, Art. 191 AEUV, para. 22.

46 Vgl. Wieduwilt, 'Article 50 TEU – The Legal Framework of a Withdrawal from the European Union', ZEuS 2015, 169 (193), who sees the consistency of Union law endangered by a partial withdrawal.

47 ECJ, Case C-41/74, 04.12.1974, *van Duyn*, ECLI:EU:C:1974:133, para. 12; Case C-148/78, 05.05.1979, *Ratti*, ECLI:EU:C:1979:110; Case C-8/81, 19.01.1982, *Becker*, ECLI: EU:C:1982:7, para. 23, cf. also W. Schroeder, in: Streinz, EUV/AEUV, 3. ed. 2018, Art. 288 AEUV, para. 88.

directives,[48] state liability[49]. All this is an expression of the uniformity of Union law aimed at a level playing field and shows that unhindered market access can only be granted at the price of the adoption of all cost-relevant (harmonised) regulations.

Finally, the link between standards and market access as a means of securing undistorted competition is very clearly reflected in the Northern Ireland Protocol to the Withdrawal Agreement of 25 November 2018. It is essentially shown by the fact that Northern Ireland and Great Britain are bound by Union law standards, graded according to the degree of market access.[50]

4. Interim Conclusion

For the purpose of this analysis, the conclusion can be drawn that uniform or aligned standards serve two objectives. On the one hand, they can make cross-border trade possible in the first place. This is the case when the country of destination makes the import of goods or services dependent on compliance with certain standards. Regulations tend to have different effects on goods and services.[51] For the service sector, regulations that are linked to the person of the service provider (e.g. professional qualifications) often prove to be prohibitive. On the other hand, standards have direct or indirect effects on the costs of cross border trade. Different regulatory costs can appreciably distort competition and thus conflict with the principle of Union competition.

Finally, it can be deduced from this that the harmonisation of standards is necessary if market access rights go beyond the requirement of equal

---

48 Potacs, ‚Effet utile als Auslegungsgrundsatz' EuR 2009, 465 (475); Heinze, in: Basedow/Hopt/Zimmermann, Handwörterbuch des europäischen Privatrechts, 2009, para. 337 ff.; Wegener, in: Callies/Ruffert, EUV/AEUV, 5. ed. 2016, Art 19 EUV, para. 16.

49 ECJ, Case C-6/90, 19.11.1991, *Francovich*, ECLI:EU:C:1991:428, para. 32 ff., 36 ff.; cf. Also Jacob/Kottman, in: Grabitz/Hilf/Nettesheim, Recht der EU, 65. suppl. 2018, Art. 340 AEUV, para. 144; Pieper, in: Dauses/Ludwigs, Handbuch des EU-Wirtschaftsrechts, 46. Suppl. 2019, B.I. para. 29 f.; Streinz, in: Streinz, EUV/AEUV, 3. ed. 2018, Art. 4 EUV, para. 34.

50 See below (sub III.4) and Kainer, Brexit, Nordirland und der Backstop: die besondere Herausforderung in: Kramme/Baldus/Schmidt-Kessel, Brexit. Privat- und wirtschaftsrechtliche Folgen (2. ed., forthcoming 2019), IV.2.c).bb).

51 ECJ, Case C-315/92, 02.02.1994, *Clinique*, ECLI:EU:C:1994:34, para 18; Case C-470/93, 06.07.1995, *Mars*, ECLI:EU:C:1995:224, para 13.

treatment of nationals. However, this is necessary if existing supply relationships and in particular 'just in time' supply chains are to be maintained as they build on the possibility to deliver at a planned time without delays due to checks and controls. The more open market access is, the more the need for convergence of standards arises.

III. Existing Mechanisms for Ensuring and Establishing Mutually Compatible Standards

So far, it has been argued that close economic cooperation between the EU and the UK after Brexit, if frictionless trade is to be possible, requires market access that is as open as possible (similar to the Internal Market), but for practical and constitutional reasons this depends on regulatory convergence as far as possible. But how can far-reaching regulatory convergence be achieved? In this respect, it makes sense to look at existing concepts: The EEA, the EU-Ukraine Association Treaty, the CETA and the EU's bilateral agreements with Switzerland.

1. Harmonisation: EEA and the EU-Ukraine Association Agreement

First, the UK could commit itself to take over EU regulations and directives into British law as long as the Internal Market is affected. This approach could be achieved if the UK would stay in the EEA. It has been discussed whether the EEA approach could be suitable for the future relationship between the EU and the UK;[52] however, this would mean that the UK would even *lose* sovereignty compared to the status quo as it would not be represented by a right to vote in the European institutions,[53] but would have to respect all four fundamental freedoms including the free movement of persons, contrary to the leave campaign and not in the interest of the London Government.

---

52 Schroeter/Nemeczek, 'The (Uncertain) Impact of Brexit on the United Kingdom's Membership in the European Economic Area' (2016) Vol. 27, Iss. 7, EBRL, p. 942 ff.

53 Hillion, 'Brexit means Br(EEA)xit: The UK withdrawal from the EU and its implications for the EEA' (2018) Vol. 55 Iss. 1, CML, p. 150 f.; Schroeter/Nemeczek, 'The (Uncertain) Impact of Brexit on the United Kingdom's Membership in the European Economic Area' (2016) Vol. 27, Iss. 7, EBRL, p. 955.

On the other hand, with regard to the regulatory approximation of the EEA Member States Iceland, Liechtenstein and Norway, which is necessary for the Internal Market, the EEA does not contain an automatic obligation to adopt the corresponding Internal Market law. The procedure under Article 102 EEA provides for an obligation to decide on the adoption of amendments to the law listed in the Annexes rather than for an obligation to adopt, whereby the EEA Joint Committee should take "every effort to find a mutually acceptable solution" (Article 102 (3) EEA). If the Joint Committee, which decides unanimously, does not reach an agreement and consequently no decision is taken to adopt the act, the affected part of EEA law is suspended (Article 102 (5)), with the practical consequences being the subject of a decision by the Joint Committee (Article 102 (6) EEA).[54]

A similar approach in this respect is taken by the EU-Ukraine Association Agreement (EUUAA) as it entails the obligation to gradually transpose most of the Internal Market law by Ukraine (i.a., Article 56 EUUAA). On a second level, the agreement links market access for Ukrainian businesses to the EU to the degree of regulatory convergence (i.a., Article 57 EUUAA). To the extent that Ukraine implements Internal Market legislation, the market is progressively opening up and mutual recognition mechanisms being "unlocked", which in particular applies to technical barriers to trade.[55]

2. Regulatory Cooperation: The CETA Approach

A possible outcome of the negotiations could be a preferential trade agreement, analogue the Comprehensive Economic Trade Agreement (CETA). CETA is an innovative trade agreement whose guarantees for free trade go far beyond the WTO-rules (which would most likely govern the UK-EU relationship in the absence of an agreement[56]), both in terms of content and

---

54 Baudenbacher, *The Handbook of EEA Law* (2015), p. 71 ff.

55 See, Kibasi/Morris, *The Shared Market. A new Proposal for a Future Partnership between the UK and the EU* (2017), 16 f.

56 Both the EU and the UK have signed the WTO Agreements (Marrakesh Protocol to the General Agreement on Tariffs and Trade 1994). The UK will therefore continue to be bound by the revised GATT and the GATS, see: Lehmann/Zetzsche, European Business Law Review 2016, 999 (1003). For a more detailed discussion of the UK's status as a WTO Member see *Bartels*, The UK's status in the WTO after Brexit, pp. 3 et seqq., https://papers.ssrn.com/sol3/papers.cfm?abstract_id=2841747.

with regard to the instruments provided by CETA.[57] In this respect, it not only goes beyond the classical approach of creating market access through prohibitions of discrimination but also enables its further development as a "living agreement" through a specific governance structure[58] including elements of a regulatory cooperation.[59] The CETA Joint Committee and specialised committees have the right to make binding decisions within defined limits and thus to further develop the agreement and its annexes. This includes the binding interpretation of the provisions of the agreement. One of the central competences is the possibility of accepting mutual recognition agreements (Article 11.3) and thus making a decision that directly allows market access.[60]

On the other hand, there is no legal power to issue binding law as a means of regulatory cooperation conferred to the Regulatory Cooperation Forum.[61] Chapter 21 of CETA contains rules on regulatory coordination, which apply to goods as well to services. The objectives of this chapter are broad (Article 21.3) and range from the protection of natural resources to improving the competitiveness and efficiency of businesses. The parties to CETA recognise the value of regulatory cooperation (Article 21.2 No. 3), but it is foreseen only on a voluntary basis (Article 21.2 No. 6) and the procedure is rather vague and does not deliver binding decisions. Each party shall consider the regulatory measures of the parties on the same or related topics. In the Regulatory Cooperation Forum, regulatory policy issues shall be discussed, regulators may be assisted, regulatory initiatives reviewed, and the development of bilateral cooperation encouraged.

---

57 Stoll, 'Mega-Regionals: Challenges, Opportunities and Research Questions' in Rensmann (ed), *Mega-Regional Trade Agreements* (2017), 3 (5); Repasi, 'Dynamisation of international trade cooperation. Powers and limits of Joint Committees in CETA' (2017) QIL 41, p. 73 f.

58 In detail Repasi, 'Dynamisation of international trade cooperation. Powers and limits of Joint Committees in CETA' (2017) QIL 41, p. 75 ff.

59 See more broadly Steger, 'Institutions for Regulatory Cooperation in 'New Generation' Economic and Trade Agreements' (2012) Vol. 39 Legal Issues of Economic Integration, p. 109 ff.

60 See Chetverikov/Zaplatina, 'Mutual Recognition of professional qualifications within the European Union Agreements with third countries' (2017) Vol. 4 Kutafin University Law Review, p. 171 ff.

61 Woolcock, What a CETA (or CETA+) free trade agreement would mean, p. 2, available at: http://eprints.lse.ac.uk/88939/1/brexit-2018-03-09-what-a-ceta-or-ceta-f ree-trade-agreement-would.pdf.

This leads to the conclusion that CETA cannot ensure an adequate amount of regulatory compatibility.[62] First, the idea of regulatory cooperation in CETA is designed for a cautious approach of two rather different parties with a rather different regulatory history and traditions and often not compatible and clearly not harmonised regulatory systems. The situation between the EU and the UK is very different as both sides by now have compatible standards. So far, the UK Government plans to take over the vast majority of EU rules into British law, meaning that Brexit will not immediately change the situation of common standards.[63] The aim of future cooperation will have to be to maintain the current high level of regulatory alignment as far as possible. Secondly, CETA's contractual framework lacks the ability to make binding decisions, so that the efficiency of the regulatory cooperation on CETA rules will be rather low. Besides, there is no link between regulatory convergence and market access rules. Therefore, CETA is not a suitable model for a trade agreement between the EU and the UK to ensure a high level of regulatory cooperation.

3. Autonomous Alignment: The Swiss Model

The trade relations between the EU and Switzerland, which are characterised by a number of bilateral treaties,[64] could serve as a further model for the United Kingdom's access to the European Internal Market. The most important of these treaties are interlinked in such a way that if one of

---

62 See also de Mestral, 'When Does the Exception Become the Rule? Conserving Regulatory Space under CETA' (2015) Journal of International Economic Law, p. 641 ff.

63 See White Paper by UK Government, March 2017, regarding 'The Repeal Bill', p. 13, available at: https://assets.publishing.service.gov.uk/government/uploads/syste m/uploads/attachment_data/file/604516/Great_repeal_bill_white_paper_accessibl e.pdf.

64 Noteworthy of these are: The Free Trade Agreement of 1972 (which liberalises trade in industrial goods and provides for the elimination of customs duties), the Bilateral Agreements I of 1999 (seven agreements in the areas of free movement of persons, land transport, air transport, recognition of conformity assessments, agriculture, procurement, research cooperation) and the Bilateral Agreements II of 2004 (cooperation, inter alia, in the areas of taxation of savings income and combating fraud as well as Switzerland's participation in Dublin and Schengen). Since 2009, a new agreement has been in force in the area of customs, in which Switzerland undertakes to adopt new EU law.

the agreements is terminated, the effect of the others shall be suspended.[65] The agreements regularly contain an obligation for Switzerland to adopt the *acquis communautaire* in force at the time of signature[66] in the relevant areas and to take account of the case law of the ECJ existing at that time.[67] However, it is practice for Swiss courts to include subsequent ECJ rulings in the decision-making process.[68] Since Switzerland follows the principle of monism in international law,[69] the agreements may be directly applicable provided they are formulated with sufficient precision.[70] This is the case, for example, with the references contained therein to EU legal acts.[71] Although a mandatory adoption of new EU legislation is generally not provided for, Switzerland has long voluntarily implemented a large part of EU law (autonomous alignment),[72] which explains the EU's open position concerning trade towards it. To this end, the agreements provide for infor-

---

65 This is the case for Bilateral Agreements I, which each contain a so-called "guillotine clause" in Article 25(4). The Bilateral Agreements II are not linked in this way but were negotiated in parallel.

66 These are so-called static contracts. See, for example, Art. 16 para. 1 Agreement between the European Community and its Member States, on the one hand, and the Swiss Confederation, on the other, on the free movement of persons, OJ L 114, 6 ("Agreement on the free movement of persons"), but different for the Schengen and Dublin agreements, the Air Transport Agreement and the Customs Agreement of 2009, where Switzerland must also adopt legal changes in the areas concerned, see Breitenmoser/Weyeneth, 'Die Abkommen zwischen der Schweiz und der EU', EuZW 2012, 854 (855).

67 See, for example, Article 16(2) of the Agreement on the Free Movement of Persons.

68 See, Federal Supreme Court, 29.11.2009, 2C 169/2009, para. 3.4: "However, the Federal Supreme Court may, without being obliged to do so, also refer to rulings of the Court of Justice handed down since then for the purpose of interpreting the Agreement on the Free Movement of Persons.".

69 Report of the Swiss Federal Council on the Relationship between International Law and National Law 05.03.2010, BBl 2010, 2263, para. 8.2; the UK, on the other hand, follows the dualistic approach, so that a future agreement with the EU would only claim domestic validity through the Transformation Act, ibid., para. 7.4 ff.

70 Breitenmoser/Weyeneth, EuZW 2012, 854 (855).

71 Breitenmoser/Weyeneth, EuZW 2012, 854 (855).

72 This is done under the title "voluntary alignment", see Baudenbacher, 'Swiss Economic Law Facing the Challenge of International and European Law. Report to the Swiss Jurists Day', ZSR 2012, 419 (611 ff.); Bundesrat, Botschaft vom 23. Juni 1999 zur Genehmigung der sektoriellen Abkommen zwischen der Schweiz und der EG, BBl 1999, 6128 (6128 ff., 6159).

mation and consultation mechanisms.[73] However, the EU is also increasingly calling on Switzerland to create an institutional framework "to guarantee homogeneity and legal certainty for citizens and businesses".[74]

In addition, Switzerland is in principle obliged to respect all four fundamental freedoms. The Agreement on the Free Movement of Persons covers the free movement of workers, freedom of establishment and freedom to provide services. It provides for a comprehensive ban on discrimination, the recognition of professional qualifications[75] and the coordination of social security systems.[76] The Free Trade Agreement[77] and the Agreement on the Recognition of Conformity Assessments[78] allow (for industrial products) the free movement of goods between the EU and Switzerland.[79] The Free Trade Agreement also contains competition rules modelled on EU law.[80]

---

73 See e.g. Art. 17 Agreement on the Free Movement of Persons; for the whole see Oesch, ‚Die bilateralen Abkommen Schweiz-EU und die Übernahme von EU-Recht‘, AJP 2017, 638.

74 Council of the European Union, Council Conclusions on EU relations with the Swiss Confederation, 28.2.2017, N5, Press release 93/17, available at: https://www.consilium.europa.eu/de/press/press-releases/2017/02/28/conclusions-eu-swiss-confe deration/. It also confirms to Switzerland that the internal market and its four freedoms are indivisible.

75 Art. 9, Annex III Agreement on the Free Movement of Persons. Annex III No. 1a refers to the Professional Qualifications Directive (Directive 2005/37/EC, 30.09.2005, OJ L 255, 22), inserted by Decision No. 2/2011 of the EU-Switzerland Joint Committee of 30.11.2011.

76 Art. 8, Annex II Agreement on the Free Movement of Persons.

77 Agreement between the European Economic Community and the Swiss Confederation 31.12.1972, OJ L 300, 189. However, the free trade agreement applies only sectorally and only to industrial goods. See Cottier/Diebold/Kolliker/Liechti-McKee/Oesch/Payosova, *The Legal Relations of Switzerland and the European Union*, (2014), para. 310 et seqq.

78 Agreement between the European Community and the Swiss Confederation on mutual recognition in relation to conformity assessment, 30.04.2002, OJ L 114, 369; see Cottier/Diebold/Kolliker/Liechti-McKee/Oesch/Payosova, *The legal relations of Switzerland and the European Union*, (2014), para. 386 et seqq.

79 On the free movement of goods with Switzerland, with particular reference to the Cassis de Dijons principle, see Zäch/Heizmann, 'Die Anwendung des Cassis de Dijon-Prinzips durch die Schweiz im Verhältnis zum EWR‘, EuZW, 2012, 876.

80 Articles 22-27 Free trade agreements. For these, however, the direct applicability was denied, see Federal Supreme Court, judgement of 03.05.1978, BGE 104 IV 175.

With regard to regulatory cooperation, the "Bilaterals" have only a weak institutional structure.[81] The so-called "mixed committees" have very limited powers to amend or supplement the agreement law.[82] The treaties between the EU and Switzerland are therefore predominantly static in nature. Since, however, there is a need for regulatory harmonisation on the Swiss side, it follows the legal developments of the EU largely autonomously.[83] It has been estimated that 30-50% of Swiss federal law is thus based on EU law.[84] This does not necessarily reflect a pure European orientation in Switzerland, but may rather reflect regulatory constraints. For example, Article 46 of Regulation (EU) No. 600/2014 requires the opening of cross-border trade in financial services to a regulatory equivalence on which Swiss financial services companies depend.[85] In this respect, the practice of autonomous alignment of EU law demonstrates the awareness that access to the Internal Market requires a certain degree of regulatory homogeneity.

4. Minimum Standards and Non-Regression: The Backstop Protocol

The Backstop Protocol, as part of the exit agreement negotiated between the UK and the EU,[86] essentially provides for Northern Ireland to remain in the Internal Market for goods. Furthermore, the UK as a whole under this solution will remain in a common customs territory with the EU with a market access for goods – even if this is (for goods entering or leaving Great Britain) a decisively weak form of economic integration compared to the Internal Market law which – (only) for goods – would continue to be

---

81 See Kibasi/Morris, 'The Shared Market. A new Proposal for a Future Partnership between the UK and the EU' (2017) Institute for Public Policy Research, p. 15.
82 Breitenmoser/Weyeneth, EuZW 2012, 854 (856).
83 See Oesch/Burghartz, in: Krenzler/Herrmann/Niestedt, EU-Außenwirtschafts- und Zollrecht, 12. ed. 2018, 132b para. 3 ff.
84 See Oesch/Burghartz, in: Krenzler/Herrmann/Niestedt, EU-Außenwirtschafts- und Zollrecht, 12. ed. 2018, 132b para. 4.
85 See Oesch/Burghartz, in: Krenzler/Herrmann/Niestedt, EU-Außenwirtschafts- und Zollrecht, 12. ed. 2018, 132b para. 5.
86 See Agreement on the Withdrawal of the UK (25. November 2018), https://www.gov.uk/government/publications/withdrawal-agreement-and-political-declaration, p. 301 ff.

applicable in Northern Ireland (cf. Article 6 (2) Protocol in conjunction with Article 2 (1) Annex 2).[87]

However, in order to prevent distortions of competition due to deviating standards, even this rather limited market access concerning free trade between the EU and Great Britain entails further regulatory requirements.[88] In this respect, Article 6 para. 1 and 3 of the Protocol in conjunction with Annex 4 provides for an obligation to observe (not apply!) numerous standards under EU law in order to achieve the objective of creating comparable framework conditions, in particular in the areas of taxation, environmental protection and employment and social protection. The standards laid down in EU law in these areas apply to the UK as "non-regression prohibitions" during the period of application of the Backstop which means that the UK must not lower its standards. The obligations under competition law go much further: European State aid law applies practically without limitation as supranational law under the continuous jurisdiction of the ECJ during the backstop (Article 12 of the protocol), and anti-trust law in principle at the level of EU law (Annex 4, Article 16 – 24). It should also be added that the UK is obliged to comply with functionally equivalent legal changes in State aid law without itself being represented or involved in legal processes.

All in all, the Backstop Protocol contains approaches for regulatory convergence. However, the Backstop solution is not suitable as a model for a future free trade agreement because it does not pursue a comprehensive approach, does not essentially address trade in services and also falls short of what is desirable in terms of its guarantees. This is evident very clearly in the present context of regulatory cooperation as the approach of a "non-regression prohibition" is not suitable for a future arrangement between the EU and the UK. On the one hand, a mere commitment to standards is not sufficiently effective and thus unsatisfactory. On the other hand, the standards are static as a reference point for the non-regression prohibition. As a result, the EU cannot change affected standards without distorting

---

87 See Kainer, Brexit, Nordirland und der Backstop: die besondere Herausforderung in: Kramme/Baldus/Schmidt-Kessel, Brexit. Privat- und wirtschaftsrechtliche Folgen (2. ed. forthcoming 2019), IV.2.b).cc); Repasi, 'A Legal Assessment of the draft Protocol on Ireland/Northern Ireland and its Implications for the Integrity of the EU Internal Market' (2018), Expert Hearing of the Constitutional Affairs Committee of the European Parliament (AFCO) on the 'The withdrawal agreement between the EU and the UK', p. 3.
88 Kainer/Persch, 'Das Prinzip der Einheit des Binnenmarktes: Keine Rosinen für Drittstaaten', EuZW 2018, 932 ff.

competition to the detriment of its own businesses.[89] Most importantly, however, there is a lack of institutional arrangements for regulatory cooperation, which consequently will not take place within the framework of the backstop, or only on an ad hoc basis.

5. Analysis

The different regulatory regimes in international trade agreements described above have not demonstrated an ideal solution for future regulatory cooperation between the EU and the UK.

First, CETA has different goals as it is designed to achieve a gradual opening of trade barriers between two economic zones. It represents a different situation and does not fit in with the much closer economic ties between the EU and the UK. Moreover, and above all, CETA does not have the necessary instruments in place to achieve regulatory cooperation with a far-reaching harmonisation of regulatory standards. The institution of a Regulatory Cooperation Forum without decision-making powers is unlikely to be successful in achieving sufficient coherence in the end. The same applies, even more so, to the Backstop protocol. Its provisions at least clearly show the connection between market access and standards. However, while the regulatory model in Northern Ireland probably provides for a too strong link to EU law, Great Britain's obligation to existing standards in certain areas is proving too inflexible. Therefore, even after an extension of the scope (e.g. to services), the Backstop would hardly be suitable as a model for a future commercial relationship.

The Swiss model, on the other hand, also does not contain any or only some institutionally sound mechanisms to guarantee regulatory coherence. In particular, there is no connection between regulatory coherence and market opening as an incentive and at the same time constitutional legitimacy from a European perspective. As a reminder, market opening similar to that of the Internal Market can only be guaranteed if comparable competitive conditions are in place. At least: The approach of an "autonomous alignment" of EU law is undoubtedly suitable to guarantee the sovereignty of the UK.

---

89 See Repasi, Stellungnahme zur Anhörung des Deutschen Bundestages, 14. January 2019, https://www.bundestag.de/resource/blob/587170/3c5e6aa7eaab220e743 5594a605f1c99/repasi-data.pdf, p. 6 f.

Finally, EEA membership would contain a mechanism which on the one hand would give the UK the sovereignty to block the adoption of EU law in the Joint Committee, but on the other hand, would have consequences for market access in the area concerned. However, an EEA membership, in addition to the aforementioned restrictions on the sovereignty of the UK and the tense relationship to the democratic principle, should not be considered for another important reason. The UK would not only have the right to block a legal act of the EU but at the same time, its veto would block market access for the businesses of the other EFTA States located in the EEA. Moreover, the sovereignty reserve expressed in the decision under Article 102 EEA is a one-way road. There is no possibility of unilaterally eliminating an act once it has been adopted. Such a binding effect could be seen as a "trap" in the UK and would, therefore, meet with considerable reservations.

IV. Voluntary Equivalence in Standards

Keeping in mind the arguments against the CETA and EEA approaches of regulatory cooperation, a future relationship between EU and UK concerning standards should follow four key objectives: First, the agreement should be comprehensive, both in scope and in the rights it guarantees. In order to facilitate the smooth movement of goods and services and, in particular, to maintain supply chains, the future arrangement should include market access similar to the Internal Market. A key chapter in this regard will be to ensure a far-reaching regulatory alignment, as standards should be as close as possible. In particular, there must be no distortion of competition due to regulatory differences. Second, out is out: There should be no automatism in obliging the UK to adopt EU regulations. Since the UK's main objective in the Brexit process is to regain sovereign and democratic control over its legislation, any agreement that degrades it to a mere rule taker would be unacceptable to the British side. Third, Brexit should not lead to impediments or delay in the legislative procedure within the EU. European legislation must not become the subject of a British veto. The EU must continue to be able to pursue an independent and efficient legal policy in the areas of competence assigned to it. Fourth, the proposed solution may not be regarded as an invitation for an à la carte Europe. In particular, it must not lead to distortions of competition, which could serve as an incentive for the other EU Member States to withdraw in order to be able to pick the cherries out of a trade regime afterwards.

Putting these elements together, the following points could serve as a solution.

1. *The Need for a Bespoke, Comprehensive, and Living Agreement*

Since the reference to an existing type of an international treaty (EEA, CETA, EU-Ukraine association, EU-Switzerland bilateral treaty or the Backstop protocol) has not proved to be helpful, the future relationship must be negotiated as a bespoke agreement that could be based, insofar regulatory cooperation is concerned, on the instruments of the EEA and the EU-Switzerland bilateral treaties. From these treaties, individual elements can be transferred to the future trade agreement. The future agreement should provide for rights similar to the fundamental freedoms, whereby market access must be strictly conditionalised in order to avoid distortions of competition. It should be left to the UK to decide on the adoption of European regulation as does Switzerland on the basis of the "Bilaterals" and do – in theory – the EFTA Members of the EEA. Here, elements of the EEA agreement can come into the play. In respect of other elements, independent design will be required. This includes, in particular, the need for an institutional framework for administering regulatory cooperation. At the same time, it should have the opportunity to propose European regulations through the joint administration and to influence the European legislative process in an advisory capacity.

2. *Regulatory Coordination Mechanism: Regulatory Coordination Office*

In a future trade agreement between the UK and the EU, there should be an institutional framework, which would fulfil three essential functions. It should first act as a forum for regulatory cooperation (a), secondly, monitor regulatory consistency between both partners (b) and finally take binding decisions as to whether the required consistency is given against the background of a competitive approach (c). These tasks lead to certain requirements in setting up the necessary administration, a Regulatory Coordination Office (RCO) (d).

a) A Forum for Regulatory Cooperation

From the end of the transition period after withdrawal, both parties would notify planned regulations to the RCO which would consider whether the new rules redress the equivalence of regulation in a specific sector. In this case, the RCO would serve as a forum to discuss possible changes or to pursue a common strategy.

b) Monitoring Regulatory Alignment

A second – challenging – task of the RCO should be to monitor the regulatory compatibility of both partners. Even if it can be established on a given date that a certain sector is sufficiently harmonised, this does not have to remain the case for the future. Since both Britain and the European Union are not surrendering their sovereignty, the future trade agreement is unlikely to be directly applicable and ultimately the ECJ is unlikely to have jurisdiction, changes in national law may lead to a divergence of regulations and, hence, to distortions of competition. It is therefore important and necessary that changes in standards are monitored and reported.

c) Decision Making

As mentioned, each party would have the possibility to adjust its sector-specific regulation or decide to differ from a given equivalence of regulation. In the event of a divergence of sectoral or general regulation that is relevant to competition, the RCO should determine this divergence with binding effect. It should then assess if and which markets and sectors are affected by the competition-distorting regulatory divergence and identify them in a second step. Finally, the RCO should determine whether the divergence threatens to distort competition in the sector concerned and, in this case, determine the consequences for market access.[90]

---

90 See below, IV.3.

d) Institutional Setting

For the coordination of regulatory measures, the EU and UK should set up a Regulatory Coordination Office. From the above-mentioned tasks of the RCO, basic principles for the personnel and material equipment can be derived. With regard to its decision-making powers, the institution would have to consist of a high-level board with equal representation. For the adoption of a decision that regulatory unity does not (no longer) exist, a mechanism should be found that does not require unanimity, otherwise, the link between regulatory convergence and market opening would not work.

At a lower level, the RCO would need to be sufficiently staffed to monitor regulatory convergence between the UK and the EU.

3. Conditionality of Market Access

In the proposal developed here, regulatory cooperation is voluntary. Neither the EU nor the UK is obliged to adopt changes in their partner's laws. Both are free to decide not to harmonise after appropriate discussions in the RCO.

Since, however, as has already been mentioned above repeatedly, regulatory differences can lead to distortions of competition, free market access must be tied to regulatory convergence. To the extent that this exists, the future agreement can guarantee access to cross-border markets analogous to the Internal Market. In particular, both sides would be obliged to mutually recognise their standards. If the contracting parties agree, it would also make sense to guarantee passporting rights so that financial services companies in London, for example, could continue to offer financial services throughout the Internal Market.

If the RCO, on the contrary, has decided that sufficient regulatory convergence no longer exists for a certain sector, market access must be limited to a right to equal treatment of nationals (National Treatment Principle). This allows companies to adapt to the law of the country of destination and thus to act across borders.

If, on the other hand, the regulatory difference affects a more fundamental aspect of the economic and social order in terms of competition, such as basic environmental standards, then consideration must be given to closing market access for the specific sectors concerned, completely. For example, the abandonment of certain filter technologies in the chemical industry could distort the production costs of the products concerned to such an extent that it would be appropriate to close market access completely in a special procedure.

4. The Need for Legal Protection

A third condition would be, in one way or another, a sufficient legal protection in order to secure the rights of individuals granted and ensure legal certainty.[91] As discussed at length above, compliance with standards to ensure comparable regulatory costs is central to maintaining an Internal Market-like trading system. A divergent interpretation or application of environmental standards, for example, could lead to considerable distortions of competition.[92] Therefore, the degree of market access rights for frictionless trading must be made dependent on judicial control instruments that ensure this comparability of market conditions.

It is one of the UK's key issues not to be subject to the ECJ's jurisdiction anymore. As the former minister of the department for exiting the EU David Davis put it, the UK will be "a third country outside the European Union [and] it would not be right for this role be performed by the European Court of Justice".[93] Convincing the UK to submit to the ECJ's jurisdiction when it comes to common standards for services will most likely be very difficult. However, a jurisdiction of the ECJ is by no means mandatory. In this book, Müller-Graff has proposed various models for guaranteeing the necessary legal protection. The decisive factor in selecting one of these models will be that it meets the above-mentioned criteria (comparability of regulatory costs).

It should only be noted here that the interpretation of Union law within the European Union must at all events remain in the final instance of the European Court of Justice.[94]

---

91 See Müller-Graff, Legal Protection and Legal Uniformity: Procedural and Institutional Rule in European-British Trade Relations after Brexit, in this book, p. 395 ff.

92 See Repasi, Stellungnahme zur Anhörung des Deutschen Bundestages, 14. January 2019, https://www.bundestag.de/resource/blob/587170/3c5e6aa7eaab220e743 5594a605f1c99/repasi-data.pdf, p. 4.

93 'David Davis claims 'decisive steps forward' in Brexit talks', BBC News, 28.09.2017, available at: http://www.bbc.com/news/uk-politics-41426620.

94 ECJ, Case 284/16, 6.3.2018, Slovak Republic/Achmea, ECLI:EU:C:2018:158.

5. Voluntary Equivalence as Case for Cherry Picking?

As far as one would follow the above considerations, there is a serious reservation against the proposal for voluntary alignment with EU standards: Giving the UK the right to opt in specific sectors might lead to a cherry-picking Europe à la carte. This could potentially have two effects. First, the UK could undertake regulatory alignment in sectors where its own industry is particularly competitive, while sectors with rather weak competitiveness could receive a protective shield by adhering to UK's national standards. Second, a Europe à la carte could serve as an incentive for other sceptical States and therefore conflict with the EU principle of an ever-closer union.[95]

However, on closer examination, these objections are not convincing. With regard to the possibility of incentives to leave the EU, the proposed system is rather unattractive. In practice, we can expect that the EU would essentially set the rules (regulatory maker), while the UK would adopt the European rules in most sectors without having voting rights in the Council or its people being represented in the European Parliament (regulatory taker).[96] Formally, sovereignty would be guaranteed, but de facto London would be largely bound to the Brussels set Internal Market rules. This applies also to the regulation of general (cross-sectoral) standards, as they are set by EU legislation in the areas of labour and social affairs, and at least in part to environmental standards. Without alignment with such general standards, there would be no single market-like market access in any sector.

Ultimately, there might be some cherry-picking which would result in possibilities to maintain regulatory differences as a protective shield. However, this effect should not be overestimated. The industry is not monolithic in its competitiveness and is highly dynamic. Shielded enterprises tend to continuously lose competitiveness with negative consequences for the overall welfare; conversely, enterprises can gain competitiveness in competition through innovations and cost reductions if this is necessary for their survival. All this suggests that the UK would prefer not to use the system of voluntary alignment specifically for protectionist purposes. Especially the financial sector, for which staying in the Internal Market is of greatest interest to the UK, would have to renounce liberalisation – although this

---

95 See, to this extent, Kainer/Persch, EuZW 2018, 932 (935).
96 It would, however, be desirable for the UK to have the right to be heard at meetings of the EU Council.

was one of the Brexit Campaign objectives – in order to factually stay in the Internal Market and benefit from its passporting rights.

V. Summary

The considerations made here can be summarised as follows.

1. The harmonisation of standards in international trade agreements has so far been the exception rather than the rule. Ambitious approaches such as CETA include initial steps towards regulatory cooperation, but do not provide for mechanisms to issue binding rules themselves. In this respect, the European Union is unique worldwide in the scope of its competences and the diversity of its standard setting.

2. The study of standards has shown two effects in a trans-national competition order. On the one hand, harmonized standards often make smooth trade possible only by enabling or facilitating the application of the principle of origin. In this sense, common standards create mutual trust. On the other hand – and of particular importance here – an approximation of standards in a broader sense, i.e. including environmental, health and safety standards, is a precondition under Union law for guaranteeing market access similar to an Internal Market. Fair competition requires a level playing field, at least in part. If the regulatory costs in one part of the market deviate too far from those in the other, free market access leads to distortions of competition which are incompatible with Union law. In this way, the call for frictionless trade, in particular, to maintain supply chains 'just in time', creates the need for regulatory alignment.

3. A look at different international trade agreements has not revealed fully-fitting models for future regulatory convergence between the EU and the UK. If the British wish to regain regulatory control is respected, only a voluntary alignment of the UK with EU standards can be considered (in exceptional cases, this can also happen vice versa). As in the case of the EEA, market access should be made conditional on the harmonisation of standards. On the one hand, this creates an incentive for the voluntary implementation of Union law, but on the other hand, it does not restrict but maintains British sovereignty.

4. An intergovernmental institution should be created for the administration of regulatory cooperation and the market access depending on regulatory alignment. This Regulatory Coordination Office could serve as an interface between regulatory coordination and free market access

under the principle of mutual recognition. In this way, both sides could further develop their regulations and also deviate from the previous regulatory framework, but at the price of restricting market access for the affected sectors from a right to barrier-free access to a right of national treatment.

Part 3 Specific Issues of Future Trade Agreements between the EU and the UK

Balancing sovereignty, trade and Northern-Irish peace: Free movement of goods post-Brexit

Armin Cuyvers[1]

1. Introduction: the enduring importance of goods

Regulating trade in goods post-Brexit is of fundamental importance, economically, legally and politically. Economically, the EU easily remains the largest trading partner for the UK. In 2017, 44% of all UK exports went to the EU, whereas 53% of all UK imports came from the EU. Goods, rather than services, made up the majority of this trade. In 2017, the UK exported £162.1 billion worth of goods to the EU, whereas UK exports in services to the EU totalled £109.6 billion. Services therefore 'only' accounted for 40% of UK-EU exports, whilst goods made up almost 60% of trade. As for imports, in 2017 the UK imported £256.6 worth of goods from the EU, whilst importing £84.4 billion in services. Consequently, goods dominated UK-EU imports with services only accounting for some 25% of UK imports from the EU. This despite the fact that services make up over 80% of the UK economy.[2] Overall, therefore, goods remain of central economic importance for EU 27-UK trade, and therefore for Brexit.

Trade in goods also creates several of the main legal challenges that complicate Brexit.[3] First, it is the regime for goods that largely determines the

---

1 Associate professor of EU law and jurisprudence, Europa Instituut of Leiden Law School. I am deeply indebted to my colleagues at the Europa Instituut for our many discussions on Brexit, but special thanks are due to Prof. S.C.G. Van den Bogaert for our many hours of Brexit brainstorming. Naturally any remaining errors remain wholly my own.
2 House of Commons Briefing Paper Number 7851, 31 July 2018, 'Statistics on UK-EU trade'. On the crucial impact of Brexit on the vital UK financial services sector see N. Moloney, 'Brexit and financial services: (Yet) another re-ordering of institutional governance for the EU financial system?', 55 *CML Rev.* (2018), 175 and K. Alexander a.o. (eds.), *Brexit and Financial Services. Law and Policy* (Hart 2018).
3 For a more general analysis of the legal challenges related to leaving the EU see inter alia A. Lazowski, 'Withdrawal from the European Union and Alternatives to Membership', 37 *EULR* (2012), 523, C. Hillion, 'Accession and Withdrawal in the Law of the European Union', in: A. Arnull & D. Chalmers (eds.), The Oxford handbook of European Law (OUP, 2015), 126, or H. Hofmeister, '"Should I Stay or

legal need for hard borders, either between Ireland and Northern Ireland or between Northern Ireland and the UK. Trade in goods, after all, involves customs duties and product standards, which in turn require border controls.[4] Second, as they concern customs duties, the future regime for goods determines the legal space for the UK to conclude future trade agreements with third countries, a key promise of Brexiteers. Third, depending on the depth and nature of the EU-UK agreement on goods, EU law may require jurisdiction for the Court of Justice of the European Union (CJEU).[5] Anything close to 'frictionless trade' in goods post-Brexit may, therefore, only be legally possible at the cost CJEU jurisdiction. Fourth, because of its singular importance for Brexit, the legal question arises if free movement of goods could be decoupled, to some extent, from the other freedoms and EU flanking rules on competition and State aid. Could some form of free movement of goods be preserved post-Brexit without the UK accepting all other parts of the internal market as well?[6] Legally, therefore, the regulation of trade in goods post-Brexit presents the EU and the UK with some very tough nuts to crack, and with some hard choices between free movement and national sovereignty.

These economic and legal stakes also underlie the political significance of goods for Brexit. Most pressingly, the regime for goods determines the need for a hard border, which has developed into the main political obstacle for an orderly Brexit. Most fundamentally, however, the future regime for trade in goods confronts the EU and the UK with existential questions about the nature of the EU, and the future of EU integration itself. Can the four freedoms and the internal market be split up, and would such a split

---

Should I Go?" – A Critical Analysis of the Right to Withdraw From the EU', *ELJ* (2010), 16. 589.

4 Free movement of services and capital do not require border controls, whereas free movement of persons between the UK and Ireland will remain covered by the Common Travel Area (CLA), also obviating the need for border checks on persons post-Brexit.

5 See more generally on the institutional challenges created by Brexit C. Tobler, 'One of many challenges after "Brexit": The Institutional Framework of an Alternative Agreement – Lessons from Switzerland and Elsewhere?', 23 *MJ* 4 (2016), 575.

6 This is legally additionally interesting as most of the foundational principles of EU free movement law were developed in the context of goods. The case law on the free movement of goods therefore provided the foundation for the EU internal market acquis as a whole. See for example CJEU Case 26/62 *Van Gend & Loos* [1963] ECR 1, CJEU Case 8/74 *Dassonville* ECLI:EU:C:1974:82 or CJEU Case C-120/78 *Cassis de Dijon* ECLI:EU:C:1979:42, as well as S.C.G. Van den Bogaert & P. Van Van Cleynenbreugel, 'Free movement of goods'. In: P.J. Kuijper et al. (eds), *The Law of the European Union* (Deventer: Wolters Kluwer).

be a first step towards a truly differentiated Union?[7] And would such structural differentiation offer much needed flexibility and more space for political self-determination to national electorates, or would it be a first step on the slippery slope towards disintegration? As shown by the perennial food-based metaphors involving cake and cherries, the EU has so far been very reluctant to consider increased flexibility. With multiple crises raging or slumbering, the institutions and most Member States do not feel this is the correct time to open a Pandora's Box of treaty change and constitutional level reforms. The political rigidity, this creates on the EU side, however, further complicates the challenge of finding a suitable future regime for goods that meets all EU and UK red lines.

Regulating trade in goods post-Brexit is therefore both important and challenging. Which options for goods are legally feasible, politically tolerable, and limit economic damage as much as possible? In light of this challenge, this contribution sets out the key legal challenges to successfully regulate trade in good post-Brexit and the regulatory models these challenges leave on the table. Considering the central importance of the Northern-Irish border issue, and the multiple affirmations by the UK and the EU that they want to prevent a hard border at all costs, this contribution takes the need to avoid a hard border as its starting point.[8] The benchmark for any regulatory regime for goods therefore is if it suffices to prevent a hard border on the Irish island, and thus pre-empts the need to apply the back-

---

7　Currently many forms of differentiation exist, but none of these are truly affecting the constitutional core of the EU legal order. Cf. on flexibility in the internal market inter alia S. Weatherill, 'The several internal markets', 36 *YEL* (2017), 125 and C. Barnard, 'Brexit and the EU internal market', in: F. Fabrini (red.), *The Law and Politics of Brexit*, Oxford: Oxford University Press 2017. For a more fundamental analysis of differenation in the EU (and its legal limits) see B. de Witte, 'An undivided Union? Differentiated integration in post-Brexit times', 55 *CML Rev.* (2018), 227 and B. De Witte, 'Near-membership, partial membership and the EU constitution', 4 *EULR* (2016), 471.

8　Cf. art. 3(1) of the draft withdrawal agreement as well as the preamble to the Northern-Ireland Protocol, clarifying that the aim is to have *no* border infrastructure: 'RECALLING the commitment of the United Kingdom to protect North-South cooperation and its guarantee of avoiding a hard border, including *any physical infrastructure or related checks and controls*, and bearing in mind that any future arrangements must be compatible with these overarching requirements'. Draft agreement on the withdrawal of the UK from the EU as agreed at negotiators' level on 14 November 2018, available at: https://www.consilium.europa.eu/media/37095/draft_withdrawal_agreement_incl_art132.pdf.

stop requirement in the current draft-withdrawal agreement.[9] This benchmark remains fully legal, as the question which regulatory regime is sufficient to avoid border checks is one of legal fact. It also has the benefit of reducing the number of regimes that need serious legal or political attention as long as the commitment to avoiding a hard border stands. Consequently, regulatory regimes that do not prevent a hard border will only be briefly touched upon here, though references will be provided to literature that discuss them in more detail.

Considering the above aims, this contribution is structured as follows. Section two first sets out the main legal components of the *current* legal framework for free movement of goods in the EU. This provides a necessary overview of what truly free movement of goods requires, and thereby allows us to establish our benchmark for alternative regimes post-Brexit that would prevent a hard border. Section three then briefly discusses the current backstop proposal in the draft withdrawal agreement which, it is argued, provides a baseline under which the future regulatory regime for goods can never go. If ratified, therefore, the backstop becomes part of the benchmark for a future regime for trade in goods. Subsequently, based on this benchmark, section four assesses the UK Chequers proposal for frictionless trade in goods. Partially in light of the serious flaws in the Chequers plan and the implicit UK commitment to an EU-UK customs union, section five then concludes that the only post-Brexit regime that remains *legally* feasible is a Norway+ model, which seems *politically* nigh impossible. This contribution subsequently concludes with some more general conclusions on the hard choices that will have to be made. Especially if the current draft withdrawal agreement is ratified, the UK will at some point in the next four years have to face the trilemma between its precious sovereignty, its equally precious union with Northern Ireland and its economic wellbeing. The EU on the other hand, will have to choose if rigidity or flexibility is the way forward, and if Brexit is seen as an opportunity to correct course or to set the existing acquis in stone.

---

9 This approach also fits with the stated intention of the EU and the UK in the joint political declaration to absolutely prevent a hard border from ever arising. See the joint Political declaration setting out the framework for the future relationship between the European Union and the United Kingdom as agreed on 22 November 2018, available at: https://www.consilium.europa.eu/media/37100/20181121-cover-political-declaration.pdf.

2. Benchmarking: the current EU legal framework for free movement of goods

What does it legally take to move a car, a prescription drug, or a piece of mutton *between* countries as freely as *within* a single country?[10] After more than 60 years of increasing economic integration, the answer is more than one might perhaps think.[11] As with water flowing through a pipe, you only have truly free movement if you remove all obstacles to free movement. What is more, removing half of all obstacles does not necessarily mean you will have 50% freer movement or even any free movement at all.[12] This is of course why, over the decades, Member States have agreed to transfer ever more far-reaching competences to the EU, and why internal market law has gradually expanded into politically sensitive fields such as health care, social security, taxation, citizenship and even monetary and economic policy. This is of course also precisely why it is so hard for the UK to reclaim sovereignty whilst still ensuring sufficient free movement of goods to prevent a hard border.[13]

This section provides a brief overview of the main categories of obstacles that need to be removed to achieve free movement of goods, as well as the legal machinery required to do so.[14] This overview provides the benchmark for the later discussion of alternative models for EU-UK trade post-

---

10 Article 26 TFEU, Case 15/81, *Gaston Schul Douane Expediteur BV v Inspecteur der Invoerrechten en Accijnzen, Roosendaal*, [1982] ECR 1409, par. 33.

11 See for a general overview inter alia C. Barnard, *The Substantive Law of the EU. The Four Freedoms* (Oxford, Oxford University Press, fifth edition, 2016). For a more sinister example of where free movement may lead you Regulation 2016/2134 concerning trade in certain goods which could be used for capital punishment, torture or other cruel, inhuman or degrading treatment or punishment OJ [2016], L 338/1.

12 As demonstrated by other aspiring but less developed internal markets such as in the East African Community or ASEAN. See for example A. Cuyvers, 'Free Movement of Goods in the EU.' In: E. Ugirashebuja, J.E. Ruhangisa, T. Ottervanger & A. Cuyvers (eds.) *East African Community Law: Institutional, Substantive and Comparative EU Aspects* (Leiden/Boston: Brill Nijhoff), 326.

13 See on the UK dilemma inter alia M. Dougan, 'An airbag for the crash test dummies? EU-UK negotiations for a post-withdrawal "status quo" transitional regime under Article 50 TEU', 55 CML Rev. (2018), 66.

14 This chapter defines goods as 'products which can be valued in money and which are capable, as such, of forming the subject of commercial transactions.' This following the CJEU in Case 7/68 *Commission v. Italy* ECLI:EU:C:1968:51. Whether an agreement would follow this definition, dynamic or static, is of course a question in itself, which would affect the entire scope of a possible agreement on goods.

Brexit. It will allow us to identify which obstacles will arise once the UK leaves the internal market, and how these obstacles might be addressed under different regulatory models for trade in goods post-Brexit.

2.1. Customs duties and charges having equivalent effect

Customs duties are all charges imposed on goods for crossing a border. For example, importers of new or used Chinese motor cars, principally designed for the transport of persons and of a cylinder capacity exceeding 1 000 cm³ but not exceeding 1 500 cm³, must pay a tariff of 10% to bring their cars into the EU.[15] Customs duties thereby increase the cost of imported products, directly hindering free movement of goods.

Considering their inherent protectionist and restrictive nature, EU law prohibits all customs duties and all charges having equivalent effect between Member States.[16] Member States are thus prohibited from imposing any customs duties on products from other Member States. For goods coming from third countries, duties are set by EU law.[17] Negotiating EU tariffs with third countries is an exclusive EU competence. Member States can therefore no longer conclude their own trade agreements concerning tariffs and duties, normally a central element of such agreements.[18]

After Brexit, the UK will become a third country. In principle, EU customs duties will then apply to trade in goods between the EU and the UK. To ensure that such duties have been paid, moreover, customs checks will in principle be required. A first question for any future agreement on trade in goods, therefore, is how it deals with customs duties and charges having equivalent effect, as well as the need to effectively enforce such duties.

---

15 Council Regulation 2658/87 on the tariff and statistical nomenclature and on the Common Customs Tariff OJ [1987] L/256, product codes 87 03 221000 and 87 03 229000.

16 Article 30 TFEU. For the broad interpretation of charges having an equivalent effect see for example Joined cases 2&3/62 *Commission v Luxembourg and Belgium (Gingerbread)* ECLI:EU:C:1962:45 or Case 24/68 *Commission v Italy* [1969] ECLI:EU:C:1969:29, par. 9.

17 For the two very limited exceptions to this prohibition see Case 132/82 *Commisison v. Belgium* ECLI:EU:C:1983:135 and Case 18/87 *Commission v. Germany* ECLI:EU:C:1988:453.

18 See for the exclusive EU competence on customs art. 3(1)(a) TFEU and for the Common Commercial Policy (CCP) art. 3(1)(e) TFEU.

2.2. *Fiscal barriers due to internal taxation*

Discriminatory internal taxation may limit free movement in similar ways as customs duties. For example, a French tax may favour French cars by imposing a higher internal tax on imported German cars.[19] For this reason, Article 110 TFEU complements Article 30 TFEU by prohibiting taxation that either discriminates between similar domestic and imported products or indirectly protects domestic products against competing imported products.[20]

To ensure full free movement, any agreement on the future relation between the EU and the UK should therefore also cover discriminatory or protectionist taxation. Failure to do so would open up possibilities of abuse whereby either the EU or the UK could protect national production via internal taxation. At the same time, circumscribing the power to taxis a far-reaching limitation on the very sovereignty so sought after by Brexiteers.

2.3. *Non-tariff barriers*

Non-tariff barriers (NTB's) are all non-financial obstacles to free movement of goods. Product norms provide a prime example. Take a fictitious Dutch rule requiring all cheese sold in the Netherlands to be made using only milk from Dutch cows. Such a rule imposes no financial barrier yet would make it almost impossible to sell imported cheese in the Netherlands.

In today's reality, where global trade agreements have removed or lowered many tariff barriers, NTB's are the main barrier to trade in goods.[21] Diverging product rules, which often serve essential purposes such as public health or consumer protection, now form the primary obstacle to moving goods between countries. To eliminate NTB's as much as is possible (and desirable), the EU relies on a combination of *positive* and *negative* integration.

---

19 CJEU Case C-112/84 *Humblot* ECLI:EU:C:1985:185.
20 See for example CJEU Case 168/78 *Commission v. France* ECLI:EU:C:2008:202, CJEU Case C-402/09, *Tatu* ECLI:EU:C:2011:219 par. 37, or CJEU Case C-167/05 *Commission v. Sweden* ECLI:EU:C:2008:202, par. 41.
21 The US-China trade war may of course change this for the worse.

Positive integration essentially entails harmonizing rules between Member States. If, for example, the safety standards for cars are the same in Sweden as in Spain, a car legally produced in Sweden will also meet product standards in Spain. Harmonization, therefore, removes NTB's by removing divergence in rules, or at least requiring Member States to accept all products on their market that meet a certain agreed minimum standard. It does so, however, at a political cost. With harmonization, Member States lose the freedom to set or enforce their own standards. Harmonization, moreover, also requires political agreement, and therefore a political process at the EU level that is able and empowered to adopt binding harmonizing measures.

Negative integration, on the other hand, removes NTB's by prohibiting them, except where a Member State is able to justify a NTB. For goods, the central provisions are Articles 34 and 35 TFEU, which in principle prohibit all quantitative import and export restrictions and measures having equivalent effect. The CJEU has given a very extensive interpretation to the concept of a 'measure having equivalent effect' (MEQR). In *Dassonville* the CJEU defined an MEQR as 'all trading rules enacted by Member States which are capable of hindering, directly or indirectly, actually or potentially, intra-Community trade.'[22] This captures almost all product norms, as any norm worth its salt will in some way make it harder to bring a good to market.[23]

In principle, all MEQR's are prohibited, unless they can be justified by the Member State under Article 36 TFEU or the so-called rule of reason.[24] To justify a restriction, Member States have to show how the restriction in question achieves a legitimate aim in a suitable and proportionate manner. Negative integration, therefore, does not automatically remove all NTB's, but it does force Member States to justify each MEQR.

After Brexit, harmonization between the EU and the UK ends. Even if the UK incorporates existing EU standards into UK law via the European Union (Withdrawal) Act, 2018, this no longer provides effective harmo-

---

22 CJEU Case 8/74 *Dassonville*, par.5.
23 See for a rather extreme CJEU Case C-470/03 *AGM-COS.MET* ECLI:EU:C:2007:213. The effect of *Dassonville* was of course somewhat curtailed by the exception of selling arrangements in CJEU Joined cases C-267/91 and C-268/91 *Keck* ECLI:EU:C:1993:905.
24 CJEU Case C-120/78 *Cassis de Dijon* ECLI:EU:C:1979:42. Negative integration, moreover, functions against the background of mutual recognition, which in principle requires Member States to accept products meeting product standards in the Member State they were produced.

nization. The EU will be under no obligation to recognize UK standards or to allow UK products that meet EU standards onto its market, just as the EU would be under no legal obligation to allow Chinese products onto its market if China would voluntarily copy EU product norms. In addition, the EU and UK would be free to start adopting diverging product norms, which would create new NTB's for trade in goods between the EU and the UK. Because after Brexit Articles 34 and 35 TFEU no longer apply, any NTB's that arise due to diverging EU and UK norms are no longer caught by negative integration and hence restrict free movement of goods.

2.4. *The legal machinery behind free movement of goods*

Having rules that protect free movement is of little use when these rules are not effectively policed and enforced. EU free movement therefore also depends on an elaborate legal machinery that ensures effective application and uniform interpretation of EU rules. Most fundamentally, this machinery rests on the principles of direct effect, supremacy and effectiveness, as well as on the jurisdiction of the CJEU to control the ultimate application and interpretation of EU law.[25]

In the context of MEQR's, for example, Article 34 TFEU has direct effect and primacy over any national conflicting rule. Consequently, any individual or company may challenge a MEQR in front of a national court, and the national court then has the authority and the obligation, based on EU law, to disapply any national law that restricts free movement, up to and including the national constitution.[26] Direct effect and supremacy thereby transform all companies and individuals into enforcers of EU law, who can identify and challenge any MEQR that may limit their free movement before their national courts.[27]

A future EU-UK agreement, however, may not have the same direct effect and supremacy as current EU law. This means that even if an agreement on the future relation prohibits, to a certain extent, MEQR's, the effectiveness of such a prohibition may be doubted. In turn, this lack of effectiveness would undermine the feasibility of mutual recognition, and hence the feasibility of abolishing borders.

---

25 CJEU Case 26/62 *Van Gend en Loos* ECLI:EU:C:1963:1, CJEU Case 6/64 Costa v. E.N.E.L. ECLI:EU:C:1964:66, CJEU Opinion 2/13 (Accession ECHR II) ECLI:EU:C:2014:2454, and CJEU Case, C-284/16 *Achmea* ECLI:EU:C:2018:158.
26 CJEU Case C-399/11 *Melloni* ECLI:EU:C:2013:107.
27 This was also the explicit aim of the CJEU in *Van Gend en Loos*.

To preserve free movement to a level that removes the need for a hard border, any future agreement should therefore not just address the different obstacles to free movement. It must also provide the legal machinery necessary to make those rules sufficiently effective. As even the short overview above demonstrates, this may prove complex. Both positive and negative integration require a level of political cooperation, transfer of competences, and supranational judicial overview that may be hard to reconcile with the UK objectives behind Brexit, especially those linked to the aim of 'taking back control'.

The already high legal threshold for ensuring free movement of goods post-Brexit is further entrenched by the backstop arrangement in the draft withdrawal agreement. The backstop obligates the UK to stay connected to the EU customs union as long as no alternative arrangement has been agreed that prevents a hard border. The next section therefore briefly examines this backstop arrangement, after which the analysis moves on to the UK's Chequers proposal and the extent to which it suffices to allow free movement of goods and thus removes the need for a hard border.

3. The backstop and the minimum content of a future arrangement for goods

Both the EU and the UK have committed themselves to *guaranteeing* that there will be no hard border between Northern Ireland and Ireland. So far, however, the EU and the UK have not been able to agree on a future relationship that would prevent a hard border. The hope is that such a model may be found during the transition period, which is envisioned to last until 31 December 2020 but may be extended to 31 December 2022.[28] If no agreement is found in this period, however, a hard border would inevitably arise after transition. It is to remove this risk of a hard border after transition that the draft withdrawal agreement contains the so-called backstop option. The backstop automatically enters into force if no sufficient agreement on the future relation is in place after transition and remains in force until a future relation has been agreed that, according to *both* the EU and

---

28 Article 126 and 132 of the draft Withdrawal Agreement. During transition all EU rules continue to apply, removing the need for a hard border. See further on transition M. Dougan, 'An airbag for the crash test dummies? EU-UK negotiations for a post-withdrawal "status quo" transitional regime under Article 50 TEU', 55 CML Rev. (2018), 66 and K. Armstrong, 'Implementing transition: Legal and political limits', (2017) University of Cambridge Faculty of Law Research Paper No. 50/2017.

the UK,[29] avoids the need for a hard border.[30] Leaving the backstop, therefore, requires joint consent.

The backstop itself essentially is a combination of four elements. First, a 'single customs territory' is created, which comprises the EU and UK customs territories.[31] Effectively this means that the *entire UK* remains part of the EU customs union and subject to EU customs rules.[32] Second, Northern Ireland remains even more closely connected to the EU internal market than the rest of the UK. To this end, Northern Ireland remains dynamically bound to significant parts of EU secondary legislation as well as to Articles 30, 34, 36 and 110 TFEU.[33] A separate regulatory regime will therefore apply to Northern Ireland, and Westminster will not be allowed to adopt acts that create MEQR's for EU-Northern-Irish trade in goods. Third, as this arrangement provides the UK a certain access to the EU internal market, so-called 'level-playing field' rules are included to avoid unfair competition from UK–based actors. These level-playing field rules include rules on environmental protection, taxation, labour and social standards, State aid, and competition law, including concentrations.[34] Fourth, to ensure the effectiveness of all these rules, the protocol incorporates significant parts of the EU legal machinery, including continued jurisdiction for EU institutions, bodies, offices, and agencies and the recognition that their acts 'shall produce in respect of and in the United Kingdom the same legal effects as those which they produce within the Union and its Member States', which is a more diplomatic term for direct effect and supremacy.[35]

Jointly, these elements create a two-tier relation between the EU and the UK for the movement of goods. The first tier comprises the whole UK and

---

29 Art. 20 Northern-Ireland Protocol.

30 Art. 1(4) and 2 Northern-Ireland protocol.

31 Art. 6 Northern-Ireland protocol and Regulation No 952/2013 (Union Customs Code) OJ [2013] L 269/1.

32 With some exceptions regarding fishery and aquaculture products, see art. 6 Northern-Ireland protocol. This in contrast to the original proposal by the EU where only Northern-Ireland would remain part of the EU customs union, creating a customs border between Northern-Ireland and the rest of the UK. See the earlier draft agreement of 19 March 2018 available at https://ec.europa.eu/commis sion/sites/beta-political/files/draft_agreement_coloured.pdf. For discussion see S.C.G. Van den Bogaert S.C.G. & A. Cuyvers, Brexit: You can't always have what you want, *Rechtsgeleerd Magazijn Themis* 2018(6), 221.

33 Art. 6(2) and 8(1) and Annex 5 Northern-Ireland protocol. See for the incorporation of EU legislation and CJEU case law adopted after the back-stop takes effect art. 15(3) and (4) Northern-Ireland protocol.

34 Art. 12 and Annex 4 Northern-Ireland protocol.

35 Art. 14(4) and (5) Northern-Ireland protocol.

entails an EU-UK customs union. Because the entire UK remains linked to the EU customs union, no customs checks will be necessary, either between Ireland and Northern Ireland or between Northern Ireland and the UK. This first tier therefore removes one of the main factors necessitating a hard border, albeit at a steep price for the UK. It is especially politically sensitive that, as long as the UK remains connected to the EU customs union, it will not be able to strike independent trade agreements with third countries on tariffs, one of the key elements of most trade deals.[36] In addition, the entire UK will remain subject to EU customs rules as interpreted by the CJEU without any say on those rules. By itself, however, even this far-reaching EU-UK customs territory is not yet *sufficient* to prevent a hard border. To completely remove the need for border checks, one also needs to remove the need to check if products meet all required product standards, including Sanitary and Phytosanitary rules, and this is where the second tier comes in.

The second tier essentially comprises the pseudo-membership of only Northern Ireland of the EU internal market for goods.[37] The alignment of Northern-Irish rules with EU standards guarantees that Northern-Irish products can enter the EU without checks. At the same time, it makes it necessary to check that other UK goods that move to the EU via Northern Ireland also meets EU standards. Although less far reaching and visible than under the original backstop, where only Northern Ireland would remain in the EU customs union, the current two-tier backstop arrangement therefore still leads to regulatory divergence between Northern Ireland and the rest of the UK. It also means that part of the UK remains directly subjected to EU rules, as interpreted by the CJEU, without any UK input in the formulation of those rules.

The backstop has not yet been accepted by the UK Parliament, and at the time of writing it is highly unsure if it may ever be. In addition, even if it is ratified, the back-stop may never enter into force if an alternative solution is found. Nevertheless, it seems legally cogent to take the current backstop as the lower limit of *any* future EU-UK agreement concerning trade in goods. Unless the UK is willing to accept a hard border or risk the union

---

36 Although the UK will therefore be legally allowed to conclude trade agreements with third countries, these trade agreements may simply not deviate from EU tariffs, greatly undermining their practical use. See further R. Wessel, 'Consequences of Brexit for international agreements concluded by the EU and its Member States', 55 *CML Rev.* (2018), 101.

37 Note that this back-stop solution, which has been sanctioned by the EU, further confirms that the internal market is not indivisible.

with Northern Ireland, after all, it will need to accept a trade regime that is at least as far-reaching as the back-stop arrangement. The chance that some kind of alternative, less far-reaching arrangement can be found, for example via novel 'technology', seems rather negligible. After two and a half years of intense negotiation and research there is not yet the beginning of such an alternative solution, whereas the 'technology' needed remains in the realm of science fiction for now. This means that as long as the EU and UK remain committed to Northern Ireland, any deal will have to be at least as far-reaching as the back-stop. If the EU and UK fail to agree on any such far-reaching deal, the only alternative seems to be a hard Brexit, and therefore a very limited WTO regime for goods,[38] or the UK remaining in the EU.[39] After all, any agreement that is less far-reaching than the current back-stop will create a hard border and will hence be unacceptable and legally impermissible under the draft withdrawal agreement.

Legally, therefore, any future agreement cannot drop below the level of the current back-stop arrangement as long as the EU commitment to avoiding a hard border and the UK commitment to preserving unity with Northern Ireland stand. Consequently, the current back-stop arrangement should be considered an integral part of the more general legal benchmark against which any future agreement on the regulation of trade in goods between the EU and the UK should be tested, including the UK's own Chequers proposal.

---

38 Of course, even the WTO regime offers nowhere near the same level of facilitation as the EU internal market and after a hard Brexit falling back on WTO norms will be far from simple or automatic. See for an overview of all obstacles awaiting the EU and UK in this context F. Baetens, '"No deal is better than a bad deal?" The fallacy of the WTO fall-back option as a post-Brexit safety net', 55 *CML Rev.* (2018), 133.

39 The CJEU has recently confirmed that the UK is legally allowed to *unilaterally* withdraw its Brexit notification up to the very last moments of its EU membership, thereby remaining a full member of the EU. See CJEU Case C-621/18 *Wightman* ECLI:EU:C:2018:999. For further discussion on the right to withdraw a notification see inter alia D. Benrath, 'Bona fide and revocation of withdrawal: how Article 50 TEU handles the potential abuse of a unilateral revocation of withdrawal', 43 *EULR* (2018), 234, I. Papageorgiou, 'The (ir-)revocability of the withdrawal notification under Article 50 TEU', Policy Department for Citizens' Rights and Constitutional Affairs European Parliament (2018), PE 596.820, A. Sari, 'Reversing a Withdrawal Notification under Article 50 TEU: Can a Member State Change Its Mind?', 42 *EULR* (2017), 451 or P. Ostendorf, 'The withdrawal cannot be withdrawn: the irrevocability of a withdrawal notification under art. 50(2) TEU', 42 *EULR* (2017), 767.

4. *Checking Chequers: please mind the gap!*

The most recent and developed UK proposal on the future EU-UK relationship is laid down in the UK white paper on 17 July 2018.[40] The white paper, however, was heavily criticized by leading Brexiteers who felt it kept the UK tied too closely to the EU. In the end, May was able to force the white paper through her own cabinet and through Parliament, but only at significant political costs, including the resignation of leading Brexiteers Boris Johnson and David Davis. Considering the intense political resistance to the white paper, as well as the even more overwhelming resistance to the draft withdrawal agreement, it must be assumed that under current political conditions the white paper represents the upper limit of what the UK is able and willing to accept in terms of the future relation.[41] Even though the white paper was immediately and categorically rejected by the EU, it therefore remains important to assess to what extent the white paper suffices to prevent a hard border, and if not, where it falls short and what would be required for it to pass muster.[42]

To this end, the current section checks the white paper against the benchmark developed above. To what extent does the white paper remove customs duties, fiscal barriers and non-tariff barriers, and more generally, suffice to prevent a hard border?

4.1. *Customs duties and charges having equivalent effect under the white paper*

The white paper proposes a *'facilitated customs arrangement'*. This 'arrangement' entails close cooperation and coordination instead of an actual customs union between the EU and the UK. The central idea is that the UK

---

40 HM Government 17 July 2018, 'The future relationship between the United Kingdom and the European Union', available via www.gov.uk/government/publication s/the-future-relationship-between-the-united-kingdom-and-the-european-union. This *White Paper* is the more developed version of the now notorious Chequers-agreement of 6 July 2018.

41 Cf. in this regard the Brady amendment adopted by a majority of 16 by the UK Parliament on 29 January ordering May to return to Brussels to renegotiate the back-stop and replace it with 'alternative arrangements' as its current form was deemed unacceptable.

42 See amongst the different public rejections especially the interview with Barnier on 2 September 2018 in the *Frankfurter Allgemeine* available via: www.faz.net/-gq5-9dxnd?premium and Barniers Op-ed of 2 August 2018, available via: https://ec.eur opa.eu/commission/news/ambitious-partnership-uk-after-brexit-2018-aug-02_en.

would collect all EU duties on goods that enter the UK but eventually move onward to the EU. Where products ultimately remain in the UK, importers would be reimbursed for any higher EU duties they might have paid, assuming UK customs tariffs will be lower. As the UK would collect all EU duties and transfer them to the EU, the UK argues that no customs checks between Ireland and Northern Ireland would be necessary, and therefore a hard border could be avoided.[43] In addition, as the UK would not be a member of the EU customs union, the UK would still be able to conclude independent trade agreements with third countries, inter alia on separate UK tariffs that deviate from EU tariffs.

Central to the proposal is the assumption that the UK will be able to track all goods that enter the UK, including goods that are ultimately used to manufacture other products. As indicated above, however, this assumption rests on as of yet non-existent or at least wholly unspecified 'technology' that would be able to track the massive flow of goods in the UK, even as products flow in and out of the country propelled by global value chains. For such a system to work, moreover, it would be insufficient to merely track trucks or containers as such. After all, most trucks or containers contain different products for different recipients. For the UK system to work, it is necessary to develop tamper-proof technology that can continually trace *each individual product*. What is more, this technology must also be able to keep tracing products as they are used to fabricate other goods, such as for example imported computer chips and batteries that are used to construct a car, and must even enable a determination to be made when products cease to qualify as individual products but instead become part of a new fabricated product. When have the Chinese chip and the American battery becomes a UK-made car?

In addition to such a quantum leap in technology, the UK proposal also assumes a very high level of trust between the EU and the UK. The EU will have to trust that the UK will correctly and faithfully collect and transfer all duties owed.[44] What is more, even if sufficient technology and trust can be found, the system would require tremendous administrative capacity as

---

43 This proposal builds on the earlier UK proposals, also rejected by the EU, concerning 'maximum facilitation'. See the 'future partnership paper' on the 'Future customs arrangements' of 15 August 2017 available at: www.gov.uk/government/publications/future-customs-arrangements-a-future-partnership-paper.

44 The fact that on 8 March 2018 the Commission claimed more than € 2 billion from the UK for consistently misapplying EU customs rules to Chinese imports does little to increase this trust.

well as other far-reaching harmonization between the EU and UK customs regimes, so as to enable the EU and UK systems to effectively connect.[45]

The white paper does not even come close to addressing these concerns, nor does it provide any alternative solution to avoid the need for customs checks as long as the required trust, technology and harmonization are not in place. Already for these reasons the white paper is not sufficient to obviate the need for customs checks at the border. Even if agreed to by all parties, therefore, the *facilitated custom arrangement* would not be sufficient to prevent the backstop from being triggered, and does not meet the benchmark set for a feasible regulatory regime for goods.

4.2. Fiscal barriers due to internal taxation and the white paper

An additional legal gap in the white paper is its complete failure to address fiscal barriers, even though these form an important obstacle to truly free movement of goods.[46] The white paper, therefore, does not provide a solution to the problem of discriminatory or protectionist taxation, as currently prohibited under Article 110 TFEU.[47] This means that both the EU and the UK could resort to discriminatory taxation post Brexit. In itself this may not immediately lead to a hard border. Internal taxes will, after all, be levied internally. Yet the possibility of discriminatory taxation, which can have an equivalent effect to customs duties, further undermines the UK proposals to do away with the need for customs checks as well as the proposal to create a common rule book for goods to prevent MEQR's. It is difficult to imagine, therefore, how one could have 'frictionless' trade in goods and completely abolish border checks without an effective regime to deal with discriminatory or protectionist taxation. Such a system would, after all, allow the EU or the UK to discriminate against imported products whilst enjoying unfettered access themselves, a competitive advantage no party is logically willing to cede to the other. Creating an effective system to combat fiscal barriers, however, would of course involve some limits on

---

45 For example, the UK would remain bound to the categories of the EU customs code but also would have to effectively adopt EU norms on when a product has been sufficiently transformed to qualify as a UK product. Cf. Ch 1, par. 17 of the White Paper.
46 Ch 1, par. 18 of the white paper only briefly touches on VAT and excises, but not on other forms of discriminatory or protectionist taxation.
47 This contrary to the back-stop, which does make Art. 110 TFEU applicable to Northern Ireland.

UK tax sovereignty, which would make Chequers even harder to swallow for Brexiteers than it already is.

4.3. Non-tariff barriers and the white paper

To prevent the need for border checks due to diverging product and safety standards the white paper suggests a 'free trade area for goods'. The free trade area is more limited than the full EU internal market and is based on a 'common rulebook'. The common rulebook essentially means that the UK will copy-paste current and future EU product rules, but several important limitations apply. To begin with, the UK will only take over those rules that are necessary to avoid the need for border checks, and hence borders.[48] Even for these norms, moreover, the sovereign UK Parliament would retain the right to deviate, even though the white paper acknowledges that any such deviation would have 'consequences'.[49] What is more, for agriculture, food and fisheries products the UK proposes even less far-reaching harmonization. For these products, the UK only wants to take over EU rules concerning the protection of human, animal and plant health including especially Sanitary and Phytosanitary (SPS) rules. 'Wider food policy rules' as well as rules relating to domestic production, would not be copied into UK law, meaning on these points UK and EU law could start to diverge.[50]

The white paper proposals do, therefore, not remove all MEQR's. To begin with, the UK proposals do not contain effective negative integration. Since there will be no equivalent to Articles 34 and 35 TFEU, individuals and companies will not be able to effectively remove national barriers that limit their access to market. In itself this may not directly necessitate border checks, but it again undermines the mutual trust required for borderless trade. In addition, the UK's proposal only envisions limited harmonization with continuing authority of the UK Parliament to deviate from EU standards. This approach denies the legal reality that for truly frictionless and borderless trade you need to remove more than just the rules narrowly related to border crossing. In a similar vein, the UK proposals also

---

48 *White Paper* Ch. 1, par. 11 and par. 24 a.o, p. 15.
49 The UK seems unwilling to admit here that one of the inevitable consequences would have to be the reinstatement of border checks to stop those goods that may no longer meet EU standards. Any use of Parliaments sovereign right to deviate from EU norms would, therefore, again comes at the cost of hard borders.
50 White Paper, ch. 1, par. 32 a.o.

do not incorporate the underlying principles of EU law such as the principles of mutual recognition and loyal cooperation that also underlie borderless trade in the EU. This unwillingness to adopt the broader and deeper legal framework required is also reflected in the refusal of the UK to accept the underlying legal machinery needed for truly free and borderless trade.

4.4. *The legal machinery behind free movement of goods and the white paper*

Substantive rules alone are not enough to remove borders. As discussed above, a rather elaborate legal machinery is necessary as well to ensure that all substantive rules are uniformly interpreted and effectively applied.[51] For truly borderless trade, all relevant actors must be able to trust that all products indeed meet required standards, and that neither the EU nor the UK can provide 'their' producers a competitive advantage by applying regulations more leniently. It is for this reason that borderless trade within the EU also depends on the supervisory authority of the Commission and the CJEU, as well as on the general principles of direct effect, supremacy, and the obligation of national courts to loyally apply EU law and refer to the CJEU where necessary.

The white paper falls far short of creating the necessary legal machinery for borderless movement. To begin with, the rules of the proposed UK-EU agreement would not have direct effect or supremacy.[52] Individuals and companies could not, therefore, rely directly on the agreement in front of national courts or administrative bodies. This also means they could not rely on the agreement to set aside national legislation that obstructs free movement in a way that conflicts with the agreement. Rights under the agreement would, therefore, be just as ineffective for individuals as rights under ordinary public international law.

What is more, even when it comes to the interpretation of national legislation that transposes the agreement into national law, the proposed system does not sufficiently guarantee uniform interpretation or effective enforcement either. The white paper proposes, for example, that EU and UK courts, when they interpret provisions of national legislation intended to give effect to the EU-UK agreement, 'could take into account the relevant

---

51 See also R.C. Tobler, 'One of Many Challenges After ,Brexit': The Institutional Framework of an Alternative Agreement – Lessons from Switzerland and Elsewhere?, 2018 *Maastricht Journal of European and Comparative Law* 23 (4): 575.

52 Cf White Paper ch. 4, par. 53.

case law of the courts of the other party.[53] This provides no guarantee of uniform interpretation. Only for rules contained in a common rulebook would UK courts be obligated under UK law, in some unspecified way, to 'pay due regard to CJEU case law', although the UK expressly rejects any right or obligation of ordinary UK courts to ask preliminary references to the CJEU in such cases.[54] Only in case of a dispute between the EU and the UK itself, and then only where this dispute concerns the interpretation of rules contained in a common rulebook, would the CJEU retain some possibility to determine the final interpretation of EU law. To this end, the white paper proposes that EU-UK disputes on the interpretation of common rulebooks should in principle be settled by the Joint Committee. The Joint Committee could then refer questions of interpretation to the CJEU, but only by mutual consent of the EU and the UK. This means that the UK could block a referral. If the Joint Committee cannot agree on the correct interpretation, the dispute would be referred to arbitration. The arbitral panel would then have a right, but no obligation, to refer a question on interpretation to the CJEU.[55]

Even for disputes between the EU and the UK on the interpretation of rules in the common rulebooks, therefore, the proposed system does not guarantee sufficient jurisdiction for the CJEU, whereas the CJEU receives no jurisdiction over the other parts of the EU-UK agreement, even though these may require, directly or indirectly, the application or interpretation of EU law. Consequently, also on the level of legal machinery and dispute resolution, the white paper seems insufficient to enable frictionless or borderless trade. To boot, the proposals in the white paper even seem to conflict with the autonomy of EU law, especially under the rather militant interpretation of this principle by the CJEU in *Opinion 2/13* and *Achmea*. Contrary to what is demanded in these judgments, after all, the CJEU does not retain the final say over the interpretation and application of EU law.[56] In addition to being insufficient to prevent a hard border, such a conflict

---

53 White Paper, ch. 4. par. 33, whereby the UK expressly adds that this would respect the 'independence' of the respective courts. The White Paper further suggests in par. 34 that the Joint Committee would be empowered 'act to preserve the consistent interpretation of the agreements' if 'significant divergences' occur, but it is difficult to see how the Joint Committee could address the case law of independent courts.

54 White Paper, ch. 4, par. 35.

55 White Paper ch. 4, par. 42, both the Joint Committee and the arbitral panel would be bound by the decision of the CJEU.

56 Also, other dispute settlement bodies may be called upon to rule on the division of competences within the EU. Since the EU-UK agreement will almost certainly

with autonomy would make it illegal for the EU to sign and ratify a deal based on the white paper.[57]

Even the short overview above makes it clear that the proposals in the white paper do not guarantee frictionless trade and are insufficient to remove the need for border checks. The white paper, therefore, does not meet the minimum benchmark for legally feasible regimes for trade in goods post-Brexit. This automatically also means that the white paper falls far short of ensuring the kind of borderless trade required to prevent the backstop from entering into force. Even if the white paper was fully accepted by the EU, therefore, the backstop would still enter into force and the UK would remain in the EU customs union until it concludes a more far-reaching trade agreement with the EU that would be sufficient to allow borderless trade. In other words, if the UK Parliament ratifies the current draft withdrawal agreement, and with it the back-stop, May's entire Chequers plan is toast. More generally, as long as the EU and/or the UK remain committed to preventing a hard border on the Irish island, Chequers is simply obsolete except as a source of inspiration for more far- reaching agreements.

---

be a mixed agreement, settling disputes under it may after all require rulings on the division of competences and responsibilities between the EU and its Member States. See especially CJEU Opinion 2/13 (Accession ECHR II) ECLI:EU:C:2014:2454, and CJEU Case, C-284/16 *Achmea* ECLI:EU:C:2018:158. For discussion see R. Wessel, 'Consequences of Brexit for international agreements concluded by the EU and its Member States', 55 *CML Rev.* (2018), 120-121, G. Van der Loo & R.A. Wessel, 'The non-ratification of mixed agreements: Legal consequences and solutions', 54 *CML Rev.* (2017), 735 and C. Hillion & R. Wessel, 'The European Union and International Dispute Settlement: Mapping Principles and Conditions', in: M. Cremona, A. Thies, & R.A. Wessel (eds.), *The European Union and International Dispute Settlement* (Oxford, Hart Publishing 2017), 7.

57　See also CJEU Opinion 1/91 (EEA I) ECLI:EU:C:1991:490, CJEU Opinion 1/92 (EEA II) ECLI:EU:C:1992:189, CJEU Opinion 1/09 (Patent court) ECLI:EU:C:2011:123, and CJEU Opinion 1/00 (European Common Aviation Area), ECLI:EU:C:2002:231. For a further analysis on autonomy see P. Koutrakos, 'What is the Principle of Autonomy Really About?', 43 *EULR* (2018), 1 and C. Hillion & R. Wessel, 'The European Union and International Dispute Settlement: Mapping Principles and Conditions', in: M. Cremona, A. Thies, & R.A. Wessel (eds.), *The European Union and International Dispute Settlement*, (Hart, 2017), 7. On autonomy and the withdrawal agreement see also A. Cuyvers, 'Solving the autonomy conundrum: Can the UK avoid a hard border in Northern Ireland without subjecting itself to EU judges?' *Edinburg University European Futures Blog* available at: https://edin.ac/2Q1EwS7 and S.C.G. Van den Bogaert S.C.G. & A. Cuyvers, Brexit: You can't always have what you want, *Rechtsgeleerd Magazijn Themis* 2018 (6), 221 a.o.

5. Between a political rock and a legal backstop: what regulatory model for goods post-Brexit?

Combining the legal benchmark developed in Section 2 with the analysis of the backstop and the white paper in Sections 3 and 4, it becomes clear that few regulatory models for trade in goods post-Brexit remain legally fit for purpose. This section first sets out several popular models which fall short of preventing a hard border and therefore do not form realistic legal options, even though they have long been considered leading candidates on both sides of the channel. Subsequently, this section explores what legal options, if any, remain, including the option of a Norway+ model or a hard border in the Irish sea.

5.1. Falling short: regulatory models for goods that do not prevent a hard border

A first regulatory model that fails to prevent a hard border, and thus falls short of our legal benchmark, is the so called WTO option. Especially popular with more radical Brexiteers, falling back on WTO rules means that the UK would not conclude a new trade agreement with the EU. Instead, EU-UK trade would take place under WTO rules. This option is so minimal that it can hardly be called a model at all. It certainly does not remove the need for borders, as the very real borders between the EU and other WTO members aptly illustrate. For example, the WTO regime does not even remove all tariff barriers, and therefore certainly does not remove the need for customs checks. In addition, WTO rules do relatively little to remove NTB's, and therefore do not remove the need for border checks to ensure that goods meet product standards.[58] These problems, in addition to a plethora of other limitations of WTO law, make the WTO option essentially a non-starter for all except supporters of a de facto hard Brexit.

More problematic is that a second option, that of a CETA style Free Trade Agreements (FTA), also falls short. Under this model the EU and UK would conclude a deep and comprehensive trade agreement modelled on the CETA FTA between the EU and Canada. Although often presented as the most feasible option in the past, including by Barnier, a CETA-like agreement would, however, not remove the need for a border either. To begin with CETA removes many but not all tariffs, which means that cus-

---

58 See F. Baetens, "'No deal is better than a bad deal?' The fallacy of the WTO fallback option as a post-Brexit safety net", 55 *CML Rev.* (2018), 133.

toms checks would remain necessary. In addition, a CETA-like agreement would not harmonize product rules sufficiently to make border checks obsolete either.[59] CETA, furthermore, also does not offer the legal machinery required for borderless trade. It for example lacks direct effect and supremacy and relies on a system of institutionalized arbitration that falls short of CJEU supervision. Again, the remaining borders between the EU and Canada offer graphic proof of the fact that CETA simply is not enough to remove borders. What is more, even a CETA+(+) agreement would not suffice in this regard, as it would still not go far enough to allow for borderless trade, including on the issue of legal machinery required for effective and uniform application. Even modern and deep FTA's like CETA or the Singapore FTA, after all, are still primarily focused on removing tariff barriers, and do not go far enough to eradicate NTB's and allow borderless trade.

A third model that falls short of allowing borderless trade is a customs arrangement between the EU and the UK modelled on the EU-Turkey relationship. Membership of the UK in the EU customs union would of course remove the need for customs checks, as also evidenced by the backstop arrangement itself. Even full UK membership of the EU customs union, however, would not remove the need for border checks on product standards. It is of course for this reason that the backstop also includes regulatory alignment between Northern Ireland and the EU.

Even a fourth model, full UK membership of the European Economic Area (EEA), would legally speaking not be sufficient to allow borderless trade and escape the back-stop. Under this so-called 'Norway' option the UK would join the EEA alongside Norway, Iceland and Liechtenstein. As an EEA member the UK would *de facto* be bound by most EU rules concerning free movement and the internal market, including most product rules. Aside from problems concerning fisheries and agriculture, however, the EEA does not include a full customs union.[60] Even between the EU and EEA members, therefore, customs checks are still required. Although these checks may be minimized using different facilitation techniques, EEA membership alone therefore still requires a hard border. Consequently, even the EEA model, as far reaching as it is, does not meet the condition

---

59 A. Cuyvers, 'The legal catch-22 of a CETA-Brexit: either too little or too much to avoid a pretty hard Brexit', *Regulating for Globalization*, 14 December 2017, http://r egulatingforglobalization.com/2017/12/14/legal-catch-22-ceta-brexit-either-little-m uch-avoid-pretty-hard-brexit/.

60 See generally C. Baudenbacher, *The Handbook of EEA Law* (Springer, 2016), especially parts VII and VIII.

of borderless trade required to prevent a hard border in Northern Ireland or escape the back-stop.[61]

5.2. Regulatory models that do prevent a hard border (at a cost)

As the analysis above shows, preventing a hard border requires a very far-reaching regulatory model for goods, which is of course why it has been so difficult for the UK to propose a viable alternative to the backstop so far. For truly removing the need for a border, any regime for trade in goods post-Brexit must seemingly *combine* a customs union, or an equivalent regime, with an EEA-level commitment to EU internal market rules.

In light of this fact, only two legally viable options seem to remain. The first option is a regulatory model that combines an EU-UK customs union with EEA membership of the UK, or at least an EU-UK relation that is equivalent to that between the EU and an EEA member. This option can be labeled the Norway+ model, as it would surpass the already far-reaching EU commitments of existing EEA members such as Norway.[62] The EEA membership, or equivalent, would de facto keep the UK in the internal market, which could remove the need for product checks at the border. The addition of a customs union, moreover, would remove the need for customs checks, as the UK would already apply EU tariffs at its external borders. Taken together with EEA rules such as those on effective enforcement, loyal cooperation, fair competition and the prohibition of discriminatory taxation, a Norway+ model could remove all need for border checks and therefore prevent a hard border.

Of course, combining membership of the EU customs union with an almost total commitment to the EU internal market comes perilously close to *de facto* EU membership. Yet by combining these elements a Norway+ model could guarantee borderless trade in goods and remove the need to apply the back-stop. By closely mimicking EU membership, a Norway+ model would also significantly limit the negative impact of Brexit on trade and the EU and UK economy. A Norway+model might furthermore avoid

---

61 See further on the EEA option, or the lack thereof, C. Hillion, 'Brexit means Br(EEA)xit: The UK withdrawal from the EU and its implications for the EEA', 55 CML Rev. (2018), 135.

62 It might be possible, however, to reduce UK alignment with the EU internal market compared to the EEA, meaning that the EU-UK relation might go further than the EEA system in terms of customs, but less far than the EEA in terms of the obligation to incorporate EU rules and standards into national law.

the need for the UK to accept direct jurisdiction of the CJEU or full supremacy of EU law. EEA law, after all, is guarded by the EFTA Court, which is formally independent of the CJEU and has not created an equivalent doctrine of supremacy, even though it is *de facto* bound to interpretations of EU law by the CJEU.[63] By joining the EEA, or negotiating an equivalent status and 'docking' at the EFTA Court, the UK might therefore 'only' have to accept the jurisdiction of the EFTA Court, at least formally escaping the jurisdiction of the CJEU.

A Norway+ model, therefore, satisfies the legal benchmark for avoiding a hard border and circumvents some sensitive issues such as CJEU jurisdiction and formal supremacy of EU law. At the same time, a Norway+ model is almost the exact opposite of what Brexiteers want and what UK voters was promised.[64] Instead of taking back control, ending payments to the EU and launching a 'Global Britain' via new trade agreements, the UK will remain bound to EU rules and foreign judges, will pay probably around 80% of current contributions, more if it loses the rebate, and will not be able to conclude meaningful own trade agreements.[65] A Norway+ model, therefore, binds the UK much closer to the EU than for example, Chequers or the backstop, options which already go too far for Brexiteers. To make matters worse, under a Norway+ model the UK will lose all say over the EU rules it will be bound to. As an EEA member the UK will lose all representation in the European Council, the Council, the Commission and the European Parliament, as well as almost all formal say in the plethora of EU agencies and bodies that create so much of the crucial regulation and soft law that affects trade. Under a Norway+ model, therefore, the UK would become a mere rule taker, which would be a far cry from 'taking back con-

---

63 Formally the EEA does not accept primacy, even though it can be wondered if this would still be an option if elements of a customs arrangement were added. The same applies to the jurisdiction of the CJEU. On the EFTA Court see H.H. Fredriksen, 'The EEA and the Case Law of the CJEU: Incorporationwithout participation', in E. Eriksen and J.E. Fossum (eds.), *The European Union's Non-Members: Independence under Hegemony?* (Routledge, 2015), Ch 6.

64 See on this tension also. P. Craig, '*Brexit*: a drama in six acts', 4 *EULR* (2016), 447.

65 See for the different contributions of the UK under different models S. Dhingra en T. Sampson, 'Life after Brexit: What are the UK's options outside the European Union?' Centre for Economic Performance, *London School of Economics Working Paper Brexit* nr. 1, 4. On the effect of Brexit on existing agreements see G. Van der Loo & R.A. Wessel, 'The non-ratification of mixed agreements: Legal consequences and solutions', 54 *CML Rev.* (2017), 735.

trol' indeed.[66] In light of these costs, one may wonder what the benefit of a Norway+ model is compared to simply retaining full EU membership as the UK could do under *Wightman*.

Getting a Norway+ model through the UK Parliament, therefore, seems an uphill battle, to put it euphemistically.[67] In addition, it is far from evident that all current EU and EEA members would be willing to accept a Norway+ model for the UK, whilst each of them wields a veto.[68] The almost comical contradiction between a Norway+ model and the original objectives of Brexit, however, may lead the UK to at least consider a second model that would avoid a hard border without trapping the entire UK in the internal market, namely only leaving Northern Ireland in the internal market and creating a hard border between the UK and Northern Ireland in the Irish sea.

The starting point for this Irish sea model is that the legal benchmark only requires avoiding a hard border *on the Irish Island*. It does not exclude the creation of a hard border somewhere else. Consequently, it would be possible to keep *only* Northern Ireland in the EU internal market and the EU customs union, whilst the rest of the UK leaves the internal market and the customs union. Such a model, which builds on the original backstop arrangement in the earlier draft withdrawal agreement, removes the need for a hard border on the Irish island as no customs or product checks would be necessary on goods that move from Northern Ireland to Ireland.[69] After all, Northern Ireland would effectively remain part of the internal market. At the same time, the rest of the UK (i.e. Great Britain) would be freed from the need to conclude a trade agreement with the EU that is far-reaching enough to avoid borders. This would open up a wide array of models for the EU-Great Britain relationship, including CETA-based models, that allows for more UK regulatory independence and would allow the UK to conclude its own trade agreements with third countries, albeit at a price in terms of access to the EU internal market.

---

66   Cf. in this regard the frank description of EEA membership as 'independence under hegemony' in E. Eriksen and J.E. Fossum (eds.), *The European Union's Non-Members: Independence under Hegemony?* (Routledge, 2015).

67   On 15 January 2019 the draft withdrawal agreement was rejected by a majority of 230 votes, the heaviest parliamentary defeat of any British Prime Minister in recent history.

68   C. Hillion, 'Brexit means Br(EEA)xit: The UK withdrawal from the EU and its implications for the EEA', 55 CML Rev. (2018), 135.

69   Draft agreement of 19 March 2018 available at https://ec.europa.eu/commission/si tes/beta-political/files/draft_agreement_coloured.pdf.

The glaring cost of this model is of course the creation of a hard border between Northern Ireland and the rest of the UK in the Irish sea. The border between Northern Ireland and the rest of the UK would effectively become an external border of the EU, meaning the UK would have to accept a hard border within its own sovereign territory, as well as the fact that part of its own territory would be governed by EU rules over which it has no say. This is of course a hefty price that amongst other problems sits uneasily with the Brexit objective of taking back control and recapturing UK sovereignty, let alone the fact that May's majority rests on the ten seats of the DUP, which abhors any separate regime for Northern Ireland. Legally speaking, however, such a separate regime for Northern Ireland seems the only viable alternative to committing the entire UK to at least a Norway+ relation with the EU, at least as long as the determination to prevent a hard border on the Irish island holds. From this perspective, Northern Ireland becomes the price for 'liberating' the rest of the UK from the EU internal market.

5.3. Time for hard choices: the UK trilemma

The commitment to prevent a hard border at all costs, therefore, forces both the EU and the UK to make some very tough choices, and the time to make them is running out. The UK will have to face the trilemma between its precious sovereignty, its equally precious union with a stable Northern Ireland and its economic well being. The first option for the UK, and the default option under Article 50 TEU if no agreement is reached on the withdrawal agreement, is a hard Brexit. This option will protect UK sovereignty, at least under a superficial definition, and will avoid regulatory divergence with Northern Ireland.[70] It will do so, however, at a tremendous cost to the UK economy and the Irish peace process. A hard Brexit, after all, simply means a hard border on the Irish island.[71] The sec-

---

70 For a more detailed discussion of an evolved conception of sovereignty that can accommodate regional integration see A. Cuyvers, *The EU as a Confederal Union of Sovereign Member Peoples – Exploring the potential of American (con)federalism and popular sovereignty for a constitutional theory of the EU* (Diss. Leiden, 2013), part. II.

71 For a devastating analysis of the costs of a hard Brexit see Bank of England, *EU withdrawal scenarios and monetary and financial stability*, report of 28 November 2018, available at https://www.bankofengland.co.uk/-/media/boe/files/report/2018/eu-withdrawal-scenarios-and-monetary-and-financial-stability.pdf?la=en&hash=B5F6EDCDF90DCC10286FC0BC599D94CAB8735DFB.

ond option is to ratify the withdrawal agreement and thereby commit itself to the backstop minimum or even a Norway+ model. This second option will safeguard its economy and Northern Ireland, but does so at the cost of UK sovereignty. The same goes for the third option of remaining in the EU, albeit that this option has the added benefit of safeguarding UK influence over EU decision-making, and in some ways, therefore, protects UK sovereignty more than the Norway+ model.[72]

The fourth and last option is to sacrifice, or at least significantly weaken, the union with Northern Ireland. Building on the backstop arrangement in the earlier draft withdrawal agreement, the UK could accept that Northern Ireland *de facto* remains in the EU customs union and internal markets.[73] This would lead to a relatively hard border between Northern Ireland and the rest of the UK, reduce UK sovereign control over a part of its own territory and still cause significant economic damage to the UK economy. Sacrificing sovereignty over one part of the UK could therefore increase UK sovereignty over the rest of its territory. Currently this option does not seem to be on the table in the UK politically. Yet come 2022 or 2024 after an (extended) transition, with a government perhaps no longer tied to the DUP, this option may become more attractive compared to the other three options available.

5.4. Time for serious self-reflection: the EU choices

Like the UK, the EU also faces some hard and fundamental choices.[74] Of course the EU has to decide what it wants in terms of withdrawal and especially concerning the future relationship itself. But behind these more immediate decisions lie choices of even more fundamental and constitutional significance. One of the most fundamental choices in this regard is between rigidity and flexibility. On the one hand, Brexit can be used to set

---

72 On the proper application or translation of the concept of sovereignty in the context of EU integration see inter alia N. Walker (ed), *Sovereignty in Transition* (Hart 2006), and N. MacCormick, *Questioning Sovereignty: Law, State and Nation in the European Commonwealth* (OUP, 1999).

73 Draft agreement of 19 March 2018 available at https://ec.europa.eu/commission/si tes/beta-political/files/draft_agreement_coloured.pdf.

74 L. Van Middelaar, 'Brexit as the European Union's "Machiavellian" moment', 55 *CML Rev.* (2018), 3, and M. Nettesheim, 'Brexit: Time for a Reflection Period about the Finalitè of European Integration' *German Law Journal Brexit Supplement* (2016), 87.

the existing acquis in stone. The internal market, for example, could politically be deified as one and indivisible. To a large extent this has indeed been the EU position so far.[75] All UK attempts to separate the different freedoms have been squarely rejected as cherry picking. It should be acknowledged, however, that the *legal* arguments behind the indivisibility of the internal market are far from ironclad.

For on the one hand it is undeniable that there is a strong correlation and interaction between the different freedoms and that the CJEU increasingly interprets the different freedoms in a uniform and integrated manner.[76] It is equally true that all freedoms jointly contribute to the shared objective of creating a single internal market, and that the different freedoms together represent a broader political compromise between Member States. One Member State, for example, will benefit more from the free movement of goods whereas another Member State may benefit relatively more from the free movement of workers and service providers. Cherry picking individual freedoms undermine this compromise, as entrenched in EU law.

On the other hand, the claim that, as a matter of *law*, the internal market is necessarily one and indivisible is hard to reconcile with the rather impressive amount of *existing* differentiation and flexibility in current internal market law.[77] Some examples suffice to illustrate this point. First, the four freedoms have historically developed along separate trajectories. In

---

75 See for example the Guidelines of the European Council (art. 50) of 29 April, p. 3, par. 1: 'Preserving the integrity of the Single Market excludes participation based on a sector-by-sector approach. A non-member of the Union, that does not live up to the same obligations as a member, cannot have the same rights and enjoy the same benefits as a member. In this context, the European Council welcomes the recognition by the British Government that the four freedoms of the Single Market are indivisible and that there can be no "cherry picking". The Union will preserve its autonomy as regards its decision-making as well as the role of the Court of Justice of the European Union.' For a later confirmation see eg. the Guidelines of the European Council (art. 50) of 23 March 2018, paras. 2 and 7. For a further analysis of the potentially positive, consolidating effects of Brexit in these regards see C. Hillion, 'Withdrawal under Article 50 TEU: An integration-friendly process,' 55 *CML Rev.* (2018), 29.

76 Cf. already CJEU Case C-55/94 *Gebhard*, ECLI:EU:C:1995:411, par. 25 as well as P. Oliver and W-H. Roth, 'The Internal Market and the Four Freedoms' 41 (2004) *CML Rev*, 407.

77 See also S. Weatherill, 'The several internal markets,' 36 *YEL* (2017), 125 and C. Barnard, 'Brexit and the EU internal market,' in: F. Fabrini (eds.), *The Law and Politics of Brexit*, (OUP, 2017). For the more general background on differentiation in the EU see B. de Witte, 'An undivided Union? Differentiated integration in post-

the early years of the internal market, the focus was largely on the free movement of goods, whereas the free movement of capital long remained the ugly duckling of the four freedoms, in part because this freedom even lacked direct effect. It was only with the Treaty of Maastricht that capital not just developed into a full blown freedom but even surpassed other freedoms by becoming the only freedom to directly apply to third countries.[78] Similarly, the free movement of persons also evolved significantly over time, and not always in sync with other freedoms.[79] For example, for a long time free movement rights were the sole preserve of the economically active and their family members. Only after Maastricht, with the introduction of EU citizenship, did non-economically active individuals gradually acquire more and more rights under EU law. In light of this gradual development of the different freedoms, often out of step with each other, it does not seem very convincing to, in the context of Brexit, suddenly present the four freedoms as one and indivisible, let alone to claim that any differentiation between the four freedoms inherently violates some core precepts of EU law.

Second, EU relations with third countries already demonstrate an impressive array of differentiated access to the internal market.[80] Examples include the customs union with Turkey, which primarily covers goods, the unique relationship between the EU and Switzerland, where over a 100 bilateral agreements allow Switzerland partial access to the internal market with differing exceptions for different freedoms, or the EEA agreement, which covers most parts of the internal market, but excludes some areas like fisheries, and also does not include a customs union.[81] All of these models only incorporate subsections of the internal market and strike a dif-

---

Brexit times', 55 *CML Rev.* (2018), 227 and B. De Witte, 'Near-membership, partial membership and the EU constitution', 4 *EULR* (2016), 471.

78 See the original Article 67 EEC as well as, amongst many others, J. Snell, 'Free movement of capital: Evolution as a non-linear process', in: P. Craig & G. De Búrca (eds.), *The Evolution of EU Law* (OUP 2011), 547-574 or L. Flynn, 'Free movement of capital', in: C. Barnard & S. Peers (eds.), *European Union Law* (OUP, 2014), 443-472. Of course, this also means that even after a hard Brexit free movement of capital will still partially apply to the UK, which in itself demonstrates a certain level of divisibility.

79 For a discussion on this point see N. Nic Shuibhne, *The Coherence of EU Free Movement Law: Constitutional Responsibility and the Court of Justice* (OUP, 2013).

80 Cf. also S. Weatherill, *The Internal Market as a Legal Concept* (OUP, 2016).

81 See also C. Tobler, 'A Look at the EEA from Switzerland', in: EFTA Court (ed.), *The EEA and the EFTA Court: Decentred Integration* (Hart, 2014), ch. 40.

ferent balance between the different freedoms, including restrictions on free movement of persons.[82] Confronted with such a variety in market access for third countries it becomes increasingly difficult to maintain that differentiation between the four freedoms is legally impossible.

A third example concerns the accession agreements of Bulgaria and Romania. These accession agreements contained transitional arrangements that limited the free movement of Bulgarian and Romanian citizens for several years *after* accession. This means that even after accession, and in the relation between Member States, it was possible to significantly limit free movement of persons and to restrict the foundational principle of non-discrimination. At least as far as the free movement of Eastern European EU citizens was concerned, therefore, the internal market did not prove inherently indivisible.[83]

A fourth and last example is provided by the so-called 'Cameron deal' agreed to by the European Council in an effort to convince the UK electorate to vote remain. Although this deal never entered into force, and although it was never subjected to CJEU scrutiny, it did allow the UK to limit some of the rights to social benefits EU citizens derive from EU law.[84] At least at this stage of the Brexit-saga, therefore, it was still considered legally feasible by the European Council to restrict the free movement of persons in the UK, under the assumption that the UK would remain a full Member State, even though all other freedoms remained fully applicable.[85]

These examples demonstrate that, as a question of law, it is not inherently impossible to differentiate between the four freedoms, although this of course does not mean that there are no legal limits to how far one can

---

82 Cf in this context also the limitations and 'emergency breaks' concerning immigration in the EEA and the EU-Switzerland relation, as discussed in C. Barnard & S. Fraser Butlin, 'Free movement vs. fair movement: Brexit and managed migration', 55 *CML Rev.* (2018), 203.

83 See N. Idriz, *Legal Constraints on EU Member States as Primary Law Makers: A Case Study of the Proposed Permanent Safeguard Clause on Free Movement of Persons in the EU Negotiating Framework for Turkey's Accession* (E.M. Meijers Instituut, No. 247, 2015).

84 See for this deal the Decision of the Heads of State and Government, meeting within the European Council, concerning a New Settlement for the United Kingdom within the European Union, Annex 1 of the European Council conclusions of 18 and 19 February. For analysis see 'Editorial comments: Presiding the Union in times of crisis: The unenviable task of the Netherlands', 53 *CML Rev.* (2016), 327.

85 See also B. de Witte, 'An undivided Union? Differentiated integration in post-Brexit times', 55 *CML Rev.* (2018), 234.

cherry pick the internal market. The rigid position of the EU concerning the indivisibility of the internal market, therefore, appears primarily driven by political considerations, not legal ones. And of course, there are good political reasons for this rigidity.[86] For understandable reasons the EU does not want to offer the UK a deal where it has most of the benefits but few of the costs of EU membership. Rigidity on the internal market also has the benefit of legal certainty and avoids the slippery slope of renegotiation the very basis of the EU legal order and the many political compromises that underlie it, and doing so in a time where EU integration is already facing a polycrisis. Reopening EU treaties now would certainly be a very high stakes gamble.

EU rigidity, however, also carries significant costs and risk. One main risk of rigidity is that it might only exacerbate popular resentment and resistance against European integration. And what does not bend may break. After a string of lost referenda and populist election victories, with Brexit so far as the most spectacular EU example, it is clear that a large portion of EU citizens disagrees with the status quo and current course of the EU.[87] Obviously the reasons for this are many and multifaceted, but one element seems to be the narrative of inevitability surrounding EU integration and the associated loss of political self-determination.[88] Often the EU is presented as the only viable option, removing the scope for further political disagreement and debate. Adrift in the currents of globalization and automation, people are told that there is no alternative to giving up authority. A Brexit that ends in a Norway+ model or even continued EU membership of the UK could feed into this narrative of inevitability. Despite a majority voting to leave, the UK would for all practical purposes remain. The additional discontent that such an outcome would create could fuel further populism and resistance, speeding up a negative spiral of distrust and ultimately disintegration.

---

86 See on the consolidating effect, and qualities, of Brexit in this regard also C. Hillion, 'Withdrawal under Article 50 TEU: An integration-friendly process', 55 *CML Rev.* (2018), 29.

87 See more generally on the democratic challenges facing the EU, in the context of Brexit, K. Nicolaïdis, 'Sustainable integration in a demoicratic polity, A new (or not so new) ambition for the EU after Brexit', or R. Bellamy, 'Losing control, Brexit and the demoi-cratic disconnect', both in B. Martill and U. Staiger (Eds.), *Brexit and Beyond, Rethinking the Futures of Europe* (UCL Press, 2018), 212 and 222.

88 Cf. A. Cuyvers, 'Recapturing popular sovereigns after Brexit: towards a compound parliamentary construct. 2017 EUSA Fifteenth Biennial Conference, Miami.

Instead of rigidity, therefore, the EU may want to seriously explore options to increase flexibility in ways that offer more political choice to national electorates on the modalities of European integration.[89] Instead of celebrating a possible Norway+ or remain outcome as a victory, this would entail treating such an outcome as only increasing the absolute necessity an urgency for the EU to find such flexibility. Even behind seemingly technical decisions on the regulation of trade in goods, therefore, fundamental choices on the future of EU integration lurk.

---

89 Clearly this touches on an already ongoing debate in EU integration, see for example B. De Witte, A. Ott, and E.Vos (Eds), *Between Flexibility and Disintegration: the Trajectory of Differentiation in EU Law* (Cheltenham: Elgar, 2017) or J-C. Piris, *The Future of Europe: Towards a Two-Speed EU?* (CUP, 2012).

Brexit and the Free Movement of Services: Challenges and Regulatory Solutions

Gavin Barrett [1]

Introduction – the Importance of Services

The services sector has become hugely significant at global level, at European Union level and for the United Kingdom, currently engaged in the process of terminating its membership of the EU.

Globally, services represent on average about two thirds of the economic output in developed economies. They account for a lower proportion of international trade as a whole – between 20% and 25% – but a growing one,[2] with growth being aided by advances in the uses and capacities of technology and by the interconnectedness and interdependence of modern economies.

At *European Union* level, it has been estimated that services make up about 70% of the EU's economic output.[3] At this level, services account for a lower proportion of cross-border trade as a whole, but still a highly significant one, with one fifth of services in the EU crossing a border.[4]

Legal provision for free movement of services is made in Articles 56 and 57 of the Treaty on the Functioning of the European Union. However, other provisions of both primary and secondary EU law also play a major role. Insofar as concerns Treaty provisions, Articles 49 and 54 TFEU are significant for providing for the freedom of establishment, thereby enabling the setting up of subsidiaries of businesses in other Member States. Most-cross border service provision is also supported by horizontal measures such as the 2006 Services Directive,[5] the 2004 Citizens' Directive,[6] which provides

---

1 Professor of Law, Sutherland School of Law, University College Dublin.
2 House of Lords European Union Committee, *Brexit: trade in non-financial services* (18th Report of Session 2016-17),(HL Paper 135), 10.
3 The City UK, 'Brexit Deal Should be Ambitious and Comprehensive', (statement published on website, 19.12.2017).
4 House of Lords European Union Committee, *op. cit.*, n. 2, 3 and 9.
5 Directive 2006/123/EC; House of Lords European Union Committee, *op. cit.*, n. 2, 18.
6 Directive 2004/38/EC.

for the free movement of persons (needed by, *inter alia*, many service providers) and the umbrella 2005 Directive consolidating the law on the recognition of professional qualifications.[7] Sectoral legislation governing particular services has also been adopted over the years. One prominent example of this is the 1977 directive on lawyers' services.[8]

The single market in services is a much more recent development than integration in the free movement of goods area. What is now the European Union has involved a customs union since 1958, but has had a Services Directive only since 2006. A digital single market in services is still under construction.[9] Services are not like goods. It is much more difficult to create a single European market in services than it is in goods. Services are far more complex and varied in their nature: thus, for example, some services can be traded online whereas others (such as medical or dental treatment) may require to be provided in person and thus require the free movement of persons to be guaranteed in order for them to be freely traded. Other services again may be embedded in goods. (The archetypal example of this is software in computers.)

Furthermore, services are delivered using a variety of methods. No less than four different ways of delivering services are provided for in the General Agreement on Trade in Services: (i) cross-border provision, *i.e.*, from one State to another; (ii) where the consumer crosses the border to the provider; (iii) where the service is provided via a subsidiary or branch of the service provider; and (iv) where the service provider crosses the border temporarily.[10] Even obstacles to services can be more complex than those to goods. Goods can be restricted by tariffs whereas services are largely unaffected by these, and instead tend to be restricted by a variety of non-tariff barriers such as licensing requirements and other regulations.[11] As Rogers puts it, "services trade is extremely hard to liberalise as you are dealing

---

7 Directive 2005/36/EC.
8 Council Directive 77/249/EEC. General practitioners, nurses, veterinary surgeons, pharmacists and architects have also been the subject of sectoral measures on the mutual recognition of qualifications, and there have also been directives concerning particular industries and sectors of the economy such as food and beverage, the coal trade, and the wholesale, intermediary and retail sectors. (See further Craig/de Búrca, *EU Law*, (6th Edition, 2015), 842 f.
9 House of Lords European Union Committee, *op. cit.*, n. 2, 90.
10 House of Lords European Union Committee, *op. cit.*, n. 2, 11.
11 See V. Romei, "Dark Matter that Matters' in UK Trade with EU', Financial Times (17.12.2017).

with entrenched cultural preferences and intractable regulatory barriers."[12] It is nonetheless by dismantling such barriers and thereby reducing trans- actions costs that the EU single market in services functions.

Because of such challenges, the single European market in services is significantly less integrated than the single market in goods (with only ap- proximately one fifth of services provided in the EU involving the crossing of a border).[13] A further reason for the comparative lack of integration in the services field at international level is that there is no equivalent to the Common Commercial Policy (which applies to the free movement of goods) in the area of the free movement of services – *i.e.*, there is no uni- form/harmonised trade regime for trading with non-single market coun- tries.[14]

If, because of considerations like these, the single market in services is significantly less integrated than the single market in goods, it is nonethe- less also the case that the European Union has the most integrated interna- tional services market in the world. Moreover, the degree of integration in- volved in it looks likely to increase.[15]

Focusing more closely on the position of the *United Kingdom* as regards services, by 2015 the UK was the second largest exporter of services in the world, providing 7.1% of total global service exports. (The United States was some way ahead as the world's leading exporter, supplying a full 15.6% of global service exports.) After the UK came China, Germany and France in that order.[16] Overall, it has been estimated that services account for ap- proximately three quarters of the UK's economic output and about 44% of the UK's international trade.[17] At the time of writing, these proportions are growing,[18] with tradeable services the fastest-growing element of UK

---

12 I. Rogers, *"Where did Brexit Come From and Where is it Going to Take the UK?"* (lec- ture, UCL European Institute, 22 January 2019), 14.

13 See generally on services in the single market, *e.g.*, Andenas/Roth, *Services and Free Movement in EU Law*, (2002); Snell, *Goods and Services in EC Law: A Study of the Relationship Between the Freedoms*, (2002); Barnard/Scott, *The Law of the Single Eu- ropean Market: Unpacking the Premises*, (2002).

14 House of Lords European Union Committee, *op. cit.*, n. 2, 86.

15 *Ibid.*, 29.

16 *Ibid.*, 10. Such statistics should come with something of a health warning regar- ding their ability to mislead: it is notoriously difficult in particular to measure the impact of (a) foreign-controlled enterprises and subsidiaries providing services and (b) services provided when a person moves from one country to another. (*Ibid.*, 11, and 13-15).

17 House of Lords European Union Committee, *op. cit.*, n. 2, 10.

18 *Ibid.*, 15.

trade.[19] A lower proportion of UK service exports than exports of goods go to the EU (37% vs. 48% for goods), but for all that it is both important and the most integrated market for services in the world.[20] The EU collectively is the UK's single largest market for services, worth over 70% more than its nearest rival, the US,[21] and worth more than all eight countries comprising the UK's next largest purchasers of services.[22] Unlike in goods, the UK has a surplus with the EU in both financial and non-financial services. Overall, service exports to the EU represent 4.8% of the UK's entire GDP.

The Particular Case of Financial Services

Some brief points may be made about the topic of financial services, in particular.[23] The significance to the European economy of financial services provided from the UK is large: in total, over a quarter of the EU 27's total demand for financial services is met by the UK financial services industry. The UK financial services centre earns between €217 and €234 billion in revenues and generates between €68 and €76 billion in taxes.[24] Dependence, of course, is mutual. The UK economy relies on EU demand for financial services. The other EU States, however, depends on the UK to supply those services.[25] Unsurprisingly, given the scale of economic activity involved, however, there is also rivalry between London and other financial centres such as Paris, Frankfurt, Luxembourg, Dublin and Amsterdam in providing such services. Nevertheless, the provision of financial services is clearly not entirely a zero-sum game. In other words, it is not necessarily the case that a decline in the fortunes of London in providing financial services will be matched by a corresponding increase in the fortunes of finan-

---

19 I. Rogers, *"Where did Brexit Come From and Where is it Going to Take the UK?"* (lecture, UCL European Institute, 22 January 2019), 14.
20 Romei, *loc. cit.*, n. 11.
21 *Ibid.*
22 See more generally S. Jack, 'Brexit: Business Secretary Greg Clark Warns on Services', BBC News website (21.06.2018).
23 See more generally Alexander/Barnard/Ferran/Lang/Moloney, *Brexit and Financial Services Law and Policy* (2018).
24 See Oliver Wyman, *The Impact of the UK's Exit from the EU on the UK-Based Financial Services Sector* (Marsh and McLennon, 2018), 2. (Figures converted into euro by the author.).
25 European Research Centre for Economic and Financial Governance, *Implications of Brexit on EU Financial Services* (Study for the ECON Committee, European Parliament (IP/A/ECON/2016-22, PE 602.058), 9.

cial service centres in the EU-27. The City of London may be regarded as constituting a financial ecosystem within the European Union of unique mass. If badly damaged, there is a danger that instead of other financial centres in the EU profiting and correspondingly increasing their business, all concerned will lose and the business pass to non-EU locations such as New York or Tokyo.[26] Another way of putting this is that, to an undetermined extent, EU States are in a state of mutual dependency on each other when it comes to financial services.[27]

Much of the discussion of financial services in the context of Brexit has focused on the issue of passporting such services, which is where meeting regulatory requirements in one Member State of the EU absolves a provider, under EU law, from the need to meet the corresponding regulatory requirements in the Member State of the service recipient. Passporting is undoubtedly a valuable right under EU law. On the other hand, a discussion of free movement of financial services cannot be reduced in consideration of this possibility. In reality, passporting is neither a universal nor a homogeneous practice by businesses established outside the EU (which is what British businesses will be once Brexit occurs). In the first place, non-EU businesses that establish a branch or subsidiary in an EU Member State no longer need to invoke any special passporting regime for non-EU companies. This is, of course, of considerable significance. Hence for example, 87% of companies that provide insurance to the EU-27 have already established a branch or subsidiary in the EU-27. Another factor limiting the importance of passporting is that equivalence regimes exist in relation to many financial services and provide some substitute for passporting, even if, admittedly, it is only a limited one: limited in that equivalence is (a) recognised at the discretion of the Commission; (b) is technically open to being withdrawn (although in practice never is); (c) has in the past sometimes taken several years to be granted; and (d) has not been provided for under EU legislation in all areas of financial services. It is not, for example, available in the field of wholesale banking (a situation which has the potential to be highly problematic post-Brexit as without equivalence, UK-based banks would no longer be able to provide services to clients across the

---

26 For a description of the EU-27's own financial interest in maintaining this ecosystem, see (the rather optimistically entitled) J. Ford, 'Why a Hard Brexit for Financial Services in Unlikely', Financial Times (10.12.2017).

27 An analogy may perhaps be drawn with the Amazonian rain forest. Were this to be destroyed, few would dispute that the world as a whole would be worse off, or expect planting trees in Germany or Norway to make up the difference.

EU from the UK). Nor is it available in the field of asset management,[28] or in relation to UCITs.

Apart from the question of passporting, another issue which has given rise to discussion in the context of free movement of financial services is the considerable risk that in a Brexit situation, there would potentially be a threat to UK businesses in clearing euro-denominated trades – specifically, were the ECB to be given power to (re-)introduce a location policy requiring that central counterparties be located in the Eurozone. Such prospects are very much alive at the time of writing, the German Finance Minister having both called for London's multi-billion pound euro-clearing business to be relocated after Brexit occurs, and (perhaps unsurprisingly) suggested Frankfurt as an alternative location. Such plans fit well with the plans of Deutsche Börse to win at least a quarter of the market for clearing euro interest rate swaps from London in the short term.[29]

For all the significance of financial services, however, what is not commonly realised is that the majority (72%) of services exported from the UK are non-financial in nature. These cover areas such as telecommunications, broadcasting, tourism and aviation as well as professional services such as accountancy and law. In 2015, these accounted for 32% of the UK's exports as a whole, with a total value of £62.9 billion, compared to financial service exports, which were worth £26 billion. While financial services constitute the biggest individual slice of UK services exports, the majority of service exports are, in fact, non-financial.[30]

Interestingly, non-financial services are not merely responsible for more exports than financial services. They also give rise to more jobs.[31]

---

28 See generally, A. Tarrant, P. Holmes, R. D. Kelemen, *Equivalence, Mutual Recognition in Financial Services and the UK Negotiating Position* (Briefing Paper 27, UK Trade Policy Observatory, University of Sussex, January 2019), 3-4.

29 See generally Storbeck/Stafford, 'Germany's Olaf Scholz Suggests Euro Clearing Be Moved to Frankfurt', Financial Times (08.06.2018). *Cf.* however Strauss, 'Why is No One Talking About the City?', Financial Times (12.06.2018), in which it is noted, however, that neither French nor German banks or companies (which benefit from London's economies of scale) are lobbying for any such change. The same article gives an up-to-date idea of the highly uncertain outcome of discussions concerning services. For a review of the overall progress of negotiations, see *e.g.*, Wolf, 'Playing Chicken Over the Post-Brexit Irish Border', Financial Times (14.06.2018).

30 See V. Romei, *loc. cit.*, n. 11.

31 House of Lords European Union Committee, *op. cit.*, n. 2, 86.

Relevant Considerations in Negotiating a Brexit Deal on Services

Some of the factors which have made agreement on free movement of services difficult to arrive at for the purposes of creating and developing a single European market were always likely to render a deal on free movement of services difficult to obtain in the negotiations concerning the UK-EU trade relationship in the wake of Brexit. As already noted, depending on the nature of the service at issue, free movement of services is frequently *intrinsically* dependent on the free movement of persons. The latter freedom facilitates the provision of certain services, such as legal or medical advice, to clients and business partners. However, beyond this, free movement of persons also facilitates recruitment to service industries in which the UK leads Europe, such as in the field of digital services. Industry seems to have been more aware of this point than the UK Government. Hence the City UK (which represents the UK's financial services industry), from the beginning of the Brexit process, lobbied for "continued access by the UK to the best talent".[32] Depending on the circumstances, the free movement of services can be intrinsically linked to more than one other economic freedom. A good example of this is that it is common practice for aircraft engine manufacturers to sell their product at a loss. Profits are then made on the sale of services: inspections, maintenance and repairs, which are provided under contracts for these services which may endure for decades. In addition, providing these services requires free movement of persons, so that skilled workers can provide such services often at short notice.[33] Beyond such linkages, the insistence of the European Union on the indivisibility of the four freedoms has resulted in the free movement of services becoming *politically* dependent on the free movement of persons. In effect, what the EU-27 are saying is that if the UK is not willing to accept EU-27 nationals in its labour market, then the UK will no longer be allowed to enjoy the same access to the EU's services market. Overall, therefore, both by reason of intrinsic links between the economic freedoms and

---

32 The City UK, 'Brexit and UK-Based Financial and Related Professional Services', statement published on The City UK website (accessed 01.06.2018). Put another way, it has pushed for a globalisation objective, not the deglobalisation agenda (in the form of opposition to migration) that motivated at least some of the support for the Brexit vote. Véron, 'Brexit: When the Banks Leave', Bruegel (01.12.2017); the City UK, 'Brexit Deal Should be Ambitious and Comprehensive' (statement published on website, (19.12.2017)).

33 S. Jack, 'Brexit: Business Secretary Greg Clark Warns on Services', BBC News website (21.06.2018).

because of the refusal of the EU to countenance separate access to each of the four market freedoms, Prime Minister May's insistence on ending free movement of persons would imply (if put into effect) the death knell for UK participation in the Single European Market.[34]

Political considerations are part of the negotiations on free movement of services in another way as well. The European Union and the Eurozone have shown themselves adept at finding solutions to seemingly intractable political difficulties. The bailouts of Eurozone States (particularly the bailouts in 2010, 2012 and 2015 of Greece); the construction from 2012 onwards of European Banking Union; and ECB's OMT and Quantitative Easing programmes of 2012 and 2015 respectively are all examples of solutions being found to crises where the legal obstacles were considerable. There is a crucial difference between these political crises and the crisis represented by Brexit however in that the solutions to these earlier problems furthered the cause of European integration. An overly-generous deal on Brexit on the other hand, might be feared to do exactly the opposite, by effectively incentivising the disintegration of the European Union, and demonstrating that it is possible to secure the benefits of a fundamental economic freedom, without paying the usual price of acceptance of all three other fundamental economic freedoms and the financial and restrictions on national discretion that form part and parcel of membership both of the European Union and of the European Economic Area. For this reason, therefore, the objective of maximum free movement of services between the European Union and the post-Brexit (and post-transition period) United Kingdom has not been sought to be attained on the part of the EU-27. In practice, the UK has been unwilling to permit the free movement of persons to the extent sought by the EU-27, and the EU-27 conversely unwilling to lower their demands (in terms of free movement of persons) to a level deemed acceptable to the United Kingdom.

Possible Negotiation Outcomes Regarding the Free Movement of Services

The UK's preparations for negotiations on the free movement of services were unorthodox, to say the least. Rather than adopting the usual course in international negotiations of setting out its proposed objectives, it did the

---

34 See Rogers, *loc. cit.*, n. 12, 21-22. From an economic perspective, exit from the Single Market seems a high price to pay for the freedom to restrict immigration in a manner, which in any case seems of dubious long-term practicality.

very opposite. Hence, for example, over the course of 2017 and 2018, it first deferred and then shelved a paper on financial services, purportedly to conceal its negotiating hand, but in reality probably because of internal disagreement within the Cabinet on what the UK itself wanted.[35] An expected broader white paper setting out the UK position regarding its future relationship with the EU in advance of the June 2018 European Council was subsequently also postponed.[36] In the wake of the 2016 Brexit referendum and the subsequent giving of Article 50 notice by the United Kingdom on 29 March 2017, a range of outcomes became – and, as shall be seen, for a surprisingly long time, has remained – possible. Indeed, the parliamentary chaos which has afflicted Westminster leading up to, at and beyond the time of Brexit's original supposed March 2019 implementation deadline means that even now no possibility can be definitively ruled out. For this reason, the entire range of possible outcomes is examined at least briefly here.

At the one extreme would be retention of EU membership with all the free movement rights this entails. However, this is an objective which could only be attained where the objective of Brexit itself abandoned, which would probably necessitate (politically speaking) a second referendum reversing the result of the original vote. At the other extreme is the situation of a no-deal Brexit, obviously implying that the desire to seek Brexit be persisted with, and yet that no EU-27–UK agreement at all be arrived at, including concerning the cross-border free movement of services. Various possible compromise positions are to be found along the route between these two extremes, on the model of stops along a tram line, travelling along a route of descending levels of integration. We can term the stops along this route an 'EEA-style agreement' (or, more optimistically, an 'EEA-plus-customs-union style-agreement')[37]; a 'CETA plus-style agreement' (or, alternatively, an 'EEA minus-style agreement')[38]; a 'Ukraine-style association agreement'; and a 'CETA/Korea-style agreement'. Any of these

---

35 Neilan, 'Government Slammed for Forcing City Firms to Plan for Brexit', City AM (05.09.2017); G. Parker, 'UK Shelves Financial Services Brexit Position Paper', Financial Times (22.01.2018).

36 See Pooley, 'May Refuses to Commit to Date for Brexit White Paper after Delay', Financial Times (06.06.2018).

37 With EEA here standing for 'European Economic Area', which came into being on 1 January 1994 on the entry into force of the EEA Agreement (signed on 2 May 1992, and adjusted by a Protocol signed on 17 March 1993).

38 With CETA here standing for the EU-Canada Comprehensive Economic and Trade Agreement signed on 30.10.2016.

would have to be preceded by a transition period, since there was never going to be enough time to negotiate any agreement dealing with such matters before 29 March 2019, the Treaty deadline for the initial Article 50 withdrawal agreement to be reached. The stop at which the Brexit tram pulls in has always depended on the willingness of the UK to make trade-offs. If it sought regulatory autonomy, then it was inevitably going to face barriers to the Single European Market. If it sought access to the Single European Market, this implied losing regulatory autonomy. The price of single market participation would be to accept all four freedoms – free movement, in other words, of goods, persons, services and capital[39] – which the EU regards as coming as an inseparable, albeit perhaps with minor concessions possible, as has been the case with the EEA States.[40] It is proposed to examine each of the possible stops/negotiation outcomes to the Brexit negotiations before turning to the topic of how EU-UK negotiations themselves have proceeded to date.

Retention of EU Membership

The first step along our imaginary tramline would consist of the UK either staying in the European Union, or else re-entering it, having left it, and thus either way would involve either the retention or recovery of all free movement rights. Discussion of either possibility need not detain us for long here. At the time of writing, the first eventuality – remaining in the EU – seems unlikely to happen, barring an extraordinary and as-yet improbable-seeming major shift in public opinion.[41] Although, ironically, opponents of Brexit are now a clear popular majority, the shift may not be radical enough to guarantee that a second referendum would be won by 'remainers' and then be duly reflected in the actions of the UK Parliament

---

39 House of Lords European Union Committee, *op. cit.*, n. 2, 9.
40 Note also the position of Switzerland and the Ukraine, although neither of these has full access to the Single Market. (See Demertzis/Sapir, 'Brexit, Phase Two (and Beyond): The Future of the EU-UK Relationship', Bruegel (13.12.2017), 3.)
41 In late February 2019, the Labour Party, subsequent to the departure of a number of its MPs objecting to its Brexit policy finally announced for the first time that it would support a referendum if its preferred version of Brexit were not accepted. However, the existence even of sufficient parliamentary support – let alone popular support - for a further referendum was not apparent, and has remained unclear since then. (See J. Pickard, *'Labour Party to Back Second Referendum on Brexit'*, Financial Times (25.02.2019)).

and government.[42] As for re-entry, once having left, it seems unlikely that re-entry into the EU would come about for many years, if ever. (It is noticeable that political resentment of the EU has grown in Switzerland since voting 'no' to membership of the EEA in 1992, with recent polls showing support for membership of the EU to have fallen to 11%.[43])

EEA-Style Agreement/EEA-plus-Customs Union-Style Agreement

Descending in terms of the level of European integration involved, a second possibility has been membership by the United Kingdom of the European Economic Area (this time as a state with a status similar to EFTA members Norway, Iceland and Liechtenstein) or else negotiation of an effectively similar relationship (whether or not combined with a similar customs relationship between the EU and the UK to that presently enjoyed by virtue of the UK's EU membership). Such a relationship would have a number of characteristics. It would bring with it continued access by the UK to the single European market in services. This would include passporting rights in the financial services area. However, the new relationship would function without the application within the United Kingdom of the doctrine of direct effect. In addition, there would be less of a guarantee that single market rules would be speedily implemented.[44] (The reason for this is, in the first place, that there is always a time lag between when a law is adopted at EU level and when it is added to the EEA Agreement. Furthermore, it has been noticeable that speedy implementation of single market rules by current non-EU EEA members has been far from guaranteed.[45]) An EEA-style relationship would be inferior to membership of the European Union in that EEA States have comparatively little power to influence the rules that will affect them, including in the field of free movement of services. Furthermore, the UK would also have to accept all four

---

42 See B. Kentish, *'Voters Want to Remain in EU by 12-Point Margin as Brexit Opposition Reaches New High, Poll Finds'*, The Independent (17.01.2019).

43 See Bolet, 'Is Switzerland a Model for the UK-EU Relationship?', LSE Brexit blog, http://blogs.lse.ac.uk/brexit/2018/01/29/continental-breakfast-6-is-switzerland-a-m odel-for-the-uk-eu-relationship/ (accessed 01.06.2018).

44 See further Alexander *et al, op. cit.,* n. 23, 16.

45 Most recently, Iceland, in particular, has attracted some criticism in this regard. (See European Commission, *Single Market Scoreboard* (Reporting period: 12/2015 – 12/2016), http://ec.europa.eu/internal_market/scoreboard/_docs/2017/transposit ion/2017-scoreboard_transposition_en.pdf (accessed 14.06.2018).

fundamental economic freedoms as part of such a relationship, although it is true that a slightly milder form of free movement of persons pertains than is the case for EU members.[46]

It is if the UK leaves the single European market that estimates of how bad the City of London will be hurt begin to be the subject of particular focus. Projections vary considerably. Véron has estimated that in the event of the UK leaving the single market, between 15% and 25% of the City's business would migrate and come to be provided from an EU-27 location.[47] To date, job losses have not been as great as feared[48] – but concern on the part of UK service providers, particularly those in the financial sector, continue to be voiced as the date of Brexit approaches.[49]

Free Trade Areas and the Free Movement of Services

Some general observations may be made concerning the next three possible steps for a Brexit – bound UK, all of which involve some or other version of a free trade area. Free trade areas involve agreements to cooperate to reduce trade barriers and thus to liberalise trade between two or more States. Usually they are concerned with trade in goods. But any comprehensive free trade agreement could target trade in services as well. Free trade agreements vary greatly in terms of the market access they provide. However, what they have in common is that they provide only access to the market. They do not exempt from the duty to comply with local laws and regulations. In contrast, single European market rules involve mutual recognition, harmonised rules and a more level playing field as regards competition, social standards, environmental standards and data protection. The single European market should thus be thought of as involving a single regulatory space, and a free trade agreement in contrast as involving two distinct regulatory spaces. Although free trade agreements are sometimes de-

---

46 See more generally Alexander *et al*, *op. cit.*, n. 23, 16-17 and 62-64.
47 Véron, 'Brexit: When the banks leave', Bruegel (01.12.2017), 2-4.
48 See *e.g.*, L. Noonan and R. Atkins 'UBS to Move Fewer London Jobs Than Initially Feared', Financial Times, (3.11.2017); and A. MacAskill, 'Brexit and the City: Taking London's Financial Pulse', Reuters (20.11.2017).
49 See H. Jones, 'Former UK Financial District Leader sees 75,000 Brexit job losses', Reuters (20.06.2018); Strauss/Jenkins, 'Hammond Vows to Fight for City Over Post-Brexit Rules', Financial Times (22.06.2018); S. Jones, 'No-deal Brexit Could Return UK to 1930s, Says Senior Banking Figure', Financial Times (10.02.2019) and P. Stafford, 'Key London Markets Would be Left in the Lurch Under a 'No-Deal' Brexit' (1.10.2018).

scribed as 'comprehensive',[50] this description is merely relative: trade agreement provisions governing services begin at a low standard – and rules concerning financial services in particular lack mutual recognition provisions and tend to be riddled with exceptions. EU-UK trade in services governed by a free trade agreement would be far less free than it has been in the Single Market.[51]

Complicating the use of free trade areas in the context of Brexit is the requirement of Article V of the General Agreement on Trade in Services (GATS), under which such agreements must have "substantial sectoral coverage" – although what this means is uncertain and the provision is rarely relied upon in disputes.

Another potential obstacle to such a deal for the UK covering services is that the 'most favoured nation' clauses in free trade deals with other countries such as Canada, South Korea, the Caribbean islands and Singapore (all of which have some provisions on services of their own)[52] might oblige the EU to offer a similarly generous deal concerning services to these countries as that offered to the UK concerning services – without, however, having secured any *quid pro quo* justifying such a concession to these other countries. There are certain exemptions for the applications of these provisions which might arguably apply.[53] However, an EU reluctant to reach an accord can seek shelter behind most favoured nation clauses in existing free trade deals.

In order to protect the UK's status as a global leader in trading services, any such EU-UK free trade agreement would need to be both radical and broader than anything seen before, including CETA – which itself has been described as "the most comprehensive free trade agreement in services ever agreed".[54] The free trade agreement would need to be *radical*, in that it would require stronger institutions than the normal State-to-State dispute settlement mechanisms in free trade agreements. (By definition, of course, such a free trade agreement would be radical in another, rather dif-

---

50 An example of this being CETA, the Comprehensive Economic Trade Agreement.
51 See Tarrant *et al, op. cit.*, n. 28, 8-9.
52 Note also the draft free trade agreement with Japan, which has a similar such clause.
53 Namely, if the EU-UK deal creates an internal market between the partners, grants the right of establishment to each side's businesses or if the deal involves "approximation of legislation", involving one party aligning its rules to the others, or else common rules. See further Hogarth, 'EU Barred from Striking Favourable Brexit deal on City', The Times (22.01.2018).
54 House of Lords European Union Committee, *op. cit.*, n. 2, 22-24.

ferent way, in that it would have as its aim the *restriction* of trade between the parties, currently set at the higher level of a customs union.) An EU-UK free trade agreement would also need to be *broad* in that the use of a free trade agreement to provide wholesale access to service market would be unprecedented. Numerous service areas would need to be facilitated, in order to prevent serious disruption to the businesses of UK service providers. To take just two examples, such an agreement would need to provide for UK airlines flying between EU-27 States and within them. Furthermore, the rights of UK broadcasters to broadcast into the single European market – which affects 60% of all UK channels – would need protection. Similar issues exist across a swathe of other sectors. Not alone has a deal of so ambitious a nature never been entered into by the European Union before, but certain areas *e.g.*, audiovisual media services have been specifically excluded from all free trade agreements until now.[55] Given the great variety in the nature of services (a topic touched upon already), it is clear that the negotiation of a free trade area covering free movement of services would take a long time, possibly necessitating a lengthy transition period, so as to avoid a regulatory cliff edge if negotiations went on too long.[56] Complicating matters, the EU does not have a harmonised third country trade policy in services. A free trade agreement in this field, unlike in the free movement of goods area, would probably be a mixed agreement with all the ratification challenges and delays that this would involve.[57] (In the latter regard, the October 2016 blocking of the CETA accord by the Wallonian Parliament, although eventually defused by a compromise acceptable to all concerned, is a far-from-distant memory.[58])

The fact that such an ambitious free trade agreement – in effect, a kind of half-way house between a normal free trade area and a single market – has never been agreed upon before does not mean that it could not be agreed in the context of Brexit. However, its negotiation and ratification would clearly be no simple matter and there must be some doubt as to whether agreement could be reached at all on many aspects.[59] Where there is a will, there tends to be a way. However, as will be seen, there has been a distinct absence of will – both on the EU side, and, far more remarkably,

---

55 *Ibid.*, 89.
56 See House of Lords European Union Committee, *op. cit.*, n. 2, 9 and 25.
57 *Ibid.*, 29.
58 See Brunsden, 'Belgium's Walloon Parliament Blocks EU-Canada Free-Trade Deal', Financial Times (14.10.2016).
59 See recently in this regard, Anon., 'Bankers to Ask May Why they Should Stay in London after Brexit', Financial Times (14.06.2018).

on the UK side – to reach an ambitious arrangement extending generally to services. On the EU side, at least, this was only to be expected. The EU must after all, be seen to confine the major benefits of membership of the European Union to Member States of the Union itself, if it wishes to safeguard the stability of the EU as an international organisation, and the attractiveness of participation in the EU to its component States.

CETA plus-style (or EEA minus-style) agreement

Continuing along our metaphorical tramline to possible future destination points for Brexit negotiations (and descending a further level in terms of ambition), one arrives at the idea of a CETA plus-style (or EEA minus-style) agreement. Some hope of what might be termed such an agreement, falling short of full membership of the single European market, was given rise to at one point by statements by leading French and German politicians referring to the possibility of a "half-way house between Norway and free trade" [60] and of creating a "model for countries like Turkey or Ukraine." [61] One advantage of such a relationship, from the EU's point of view, would be that it would keep the United Kingdom safely within the EU's orbit as a kind of economic satellite.[62] A second advantage is that it would also help fill the Brexit-shaped hole in the EU budget, because the UK would of course be expected to pay for the privilege of such a relationship.[63] Thirdly, and as already indicated, such a relationship could function as a model for countries that want to be close to the European Union, without however joining it.[64]

---

60 G. Parker, 'Macron Boosts May's Hopes of Bespoke EU Trade Deal', Financial Times (20.01.2018).
61 Anon., 'Brexit Model Could Influence Turkey and Ukraine Deals', RTE News online (26.12.2017), (accessed 01.06.2018).
62 Duff, 'Brexit: Launching Satellite Britain', European Policy Centre Discussion Paper, (05.12.2017).
63 G. Parker/Hughes/Milne, 'May Urged to Back 'Norway-Style' Payments', Financial Times (22.01.2018).
64 Anon., 'Brexit Model Could Influence Turkey and Ukraine Deals', RTE News online (26.12.2017), (accessed 01.06.2018).

Ukraine-style association agreement

To continue our imaginary tram-ride, less extensive free trade agreements would also be possible. The EU-Ukraine agreement, sometimes referred to as a "deep and comprehensive free trade agreement" was signed in 2014 and entered into full effect in September of that year. It does not involve membership of the single European market but does include extensive market access for goods and services, although less in the case of services than that of goods. It involves a certain level of free movement of persons, with visa liberalisation and a work permit scheme. (The enforcement aspect of the agreement at least initially might have been thought unacceptable to the UK – it involves an arbitration panel, bound by the European Court of Justice. Furthermore, the agreement requires 'regulatory alignment',[65] which might also have been expected to incur the dislike of Brexit advocates. However, as shall be seen, in *both* respects, initial red lines in the UK's negotiating approach proved more malleable than might have been thought.

CETA/Korea-style agreement.

Moving onwards (and downwards) from the 'deep and comprehensive' Ukraine free trade agreement to 'ordinary' free trade agreements, free trade agreements of this latter kind have not led to very extensive liberalisation of trade in services, although they have had *some* coverage of services. Examples are the Swiss-EU bilateral agreements (which cover public procurement, air transport and the free movement of persons); the EU – South Korea free trade agreement (which covers intellectual property, lawyers, telecommunications and transport); and the EU-Canada CETA agreement (which covers post, telecommunications and marine transport).[66]

As regards to their modus operandi, such agreements adopt one of two approaches. Either they list sectors they liberalise (the so-called 'positive list' approach) or, like CETA, they have a 'negative list' of sectors that they do *not* liberalise.

The very limited nature of agreements of this nature adopted by the EU to date should also be borne in mind. For example, there is no adoption of

---

65 Barber, 'Ukraine May be Closer than Norway to UK Post-Brexit', Financial Times (09.01.2018).

66 House of Lords European Union Committee, *op. cit.*, n. 2, 20-21.

the EU *acquis* in CETA. It is purely an international law agreement. Adopting such an arrangement would involve a major deterioration from the present position.[67] For example, under such a system, no passporting would be allowed. Although CETA is a good deal in services by world standards, it has been accurately described as failing to give Canada or the EU a uniform position in each other's markets. Over 500 exemptions of either a regional or sectoral nature (and regarding matters as diverse as the qualifications required of service providers, nationality requirements and stipulations as to their corporate form) take from CETA's general provisions liberalising services. Adherence to such a regime would potentially involve a loss of a large proportion of UK service exports to the EU.[68]

As for the Swiss agreement on access, this applies only to a very limited section of financial services, and in any case, largely involves only the WTO GATS regime. It was never clear that a Swiss-style arrangement would be on offer in any case, as the European Union had clearly become unhappy with the EU-Switzerland agreement itself, and is currently pursuing the objective of an 'institutional framework agreement' replacing and updating the proliferation of bilateral agreements which provide for Swiss access to the single market, and providing for a role for the European Court of Justice – something an unenthusiastic Switzerland had managed to avoid up until now.[69]

The 'No Deal' Scenario

The stop along the line for the Brexit process involving the least degree of integration would be a 'no deal' scenario. This possibility was trumpeted rather puzzlingly by Theresa May for sometime as being "better than a bad deal".[70] It would leave the United Kingdom trading services with European

---

67 European Research Centre for Economic and Financial Governance, See more generally Alexander *et al, op. cit.*, n. 23, 18.
68 See generally, Rogers, *loc. cit.*, n. 12, 14.
69 See Atkins, 'Switzerland Readies Counter Measures as Bourse Row with EU Intensifies', Financial Times (08.06.2018).
70 Mrs May was originally quoted as saying that "I am... clear that no deal for Britain is better than a bad deal for Britain" on 17 January 2017. The expression subsequently found its way into the Conservative Party manifesto for the June 2017 election, although its use has become increasingly rarer as time has gone on. (See for one commentary on this Chu, 'Theresa May's 'No Deal is Better Than a Bad Deal' Brexit Logic Could End Up Destroying the British Economy', The Independent (28.05.2017).)

Union Member States on the basis of WTO rules. The General Agreement on Trade in Services, in force since 1995, would be the main treaty governing trade in services in such a scenario. The UK would have to have its own schedule of concessions and commitments regarding international trade and to have that certified by other WTO countries. It would be likely to seek to replicate the existing schedule, which relates to EU Member States. Obviously, WTO rules would be worse than trading services on the basis of the single European market, or under free trade agreement rules of any description. But it is nonetheless capable of being done. Trade in services with the US (the UK's biggest trading partner for services) is, after all, governed by WTO rules. The effect would vary depending on the service sector involved. Regulated sectors (lawyers, doctors, accountancy firms *etc.*) would face barriers to trading (perhaps complete barriers). Unregulated sectors would not. Potential problems with the WTO regime include (1) the fact that enforcement would be problematic for private parties under a WTO-based regime because the WTO's dispute resolution process is State-led; (2) the fact that, as they are based on a global organisation, the WTO's rules are not a system well adjusted to fast-changing industries *e.g.*, digital services; (3) the fact that some services are not covered by the EU's GATS Schedule of Commitments (*e.g.*, audiovisual media services, air services, and publicly-funded services, so that the areas of health and education, for example, would only be covered to a restricted extent);[71] and (4) the fact that free movement of persons and data protection are not provided for under WTO rules. Overall, the choice to leave without a deal and therefore to have resort to WTO-only freedoms would be an astonishing one to take from an economic point of view. Rogers has asked pointedly "how one can seriously argue that the *only* bloc with which one does not need a free trade deal is that one with which one does easily the largest amount of trade?", pointed out that choosing the WTO option involves "having to try and scramble your way back up the hill to a preferential deal, under huge time pressure, notably in those many sectors and issues on which a resort to WTO rules gives you nothing" and observed that "the reality is that you would in exiting to WTO terms reset the baseline for future FTA talks in the worst possible place for UK negotiators," WTO rules providing merely a foundation on which to build in seeking deeper freeing up of trade.[72]

---

71 House of Lords European Union Committee, *op. cit.*, n. 2, 89 and 90. Other areas are protected to a lower standard *e.g.*, intellectual property rights which are protected under the Agreement on Trade-Related Aspects of Intellectual Property Rights ('TRIPS').

72 See Rogers, *loc. cit.*, n. 12, 14.

Developments During the Negotiations on Brexit and their Relevance to the Free Movement of Services

The above section has addressed the various possible future scenarios which offered themselves from the time the path towards Brexit was first embarked upon, and indeed – given the lack of substantive progress made along that path –*still* exist. Nevertheless, time has not stood still since Article 50 notice was first given and it is proposed to consider the course of the negotiations to date and how this relates to the free movement of services. A brief timeline of negotiations to date is that on 29 March 2017, Prime Minister May notified the European Council under Article 50 TEU of the UK's intention to withdraw from the EU. Negotiations began on 19 June.[73] An EU-UK Joint Report was published on 8 December 2017 setting out areas of agreement (in particular on citizens' rights, a financial settlement and the Northern Irish border). This was followed by various stages[74] before the European Commission and UK negotiators agreed on both a Withdrawal Agreement and an outline of the political declaration on the future EU-UK relationship on 14 November 2018.

Certain steps along the way were of particular importance as regards free movement of services, however, namely Theresa May's March 2018 Mansion House speech, the Chequers declaration and then UK Government White Paper of the following July.

Mansion House speech

Some idea of the UK Government's original vision for financial services in particular, was finally (belatedly) expressed by Theresa May in her Mansion House speech in March 2018, in which she called – albeit remaining somewhat vague as regards the details [75] – for a "comprehensive system of mutual recognition" including establishing in the financial services field in par-

---

73 Their commencement was delayed by the UK's general election in which May's Conservatives returned to power but only as a minority administration.

74 Namely, a February 2018 Commission draft Withdrawal Agreement, a March 2018 amended version (with highlighted areas of agreement and disagreement) and a June 2018 Joint Statement.

75 See for one attempt at deciphering what was intended, Tarrant *et al, op. cit.*, n. 28, 5.

ticular "the ability to access each other's markets, based on the UK and the EU maintaining the same regulatory outcomes over time".[76]

As Tarrant *et al* explain, in general terms "equivalence" and "mutual recognition" can both be described as processes by which goods or services produced in a first country (the "home country") are recognised as being compatible with the standards set in a second (the "host country"). However,

> "mutual recognition is in principle comprehensive: it allows all goods and services meeting the regulatory standards set in the home country to be sold in another without any further assessment beyond those applied in the home country. Equivalence, conversely, requires that the host country assess whether the regulatory standards of the home country meet the regulatory requirements of the host country, with respect to particular sets of home country products, before they are allowed to enter the host market. The application of mutual recognition in financial services within the EU provides for "passporting", the process by which a service provider authorised in one member state does not require authorisation in another Member State in order to offer services in the latter." [77]

There are clear problems with any vision of EU-UK relations in financial services being based essentially on mutual recognition and passporting, however. In the first place, it is anachronistic, a vision gradually being left behind even within the EU. Thus, since the 2008 financial crisis, the EU has distanced itself from mutual recognition in favour of a more centralised harmonisation approach.[78] Harmonisation provides more confidence that a foreign service providers will be effectively regulated, and that host country interests will be taken into account in the event of a crash, assuran-

---

76 See T. May, *Speech on our Future Economic Partnership with the European Union*, 2 March 2018, available at https://www.gov.uk/government/speeches/pm-speech-on-our-future-economic-partnership-with-the-european-union.

77 Tarrant *et al, op. cit.,* n. 28, 5-7.

78 As Stefaan de Rynck, adviser to EU Chief Brexit negotiator, Michel Barnier noted in a speech delivered in the London School of Economics, "the EU has moved away in the wake of the financial crisis from mutual recognition of national standards to a centralised approach with a single EU rule book and common enforcement structures and single supervisory structures." (Quoted in P. Wintour, 'EU Brexit Adviser Deals Blow to Theresa May's Free-Trade Proposal', The Guardian (6.03.2018.).

ces that are absent in a mutual recognition regime.[79] May's approach involved rejecting any such harmonisation however.[80]

Secondly, in looking for a comprehensive system of mutual recognition,
Mrs May looked for something which actually never existed within the
Single Market, where various excuses (*e.g.*, health protection, consumer
protection and environmental protection) have been accepted allowing
Member States to derogate from recognising each other's standards. Even
inside the Single Market, therefore, mutual recognition is non-absolute
and conditional, and expecting more than this for a State outside the Single Market was never realistic.[81]

Thirdly, and most seriously, May's idea of mutual recognition based on
binding commitments to EU-level regulatory standards failed to recognise
that the EU "is a rules-*plus* system. It is based on common rules but also
common institutions and common constitutional principles". As Weatherill has pointed out, in order to generate the trust needed to facilitate frictionless trade in the Single European Market, the "EU…built on rules
and…built on trust…is also built on institutional and constitutional
frameworks that underpin those rules and verify that trust is warranted…
what the Commission has lately taken to describing as the EU's 'ecosystem'".[82] In a speech thus demanding simultaneously the right to leave the
Single Market, its institutions and principles behind and yet the ability to
keep greater rights of access to it even than EU States possessed, May came "perilously close to asking for the obligations of Canada and the rights
of Norway".[83] Her speech failed to appreciate "the intensity of the obligati-

---

79 Tarrant *et al*, *op. cit.*, n. 28, 4-5.
80 The former Head of the UK's International Trade Department, Sir Martin Don-
    nelly had already pithily pointed out the difficulty here, asking "can we negotiate
    equal access in all those areas of services without agreeing to obey the same rules
    as everybody else? I'm afraid I think that's not a negotiation, that is something for
    a fairy godmother. It's not going to happen". (See D. Staunton, 'Liam Fox Says
    Post-Brexit Customs Union Would be 'Sellout'', Irish Times (27.02.2018)).
81 See S. Weatherill, '*What 'Mutual Recognition' Really Entails: Analysis of the Prime
    Minister's Mansion House Brexit Policy Speech*', EU Law Analysis, 4.03.2018), 2.
82 *Ibid.*, 3 and note by the same author the observation that "the EU is not simply a
    system of rules, it is a system too that involves the oversight of the Commission,
    the place of sector-specific agencies, the authority of the Court of Justice and the
    everyday involvement of national courts and administrative agencies. Rules – but
    also supervision, administrative cooperation, interpretation and enforcement too".
    (*Ibid.*, 2).
83 *Ibid.* While simultaneously expressly asserting that the UK would not accept the
    rights of Canada and the obligations of Norway – something, however, no-one
    had ever demanded.

ons that are required to generate trade integration on the truly deep and special scale that the EU's internal market has achieved." [84] These include the role of institutions like the Commission and the Court of Justice, and the role of principles like direct effect and supremacy. [85]

Chequers

Notwithstanding whatever light was shed on matters by the Mansion House speech, throughout most of the Article 50 notice period, negotiations to structure the arrangements of the UK's withdrawal from the UK and to identify a framework for its future relationship with the EU, [86] including in the area of services, were handicapped by the failure of a badly divided UK Government to identify what precisely its negotiating objectives were. This situation ended in July 2018, when after ten hours of intense discussion at the Prime Minister's official residence at Chequers, a declaration, and a more detailed communiqué, were issued, announcing the Cabinet had endorsed Prime Minister May's plan for a UK-EU free trade area and closely linked customs relationship with the EU. [87] The Chequers proposal envisaged a UK-EU free trade area with a common rule book for industrial goods and agricultural products. Remarkably, however – given the importance of services – it envisaged that a more restrictive regime would apply limiting mutual access by the UK and the EU to each other's services markets – the explicit aim being that by retaining regulatory flexibility for this sector, restricted access to EU markets would be compensated for because "potential trading opportunities outside the EU are the largest". [88] There was, however, a strong element of the UK trying to have its cake and eat it

---

84 *Ibid.*
85 May's Mansion House approach is open to a fourth criticism that it would also have undermined the Single Market by separating the four fundamental economic freedoms from one another. This is a topic returned to in the text below however, and so can be left aside for now.
86 See Article 50 TEU.
87 See T. McTague, 'Theresa May Wins Agreement for New UK Brexit Offer', Politico (6.07.2018).
88 See para. 6(b) of the Chequers statement (HM Government, 6 July 2018) and for a useful summary of the Chequers proposals, Anon., *'Key Points of Post-Brexit Trade Plan'*, RTÉ news website (9.07.2018). The irony involved here did not escape Rogers, who observed that "as for Westminster...we are deep in the Alice in Wonderland world of politics where the vast bulk of the peculiarly antiquated debate about our trading future has been focused on goods and tariffs issues." (Rogers,

with these plans [89] since although nominally giving up on its mutual recognition model in the financial services field, the UK Government effectively merely repackaged it, indicated it was going to seek "arrangements on financial services that preserve the mutual benefits of integrated markets"[90]

Chequers – a tortuously arrived-at attempt to create some kind of consensus within the UK's ruling Conservative Party – was effectively stillborn as a viable negotiation strategy, however, with Barnier reportedly regarding it as an attempt to achieve what David Cameron had sought but failed to obtain in his negotiations with the EU prior to the June 2016 Brexit referendum: effectively providing billions in savings for UK service providers by releasing them from the application of EU regulations.[91]

The July White Paper

Shortly after the Chequers declaration, the UK Government released a White Paper outlining in more detail its desired terms for the future UK-EU relationship.[92] Its terms regarding services did indeed seem improbably ambitious for a country explicitly renouncing participation in the Single

---

loc. cit., n. 12, 14.) See for expressions of concern from the world of business that services could become an afterthought in the Brexit negotiations, C. Kepple, 'Draft Text of Brexit Withdrawal Agreement to be Published 'Within Two Weeks' – Varadkar', Irish Independent (23.02.2018).

89 Perhaps not surprisingly, given the previous insistence by Government ministers that services must be part of any Brexit deal. (See S. Jack, 'Brexit: Business Secretary Greg Clark Warns on Services' BBC News (21.06.2018); and J Rankin, '*UK Cannot Have a Special Deal for the City, Says EU's Brexit Negotiator*', The Guardian (18.12.2017), in which David Davis, the then Brexit minister was reported to have asserted (with a remarkable degree of chutzpah) that he would not allow the Commission to 'cherry-pick some sectors' in negotiations or allow services to be separated from goods.

90 *Ibid.*, para. 6(b). See also Tarrant *et al*, *op. cit.*, n. 28, 2. The Prime Minister's apparent quest to attain EU-UK customs unity, regulatory alignment and the simultaneous delivery of a fully sovereign trade policy across both goods and services was sardonically described by former UK Permanent Representative to the EU, Sir Ivan Rogers as an aspiration to achieve an "an amazing three card trick" involving painfully obvious internal contradictions. (See Rogers, *loc. cit.*, n. 12, 15.).

91 See J. Barigazzi, '*Brussels: May's Brexit Plan Would Save UK Business Billions*', Politico (27.08.2018).

92 HM Government, *The Future Relationship Between the United Kingdom and the European Union* (Cm 9593, 12 July 2018).

Market.[93] Among such expressly declared objectives were an unprecedented level of EU-UK mutual recognition of professional qualifications for a non-EU Member State;[94] and a special regime for professional and business service providers (including legal, accounting and audit services).[95] In the field of financial services, although the UK's (in any case hopeless) quest for a passporting regime was explicitly abandoned (as something 'intrinsic' to a Single Market itself now being left behind), language suggesting mutual recognition nonetheless remained, with references to 'a coordinated approach leading to compatible regulation', a proposal for "a new economic and regulatory arrangement with the EU in financial services" and stress being put on an approach based on a "judgement of the equivalence of outcomes achieved by the respective regulatory and supervisory regimes". The White Paper argued that existing frameworks for equivalence "would need to be expanded, to reflect the fact that equivalence as it exists today is not sufficient in scope for the breadth of the interconnectedness of UK-EU financial services provision." [96] The Paper also proposed regulatory dialogue, with the UK and the EU being able to comment on each other's proposals at an early stage.[97]

The White Paper was coolly received by the EU. In the first place, the EU objected to any suggestion that the White Paper's proposal for institutional arrangements including arbitration to govern a future EU-UK relationship[98] might apply to equivalence decisions in the financial services area (and would give the UK more influence over such decisions outside the EU than it had inside it [99]) and any such suggestion was quickly retreated from.[100] Furthermore, EU Chief Brexit negotiator Michel Barnier also objected to the undermining of the Single Market involved in the White

---

93 And insisting on an end to free movement, although nonetheless seeking reciprocal arrangements allowing businesses to "move their talented people". (See Rubric 1.4.2) See for a prescient prediction that there would be no single market access for financial services outside the single market, however, W. Münchau, 'An Old-Fashioned Economy Heads Towards a Downfall', *Financial Times* (20.11.2017).
94 See Rubric 1.3.2 of the White Paper.
95 Rubric 1.3.3 of the White Paper.
96 See generally Rubric 1.3.4 of the White Paper.
97 See para. 69 of the White Paper. This was in addition to proposed extensive supervisory cooperation. (*Ibid.*).
98 See Chapter 4 of the White Paper.
99 See for further elucidation in this regard, Tarrant *et al*, *op. cit.*, n. 28, 7 and 9.
100 See A. Barker, 'Barnier Eases Opposition to May's Brexit Plan for City of London', *Financial Times* (30.07.2018).

Paper's broad aim of the UK keeping the free movement of goods but ridding itself of the obligation to allow free movement either of people or of services.[101]

Unsurprisingly, the future relationship later agreed upon in framework form by the UK and the EU looked nothing like what had been envisaged at Chequers or in the UK Government's July White Paper.

The Withdrawal Agreement and Associated Political Declaration

After lengthy negotiations, a 585-page *Agreement on the withdrawal of the United Kingdom of Great Britain and Northern Ireland from the European Union and the European Atomic Energy Community* (the so-called 'draft Withdrawal Agreement' was eventually published on 14 November 2018. Concerned (as its title might suggest) with the departure of the UK from the European Union, rather than the subsequent economic relationship between the UK and the EU, the Agreement nonetheless contained at least two articles of particular relevance to the free movement of services: Article 126 which provides that there has to be a transition period, starting on the date of entry into force of this Agreement and supposedly ending on 31 December 2020;[102] and Article 127, paragraph 1 of which provides that Union law – in other words, the whole *acquis* including the law on the free movement of services – is to be applicable to and in the United Kingdom during this transition period.[103]

In a vote on the withdrawal agreement held on 15 January 2019 the House of Commons rejected the Withdrawal Agreement by a margin of

---

101 See C. Cooper, 'Michel Barnier: UK Brexit Plan 'Undermines' Single Market', Politico, (2.08.2018). Weatherill's comment that much of what happened after the giving of Article 50 notice in March 2017 "involved a desire to retain the benefits of EU membership while shrugging off the status and responsibilities of membership" seems apposite here. (See Weatherill, *loc. cit.*, n. 83, 1.).

102 Under Article 132, this period is extendable for up to two years however.

103 However, the UK will no longer be represented in EU institutions or participate in the decision-making and decision-shaping process of the EU. See generally Part IV of the Agreement. A useful brief summary of the Agreement is to be found in the *Proposal for a Council Decision on the conclusion of the Agreement on the withdrawal of the United Kingdom of Great Britain and Northern Ireland from the European Union and the European Atomic Energy Community* (COM (2018) 834 final (Brussels, 5 December 2018)).

230 votes (432 to 202),[104] however, thereby risking that the Article 126 transition period (along with the rest of the Withdrawal Agreement) would never enter into force, and thus that no transition period would ever occur.[105]

A *Political declaration setting out the framework for the future relationship between the European Union and the United Kingdom*[106] accompanied the Withdrawal Agreement. Unlike the Withdrawal Agreement itself, this is legally non-binding. It set out some broad principles (although lacking important details), which would supposedly guide post-Brexit transition period negotiations, including on services. Hence it declared that

> "the Parties should conclude ambitious, comprehensive and balanced arrangements on trade in services and investment in services...respecting each Party's right to regulate. The Parties should aim to deliver a level of liberalisation in trade in services well beyond the Parties' World Trade Organisation (WTO) commitments and building on recent Union Free Trade Agreements (FTAs).
>
> In line with Article V of the General Agreement on Trade in Services, the Parties should aim at substantial sectoral coverage, covering all modes of supply and providing for the absence of substantially all discrimination in the covered sectors, with exceptions and limitations as appropriate. The arrangements should therefore cover sectors including professional and business services, telecommunications services, courier and postal services, distributions services, environmental services, financial services, transport services and other services of mutual interest." [107]

A number of further paragraphs followed in the declaration setting out aspirational objectives concerning market access and non-discrimination; approaches to regulation, regulatory cooperation and professional qualifications; financial services (with emphasis here, however, being put on the Parties' regulatory and decision-making autonomy, equivalence frameworks

---

104 See H. Stewart, 'May Suffers Heaviest Parliamentary Defeat of a British PM in the Democratic Era', The Guardian (16.01.2019).

105 This long-anticipated transition period gradually diminished in value the longer it took to be agreed, however, and then subsequently continued diminishing the longer it took to secure parliamentary approval as part of the Withdrawal Agreement. (See P. Jenkins, 'Banking on a Back-to-Back Brexit', Financial Times (11.03.2017)).

106 XT 21095/18 (Council of the European Union, Brussels, 22 November 2018.)

107 See Paras. 29-30 of the Political declaration.

and cooperation on regulatory and supervisory matters); the facilitation of electronic commerce; free movement of capital and payments related to transactions covered by any deal; intellectual property; public procurement, mobility and transport.[108]

Notwithstanding all the impressive-sounding language, however, the political declaration (its ambition inevitably curtailed because of Prime Minister May's rigid adherence to her anti-free movement red line) has been justifiably panned for its lack of ambition, and for having explicitly endorsed the *'tabula rasa'* route, meaning that "both sides will begin with their WTO commitments, and the EU side with its commitments in existing FTAs, and work up from there." [109] Rogers (a former UK Permanent Representative to the EU) has predicted

> "when we get into [post-Brexit talks], we will discover, at a granular level, just how bad it is to start from a *tabula rasa* third country baseline on services. And we shall then spend a lot of negotiating capital and use a lot of concessions on other issues – and the free movement of people question is, as we have seen, intimately linked to services provision – to try and lever up our level of market access into what used to be our home market to something nearer Single Market levels." [110]

The Political declaration manifested no intent to adjust the EU's existing equivalence regime. As is clear from the text above, what the UK had been seeking had evolved from explicitly seeking mutual recognition to accepting equivalence – but in "a bespoke form...that would include significant elements of a mutual recognition regime".[111] What is on offer is less appealing, however, and it seems more unlikely than ever that UK financial service providers outside the Single Market will ever gain access to EU mar-

---

108 See paras. 31-65 of the Political declaration. See also H. McGrath, 'FS Free Movement of Capital under Brexit Deal', FS Tech (15.11.2018).

109 Rogers, *loc. cit.*, n. 12, 13, where he points out that "the Political declaration cites Article V of the GATS (General Agreement on Trade in Services) which just sets out the basic requirements for two WTO members trading solely on WTO terms which seek to embark on Free Trade Agreement negotiations."

110 *Ibid.*, 15. A similarly downbeat assessment of the deal is given in J. Johnson, 'Politicians Must Stand up for the City after EU exit' Financial Times (21.02.2019), which was written by a former Minister for Transport in Theresa May's government.

111 Tarrant *et al*, *op. cit.*, n. 28, 2. Judging by subsequent economic analysis published by the UK Government, such an adjustment nonetheless still appears to be an objective of the UK Government in future trade negotiations, however. (*Ibid.*).

kets in post-Brexit negotiations on the basis of any mutual recognition regime.[112] It is not for nothing that the chief executive of UK Finance (the trade body for the UK banking industry) has described the Political declaration as being "quite frankly...not worth the paper it is written on." [113]

Ground Zero: the Looming Danger of a No Deal Scenario

Whatever the flaws of the Political declaration, as the date of expiry of the UK's Article 50 notice in March 2019 has approached without parliamentary approval at Westminster of the negotiated deal, the far less appealing prospect of a no-deal Brexit has reared its frightening head to an ever-growing extent.[114] Already, in November 2018, the Commission had launched a Contingency Action Plan announcing that there would be unilateral measures to limit damage and mitigate the most severe consequences of a no-deal Brexit. A month later (and in line with the December European Council conclusions), the Commission adopted all legislative proposals and delegated acts that had been announced in the Contingency plan. The idea is that contingency measures will not mitigate the overall impact of a 'no-deal' scenario or in any way compensate for the lack of stakeholder preparedness or replicate the benefits of EU membership or the terms of any transition period.[115] Moreover, they will be limited to specific areas where it is absolutely necessary to protect the vital interests of the EU (and where preparedness measures alone are insufficient); will be temporary in nature; will be unilaterally adopted by the EU in pursuit of its own interests and be revocable at any time.[116]

---

112 *Ibid.* It was concerns about a potential lack of availability of passporting rights (*i.e.*, mutual recognition) which led Britain's second largest insurer Aviva to decide to move a reputed £9 billion worth of assets to Ireland in February 2019. (See S. Khan, 'Brexit: Aviva to move £9bn worth of assets to Ireland as it prepares for no-deal outcome', The Independent (20.02.2019).)

113 See S. Jones, 'No-deal Brexit Could Return UK to 1930s, Says Senior Banking Figure', Financial Times (14.01.2019).

114 And thus, as Grey has put it, that "a project cloaked in the sacred cloth of the 'will of the people' [was] going to end up being the will of almost no one." See, C. Grey, 'Britain in a Tailspin', The Brexit Blog (8.02.2019).

115 *I.e.*, as provided in the draft Withdrawal Agreement.

116 See European Commission, *Preparing for the Withdrawal of the United Kingdom from the European Union on 30 March 2019: Implementing the Commission's Contingency Action Plan* (COM (2018) 890 final, Brussels, 19 December 2018), 2-3; European Commission, *"European Commission Implements 'No-Deal' Contingency*

Six sector-specific contingency measures were proposed or adopted by the Commission in the services field.[117]

In the financial services field, where the imposition of a uniformly harsh regime in the event of a no-deal Brexit would risk hurting the EU 27's financial sector more than the UK,[118] the Commission adopted a temporary equivalence decision for twelve months to avoid disruption in the central clearing of derivatives (by allowing the European Securities and Market Authority to recognise temporarily central counterparties established in the UK); a temporary equivalence decision for 24 months to avoid disruption in services provided by UK central securities depositories (allowing them to continue providing notary and central maintenance services to operators in the EU); and two delegated regulations facilitating novation, for a fixed period, of certain over-the-counter derivatives contracts with a counterparty established in the UK (allowing the transfer of such contracts to an EU 27 counterparty while maintaining their exempted status under the European Market Infrastructures Regulation).[119]

In the field of air transport, a no deal Brexit would threaten the continuation of basic connectivity.[120] The Commission thus adopted a draft regulation aimed at ensuring, for twelve months, the provision of 'point-to-point' (*i.e.*, UK to EU 27 and vice versa) air services,[121] as well as a draft

---

Action Plan in Specific Sectors" (Press Release, Brussels, 19 December 2018) and J. Quonn, 'European Commission Unveils Plans in the Event of a No-Deal Brexit', Newstalk.com News (2.10.2019).

117 Of a total of fourteen measures.

118 See in this regard the prescient article by J. Ford, 'Why a Hard Brexit for Financial Services is Unlikely', Financial Times (10.12.2017). Regulators and industry participants could forestall difficulties in certain financial service areas without the need for the intervention of legislation. See regarding the asset management industry, C. Flood, 'European Financial Regulators Move to Mitigate Brexit Threat', Financial Times (10.12.2017).

119 See regarding earlier concerns expressed in this field, C. Binham, 'BoE Calls for Brexit Withdrawal Bill to Address Cross-Border Financial Contracts', Financial Times (1.11.2017).

120 See further in this regard the European Commission Memorandum, *Questions and Answers: the Consequences of the United Kingdom Leaving the European Union Without a Ratified Withdrawal Agreement (No Deal Brexit)* (Memo/16/, Brussels, 19 December 2018), 4.

121 Subject to the UK conferring equivalent rights on EU carriers and ensuring conditions of fair competition. If reciprocity is not forthcoming, the draft measure will enable the Commission to adopt appropriate measures *e.g.*, adjusting the allowable capacity available to UK carriers, or requiring Member States to adapt, refuse, suspend or revoke the operating authorisations of UK air carriers. (*Ibid.*, 5.)

regulation on aviation safety extending the validity of certain existing licences (thereby covering the basic needs of Member State economies and mitigating to some extent the impact of withdrawal without guaranteeing the continuation of all air transport services under their present terms).[122] Both draft measures were aimed at avoiding the abrupt interruption of air traffic between the EU and the UK as of the date of Brexit.

In the field of road haulage, the Commission adopted a draft regulation [123] allowing temporarily for 9 months UK-licensed road haulage operators to carry goods between the UK and the EU 27 and thereby avoiding the severe restriction of road haulage between the EU and the UK and the introduction of an international system of limited quotas.[124]

UK unpreparedness rendered unavoidable the extension of the original deadline for Brexit happening beyond the appointed date of 29 March 2019. In late March, a (shorter-than-requested) unconditional delay until 12 April was thus acceded to by the European Council. [125] Subsequently, in April 2019 EU leaders agreed to permit a further, longer – and purportedly final – maximum six-month postponement until 31 October of this year.[126] Whether this indeed proves the final postponement remains to be seen. Further uncertainty – and an increased prospect of a no-deal Brexit - was injected into the situation by the announcement in late May by Theresa May, following the disastrous performance of her party in the local and European elections, that she would resign as leader of the Conservative Party on June 7 and would remain on as caretaker prime minister only until her successor was elected.[127]

---

122 *Ibid.*
123 To operate subject to the UK conferring the equivalent rights on Union road haulage operators and subject to conditions ensuring fair competition.
124 See generally in relation to all six measures European Commission, *Preparing for the Withdrawal of the United Kingdom from the European Union on 30 March 2019: Implementing the Commission's Contingency Action Plan* (COM (2018) 890 final, Brussels, 19 December 2018) 5-7.
125 See J. Kirby, 'Mark your calendars: the new Brexit deadline is April 12', Vox (22.03.2019.) See earlier G. Parker, J. Pickard and J. Blitz, 'May opens way for 'short' Brexit delay to appease pro-EU Tories', Financial Times (27.02.2019.) See for an earlier discussion of the possibility of a delay *e.g.*, A. Gostyńka-Jakubowska, *Can the UK Extend the Brexit Deadline?* (Centre for European Reform, February 2019), 4.
126 See Anon., 'EU leaders agree to six-month Brexit delay', Financial Times (11.04.2019.).
127 (See G. Parker, J. Pickard and S. Payne,'Theresa May resigns after Brexit failure' Financial Times (24.05.2019).

Endnote?

To date, the process of negotiating Brexit and of commencing the process of teasing out its potential implications for the free movement of services has demonstrated three important truths.

First, due to the imbalance of power between the departing State and the EU, exit 'negotiations' (rather like accession negotiations) are more accurately characterised as involving the effective imposition of a new trading relationship by the EU.[128]

Secondly, a failure by a departing State to produce its own proposals in a timely fashion will inevitably lead, to the EU setting the agenda.[129] The successful deployment of Article 50 requires an exiting country to be clear-sighted and united both about its objectives and the losses it is prepared to accept in order to attain them.[130] As has been seen, however, the UK's Chequers plan emerged only in July 2018. The failure of the UK Government to indicate any earlier in Brexit negotiations the nature of the trading relationship it wanted with the EU was scarcely surprising: the pro-Brexit side had shrewdly declined to define its preferred relationship prior to the June 2016 referendum, thus carrying the maximum number of voters with it. This approach carried with it, however, the inevitable handicap that once the referendum was won, no consensus existed on the direction the country should take: including as regards trade in services, making it well nigh impossible for the UK to set the agenda in any discussions on the future trading relationship.[131]

---

128   As Grant has pointed out,

> "leaving the EU is like joining it. Countries wanting to join engage in 'accession negotiations', but that is a misnomer. The accession process in fact involves the EU imposing its terms on the country concerned. If it does not like those terms it does not have to join. The details can be debated but not the basic deal that the EU offers. Every country that has joined the EU has put up with this unequal 'negotiation' in order to get into the club. Leaving the EU is a similar process...the EU decides what kind of deal will work. Then the exiting country has to accept those terms – if it wants a deal, and it will, since leaving without one would be hugely damaging to its economy."

(C. Grant, *The Lessons of Brexit* (Centre for European Reform, London, 2019) 3 at 4.).

129   *Ibid.*, 5.
130   Rogers, *loc. cit.*, n. 12, 27.
131   *Ibid.*, 8.

Thirdly, the need to safeguard the Union and the Single Market will always rank ahead of immediate trade considerations as far as the EU is concerned. In the Brexit negotiations, this factor, allied to an unwillingness to establishing a risky precedent for other States both inside and outside the EU – has led to an insistence by the EU 27 on the indivisibility of the four freedoms in the Brexit negotiations, notwithstanding UK confidence that its importance as a trading partner would inevitably lead to its being accorded a more favourable approach than had heretofore been made available in trade negotiations.[132] Instead, the EU's adherence to its usual approach effectively restricted the UK to a choice between a Norway-style regime – completely in the Single Market – or a Canada-style free trade agreement, completely outside it.[133]

As regards the future, the UK now stands in great danger of being about to discover by experience – the bitterest way of learning [134] two painful lessons. First, that "it is fatuous to suggest that when you immediately substantially worsen your terms of trade in services with massively your largest market...instant trade deals with other fast-growing regions will, on services, substitute for the loss" (for in reality, the losses incurred will be sizeable and certain, the potential gains merely speculative).[135] Secondly, and for an indefinite period stretching far into the future, the UK may find itself ruefully reflecting on the wisdom of the advice of its own former Permanent Representative to the European Union that "deeper liberalisation,

---

132 See T. Connelly, 'Brexit: Hell, High Water and the Return of Chequers', RTE News (9.02.2019), 15.

133 See W. Münchau, 'An Old-Fashioned Economy Heads Towards a Downfall', Financial Times (20.11.2017); Grant, *op. cit.*, n.138, 7-8.

134 To the fifth-sixth century BC Chinese philosopher and teacher, Confucius, is attributed the saying "by three methods we may learn wisdom: first, by reflection, which is the noblest; secondly by imitation, which is the easiest; and third by experience, which is the bitterest."

135 Rogers, *loc. cit.*, n. 12, 17-18. As another former eminent civil servant Sir Martin Donnelly characterised such an approach,

"you're giving up a three-course meal, the depth and intensity of our trade relationship across the European Union and partners now, for the promise of a packet of crisps in the future, if we manage to do trade deals in the future outside the EU which aren't going to compensate for what we're giving up."

(See J. Elgot, 'Leaving Single Market 'Like Swapping a Meal for a Packet of Crisps', Warns Ex-Trade Chief', The Guardian (27.2.2018)).

notably on services... is much tougher to achieve than on tariffs and is always easier within a bloc than with markets outside it".[136]

---

136 Emphasis added. Cf. the comments of the Chair of the Commons Treasury Committee reported in P. Jenkins and O. Ralph, 'Morgan Backs 'Passporting' Pacts for City Beyond Europe', Financial Times (25.01.2019).

Brexit and Financial Regulation

*Wolf-Georg Ringe**

Abstract

Among participants in the global financial market, Brexit is commonly painted as an almost apocalypse-like scenario. The threat of a British exit from the European Union (EU) arguably involves a significant disruption to financial integration in Europe, which will threaten the pre-eminence of London as a global financial centre, and impose significant costs on all market participants.

This paper takes a different position on the significance of Brexit for the European financial market. It argues that, in reality, the impact of Brexit for financial services will be minuscule, if not irrelevant. Such optimism is grounded in the economic stakes for both sides, the United Kingdom (UK) and the remaining EU countries (EU 27), in retaining the benefits of access to the European Single Market for financial services. Given the joint economic interests, a likely outcome of the Brexit negotiations will be a solution that formally satisfies the 2016 referendum result, but in substance keeps Britain closely involved in the EU financial market. Alternatively, one should expect an agreement on the basis of regulatory equivalence. If an agreement is not achieved, private solutions by market actors are to be expected.

The paper borrows from past examples in EU financial market integration that saw ingenious creativity at work in facilitating a desired outcome

---

* Professor of Law and Director of the Institute of Law & Economics, University of Hamburg; Visiting Professor, Faculty of Law, University of Oxford. This chapter is an updated and revised version of the article 'The Irrelevance of Brexit for the European Financial Market', which was originally published in European Business Organization Law Review 19 (2018), 1. I thank participants at the NCMF meeting in Helsinki, a lunch seminar at the Danish National Bank, Copenhagen, a Law & Finance conference on the future of European capital markets, hosted by Oxford, Columbia and ECGI, a routable discussion on 'Negotiating Brexit' at the University of Oxford, a conference on 'Financial Regulation and the Rule of Law' at Wharton, University of Pennsylvania, and the symposium at ZEW Mannheim for very helpful comments on earlier versions of this paper.

within the existing convoluted legal framework. These past experiences lead to the prediction of a similar approach being used for accommodating Brexit. The broader point is then that the EU financial services framework repeatedly sees a victory of politics or economics over the law—that is, formal legal problems or structures are brushed aside when political necessities or economic exigencies so require.

1. Introduction

There is no doubt that the result of the 2016 referendum in favour of the UK to leave the European Union is of epochal significance. For the first time in its history, one of the EU's Member States deliberately decided to end its membership. After 60 years of European integration, is this now the first step towards the bloc's disintegration?

A long period of uncertainty followed the referendum, during which it was unclear which direction the future EU/UK relationship would develop. This situation was somewhat mitigated by the July 2018 White Paper and Chequers Plan, where the UK Government for this first time made some forays into a concrete negotiation strategy.[1] Setting out the UK ambitions, the White Paper proposed a two-part strategy: first, to negotiate a de facto continuation of the Single Market for goods – including a common free trade area, a common rulebook and a commitment to ongoing harmonisation with EU rules on goods. Secondly, however, as regard services, and in particular financial services, the government did not propose to seek continued access to the Single Market and pursued a more nuanced approach, relying on an enhanced version of the 'equivalence' principle[2] and abandoning the 'passporting' approach[3].

The protracted negotiations during 2019 have, so far, not brought any clarity as to the outcome of the negotiations. Whether the EU will agree to this bifurcation is as yet unclear, and time is pressing. If the parties reach no agreement on their future relationship, the UK will cease to be an EU Member State by the end of October 2019. Immediately after publication,

---

1 UK Government, *The Future Relationship between the United Kingdom and the European Union – Presented to Parliament by the Prime Minister by Command of Her Majesty* (Cm 9593, July 2018).
2 On this further below section 5.2.
3 On this further below section 2.1.

EU chief negotiator Michel Barnier rejected the White Paper approach,[4] and the outcome of the negotiation process is open yet again. Bank of England Governor Mark Carney recently said that there was an 'uncomfortably high' risk of the UK leaving the EU without any deal at all.[5] All of this has triggered the alarm bells in the City of London, as the priced access to the EU Single Market is seriously under threat.

In political terms, the current debate is polarised between a 'hard' type of a Brexit versus a 'softer' version of the same.[6] Whereas the exact content of these two terms is not entirely clear, proponents of a soft Brexit seem to favour some form of continued attachment to the Single Market, whereas hard Brexiteers call for a more radical end to any EU involvement altogether. A continued membership in the European Economic Area (the 'Norway' option) or a comprehensive free trade agreement ('Canada option') are variants of a soft Brexit, whereas 'hard' Brexit would mean a more radical detachment from the EU framework (styled as the 'New York' or 'Singapore' options). The UK Government currently appears to be poised to steer into the 'hard' Brexit direction for services, and a 'soft' Brexit for goods.[7]

Whatever the outcome, the common element of all of these perspectives is that Brexit means a threat to the UK membership in the Single Market. It is precisely this threat which prompts serious critique from many financial market participants. Since the UK economy is so dependent on the financial sector, and since the City of London is the largest financial centre in Europe, a British exit from the European Union arguably involves a significant disruption to financial integration in Europe, may affect financi-

---

4 Herszenhorn/de la Baume, 'Barnier dismantles UK's Brexit white paper', Politico, https://www.politico.eu/article/michel-barnier-brexit-white-paper-analysis/, 20.07.2018, all sources last accessed on 13.12.2018.

5 G. Jackson/Pooley, 'BoE's Mark Carney sees 'uncomfortably high' risk of no-deal Brexit', FT.com, https://www.ft.com/content/8c43735e-96f1-11e8-b747-fb1e803ee64 e (03.08.2018).

6 For a comprehensive overview and discussion of the various options, see Armour, 'Brexit to the European Economic Area: What would it mean?' Oxford Business Law Blog, https://www.law.ox.ac.uk/business-law-blog/blog/2016/07/brexit-eur opean-economic-area-what-would-it-mean (19.07.2016).

7 Watts, 'Theresa May indicates "hard Brexit" and dismisses free movement deal to keep single market access', The Telegraph, http://www.independent.co.uk/news/uk/ politics/theresa-may-hard-brexit-soft-article-free-movement-deal-single-market-acces s-a7341886.html (02.10.2016).

al stability across the continent, and threatens to jeopardise the pre-eminence of London as a global financial centre.[8]

It is at exactly this point that this paper takes a different position on the significance of Brexit. This paper argues that, in reality, the impact of Brexit for financial services will be minuscule, if not irrelevant. Such optimism is grounded in the economic stakes for both sides, the UK and the EU 27, in retaining the joint benefits of the EU Single Market for financial services. Given the joint economic interests, a likely outcome of negotiations will be a solution that formally satisfies the letter of the 2016 referendum result by delivering a formal 'Brexit', but in substance keeps Britain closely involved in the EU financial market. If such an agreement cannot be achieved, a second-best solution may be to ensure that City firms can continue operating in the EU on the basis of a 'third-country' passport, relying on regulatory equivalence. Finally, if the negotiating parties fail to reach consensus on even that aspect, private solutions are to be expected: financial services firms will respond to the Brexit by reorganising themselves so that they can enjoy future Single Market access.

The paper borrows from past examples in EU financial market integration that saw ingenious creativity at work in facilitating a desired outcome within the existing complex legal framework. The broader point is then that the EU financial services framework has repeatedly witnessed a victory of politics or economics over the law—that is, formal legal problems or structures are brushed aside when political necessities or economic exigencies so require.

The remainder of this paper is organised as follows. Section 2 describes the worst-case scenario of a complete end to Single Market access and explains why many commentators in the present discourse fear that this scenario could materialise. In contrast, Section 3 turns to the economic incentives of both the negotiating parties and explains how a continued access to the Single Market would be beneficial to both sides. Section 4 considers the historical development of EU financial integration and shows how it has repeatedly been possible to implement a desired outcome into the existing legal framework. This development suggests that economic imperatives will eventually trump legal formalities, and the same should be expec-

---

8 House of Lords European Union Committee, *Brexit: the future of financial regulation and supervision* (11th Report of Session 2017–19), (HL Paper 66); Noonan/ Arnold, 'Banks braced for 'hundreds of millions' in Brexit costs', Financial Times (15.05.2017), 15.

ted of Brexit. Sections 5 and 6 conclude by exploring how a concrete solution may look like.

2. The Doom Scenario

2.1 No More Passporting Post Brexit

As explained above, the greatest concern for the City of London is to lose access to the Single Market. In particular, the most cherished element of it is the principle of 'passporting' for providers of financial services, which allows them to offer their products across the entire market.[9]

This principle is enshrined in the rules on free movement, as specified in the EU Treaties. Depending on the context, the free movement of capital will be the most significant, although the freedoms of establishment and services may also be relevant. To illustrate, the concept of free movement of capital, governed by Articles 56-65 of the Treaty on the Functioning of the European Union (TFEU), holds that all restrictions on the movement of capital between EU Member States and third countries are prohibited. Put differently, EU Member States must accept capital movements from each other without imposing any restrictions on them. This requirement has long been understood as going beyond a pure discrimination-based approach to capture any potential impediments that are found to render market access more difficult.[10]

Common to all four EU freedoms—goods, services, persons and capital—is the idea of 'home State control', according to which a product, service, or investment may be freely traded or operated across the EU once it has been lawfully admitted in one Member State. The country of origin is thus responsible for admitting a certain product, entity or service to the market, and other Member States have to trust that decision and may not impose any additional requirements themselves.

This concept has found further support and has been reinforced by a number of pieces of EU secondary legislation concerning the financial market. All major relevant laws in this field now allow passporting in the

---

9 Finch, 'Banks' Brexit Future Hinges on Passporting Rights', Bloomberg, http://ww w.bloomberg.com/news/articles/2016-10-19/u-k-banks-brexit-hopes-boil-down-to-o ne-word-quicktake-q-a (20.10.2016).

10 See, for example, Case C-98/01, 13.05.2003, *Commission v UK*, ECR I-4641 (the *BAA* case) concerning a rule which limited the acquisition levels in shares. This was not discriminatory, but was held to deter foreign investment.

sense that once a provider of financial services has been authorised in one country, no further scrutiny elsewhere is permitted. UK authorised financial institutions can thus carry out their activities across the EU without setting up a separate entity in the destination market and/or obtaining authorisation in each EU Member State. This allows the financial services industry to operate with a branch structure across Europe, or even to offer cross-border services directly to clients. Once a financial product has been authorised by one Member State, it can be marketed freely across the Union. Examples are the well-known cornerstones of the EU financial market framework known as the Markets in Financial Instruments framework (MiFID/MiFIR),[11] the Capital Requirements Directive IV (CRD IV),[12] the Payment Services Directive II (PSD II),[13] the Second E-Money Directive (2EMD),[14] the Insurance Distribution Directive (IDD),[15] the UCITS frame-

---

11 Directive 2014/65/EU of the European Parliament and of the Council of 15 May 2014 on markets in financial instruments and amending Directive 2002/92/EC and Directive 2011/61/EU (MiFID II), [2014] OJ L173/349; Regulation (EU) No. 600/2014 of the European Parliament and of the Council of 15 May 2014 on markets in financial instruments and amending Regulation (EU) No. 648/2012 (MiFIR), [2014] OJ L173/84. Both instruments apply from 3 January 2018.

12 Directive 2013/36/EU of the European Parliament and of the Council of 26 June 2013 on access to the activity of credit institutions and the prudential supervision of credit institutions and investment firms, amending Directive 2002/87/EC and repealing Directives 2006/48/EC and 2006/49/EC (CRD IV), [2013] OJ L176/338.

13 Directive (EU) 2015/2366 of the European Parliament and of the Council of 25 November 2015 on payment services in the internal market, amending Directives 2002/65/EC, 2009/110/EC and 2013/36/EU and Regulation (EU) No. 1093/2010, and repealing Directive 2007/64/EC (PSD II), [2015] OJ L337/35, applicable from 13 January 2018.

14 Directive 2009/110/EC of the European Parliament and of the Council of 16 September 2009 on the taking up, pursuit and prudential supervision of the business of electronic money institutions amending Directives 2005/60/EC and 2006/48/EC and repealing Directive 2000/46/EC (2EMD), [2009] OJ L267/7.

15 Directive (EU) 2016/97 of the European Parliament and of the Council of 20 January 2016 on insurance distribution (recast) (IDD), [2016] OJ L26/19, applicable from 23 February 2018.

work for funds,[16] and the Alternative Investment Fund Managers Directive (AIFMD).[17]

The passport concept has been very attractive for financial institutions based in London, as it contributes to substantial cost savings for pan-European groups. In fact, the regime has even allowed third-country operators, for example, from the United States or from Japan, to set up a single European subsidiary in London and serve the entire EU from there. For example, it is estimated that the top five US investment banks (Goldman Sachs, JP Morgan, Citigroup, Morgan Stanley, and Bank of America Merrill Lynch) locate about 90% of their European operations in the City.[18]

Against this backdrop, it is understandable that the loss of passporting rights is one of the greatest worries of UK-based financial institutions and of third-country firms which operate through London.[19] A formal exit from the EU would bring the application of the passporting framework to an end, and UK-based institutions would have to encounter much higher costs of operation—for example, by setting up another subsidiary within the remaining EU 27.[20]

---

16 Directive 2009/65/EC of the European Parliament and of the Council of 13 July 2009 on the coordination of laws, regulations and administrative provisions relating to undertakings for collective investment in transferable securities (UCITS) (recast), [2009] OJ L302/32, as amended by Directive 2014/91/EU of the European Parliament and of the Council of 23 July 2014 amending Directive 2009/65/EC on the coordination of laws, regulations and administrative provisions relating to undertakings for collective investment in transferable securities (UCITS) as regards depositary functions, remuneration policies and sanctions, [2014] OJ L257/186.

17 Directive 2011/61/EU of the European Parliament and of the Council of 8 June 2011 on Alternative Investment Fund Managers and amending Directives 2003/41/EC and 2009/65/EC and Regulations (EC) No. 1060/2009 and (EU) No. 1095/2010 (AIFMD), [2011] OJ L174/1.

18 Schoenmaker, 'Lost passports: a guide to the Brexit fallout for the City of London', Bruegel, http://bruegel.org/2016/06/lost-passports-a-guide-to-the-brexit-fallout-for-t he-city-of-london/ (30.06.2016).

19 See DLA Piper Client Alert, 'No more passporting post-Brexit', Financial Services Regulation Alert, https://www.dlapiper.com/en/uk/insights/publications/2016/07/ no-more-passporting-post-brexit/ (27.07.2016).

20 See below section 5.3.

2.2 No alternative—EEA Membership or Bespoke Arrangement

By some accounts, the 'Norway model', or some variant of it, has been put forward as an alternative and viable destination for post-Brexit Britain.[21] As a member of the European Economic Area (EEA), Norway (along with Iceland and Liechtenstein) enjoys full access to the EU Single Market. At the same time, however, Norway is not part of the political structure of the EU, an arrangement which should also appear attractive to the UK. So, the country does not subscribe to justice and home affairs, it is not under the obligation to join the single currency and is not part of the common agricultural nor fishing policy. Norway is also free to conclude its own bilateral trade deals with third countries. It has control of its fisheries too.

Although all EU Member States presently are members of the EEA, the EEA agreement is formally separate from the EU Treaties. Much of the legal detail is unclear, but it appears that the UK would have to also withdraw from the EEA agreement if it wanted to undo Single Market access entirely.[22] An attempt to prevent the Government from doing so was unsuccessful in the High Court of England and Wales.[23]

Despite all of this, the Norway option does not seem to be attractive to the large majority of the UK public nor its policy-makers.[24] Most importantly, membership of the EEA and the Single Market means that EEA countries also need to comply with EU law concerning the Single Market. It is for this reason that Norway implements most EU laws domestically. Yet as a non-EU member it has no influence on shaping those same laws, or the evolution of the Single Market. Norway has no representation in the European Commission, no European parliamentarians, no seat at the Eu-

---

21 Green, 'Brexit: can and should the UK remain in the EEA?', FT Online, https://www.ft.com/content/16b50be8-161c-38d3-83b8-14b04faa9580 (02.08.2017). For an analysis of the various options, see European Parliament (Economic and Monetary Affairs), *Potential concepts for the future EU-UK relationship in financial services—Study for the ECON Committee* (January 2017).

22 Schroeter/Nemeczek, 'The (uncertain) impact of Brexit on the United Kingdom's membership in the European Economic Area' (2016) 27 European Business Law Review 921; Green, (fn. 21).

23 Croft, 'High Court throws out second legal challenge to UK's exit', Financial Times (04.02.2017), 3.

24 See Oliver/Milne, 'Norway's offshore drilling fight with EU a cautionary tale for UK', FT Online, https://www.ft.com/content/9ed984b0-bab0-11e5-b151-8e15c9a029fb (18.01.2016); Pisary-Ferry/others, 'Europe after Brexit: A proposal for a continental partnership', Bruegel, http://bruegel.org/2016/08/europe-after-brexit-a-proposal-for-a-continental-partnership/ (25.08.2016).

ropean Council table of ministers. Many Norwegian officials have long deplored their position. Erna Solberg, Norway's Prime Minister, even actively discouraged the UK from copying her country's position by saying that 'You will hate it.'[25] To the UK public, such an arrangement would indeed be hard to sell—and it would be difficult to reconcile with the Leave Campaign's referendum slogan of 'taking back control.'

Apart from this principal issue, there are several other problems with the Norway model. For example, Norway is still obliged to contribute to the EU budget. The EEA member contributions are not as high as the contributions by full EU members, but the UK could still expect to face a substantial sum to pay every year.[26]

Finally, membership of the EEA brings the benefits of the Single Market, but also means subscribing to free movement of persons.[27] Arguably, one of the main motivating factors behind the UK referendum outcome was the objective of controlling immigration again. This goal would not be fully under the control of the UK as an EEA member. There is, admittedly, an emergency brake under the EEA agreement on immigration when 'serious economic, societal or environmental difficulties' arise.[28] But this safeguard provision is only of temporary character and has never been tested. Indeed, Norway currently has higher levels of immigration from the EU per head than the UK.

Alongside these disadvantages with EEA membership, perhaps the most surprising obstacle is that Norway appears critical of accepting a potential UK membership in the European Free Trade Agreement (EFTA).[29] The fear is that integrating a much larger new member to the small club would jeopardise the power balance within EFTA.[30] Another concern is that EFTA's

---

25 Gurzu, 'Norway to Britain: Don't leave, you'll hate it', Politico, http://www.politic
    o.eu/article/eu-referendum-look-before-you-leap-norways-pm-tells-brexiteers/
    (15.06.2016).
26 Norway currently contributes more than €800m a year to the EU budget. See Norway Mission to the EU, 'Financial contributions', https://www.norway.no/en/missi
    ons/eu/areas-of-cooperation/financial-contribution/.
27 EEA Agreement, Art. 28.
28 EEA Agreement, Art. 112.
29 Singing EFTA would be vital, as only EU or EFTA members may be part of EEA.
30 Ask, 'Norge er skeptisk til å slippe britene inn i EFTA', Aftenposten, http://www.af
    tenposten.no/verden/Norge-er-skeptisk-til-a-slippe-britene-inn-i-EFTA-601643b.ht
    ml (09.08.2016); Wintour, 'Norway may block UK return to European Free Trade
    Association', The Guardian, https://www.theguardian.com/world/2016/aug/09/nor
    way-may-block-uk-return-to-european-free-trade-association (09.08.2016). But see

trade agreements with many countries worldwide might have to be renegotiated and future trade deals would become more complex.[31]

In sum, EEA membership for the UK looks like a rather unlikely if not unattractive option. If not the EEA, other commentators argue, the UK could seek its own, tailor-made agreement with the EU. The difficulty with this appears to be the starkly contrasting standpoints that both sides currently take. The media reports that the UK Government would prefer a solution whereby free movement of services and capital could be maintained, while the free movement of workers would come to an end—in line with the demand to regain control over immigration. The EU, by contrast, has made it abundantly clear that the four freedoms only come as a package—and that cherry picking will not be permissible.[32] EU officials seem so determined about this that agreement currently does not appear possible.

2.3 Anticipatory Action and Fait Accompli

By some accounts, both camps are already moving to create facts—both the UK and the EU have over the past several months implemented policies or announced proposals to present the other side with a *fait accompli* that promises advantages or benefits for the respective side.

For example, the EU in November 2016 proposed new rules on bank capital, revising the CRD IV package.[33] One of the elements proposed is the controversial requirement for a non-EU bank with two or more affiliates within the EU to establish an 'intermediate parent undertaking', in effect a holding company that would be subject to EU capital require-

---

Ruparel, 'Norway has little to lose from having the UK in EFTA', Open Europe Blog, http://openeurope.org.uk/today/blog/norway-has-little-to-lose-from-having-the-uk-in-efta/ (10.08.2016).

31 Wintour *ibid.*

32 See, for example, the Statement after an Informal meeting of the Heads of State or Government of 27 Member States, as well as the Presidents of the European Council and the European Commission at Brussels, http://www.consilium.europa.eu/press-releases-pdf/2016/12/47244652443_en.pdf (15.12.2016): 'We reiterate that any agreement will have to be based on a balance of rights and obligations, and that access to the Single Market requires acceptance of all four freedoms'.

33 European Commission, Proposal for a Directive of the European Parliament and of the Council amending Directive 2013/36/EU as regards exempted entities, financial holding companies, mixed financial holding companies, remuneration, supervisory measures and powers and capital conservation measures, COM(2016) 854 final (23 November 2016).

ments.[34] Simultaneously, the EU implementation of the G20 Total Loss-Absorbing Capacity (TLAC) standard to facilitate bail-in would be extended to subsidiaries of non-EU banks that are globally systemic or those with total assets of more than €30bn.

While these proposals have primarily been drafted as a retaliation to the US rules on 'intermediate holding companies' for foreign banks, they could potentially affect the UK once it is no longer part of the EU.[35] Such rules would add costs and complexity to UK-based banks by forcing them to establish a separate capitalised subsidiary in the EU after the country leaves. Moreover, the need for a separately capitalised holding company in the EU 27 would make London less attractive as the headquarter for European operations of third-country banks. It is no surprise that the UK Government is heavily reluctant to support the proposal.[36]

As part of a separate exercise, the EU Commission is currently re-evaluating the process of granting Single Market access to non-EU financial institutions under the so-called 'third-country passport'.[37] The outcome of this review will potentially make it harder for UK financial services to use the EU's 'equivalence' arrangements to maintain Single Market access as a third country.[38] Whilst Commission officials insist that this review is unrelated to Brexit, commentators believe that this assertion is not credible.[39] It appears that in particular France is driving a hard line on third-country access, and other Member States do not oppose the move. Interestingly, some argue that the UK should strive to achieve the exact opposite: a 2016 Politeia policy report argues that the UK should use its remaining time as an

---

34 See proposed CRD IV, Art. 21b.

35 H. Jones, 'Foreign banks face new EU set-up to allow more scrutiny', Reuters, https://www.reuters.com/article/eu-banks-regulations/foreign-banks-face-new-eu-s et-up-to-allow-more-scrutiny-idUSL8N1LL1RO (04.09.2017).

36 House of Commons, EU Scrutiny Committee, meeting of 16.05.2018 on 'Banking reform: risk reduction measures', section 2.3, https://publications.parliament.uk/p a/cm201719/cmselect/cmeuleg/301-xxvii/30105.htm.

37 See European Commission, Commission Staff Working Document—EU equivalence decisions in financial services policy: an assessment (27.02.2017) SWD(2017) 102 final.

38 For a discussion of equivalence as a potential solution to the market access problem see below section 5.2.

39 Charles Grant, director of the Centre for European Reform, said Commission officials insist 'not entirely convincingly' that this tightening is unrelated to Brexit.

EU member to strengthen the equivalence regime with the goal of profiting from it once the country has left.[40]

A third leg of current activities could come through more restrictive 'location' policies, prescribing where EU-related financial activities can take place. The European Commission released proposals concerning the regulation of clearing houses in June 2017.[41] These target the lucrative clearing of euro-denominated securities trading in the UK. The proposed changes to the regime would allow the European Securities and Markets Authority (ESMA) to classify certain third-country clearing houses as systemically important and thus attach a number of substantial requirements to them. In extreme cases, the European Commission could even instruct them to relocate to the EU if they want to maintain access to the Single Market. Under related plans, the European Central Bank could receive powers to repatriate clearing of Euro-denominated securities to the Eurozone already pre-Brexit.[42]

2.4 Conclusion: End of Access to Financial Market?

Drawing all of these issues together, the consequence would be that the UK is inevitably drifting towards the 'cliff edge': an EU exit without a safety net. This would mean the end of passporting and Single Market access, and would indeed be a dramatic turning point for the UK economy. It would hit the financial sector particularly hard. The assumption of such an outcome of Brexit is wide-spread in a recent survey conducted by PwC among UK-based investment professionals, 70% believed that UK asset managers would not be able to rely on passporting rights after Brexit.[43]

---

40 Reynolds, *A blueprint for Brexit: the future of global financial services and markets in the UK*, (2016).
41 European Commission, Proposal for a Regulation of the European Parliament and of the Council amending Regulation (EU) No. 1095/2010 establishing a European Supervisory Authority (European Securities and Markets Authority) and amending Regulation (EU) No. 648/2012 as regards the procedures and authorities involved for the authorisation of CCPs and requirements for the recognition of third-country CCPs (13 June 2017), COM(2017) 331 final.
42 See already Barker/Brunsden, 'EU plan to curb City's euro clearing set to be flashpoint in Brexit talks', Financial Times (16.12.2016), 1. The lack of competence was the reason the UK successfully challenged the first ECB location decision back in 2011.
43 Flood, '70% of asset managers fear Brexit fund passport loss', Financial Times (05.12.2016), FTfm 1.

3. A More Realistic Scenario

Against this pessimistic outlook, this section now turns to assess a more realistic picture of the future EU-UK relationship. It will demonstrate that the economic incentives of both the UK and of the EU 27 are strongly in favour of maintaining Single Market access for financial services. Political considerations also push the two sides into this direction.

3.1 The Economic Case for Access to the Internal Market—for the UK

To understand what a hard Brexit would mean for the UK, one first needs to understand the importance of the financial sector for the UK economy. Financial services are undoubtedly the UK's biggest industry sector, worth almost 10 per cent of national GDP.[44] Data from the Office for National Statistics (ONS) suggests that the sector annually earns approximately £190-205 bn in revenues, contributes £120-125 bn in Gross Value Added (GVA), and, together with the 1.1 million people working in financial services in the country, generates an estimated £60-67 bn of taxes each year. It contributes a trade surplus of approximately £58 bn to the UK's balance of payments.

This remarkable sector is closely linked to the UK's role in and access to the EU-wide market. Nearly 11 per cent of the City's employees come from elsewhere in the EU, according to the latest census, and nearly 5,500 British registered companies use the 'passporting' mechanism as described above to access the EU market.[45] Consultancy firm Oliver Wyman estimates that around 20% of the UK's financial sector's annual revenue—between GBP 23 and 27 billion—is based on passporting access.[46]

---

44 Burgess, 'Measuring financial sector output and its contribution to UK GDP' (2011) 51 Quarterly Bulletin of the Bank of England 234; G. Tyler, 'Financial Services: contribution to the UK economy', House of Commons Standard Note (26.02.2015).

45 Financial Conduct Authority (FCA), Letter to Andrew Tyrie, Chairman of the House of Commons Treasury Committee, https://www.parliament.uk/documents/commons-committees/treasury/Correspondence/AJB-to-Andrew-Tyrie-Passporting.pdf (17.08.2016).

46 Oliver Wyman, *The impact of the UK's exit from the EU on the UK-based financial services sector* (2016), http://www.oliverwyman.com/content/dam/oliver-wyman/global/en/2016/oct/Brexit_POV.PDF.

Numerous studies have been undertaken to assess the potential impact of what a *Brexit* would mean for the financial sector. In a comprehensive assessment, consultancy firm Oliver Wyman comes to the conclusion that a UK exit from the Single Market could jeopardise 40-50% of EU-related activity (approximately £18-20 bn in revenue) and up to an estimated 35,000 jobs, along with approximately £3-5 bn of tax revenue per year.[47] Individual firms, such as Credit Suisse, for example, have calculated that the loss of passporting would affect up to 20% of their London activity.[48] Indeed, third-country banks with a comparably smaller base in the UK than domestic banks and with a presumably weaker emotional attachment to Britain are more likely to move first.

Crucially, the Oliver Wyman report suggests that knock-on effects would have to be added to this calculation.[49] This is because leaving the Single Market could result in the loss of activities that operate alongside the leaving parts of business, the shifting of entire business units, or the closure of lines of business due to increased costs. When taking this into account, an estimated further £14-18 bn of revenue, 34-40,000 jobs and around £5 bn in tax revenue per annum might be at risk.[50] These estimations are conservative by comparison. Former Chancellor of the Exchequer George Osborne even more dramatically claimed pre-referendum that 285,000 jobs in the City were linked to Europe and might be at risk.[51]

It is not only the threat of losing passporting rights that accounts for these figures. As mentioned before, London is the world's principal place for trading and clearing euro-denominated securities, an enormous market worth about $2tn per day.[52] Other EU financial centres have long sought to get their piece of this lucrative cake. Even under the present, pre-Brexit

---

47 *Ibid* 3.
48 Griffin/Suess, 'Thiam Says Passport Loss Risks 20% of His Bank's U.K. Volume', Bloomberg, http://www.bloomberg.com/news/articles/2016-09-28/credit-suisse-ce o-says-no-passporting-risks-20-of-london-volume (28.09.2016).
49 Oliver Wyman, *The impact of the UK's exit from the EU on the UK-based financial services sector* (2016), 4, http://www.oliverwyman.com/content/dam/oliver-wyman/gl obal/en/2016/oct/Brexit_POV.PDF.
50 Oliver Wyman, *The impact of the UK's exit from the EU on the UK-based financial services sector* (2016), 4, http://www.oliverwyman.com/content/dam/oliver-wyman/gl obal/en/2016/oct/Brexit_POV.PDF.
51 G. Parker/Pickard, 'Osborne warns Gove of economic "catastrophe"', Financial Times (10.05.2016), 3.
52 On this aspect of the Brexit debate, see European Parliament, Brexit, financial stability and the supervision of clearing systems (In-depth Analysis, February 2018), http://www.europarl.europa.eu/cmsdata/138403/MD%20DIW%20final.pdf.

set-up, the European Central Bank (ECB) launched an (unsuccessful) legal attack on this business, claiming that the clearing of Euro-denominated securities must be carried out within the territory of a Member State that is part of the Eurozone.[53] These attempts are currently being resumed.[54] Xavier Rolet, former CEO of the London Stock Exchange, has already claimed that as many as 100,000 City jobs could be lost if Britain left the EU, a loss linked to moving the clearing of euro-denominated securities out of London.[55]

The problem is that none of these startling numbers mattered much during the pre-referendum campaign. The debate exhibited strong elements of post-truth politics and culminated in Michael Gove, a leading Brexiteer, saying in an interview that 'People in this country have had enough of experts.'[56] The reasons are manifold and do not need to be discussed in detail here—suffice it to point out that referenda may frequently tend to lead to emotional rather than rational decisions, and that the June 2016 referendum was probably mostly about reclaiming national sovereignty, anti-establishment feelings, a rejection of uncontrolled immigration and dissatisfaction with EU bureaucracy.[57]

Crucially, however, the post-referendum government is not the 'man in the street' who is immune to economic outlook scenarios or does not understand them. The present decision-makers are accountable to the economic success of the country and will mostly stand for re-election in the future. That makes them much more susceptible to economic realities than a plebiscite which was tainted by emotions.

---

53 Case T-496/11, 04.03.2015, *United Kingdom of Great Britain and Northern Ireland v European Central Bank* ECLI:EU:T:2015:133.

54 Stéphane Boujnah, chief executive of Euronext, has already said that, at present, 30-45 per cent of trading in euro-denominated assets is done out of London, which is 'only acceptable while the UK is part of the EU and the single market.' See Stothard, 'Brexit would end City's dominance of euro trading', Financial Times (online), https://www.ft.com/content/9a52a97c-36ba-11e6-a780-b48ed7b6126 f (20.06.2016). See also Barker/Brunsden, 'EU plan to curb City's euro clearing set to be flashpoint in Brexit talks', Financial Times (16.12.2016), 1.

55 G. Parker/Pickard, 'Osborne warns Gove of economic "catastrophe"', Financial Times (10.05.2016), 3.

56 P. Stevens, 'The perils of a populist paean to ignorance', Financial Time (24.06.2016), 13.

57 Hobolt, 'The Brexit vote: a divided nation, a divided continent' (2016) 23 Journal of European Public Policy 1259.

3.2 The Case for Continental Europe to Stay with Britain

After discussing the UK's economic exposure to the European Union, it is important to also understand that the EU 27 is equally dependent on the UK. This is frequently underestimated and not fully understood in the present policy debate.[58] Some officials hope the EU's position will soften once the collective costs of retrenchment become clear.

For example, as mentioned above, 5,500 UK firms enjoy passporting rights when engaging with European clients. For the EU 27, this number is even higher: About 8,000 EU firms use passporting to access the UK market.[59] Some of these are large groups. Deutsche Bank and Commerzbank, for example, use passporting to run their businesses as 'branches' in the UK, rather than as separately capitalised subsidiaries. Evidently, passporting is therefore a 'two-way street',[60] where European firms benefit as much if not more than UK firms. Fragmenting a complex financial ecosystem inevitably puts up finance costs across Europe, and the risk is that both Britain and the EU lose out as barriers go up.

More than this, Brexit threatens to derail the entire process of EU financial integration. The willingness of continental jurisdictions to subscribe to a single market for financial services has partly been related to the expectation to profit from alignment with the most developed European market-based system, the UK.[61] Following Brexit, the appetite for further integration will be lower. The prospect of continuing the present project of a 'Capital Markets Union' (CMU) without the continent's most developed capital market appears daunting, to say the very least, although Commission officials claim that the project is now 'more important than ever'.[62] Clearly, the political momentum has been lost already, and the bargaining power be-

---

58 But see Ford, 'Why a hard Brexit would hurt European banks the most', Financial Times (11.12.2017), 18.

59 Financial Conduct Authority (FCA), Letter to Andrew Tyrie, Chairman of the House of Commons Treasury Committee, https://www.parliament.uk/documents/commons-committees/treasury/Correspondence/AJB-to-Andrew-Tyrie-Passporting.pdf (17.08.2016).

60 Borrowing from Anthony Browne, chief executive of the BBA.

61 See Armour/Ringe, 'European Company Law 1999-2010: renaissance and crisis' (2011) 48 Common Market Law Review 125, 155.

62 Brunsden, 'EU finance pact "more urgent" since Brexit', Financial Times (15.09.2016), 28. Other commentators agree and opine that Brexit will give a positive push to the remaining Member States to carry on with implementing CMU. See Price, 'Why the CMU could benefit from Brexit' (2016) 35(28) International Financial Law Review, 1.

tween industry and Member States has changed with the prospect of the UK's departure.[63] Market integration projects critically depend on the size and the depth of integration, and pursuing the project without the most advanced of its number, the CMU project looks less promising.[64] Some commentators even suggest that the future of the entire project is now thrown into jeopardy.[65]

Beyond passporting, it is obvious that the EU 27 cannot be interested in looser economic ties with the UK, as higher costs of doing business would negatively affect continental firms. A weakened British demand for goods would severely hit European exports to the UK. Moreover, UK banking services are vital for the industry all over Europe, leading Mark Carney, Governor of the Bank of England, to aptly call London 'the investment banker for Europe'.[66] Carney pointed out that over half of the equity and debt raised by Eurozone firms was issued 'in the UK, by firms based in the UK, quite often to investors in the UK'.[67] It is this close relationship of mutual economic dependency between the UK and the EU 27 which underlies much of their common interests.[68]

Another important consideration to understand is the threat of competition that aderegulated City of London could pose to the rest of Europe. The problem of regulatory competition in financial markets regulation has

---

63 Mooney, 'Fears Brexit will slow Capital Markets Union', Financial Times (18.07.2016), FTfm 3; Burke, 'Deutsche economist: Brexit could "seriously hurt" EU's capital markets', http://www.efinancialnews.com/story/2016-10-20/david-folk erts-landau-deutsche-bank-brexit-european-capital-markets, Financial News (20.10.2016); Davis Polk Client Memorandum, 'Lex et Brexit—the Law and Brexit' (Issue 5, 01.09.2016), https://www.davispolk.com/sites/default/files/2016-09 -01-lex-et-brexit-the-law-brexit-issue-5.pdf.

64 Steven Maijoor, chairman of the European Securities and Markets Authority (ESMA), speaking at a Reuters regulation summit: see H. Jones, 'Brexit would damage EU capital markets union: watchdog says', Reuters, http://www.reuters.com/ article/us-finance-summit-britain-eu-idUSKCN0Y91J8 (18.05.2016).

65 Michael Cole-Fontayn, chairman of the Association for Financial Markets in Europe (AFME), in an interview with Handelsblatt Global Edition, https://global.ha ndelsblatt.com/finance/brexit-threatens-e-u-financial-union-539886 (13.06.2016).

66 Giles, 'Carney warns EU over "crucial" City', Financial Times (01.12.2016), 2.

67 *Ibid.*

68 Clemens Fuest, Interview with Bloomberg, http://www.bloomberg.com/news/vid eos/2016-09-20/an-easy-brexit-break-up-best-for-both-sides-says-fuest (20.09.2016): 'If there is limited or no access to the internal market for British industry and banks it would be bad for Britain but it would also be bad for Europe. Exports to Britain would suffer because, if London suffers as a financial centre, German and French exports to Britain would suffer. So we have a common interest in limiting the economic damage'.

long been understood as a threat to lawmakers, as the stakes of keeping banks and other financial institutions in the country are very high.[69] In the context of Brexit, the risk is that a UK financial regulator, freed from any EU requirements, might be tempted to deregulate the sector even more, with the goal of further luring EU business to Britain. Brexit minister David Davis has warned that if the EU pushed for a punishing settlement, Britain would switch to a tougher 'alternative strategy', looking to fight for business with 'lower tax, softer regulation and other strong business incentives'.[70] This could undermine the standards agreed in the EU and pose a serious threat to the balance of powers on the European continent. A deregulated City of London at its gates would be an even more attractive jurisdiction to relocate to and might entice away even more financial services from Paris and Frankfurt.[71]

Continental financial centres (like Frankfurt and Paris) try to turn the problem into a virtue: they actively promote themselves as a substitute for London with Single Market access, hoping to lure business to the continent.[72] However, poaching part of the UK's financial business runs the risk of producing a lose-lose situation for both sides. Financial market activities benefit from agglomeration: the concentration of financial services in a single hub allows for economies of scale and a depth of capital market activity that cannot be easily replicated. Moving parts of the pie to the continent will therefore reduce the size of the overall pie. Put differently, it may be to the EU's advantage to leave the formidable ecosystem of the City of London intact.[73]

---

69 See, for a recent discussion, Ringe, 'Regulatory competition in global financial markets—the case for a special resolution regime' (2016) 1 Annals of Corporate Governance, 175-247.

70 This is according to a leaked memo of a conversation between Mr Davis and City representatives in mid-November 2016, as published by the Financial Times.

71 For example, the UK's secret arrangements with carmaker Nissan and speculation about sweetheart terms to convince the firm to build new models in the north of England have touched a nerve with continental rivals. See Barker, 'UK ally takes hard Brexit line', Financial Times (21.11.2016), 11, reporting on Denmark's position: 'Denmark is also fixated on its competitiveness. Britain is seen as a rival for investment, whatever direction it takes with Brexit. Danes fear London will relax regulations, standards or taxes to entice business.'

72 See, for example, Wessel, 'With Brexit on the horizon, Frankfurt's star is on the rise', BBC Capital, http://www.bbc.com/capital/story/20161025-with-brexit-on-the-horizon-frankfurts-star-is-on-the-rise (27.10.2016).

73 House of Lords European Union Committee, *Brexit: financial services* (9th report of session 2016-2017), (HL Paper 81, 15.12.2016), para. 37.

Moreover, a competition between London and other EU financial centres might herald the possibility of a downward spiral in regulatory and supervisory standards, which would be fatal to the stability of global financial markets. It may also be accompanied by protectionism and retaliation sentiments, as the example of a requirement for intermediate holding companies in international banking groups illustrates. Ironically, it is possible that the 'winner' of such competition may be neither of the two or three direct competitors, but an outsider such as New York. There are many reasons to believe, therefore, that the much-discussed 'competition' by the likes of Frankfurt and Paris is nothing more than a welcome opportunity for local city marketing, rather than aggressive competition, undermining the business model of others.

Maybe the best example to understand how Brexit would be a lose-lose situation is the attempt by Eurozone officials to repatriate clearing activities of Euro-denominated securities, as mentioned above. Following the UK referendum, leading politicians have renewed their calls to move all Euro clearing business from the City to the EU 27,[74] and the Commission has published a legislative proposal that would allow such a repatriation.[75] However, it has now been revealed that such a move would substantially weaken the Euro's attempt to become a global reserve currency. Research by Standard & Poor's found that it would impose a massive extra burden of margin collateral on market participants and heap pressure on financial institutions on both sides.[76] And a policy paper released by the Intercontinental Exchange (ICE) argues that 'forced repatriation' of euro clearing to the Eurozone would 'deprive European banks of access to liquid trading and clearing facilities and create fragmentation.'[77] Repatriation to mainland Europe would result in additional costs and lower efficiencies for all of the affected global clearing houses, and could also vastly increase margin collateral requirements for their clearing members, 'at a time when collateral requirements are already rising and high quality collateral is becom-

---

74 Barker/Brunsden, 'EU plan to curb City's euro clearing set to be flashpoint in Brexit talks', Financial Times (16.12.2016), 1.
75 See above n 41 and accompanying text.
76 S&P Global Ratings, 'Requiring Euro-Denominated Contracts' Clearing Within The EU Would Be Disruptive But Could Have Limited Impact On Ratings', https://www.globalcreditportal.com/ratingsdirect/renderArticle.do?articleId=1758126&SctArtId=408068&from=CM&nsl_code=LIME&sourceObjectId=9876220&sourceRevId=3&fee_ind=N&exp_date=20261117-15:33:02 (17.11.2016).
77 Cited according to Barker/Brunsden, 'EU plan to curb City's euro clearing set to be flashpoint in Brexit talks', Financial Times (16.12.2016).

ing more scarce.[78] In other words, the repatriation would not just hurt the City of London, but also EU 27 banks as the costs for all financial market participants will soar.

3.3 Avoiding a Precedent?

Taken together, it becomes apparent that the EU 27 side has as much interest in keeping the UK in the Single Market as the UK has in staying. The only serious obstacle for European policy-makers to confessing this attitude in public is the powerful imperative that is constantly reiterated in Europe: allowing a bespoke arrangement for the UK would set a dangerous precedent—with potentially inviting other EU jurisdictions to come with their own demands later. Thus, EU officials have warned against allowing the UK to 'cherry-pick' parts of the Single Market architecture for fear of becoming a menu à la carte. More than that, there may be a temptation to apply punitive terms to the UK's exit and the EU-UK relationship. This also explains the insistence, on the EU side, to emphasise that the four freedoms are indivisible and cannot be selected or adopted in part.[79]

As much as this rhetoric makes sense in political terms, the threats depicted by its supporters do not stand up to the realities. The truth is that cherry picking is and has always been present in EU integration over time, and has not had the disastrous consequences that its opponents claimed.

Consider the case of the British 'rebate' or 'discount' for its contributions to the EU budget. During the 1980s, then Prime Minister Margaret Thatcher fought hard to achieve a special treatment for the UK's contribution to the common EU budget. She was successful at the European Council in June 1984, held in Fontainebleau, and a substantial 'correction' in fa-

---

78 S&P Global Ratings, 'Requiring Euro-Denominated Contracts' Clearing Within The EU Would Be Disruptive But Could Have Limited Impact On Ratings', https://www.globalcreditportal.com/ratingsdirect/renderArticle.do?articleId=1758126&SctArtId=408068&from=CM&nsl_code=LIME&sourceObjectId=9876220&source RevId=3&fee_ind=N&exp_date=20261117-15:33:02 (17.11.2016).

79 See, for example the Statement after an Informal meeting of the Heads of State or Government of 27 Member States, as well as the Presidents of the European Council and the European Commission at Brussels (15.12.2016), http://www.cons ilium.europa.eu/media/24173/15-euco-statement.pdf: 'We reiterate that any agreement will have to be based on a balance of rights and obligations, and that access to the Single Market requires acceptance of all four freedoms'.

vour of the UK contribution was adopted by a 1985 Council decision.[80] It has been in place ever since.[81] Critics at the time were scared of the very same thing as the EU Brexit negotiators are today—that once you allow a special treatment for one country, others will ask for the same. Yet despite all prophesies to the contrary, there has not been another case of budget adjustment for another Member State ever since.

In truth, all comes down to the strength of the relative bargaining positions. The UK's exceptionally sized financial market is unmatched by any other Member State, and will be a decisive bargaining chip in the Brexit negotiations. Other Member States have too much political capital tied up in the joint European project and too much to lose economically to risk walking out. An exceedingly unfavourable deal with the UK would be liable to damage everybody and would not achieve cohesiveness within the EU 27 itself. The prediction is thus that the EU 27 will most probably jump over its shadow and grant the UK yet another 'special treatment.'

Further, whoever argues that cherry-picking has no place in the EU framework does not realise that a multi-speed Europe with a complex web of different treaties, exceptions, and principles, has long been a reality. The Economic and Monetary Union (EMU) is the most prominent example, where the UK and Denmark have negotiated a permanent opt-out.[82] But a number of other Member States are presently not part of the Eurozone either.[83] To take a few other examples, the Banking Union is, at its core, a Eurozone project: all Eurozone Member States are automatically part of the Banking Union. But the Banking Union remains open for other Member States, and several non-Euro countries are planning to join, while others

---

80 Council Decision of 7 May 1985 on the Communities' system of own resources, [1985] OJ L128/15, Art. 3.

81 The rebate is negotiated as part of the Multiannual Financial Framework (MFF) every seven years and must be unanimously agreed. See European Commission, Commission Working Document on calculation, financing, payment and entry in the budget of the correction of budgetary imbalances in favour of the United Kingdom ('the UK correction') in accordance with Articles 4 and 5 of Council Decision 2014/xxx/EU, Euratom on the system of own resources of the European Union, COM(2014) 271 final.

82 See the Protocols attached to the TEU: Protocol (No. 15) on Certain Provisions Relating to the United Kingdom of Great Britain and Northern Ireland, and Protocol (No. 16) on Certain Provisions Relating to Denmark.

83 Formally, however, these other 'Outs' are obliged to join the common currency once they fulfil the legal criteria for Euro membership.

prefer to remain outside.[84] The European Stability Mechanism (ESM) is a European bail-out fund set up at the height of the sovereign debt crisis in 2012. The ESM is formally not part of the EU legal framework, as it is enshrined in a separate international treaty, signed by the Eurozone members only.[85] By contrast, several instruments concerning fiscal coordination in the EU have been adopted over the past few years. They all apply with different intensity to a different group of members, creating a complex and an opaque web of commitments and obligations.[86]

These examples are all drawn from the sphere of the financial market; when broadening the view, it becomes apparent that the same phenomenon can be observed in the EU architecture as a whole—the EU Treaties TEU and TFEU with their numerous exceptions, opt-outs and protocols,[87] the existence of sister frameworks like the European Economic Area and EFTA, the Schengen Agreement guaranteeing passport-free travel,[88] and the European Customs Union. This list could be continued indefinitely, and is an expression of the fact that 'special deals' have been struck as long as European integration has existed. Although formally insisting on an 'ever closer Union', most officials nowadays accept the realities of a multi-speed Europe and put their hopes in a 'coalition of the willing' to move forward and to inspire others. At the celebrations of the 60th anniversary of the Treaty of Rome, EU Member States officially endorsed the idea of a multi-speed integration.[89] Even Wolfgang Schäuble, a longstanding Euro-

---

84 Hüttl/Schoenmaker, 'Should the 'outs' join the European Banking Union?' Bruegel Policy Contribution 2016/03, http://bruegel.org/wp-content/uploads/2016/02/pc_2016_03.pdf (February 2016).

85 Formally, the ESM is an intergovernmental organisation located in Luxembourg, which operates under public international law for all Eurozone Member States.

86 The most prominent examples are Euro Plus Pact 2011; the 'Six Pack' 2011 (which applies to all EU Member States but with some special rules for the Eurozone); the Fiscal Compact 2013 (an intergovernmental agreement, involving all EU28 except the UK and the Czech Republic); and the 'Two Pack' 2013 (mostly concerning the Eurozone).

87 For example, concerning the Area of freedom, security and justice and the Charter of Fundamental Rights are both subject to numerous opt-outs.

88 The UK and Ireland opted out of Schengen when it became part of EU law in 1997.

89 The anniversary declaration states that 'We will act together, at different paces and intensity where necessary' and that 'We will allow for the necessary room for manoeuvre at the various levels to strengthen Europe's innovation and growth potential.' See the Rome Declaration of the Leaders of 27 Member States and of the European Council, the European Parliament and the European Commission (25.03.2017), http://europa.eu/rapid/press-release_STATEMENT-17-767_en.htm.

pean hard-core federalist, recently backed away from the notion of ever closer integration, supporting a multi-speed governance approach instead.[90]

All of this suggests that the current EU position to not allowing the UK a tailor-made solution are nothing more than an attempt to build up a negotiating position. To claim that the four freedoms are indivisible is simply an axiomatic postulation, but nothing more. To go even further: the EU 27 negotiating team has as much to fear from a failure of the Article 50 talks as the UK, since a failure to conclude a deal with the two years after negotiations were started would mean a UK exit from the Single Market with disastrous consequences for mainland Europe too. This is where the real risk of setting a precedent lies.

3.4 Political Constraints

Alongside economic considerations, there are also a number of powerful political circumstances that are nudging the UK away from moving towards a 'hard' form of Brexit at least for services. This is a common phenomenon of any complex process. The decision about leaving the European Union is multifaceted, involves many different decision-makers and players, and spans a significant period of time. Such complex processes typically end up with some form of compromise.

The most well-known conflict over Brexit was the initial rivalry between the UK Government and Parliament over which institution is entitled to start the process of leaving the EU under TEU Article 50. When it became apparent that the Government leant towards hard Brexit, Parliament began what may be termed a soft 'rebellion'.[91] Many MPs feared the consequences for UK trade that Brexit might entail, demanding a vote on the terms of the EU exit. In any case, they protested against the risk of being sidelined in the decision-making process and against the Government's penchant for secrecy on the different exit options.

This led to the widely-reported decision by the UK Supreme Court, holding that the right to give notice under Article 50 is within the prerogative of Parliament, thus quashing the hopes of Prime Minister Theresa May to

---

90 Wagstyl/Chazan, 'Schäuble backs away from EU of "ever closer union"', Financial Times (24.03.2017), 6.

91 Blitz, 'Commons rebellion over Brexit', Financial Times Brexit Briefing (10.10.2016).

control the whole process herself.[92] The Government was thus forced to seek parliamentary authorisation for the move to trigger the Brexit negotiation process, which they ultimately did. Although most MPs are pro-remain,[93] few sought to pursue a complete reversal of the Brexit decision for fear of angering the public by defying a clear referendum decision. Therefore, it was not expected that the *Miller* decision would stop the Brexit process, but that it would encourage parliamentary reflection and debate.[94] Moreover, the ruling gave some momentum to the view that the Government must be more explicit about the type of Brexit it is seeking, and that it needed to provide that clarity before Article 50 would be invoked.

Another instance of this conflict emerged several months later over the requirement of a parliamentary vote on the outcome of an eventual Brexit agreement. In December 2017, a coalition of twelve pro-European Conservative MPs joined forces with nearly all labour, Scottish National Party and liberal democrat members, causing a major legislative defeat of the Government over the Brexit Withdrawal Bill. The 'rebels' were successful in pushing through an amendment to that Bill, requiring that the Government pass any withdrawal deal agreed with the EU via primary legislation before implementing it, and thus giving Parliament a full vote on the outcome of the Brexit negotiations.[95]

The simmering battle between Government and Parliament is however not the only internal conflict. Of similar quality is the divergence of views between the UK Government and regional policy-makers inside the UK. For example, it is well known that the Scottish public is more sympathetic to the EU than the rest of the UK, and 62% of the Scottish electorate voted Remain in the referendum. This has prompted Scottish politician to explore ways of obstructing the Brexit process. One potential avenue would be to hold another Scottish independence referendum, but the outcome of

---

92 *R (Gina Miller) v. Secretary of State for Exiting the European Union* [2016] EWHC 2768 (Admin).

93 In the House of Commons, there were about 480 MPs in favour of Remain just before the Brexit referendum compared with 150 opposed. The House of Lords was also highly supportive of the Remain camp.

94 Alison Young 'R *(Miller) v The Secretary of State for exiting the European Union* [2016] EWHC 2768 (Admin): Constitutional adjudication—reality over legality?', UK Constitutional Law Blog, https://ukconstitutionallaw.org (09.09.2016).

95 Mance, 'May dealt Brexit blow at hands of Tory rebels', Financial Times (14.12.2017), 2.

that would be very uncertain according to pollsters.[96] In the *Miller* case, First Minister Nicola Sturgeon intervened in the Supreme Court hearing, seeking a declaration that Scotland must be consulted before Brexit.[97] Whilst this claim failed, Scottish officials still explore ways of securing an alternative position for Scotland towards the EU. The Scottish Government recently adopted an official proposal for maintaining access to the Single Market.[98] A similar proposal has been put forward by political leaders in Wales.[99] Finally, Northern Ireland has been the source of much debate as negotiators sought to avoid the installation of a hard border between Northern Ireland and the Republic of Ireland. This led to the UK's promise to maintain 'regulatory alignment' with much of the EU Single Market regulation.[100]

A third and perhaps most significant conflict line lies between the UK Government and the British public in general. The outcome of the referendum was clear, and it seems that the public (although still divided) has no regret over the decision to leave the European Union. However, the choice of which course to pursue instead is ultimately very controversial. In a revealing independent study from November 2016, an overwhelming 90 percent of the public was in favour of continuing free trade with the EU.[101] And in September 2017, new figures showed that a majority of the British

---

96 Jamieson, 'Scotland Seeks Independence Again After U.K. "Brexit" Vote", NBC News, http://www.nbcnews.com/storyline/brexit-referendum/scotland-could-see k-independence-again-after-u-k-brexit-vote-n598166 (24.06.2016).

97 Ross, 'Sturgeon Launches Legal Case To Stop The UK Government Triggering Article 50', https://www.buzzfeed.com/jamieross/sturgeon-launches-legal-case-to-s top-the-uk-government-trigg (08.09.2016). See also Faulconbridge/Holden, 'In a battle over Brexit, court challenger fears Britain's demons have been unleashed', Reuters, http://uk.reuters.com/article/uk-britain-eu-article50-miller-idUKKBN13 P1SI (30.09.2016).

98 The Scottish Government, 'Scotland's Place in Europe', http://www.gov.scot/Res ource/0051/00512073.pdf (December 2016).

99 Welsh Government, 'Securing Wales' Future: Transition from the European Union to a new relationship with Europe', https://beta.gov.wales/sites/default/files/20 17-01/30683%20Securing%20Wales%C2%B9%20Future_ENGLISH_WEB.pdf (January 2017).

100 Stone, 'Britain agrees Northern Ireland can keep EU regulations after Brexit, leaked draft agreement suggests', The Independent, http://www.independent.co.uk/ news/uk/politics/brexit-northern-ireland-border-single-market-customs-union-th eresa-may-michel-barnier-david-davis-a8090561.html (4 December 2017).

101 Curtice, 'What do Voters Want from Brexit?', http://whatukthinks.org/eu/wp-cont ent/uploads/2016/11/Analysis-paper-9-What-do-voters-want-from-Brexit.pdf' (2016).

public for the first time since the referendum believed the country should remain in the EU.[102] The Government will find it difficult to ignore this position, as most of its members will face re-election in 2022 at the latest.

3.5 Currently Hardening Stances

The essence of the argument so far has been that both sides, the UK and the EU 27, have powerful incentives to seek an agreement about continued Single Market cooperation.

On the face of it, this conclusion seems to run contrary to the volatile political climate. Moods and attitudes towards Brexit are changing by the week. During most of 2017, the UK Government was sharpening its rhetoric and appeared to be drifting towards a 'hard' version of a Brexit.[103] In particular, the Prime Minister's Brexit speech in January 2017 emphasised the UK's readiness to 'walk away' from negotiations if no deal could be achieved.[104] And the ensuing Government White Paper explicitly rejected any future Single Market membership.[105] Other government ministers have gone beyond this and made hawkish remarks, suggesting their readiness to leave the EU at all costs. A number of comments have even ridiculed their EU partners' economic position.[106] Finally, in the run-up to the start of the official negotiations, the British EU ambassador surprising-

---

102 Watts, 'Brexit: Majority of British people believe UK should stay in the EU, finds latest poll', The Independent, http://www.independent.co.uk/news/uk/politics/br exit-majority-uk-british-people-stay-in-eu-not-leave-latest-poll-theresa-may-florenc e-speech-tory-a7960226.html (21.09.2017).

103 At the Birmingham Conservative party conference in October 2016, Prime Minister May made it clear that she preferred to maintain Single Market access, but that she was adamant to restrict immigration and to strive off the jurisdiction of the European Court of Justice. If given a choice between the two—if they are irreconcilable—she suggested preferring the latter. This speech has widely been interpreted as her first true announcement of a hard Brexit. See Eaton, 'Theresa May signals that the UK is heading for hard Brexit', New Statesman, http://www. newstatesman.com/politics/uk/2016/10/theresa-may-signals-uk-heading-hard-brex it (02.10.2016); Allen/G. Parker/Barker, 'May sets Brexit course with hint of clean break from single market', Financial Times (03.10.2016), 1.

104 G. Parker/Barker, 'May eases Brexit fears but warns UK will walk away from "bad deal"', Financial Times (18.01.2017), 1.

105 HM Government, *The United Kingdom's exit from and new partnership with the European Union* (Cm 9417, February 2017), 35.

106 For example, foreign secretary Boris Johnson claimed that it is 'baloney' that the UK cannot get a free trade agreement if it ends free movement for EU workers.

ly quit his post, explaining his frustration with the lack of engagement of the UK Government with Brussels. This move was also interpreted as heralding an unamicable variant of Brexit.[107]

However, the conclusion of phase 1 of the Brexit negotiations in December 2017 fuelled hopes of a rather 'soft' Brexit. In the attempt of both satisfying the continuity of Irish north-south relationship (in particular, the avoidance of any hard border) and the inner-UK trade relationship, the UK committed to maintain 'regulatory alignment' with the Single Market. The decisive passage of the Joint Report reads: 'In the absence of agreed solutions, the United Kingdom will maintain full alignment with those rules of the Internal Market and the Customs Union, which, now or in the future, support North-South cooperation, the all-island economy and the protection of the 1998 Agreement.'[108] This passage has been interpreted as paving the way for a soft Brexit.[109]

The July 2018 White Paper, as mentioned before, now testifies to this ambiguity. It proposes a version of soft Brexit for goods, and a medium position for services – including financial services.[110]

Conversely, on the European side, policy-makers are also uniting behind a hard bargaining line. To the frustration of UK officials, EU chief negotiator Michel Barnier was quick to reject the proposals made by Theresa May at Chequers and spelled out in the White Paper.[111] In substance, EU policy-makers across the board are constantly insisting that the four freedoms are indivisible and that a restriction on free movement of workers means an end to Single Market membership. The EU's chief negotiator has recently

---

107 Wishart/Ross, 'A Hard Brexit Looms Large With Resignation of U.K. Envoy to EU', Bloomberg, https://www.bloomberg.com/politics/articles/2017-01-03/a-hard-brexit-looms-large-with-resignation-of-u-k-envoy-to-eu (04.01.2017).

108 Joint report from the negotiators of the European Union and the United Kingdom Government on progress during phase 1 of negotiations under Article 50 TEU on the United Kingdom's orderly withdrawal from the European Union (8 December 2017), para 49, https://ec.europa.eu/commission/sites/beta-political/files/joint_report.pdf.

109 Green, 'Brexit: what regulatory alignment means and does not mean', Financial Times, https://www.ft.com/content/4fddeb2e-7e92-3d81-b0a7-9dfeb6055510 (08.12.2017).

110 UK Government, *The Future Relationship between the United Kingdom and the European Union – Presented to Parliament by the Prime Minister by Command of Her Majesty* (Cm 9593, July 2018).

111 Herszenhorn/de la Baume, 'Barnier dismantles UK's Brexit white paper', Politico, https://www.politico.eu/article/michel-barnier-brexit-white-paper-analysis/ (20 July 2018).

insisted that there would definitely be no 'special deal' for financial services with the UK and that passports would be lost.[112]

In a similar vein, a much-discussed contribution by Christian Noyer, former governor of the Banque de France, takes a particularly hard stance. He puts forward a number of conditions for Single Market access, which run against the current UK Government position. Further, Noyer denounces easy access by means of regulatory equivalence, contending that 'the foundations of the single market would be undermined [and] a key element of EU cohesion would be destroyed.'[113]

These positions, as reported by the press and as irreconcilable as they seem, should be interpreted as what they are: pre-bargaining rhetoric. It is common knowledge in negotiation strategy not to put one's demand too low. The negotiating strategies to be expected on both sides are therefore to aim for the 'best' outcome first, and scale down their expectations once these prove unattainable.[114]

Prime Minister Theresa May's dilemma is the following: domestically, she needs to speak tough to honour the outcome of the referendum, to pacify conservative backbenchers and to fend off the UK Independence Party. This explains her tough talk on controlling immigration, reclaiming lost sovereignty, and escaping the jurisdiction of the European Court of Justice (CJEU).[115] However, such radical positions provoke a backlash in Europe and prevent her from getting a favourable deal with her European partners. Worse, they create counterreactions and even tougher rhetoric from the EU 27 side, which in turn hardens the UK position even more. This vicious circle explains the phenomenon of seemingly irreconcilable positions on both sides of the Channel.

How then to overcome this dilemma? There are good reasons to expect an appeasement process once negotiations on the trade deal begin in ear-

---

112 Rankin, 'UK cannot have a special deal for the City, says EU's Brexit negotiator', The Guardian, https://www.theguardian.com/politics/2017/dec/18/uk-cannot-ha ve-a-special-deal-for-the-city-says-eu-brexit-negotiator-barnier (18 December 2017).

113 Noyer, 'Brexit means the end of single market access for London', Financial Times (16.03.2017), 13.

114 See Eidenmüller, 'Negotiating and mediating Brexit' [2016] Pepperdine Law Review 39.

115 Her speech at the Birmingham party conference is available in full length at http://www.independent.co.uk/news/uk/politics/theresa-may-speech-tory-confere nce-2016-in-full-transcript-a7346171.html.

nest.[116] For the most part, these negotiations on a daily basis will be led by technocrats, who are to work out the details of a leaving pact. These are free from populist pressure and will motivate to produce workable outcomes. But even the main political figures in charge of Brexit will moderate their stances, given the high economic and political costs involved in an unfavourable Brexit deal. Accountability to the public, pressure group influence and looming elections mean that politicians will not score in the long run with producing a Brexit that triggers disastrous economic consequences. A realistic expectation is therefore that phase 2 of the official Brexit negotiations on the future relationship will eventually show common ground to both sides.

4. Malleable Legal Rules Accommodate Flexible Solutions

The cautiously optimistic line developed thus far faces one undeniable problem: 'Brexit means Brexit'. This means that the UK leaving the EU as such is a near-certain fact that cannot be ignored or overcome. All faint hopes by some that the referendum decision may be reversed or that a second referendum could be held are rightly criticised as unrealistic. Reversing Brexit itself would provoke outspoken public anger. Former UKIP leader Nigel Farage and other Brexiteers have already hinted at a possible outburst of violent protests should the Brexit decision be reversed.[117]

Importantly, therefore, two things are likely to happen: First, the UK will formally and officially leave the EU. The two-year period under Article 50 is running, and the process of leaving by March 2019 is very hard if not impossible to reverse.[118] Secondly, however, this paper has demonstrated that both sides have powerful incentives to keep the Single Market for financial services intact. It is therefore fair to expect a creative solution

---

116 See Eidenmüller, 'Negotiating and mediating Brexit' [2016] Pepperdine Law Review 39.

117 Ashmore, 'Nigel Farage warns of unprecedented "political anger" after High Court ruling', Politics Home, https://www.politicshome.com/news/europe/eu-pol icy-agenda/brexit/news/80540/nigel-farage-warns-unprecedented-political-anger (06.11.2016).

118 There is a legal debate on whether the notice given under Article 50 is revocable. See Payne/Edwards/Brinded, 'Can Article 50 be reversed?', Business Insider UK, http://www.businessinsider.de/can-brexit-be-reversed-2017-6 (14.06.2017). The legal position is unclear. Politically, however, a reversal would amount to suicide for the British Government; moreover, it is not clear that the EU would be willing to unconditionally welcome the UK back at this stage.

alongside the leaving decision to maintain the substance of the UK's financial services access to Europe.

Is it realistic to see such a combination of formal exit and economic substance? Historical precedent of the EU financial market framework confirms that creative solutions to formal problems are very common. Put into a broader context, economic or political considerations have frequently triumphed over formal legal positions, to an extent that 'the law' can be seen as the constant loser.

4.1 Lessons from EU Financial Integration

To understand this, it is worth exploring in some more detail one of the key lessons from EU financial integration: that politics and economics frequently trump formal rules. The EU legal system has proven to be particularly malleable during the process of building an EU financial market. This became apparent during the 2008/09 Global Financial Crisis and the ensuing 2010-12 Sovereign Debt Crisis. One of the central tenets of policymakers, regulators and supervisors has always been to put economic necessities over formal legal problems. As put by *The Economist*, 'Given a choice between financial stability and the rule book, ditch the rule book.'[119]

The genesis of the EU financial market framework is full of such examples. Amongst the most well-known is the attitude towards the famous Euro convergence criteria. As is well known, membership of the third stage of the Economic and Monetary Union (EMU) requires certain criteria, among them that the ratio of the annual government deficit relative to gross domestic product (GDP) in each Member State must not exceed 3% at the end of the preceding fiscal year.[120] This requirement (and the other criteria) has constantly been violated by several Eurozone Member States, famously once including both heavyweights, France and Germany. Yet, the various sanctions—the Treaty's Excessive Deficit Procedure[121] and the separate Stability and Growth Pact—have never been properly used.[122] Mem-

---

119 The Economist, 'The Rule of Flaw', http://www.economist.com/news/leaders/216 98650-italy-has-been-flirting-banking-crisisand-brussels-partly-blame-rule-flaw (12.05.2016).

120 See formerly EC Treaty Art. 121, now modified to TFEU Art. 140.

121 Now TFEU Art. 126.

122 Ngai, 'Stability and growth pact and fiscal discipline in the Eurozone' Wharton Financial Institutions Working Paper 12-10, University of Pennsylvania, https://fi c.wharton.upenn.edu/wp-content/uploads/2016/11/12-10.pdf (04.05.2012).

ber States have been very creative over time in convincing the EU institutions that violations of the criteria were due to exceptional circumstances, hardship, or internal crisis. Conversely, the Commission has mostly found it inappropriate to intervene for political reasons. In sum, the convergence criteria are now predominantly seen as political tools, not as a pure legal instrument.[123]

The 2007-09 Global Financial Crisis brought the weakness of the EU legal framework to the fore. Nowhere can this be better observed than when looking at the conflict between EU State aid rules and bank bail-outs.[124] The massive scale of taxpayer-financed rescue operations for domestic banks carried out by many EU Member States ran directly contrary to the prohibition to support local firms because of market distortion risks.[125] However, faced with an unprecedented risk of a global meltdown, the EU institutions had no other choice than to rubber-stamp all those bail-outs, using the exceptions provided by the Treaties.[126] The many decisions and communications on State aid during the Crisis arguably bent State aid rules to the point of almost no recognition.

Another major crisis player, acting in a grey area, turned out to be the European Central Bank. Arguably, the ECB was the only EU institution with serious powers who was willing to use them. It has intervened numerous times during the crisis, starting with the traditional monetary policy tool of adjusting interest rates, over the so-called Long-Term Refinancing Operations for banks (LTRO) since 2008, to direct intervention in the securities market. The latter includes a number of programmes, *inter alia* the Securities Markets Programme (SMP) of 2010, a purchase programme for bank-issued covered bonds in 2011, and the announcement of the controversial 'Outright Monetary Transactions' (OMT) in 2012 with the famous announcement by ECB President Mario Draghi to do 'whatever it takes' to preserve the Euro. This triggered a legal challenge by Germany as being

---

123 De Grauwe, 'The politics of the Maastricht convergence criteria', Vox CEPR Policy Portal, http://voxeu.org/article/politics-maastricht-convergence-criteria (15.04.2009).

124 See on this Quigley, 'State aid and the financial crisis' Ringe/Huber (eds), *Legal challenges in the global financial crisis: bail-outs, the euro and regulation* (2014), 131.

125 TFEU Arts. 107, 108.

126 Initially, the Commission relied on Art. 107(3)(c) to allow for exceptions. This requires the recipient to be in financial difficulty—as the crisis progressed, it became apparent that it did not work for wider systemic issues and liquidity problems. In consequence, the Commission's approach shifted to use Art. 107(3)(b) ('serious disturbance in the economy of a Member State') as the predominant exception, which granted more leeway.

beyond the ECB's mandate.[127] The challenge was ultimately unsuccessful, but the ECB's actions have been widely criticised by legal scholars as violating the rule of law and the European Treaties.[128] Tellingly, economists have underscored the pressing need for ECB activity.

The ECB went on to embark on an impressive quantitative easing programme in 2015, which is still ongoing and which is also subject to a legal challenge in Germany, currently pending at the CJEU.[129] Part of the problem is that the ECB itself is not able to mitigate imbalances in competitiveness within the Eurozone. Ultimately, it can only buy time.

Similar criticism was voiced against the creation of the European Stability Mechanism (ESM),[130] a European bail-out fund with a maximum 'firepower' of € 500 bn.[131] The mandate of the ESM was only to provide rescue operations for EU Member States that were in financial difficulties. Direct payments to banks were not allowed before the completion of the Banking Union. Another legal challenge was launched against the legality of the ESM, arguing that it violated the 'no bail-out' clause specified in Article 125 TFEU. Although the CJEU ultimately upheld the constitutionality of the ESM, many commentators believed that it was erected on shaky grounds.[132]

The most recent example is the attempt to circumvent bail-in legislation in various situations in the course of 2016. Ironically, this concerned a major piece of the EU crisis response, the Bank Recovery and Resolution Directive (BRRD). The crucial part of this directive came into force in January 2016 and mandates the participation of private investors in the losses of a failing bank—before the taxpayer becomes liable for a public bail-out. The broader objective is to avoid the unpopular bail-outs of the crisis years. However, first practice tests during 2016 laid bare strong incentives to arbitrage around BRRD. The clearest example of this is the Italian banking cri-

---

127 Case C-62/14, 16.06.2015, *Gauweiler*, OJ C 279, 24.8.2015, p. 12–13.

128 See, *inter alia*, Yowell, 'Why the ECB cannot save the euro', in: Ringe/Huber (eds), *Legal challenges in the global financial crisis: bail-outs, the euro and regulation* (2014), 81.

129 The German Constitutional Court referred the case to the CJEU: see decision of 18.07.2017 – 2 BvR 859/15, 2 BvR 980/16, 2 BvR 2006/15, 2 BvR 1651/15.

130 The ESM is the permanent successor to the interim solutions European Financial Stabilisation Mechanism (EFSM) and European Financial Stability Facility (EFSF).

131 Formally, the ESM is an intergovernmental organisation located in Luxembourg, which operates under public international law for all Eurozone Member States.

132 Case C-370/12, 27.11.2012, *Thomas Pringle v Government of Ireland*, OJ C 26, 26.1.2013, p. 15–16.

sis, notably encompassing Banca Monte dei Paschi di Siena. When it became clear in 2016 that this bank (and others) were struggling and nearing
insolvency, the Italian Government sought to secure a public rescue programme—going the correct way of bailing in private creditors under the
BRRD seemed politically toxic, as many bondholders were in fact retail investors.[133] At some point, faced with the legal necessity to respect BRRD,
the Government openly considered simply ignoring the law.[134]

This list could be continued indefinitely. Other examples from the rich
EU financial history include the creation of the EU supervisory architecture on weak legal grounds; the framework designed to ensure fiscal discipline (Sixpack 2011 and Fiscal Compact 2013, among others); and the creation of the European Banking Union, the legal basis of which was unclear.
The claim that the adoption of such legal instruments or institutions lies
beyond the competence of the EU lawmakers may have legal force, but
does not matter much in real life. The CJEU has traditionally been generous in interpreting the Treaty powers widely.[135] Even the possibility of
creating separate EU agencies with independent discretionary powers—a
contentious area—has recently been made more flexible.[136] The message is
clear: pure legal arguments will not stand in the way of sensible economic
choices or political deals if only the pressure is high enough to come to a
deal.

4.2 Reason to Worry?

The more important question is this: Does the relaxation of legal principles in the name of economic and political goals give cause for concern?

---

133 Barker/Brunsden, 'Failing banks regime faces tough test', Financial Times
(06.12.2016), 4.
134 Sanderson/Barker, 'Renzi ready to defy Brussels over bailout for Italy's troubled
banks', Financial Times (04.07.2016), 1; Scherer, 'Renzi says wants to avoid
EU's "bail-in" to restructure banks', Reuters, http://www.reuters.com/article/euro
zone-banks-italy-idUSL8N1AJ38A (02.08.2016).
135 In the 60 years of the EU's existence, there is only one single real CJEU decision
where an EU legal act failed the test of competence: Case C-376/98, 05.10.2000,
Germany v Parliament and Council(Tobacco Advertising I), ECR I-8419.
136 See Case C-270/12, 22.01.2014, *United Kingdom v European Parliament and Council*, ECLI:EU:C:2014:18, concerning a Regulation on Short Selling.

This may certainly be so from a rule of law perspective.[137] In particular the German Government has been seeking to establish a rules-based culture in the EU financial market and discourages every attempt to insert some flexibility into the system out of fear that the entire system might be undermined. This explains the long tradition of German officials to oppose almost all the initiatives discussed above, with the ECB probably being their most obvious target.

Another view stands in stark contrast to this position. A number of scholars have argued that it is the precise genius of a legal framework to be flexible in exceptional crisis situations.[138] Katharina Pistor has argued that a conflict between legal imperative and financial necessities tends to be resolved by suspending the full force of law. It is here that power rather than law becomes salient.[139] In the context of the global financial crisis, the malleability of the legal framework has proved critical for avoiding a complete financial meltdown. This is substantially different from the Great Depression of the 1930s, where the Federal Reserve's refusal to buy any assets apart from those which were stipulated in legal rules contributed to the system's collapse.[140]

4.3 Implications for Brexit

What does all of this mean for Brexit? This section shows how flexible legal rules can be. In fact, the higher the economic stakes, the more elastic they become. The prediction for Brexit is that the same considerations will apply. Given that the economic stakes are extremely high for both sides, as demonstrated above, there is reason to expect that legal principles will not stay in the way of a reasonable deal between the UK and the remaining Member States.

The implication is of high importance for a number of issues that are relevant in the exit negotiations. It is relevant, for example, for the EU's mantra that the four freedoms (of goods, persons, services and capital) are

---

137 For example, Yowell, 'Why the ECB cannot save the euro', in: Ringe/Huber (eds), Legal challenges in the global financial crisis: bail-outs, the euro and regulation (2014), 81.

138 See, for example, Pistor, 'A legal theory of finance' (2013) 41 Journal of Comparative Economics, 315.

139 *Ibid.*

140 Mehrling, *The New Lombard Street: How the Fed Became the Dealer of Last Resort* (2010), 34-35.

indivisible. As mentioned above, this assertion is not God-given, and a reconsideration of this stance in the light of past experiences can be expected. At least partial exceptions from the freedoms will probably be on the negotiating table soon. Another implication is that substance will most likely triumph over form: while there is probably no way to reverse the decision of Brexit as such, it should be expected that the formal legal exit from the European Union does not necessarily mean an exit of the substance of the Single Market.[141] This is the essence of the 'irrelevance' claim of the present paper.

As of yet, it is of course impossible to predict where exactly the phase 2 negotiations will lead and what type of agreement the parties will seek. There are, nevertheless, a few likely key considerations that allow the development of three main scenarios, to which the following section now turns.

5. What Could a Solution Look Like?

As the parties are making progress with phase 2 of the Brexit negotiations,[142] dedicated to their future trade relationship, two things are clear. The two-year period set by Article 50 seems rather short, in particular since this period must include the ratification of the deal agreed by all 28 Member States.[143] It is further complicated by the fact that 2017 saw national elections in France and Germany, and negotiations only started in earnest after these were over. In sum, the window of opportunity for negotiations shrunk to just over a year. Against this backdrop, the UK asked for a two-year transition period. It is therefore expected that the UK will officially leave the EU in March 2019 but remain subject to EU legislation until ear-

---

141 HM Government, *The United Kingdom's exit from and new partnership with the European Union* (Cm 9417, February 2017), also hints at this by proposing a 'new strategic partnership agreement' with the EU, which should include 'the freest possible trade in financial services between the UK and EU Member States'. *Ibid.* para 8.25.

142 Phase 1, the terms of the separation, was completed in December 2017. Phase 2 began in March 2018.

143 Foster, 'Brexit deal could be reached by October 2018, says lead EU negotiator Michel Barnier', The Telegraph, http://www.telegraph.co.uk/news/2016/12/06/eu-brexit-negotiator-michel-barnier-reiterate-no-cherry-picking/ (06.12.2016).

ly 2021.[144] Still, given the recent experience with negotiating free trade agreements in general, and the complications in the EU in particular, even that extended time period appears rather short for concluding a comprehensive trade agreement.[145] It is these time constraints that need to be kept in mind when exploring the potential outcomes of the trade negotiations.[146]

5.1 'Special Deal' As Most Likely Outcome

Following the logic of this article, a 'special deal' between the UK and the EU 27 is the most likely scenario going forward. This would ensure that, on the one hand, the UK is formally leaving the bloc and thereby honouring the outcome of the referendum, and on the other, still retains access to the Single Market in substance. This is at least to be expected for the financial services sector, the topic of interest here, where the economic case is so compelling on both sides.

A 'sector by sector' approach appears likely in this context, whereby negotiators reach consensus on Single Market inclusion of particular industry sectors. Such an approach was first unofficially discussed for the car industry, following the secret agreement the UK Government reached with carmaker Nissan. In this deal, Nissan is assumed to have been promised continued Single Market membership for the car industry. A similar status could be achieved for the financial sector.

However, as a quid pro quo, it appears likely that the UK Government will have to give ground on its position towards limiting immigration.[147] It is to be assumed that such a concession will officially be made with reluctance—but in secret Theresa May will be aware that this type of immigration would be of actual benefit to the UK economy. The supply of workers and students from the EU has helped the UK grow faster than any other Member State in the past. To avoid suffocating the domestic industry, UK officials have already indicated that they may continue to let in financial

---

144 In contrast, Michel Barnier insists that the transition period should end by December 2020. See Barker/Brunsden/Mance, 'Brexit transition should end by 2021, says Barnier', Financial Times (21.12.2017), 4.

145 A Davis Polk Client Memorandum, 'Lex and Brexit—The Law and Brexit', issue 9 (30.11.2016) expects negotiations to last between five and ten years.

146 See also Ringe, 'A Brexit deal for financial services', in: Armour/Eidenmüller (eds), *Negotiating Brexit* (2017), 45.

147 'The Road to Brexit', Leader, The Economist (08.10.2016).

services employees.[148] For example, Philip Hammond, the UK Chancellor of the Exchequer, openly discussed the possibility of granting special work permit exemptions to EU citizens working in financial services.[149] In terms of the legal design of the agreement, different variations are possible, depending on the bargaining power and negotiation outcome. Either the UK opts out of free movement, but allows for a number of back exceptions, or the UK remains subject to free movement but is allowed to deviate in a number of pre-defined areas. In substance, both approaches would probably yield very similar outcomes.

The result would be a bespoke agreement between the UK and the EU, not entirely dissimilar from the relationship between Switzerland and the EU. A far-reaching Single Market access for the UK appears to be the optimal solution. Political forces and populist influence on both sides of the Channel may, however jeopardise this outcome, and for a long time the consensus prevailed that no such solution could be achieved. However, the conclusion of phase 1 of the Brexit negotiations in December 2017 gave renewed support to the idea. In the attempt to satisfy both the continuity of Irish north-south relationship (in particular, the avoidance of any hard border) and the inner-UK trade relationship, the UK committed to maintain 'regulatory alignment' with the Single Market. The decisive passage of the Joint Report reads: 'In the absence of agreed solutions, the United Kingdom will maintain full alignment with those rules of the Internal Market and the Customs Union which, now or in the future, support North-South cooperation, the all-island economy and the protection of the 1998 Agreement.'[150] This passage has been interpreted as paving the way for a soft Brexit.[151]

A pragmatic concept along these lines is a so-called 'Continental Partnership', proposed in a recent policy paper. This is the idea of an idiosyncratic and innovative relationship between the UK and the EU, resting on

---

148 *Ibid.*
149 G. Parker/Blitz, 'Hammond draws fire for Brexit caution', Financial Times (18.10.2016), 3.
150 Joint report from the negotiators of the European Union and the United Kingdom Government on progress during phase 1 of negotiations under Article 50 TEU on the United Kingdom's orderly withdrawal from the European Union (08.12.2017) para 49, https://ec.europa.eu/commission/sites/beta-political/files/joint_report.pdf.
151 Green, 'Brexit: what regulatory alignment means and does not mean', FT.com, https://www.ft.com/content/4fddeb2e-7e92-3d81-b0a7-9dfeb6055510 (08.12.2017); Münchau, 'Sneaking back into the Single Market', Financial Times (11.12.2017), 13.

the UK's participation in a series of selected common policies consistent with access to the Single Market.[152] Although the details obviously need to be worked out, this idea may helpfully inform the debate and serve as a focal point and role model for future collaboration.

5.2 Alternative: Equivalence and Third-Country Passport

If full market membership for the financial industry cannot be successfully negotiated, a second-best scenario is conceivable. Such a 'Plan B' would assume that the UK counts as a 'third country' for EU financial regulation; as such, it could still rely on being classified as an 'equivalent' legal system and thereby profit from a third-country passport under relevant EU legislation.[153] This is the approach favoured by the 2018 UK Government White Paper for financial services.[154]

The EU utilises an equivalence test in many areas to reduce overlaps and capital costs for EU institutions that comply with rules in other countries.[155] To illustrate, Articles 46 and 47 of MiFIR[156] set out an elaborate system of conditions that are to be satisfied for 'third-country firms' to perform investment activities with or without any ancillary services to EU counterparties and to professional clients.

---

152 Pisani-Ferry/Röttgen/Sapir/Tucker/Wolff, 'Europe after Brexit: A proposal for a continental partnership', Bruegel, http://bruegel.org/2016/08/europe-after-brexit-a-proposal-for-a-continental-partnership/ (25.08.2016).

153 See European Parliament, Directorate-General for Internal Policies/Economic Governance Support Unit, 'Briefing: Third-country equivalence in EU banking legislation' (07.11.2016); Scarpetta, 'Understanding regulatory equivalence—an effective fall-back option for UK financial services after Brexit', OpenEurope blog post, http://openeurope.org.uk/today/blog/understanding-regulatory-equiva lence-an-effective-fall-back-option-for-uk-financial-services-after-brexit/ (19.10.2016). For an overview, see the equivalence table at http://ec.europa.eu/fin ance/general-policy/docs/global/equivalence-table_en.pdf.

154 UK Government, *The Future Relationship between the United Kingdom and the European Union – Presented to Parliament by the Prime Minister by Command of Her Majesty* (Cm 9593, July 2018).

155 Ferran, 'The UK as a third country actor in EU financial services regulation' (2017) 3 Journal of Financial Regulation, 40.

156 Regulation (EU) No 600/2014 of the European Parliament and of the Council of 15 May 2014 on markets in financial instruments and amending Regulation (EU) No. 648/2012, [2014] OJ L173/84.

Central to the requirements is the condition that the Commission has adopted an equivalence decision in accordance with Article 47(1).[157] Under that article, the Commission may adopt a 'decision [...] in relation to a third country stating that the legal and supervisory arrangements of that third country ensure that firms authorised in that third country comply with legally binding prudential and business conduct requirements which have equivalent effect to the requirements set out in this Regulation, in [the Capital Requirements Directive], in [MiFID 2], and in the implementing measures adopted under this Regulation and under those Directives and that the legal framework of that third country provides for an effective equivalent system for the recognition of investment firms authorised under third-country legal regimes'.

Such third-country clauses have become the norm in many pieces of financial markets architecture, and the UK places high hopes on relying on them as a fall-back position or 'safety net'.[158] There are a number of problems attached to using a third-country status for the Single Market, however.

The first issue is that the third-country passporting rights tend to be restricted to wholesale financial services, whereas marketing of services to retail customers is typically not allowed. Thus, equivalence does not cover some core banking activities such as deposit taking and cross-border lending. That might not be a serious obstacle in practice, as the UK financial industry is arguably mostly focused on wholesale markets anyhow, which are the more lucrative part of the market overall.[159]

But two other considerations may make third-country access less palatable. First, the availability of third-country access is rather patchy. Several pieces of EU legislation do include the principle, but others do not. For example, the legal framework for UCITS[160] (mutual funds) in the EU does not allow third-country passporting at all.[161] Even where the principle exists, its requirements and thresholds vary. This may jeopardise the possi-

---

157 See MiFIR Art. 46(2)(a).
158 See Scarpetta, 'Understanding regulatory equivalence—an effective fall-back option for UK financial services after Brexit', OpenEurope blog post, http://openeurope.org.uk/today/blog/understanding-regulatory-equivalence-an-effective-fall-back-option-for-uk-financial-services-after-brexit/ (19.10.2016).
159 European Parliament Economic Governance Support Unit, 'Briefing—Brexit: the United-Kingdom and EU financial services' (09.12.2016), 3-4.
160 Undertakings for the Collective Investment of Transferable Securities.
161 Other examples of legal acts that do not provide for a passport are CRD IV and (in parts) Solvency II.

bility of a holistic Single Market access for the entirety of the UK financial sector. For example, in the field of hedge funds' access to the European market, the relevant piece of EU legislation—the Alternative Investment Fund Managers Directive (AIFMD)—in theory provides for an equivalence rule. However, the Commission has not used it to date—and it does not seem inclined to do so.[162]

Even more serious is the risk of *political* exploitation attached to the vetting process steered by the European Commission. The Commission is *de facto* the sole body responsible for assessing whether a third-country system really is 'equivalent' to EU standards.[163] Given that the UK has long been an EU member and has faithfully implemented all of EU financial legislation over past decades, one would assume that the UK must be the paradigm example of an 'equivalent' jurisdiction. However, the risk remains that the equivalence decision is hijacked for political motives, unrelated to substantial reasons.[164] Unlike genuine Single Market access, equivalence is not an entitlement, but a privilege which can be unilaterally withdrawn by the European Commission at short notice.[165]

There are already signs of political tactics over equivalence emerging right now, before the UK has even left: the EU recently initiated a process to review the equivalence regime overall, with a view of streamlining the process and toughening the approval criteria, in particular for systemically important financial institutions.[166] In its recent reflection document on the equivalence process, the European Commission uses remarkably strong rhetoric to underline the fact that equivalence is primarily an instrument in the interest of the EU, and may only indirectly benefit the third country

---

162 Tuffy, 'Hedge funds in the UK need a hard-Brexit contingency plan', Financial Times (05.12.2016), FTfm 9.

163 Wymeersch, 'Third-Country Equivalence and Access to the EU Financial Markets Including in Case of Brexit', (2018) 4 Journal of Financial Regulation, 209.

164 Scarpetta, 'Understanding regulatory equivalence—an effective fall-back option for UK financial services after Brexit', OpenEurope blog post, http://openeurope. org.uk/today/blog/understanding-regulatory-equivalence-an-effective-fall-back-op tion-for-uk-financial-services-after-brexit/ (19.10.2016): the process 'can easily trespass into politics—not least because the Commission can wait as long as it wishes to issue its final verdict'.

165 Ford, 'Brexit equivalence deal could spare City pain of Morton's fork', *Financial Times* (12.12.2016), 20.

166 Barker/Brunsden, 'EU review casts doubt on City's hopes for "equivalence" as Brexit last resort', Financial Times (07.11.2016), 1.

too.[167] Further, the Commission insists that '[e]quivalence is not a vehicle for liberalising international trade' and '[t]he [equivalence] decision is a unilateral and discretionary act of the EU, both for its adoption and any possible amendment or repeal.'[168] This suggests that equivalence may be a rather unreliable last resort indeed. Reportedly, EU officials are already wary of setting precedents for Brexit when deciding about the equivalence with third countries today.[169]

Add to this the general thrust of Brexit: its perceived goal is precisely to be freed from EU legislation, and to reverse EU rules where they can. This could mean that every step of the UK legal order away from the EU acquis could be interpreted—or serve as a pretext—that the UK regulatory and supervisory standards are *not* equivalent (any more) to the EU legal order. Moreover, if the EU financial laws change over time, the UK would have to constantly adapt its own legislation to maintain continued market access for its financial services sector. This would be a politically very daunting exercise.

The only relief could come from a legally binding agreement between the third country and the EU that the former's rules are deemed equivalent.[170] It is along these lines that the 2018 White Paper proposes to develop its version of 'equivalence'. This includes a number of processes designed to encourage continued convergence and to manage the process if the legal rules between the UK and the EU diverge in the future. For example, the government would like to see a transparent methodology for assessing whether regulations are equivalent, based on clear and common objectives. Further, the White Paper proposes a structured process for withdrawing a finding of equivalence with clear timelines and notice periods to allow businesses to plan if regulatory equivalence is not maintained.[171]

These proposals are helpful to make equivalence work and turn the patchy regime into a reliable framework that business can rely on. Howe-

---

167 European Commission, *Commission Staff Working Document—EU equivalence decisions in financial services policy: an assessment* (27.02.2017) SWD(2017) 102 final.
168 *Ibid.*
169 Barker/Brunsden, 'EU review casts doubt on City's hopes for "equivalence" as Brexit last resort', Financial Times (07.11.2016), 3.
170 Armour, 'Brexit and financial services' (2017) 33 Oxford Review of Economic Policy, S54. See, for example, the 'expanded equivalence' proposal made by Reynolds: Reynolds, A blueprint for Brexit: the future of global financial services and markets in the UK, (2016).
171 UK Government, *The Future Relationship between the United Kingdom and the European Union – Presented to Parliament by the Prime Minister by Command of Her Majesty* (Cm 9593, July 2018).

ver, it is uncertain whether such an agreement is acceptable to the EU.[172] In any case, it would take a long time to negotiate, and firms may have to endure a long period of uncertainty during this period. For example, it took the EU four years to negotiate a recent agreement with the US Commodity Futures Trading Commission (CFTC) on the equivalence of central counterparty clearing.[173]

5.3 Private Solutions

Were the UK and the EU to fail reaching an agreement, and the UK to cease being a Member State by way of a 'hard' Brexit, private solutions by market participants are to be expected. Financial services providers would almost certainly pursue some strategy to mitigate the loss of passporting rights in the absence of a political deal.

An open question is whether individual firms could gain market access by volunteering to be subject to EU rules. The regulatory concept of 'voluntarism' may grant individual third-country firms access to local markets where these firms voluntarily commit to comply with local rules.[174] The beauty of such an approach would be that it could be achieved in the absence of any political deal.

Importantly, however, such regimes currently only exist in some singular parts of the financial regulation framework, and where they exist, they exist only at the national level, but not for the EU as a whole.[175] That is to say that at best, UK firms may privately gain access to one particular area, in one particular jurisdiction, by striking an individual deal directly with another EU country. Further, EU law sometimes imposes limits on such national deals: for example, Article 54 of MiFIR permits such national regimes only for three years after an equivalence assessment.

It does not appear, therefore, that such agreements would offer a stable perspective of market access for City firms. They would probably be rather

---

172 For a critical comment, see Wolf, 'A post-Brexit transition must be the priority', *Financial Times* (30.11.2016), 13.

173 See Brush/Bain, 'EU Banks Closer to $5 Billion Respite With SEC Clearing Rule', Bloomberg, https://www.bloomberg.com/news/articles/2016-09-28/eu-banks-eye-5-billion-capital-reprieve-as-sec-votes-on-rules (28.09.2016).

174 Ford, 'City probes ways to access EU market after Brexit', *Financial Times* (11.04.2017), 3.

175 One example is the UK concept of 'overseas persons exclusion' under Financial Services and Markets Act 2000 (Regulated Activities) Order 2001 Art. 72.

piecemeal, complex and costly, and very much dependent on the goodwill of individual countries.

In reality, instead, UK financial firms may only truly secure Single Market access by way of setting up a subsidiary in one of the EU 27 Member States which could provide financial services as a separately regulated and capitalised legal entity.[176] However, such 'subsidiarisation' would not be a cost-free exercise. The EU financial law framework has specific provisions to ensure that a subsidiary does not become a letterbox entity, where the company exists on paper and the work is done elsewhere.[177] In the case of banking, the subsidiary would require separate capitalisation, separate staff, and supervision of the host Member State.

Even under that scenario, some banks are hoping to keep much of their current UK operations in place and set up only a formal 'brass plate' subsidiary without much substantial business activity in the EU. Various structures are considered to achieve this, such as 'back-to-back' trades to transfer the economic risk of individual transactions back to the main UK banking entity, or a 'branch-back' model, where a lightweight or shell operation in the EU 27 would carry out most of its business through a UK affiliate.[178] The European Banking Authority (EBA) predictably adopted a reluctant stance towards such ideas, warning that such an EU-based entity 'must not operate as an "empty shell", but have appropriate governance and risk management arrangements in place to be able to take on identification and management of the risks that it has generated, and that in the event of a crisis, it could rapidly deploy scaled up risk management arrangements.'[179] The UK Government has also conceded that the present regulatory framework makes it very difficult to devise a set-up where UK banks would con-

---

176 Lehmann/Zetzsche, 'How does it feel to be a Third Country? The Consequences of Brexit for Financial Market Law', CIGI/BIICL Working Paper No. 14 (February 2018), 12 ff.

177 For example, in the AIFMD: Directive 2011/61/EU of the European Parliament and of the Council of 8 June 2011 on Alternative Investment Fund Managers and amending Directives 2003/41/EC and 2009/65/EC and Regulations (EC) No. 1060/2009 and (EU) No. 1095/2010 (AIFMD), [2011] OJ L174/1.

178 Jenkins, 'Banking on a back-to-back Brexit', FT Brexit Briefing, https://www.ft.co m/content/4fa2fc60-c093-11e7-b8a3-38a6e068f464 (03.11.2017).

179 European Banking Authority, *Opinion of the European Banking Authority on issues related to the departure of the United Kingdom from the European Union* (EBA/Op/ 2017/12, 12.10.2017).

tinue their operations unaffected without a substantial establishment in the EU 27.[180]

Chances are that some large banking groups already have a substantial EU subsidiary in place. For example, Credit Suisse CEO Tidjane Thiam explained that (despite substantial costs) the Swiss bank is in a 'reasonable position' to deal with any Brexit outcome, thanks to its existing subsidiaries in Dublin and Luxembourg.[181] Likewise, insurance giant Lloyd's claims that the impact of Brexit on its operations will be minimal, and that contingency plans within its group structure are already underway.[182]

These two statements reveal an important point of information: size matters. Whereas large financial services groups are likely to already have an EU 27-based subsidiary in place or to set one up at relatively low cost, the disruption of Brexit will be felt most severely by smaller and medium-sized financial institutions, for which the costs of adjusting will be grave. A report by the Boston Consulting Group estimates that a requirement to set up a subsidiary in the EU 27 would increase investment banks' global costs by 3% to 8%, depending on their current operational model.[183] Private solutions are clearly the second-best solution only.

6. Conclusion

Brexit will inevitably come, but more in form than in substance. That is, in a nutshell, the central message of this paper for the future of European financial integration and the UK. This expectation is grounded in a combination of economic necessities and political constellations on both sides,

---

180 Pickard, 'UK's sector-by-sector Brexit assessments released', FT.com, https://www.f t.com/content/bcebe3f8- e664-11e7-8b99-0191e45377ec (21.12.2017).

181 Griffin/Suess, 'Thiam Says Passport Loss Risks 20% of His Bank's U.K. Volume', Bloomberg, https://www.bloomberg.com/news/articles/2016-09-28/credit-suisse-c eo-says-no-passporting-risks-20-of-london-volume (28.09.2016).

182 'This will not impact Lloyd's', Interview of Lloyd's Chairman John Nelson with Versicherungswirtschaft, http://versicherungswirtschaft-heute.de/dossier/this-will -not-impact-lloyds/ (21.10.2016). In December 2016, Lloyd's announced to set up a separate subsidiary in Germany or the Netherlands. See Dunkley/ Arnold, 'Lloyds eyes European arm if UK loses market access', Financial Times (28.12.2016), 17.

183 Morel/Teschner/Martin/Rhode/Bohn, 'Global Capital Markets 2016: The Value Migration (Part 2)—Assessing the Impact of Brexit' (BCG White Paper 2016), http://image-src.bcg.com/BCG_COM/BCG-Impact-of-Brexit-on-Capital-Markets-July-2016_tcm9-38972.pdf.

the EU 27 and the UK. Most importantly, the paper draws on the rich experience of the trajectory of financial integration in the EU, where legal formality has frequently bowed to political reasoning and economic necessities.

One recent example serves as an ideal illustration: Switzerland. In a parallel case to Brexit, Switzerland has long been in a similar conflict between market access and its own political exigencies. Whilst the political elite has sought to uphold an agreement with the EU guaranteeing free movement of people, a 2014 referendum demanded immigration quotas for foreigners.

Just recently, Swiss parliamentarians *de facto* undermined the outcome of the referendum by approving a carefully crafted package of measures aimed at boosting the employment prospects of locals without violating the free movement deal with the EU.

In a remarkably lucid analysis, one leading commentator summed up the outcome of the process very much along the lines of analysis pursued here: that 'we have created a Swiss exception—but tried to conform with the rules of the game, so it's not actually an exception'.[184] This, it is submitted, matches the course of the Brexit showdown expected here: legal creativity will engineer a solution that both formally satisfies the referendum outcome but protects vital economic interests of business.

---

184 MaxStern, cofounder of Foraus, a foreign policy forum (cited according to Ralph Atkins, 'Swiss head for EU immigration climbdown', Financial Times (14.12.2016), 8.

Citizens' Rights after Brexit: The Withdrawal Agreement and the Future Mobility Framework

*Menelaos Markakis**

I. Introduction

This chapter looks at the impact of Brexit on EU citizenship rights and free movement of persons. In doing so, it primarily focuses on three documents: the Joint Report from the negotiators of the EU and the UK Government on progress during the first phase of the negotiations ('Joint Report'); the draft Withdrawal Agreement (WA or 'Agreement'); and the political declaration setting out the framework for the future relationship between the EU and the UK ('political declaration'). First, the Joint Report, which was published on 8 December 2017, sets out joint commitments which 'shall be reflected in the Withdrawal Agreement in full detail.'[1] However, '[t]his does not prejudge any adaptations that might be appropriate in case transitional arrangements were to be agreed in the second phase of the negotiations, and is without prejudice to discussions on the framework of the future relationship.'[2] Second, the draft WA is based on Treaty on European Union (TEU) Article 50.[3] It sets out the arrangements for the withdrawal of the UK from the EU and from the European Atomic Energy

---

* Postdoctoral Researcher, Erasmus University Rotterdam. I have benefitted from discussions with Hayley Hooper, Beth Houghton and René Repasi. The usual disclaimer applies.
1 'Joint report from the negotiators of the European Union and the United Kingdom Government on progress during phase 1 of negotiations under Article 50 TEU on the United Kingdom's orderly withdrawal from the European Union' TF50 (2017) 19 – Commission to EU 27 (8 December 2017) <https://ec.europa.eu/commission/s ites/beta-political/files/joint_report.pdf> accessed 8 June 2018.
2 Ibid.
3 For the arrangements governing the adoption of the Withdrawal Agreement and the agreement(s) governing the future relationship between the EU and the UK, see further Fabian Amtenbrink, Menelaos Markakis and René Repasi, 'Legal Implications of Brexit: Customs Union, Internal Market Acquis for Goods and Services, Consumer Protection Law, Public Procurement' (August 2017) <http://www.europ arl.europa.eu/RegData/etudes/STUD/2017/607328/IPOL_STU(201 7)607328_EN.pdf> accessed 6 July 2018, 17-31.

Community (EURATOM). It is important to distinguish between two different texts. The draft WA published by the European Commission on 19 March 2018 translated into legal prose the Joint Report and proposed text for those outstanding withdrawal issues which were mentioned, but were not set out in detail, in the Joint Report.[4] The EU and the UK recently reached agreement at negotiators' level on the draft WA, which inevitably differs in some respects from the earlier draft.[5] Third, the WA is accompanied by a political declaration setting out the framework for the future relationship between the EU and the UK.[6] At the time of writing, the UK Prime Minister has not yet secured the requisite parliamentary majority in favour of her deal.

The twin challenge in this chapter is to assess the impact of those documents on the livelihoods of UK and EU nationals affected by Brexit; and to highlight the legal question marks that may hang over the rights granted to the persons affected. Generally, there are three models or ideal types for

4 European Commission, 'Draft Agreement on the withdrawal of the United Kingdom of Great Britain and Northern Ireland from the European Union and the European Atomic Energy Community highlighting the progress made (coloured version) in the negotiation round with the UK of 16-19 March 2018' TF50 (2018) 35 – Commission to EU27 (19 March 2018) <https://ec.europa.eu/commission/sites/beta-political/files/draft_agreement_coloured.pdf> accessed 8 June 2018; European Commission, 'Brexit: European Commission publishes draft Article 50 Withdrawal Agreement' (28 February 2018) <http://europa.eu/rapid/press-release_IP-18-1243_e n.htm> accessed 8 June 2018.

5 European Commission, 'Draft Agreement on the withdrawal of the United Kingdom of Great Britain and Northern Ireland from the European Union and the European Atomic Energy Community, as agreed at negotiators' level on 14 November 2018' TF50 (2018) 55 – Commission to EU27 (14 November 2018) <https://ec.e uropa.eu/commission/sites/beta-political/files/draft_withdrawal_agreement_0.pdf> accessed 25 November 2018. See also European Commission, 'Instrument relating to the agreement on the withdrawal of the United Kingdom of Great Britain and Northern Ireland from the European Union and the European Atomic Energy Community' TF50 (2019) 61 – Commission to EU27 (11 March 2019) <https://ec.e uropa.eu/commission/sites/beta-political/files/instrument_0.pdf> accessed 15 May 2019.

6 Council of the European Union, 'Political declaration setting out the framework for the future relationship between the European Union and the United Kingdom' (22 November 2018) <https://www.consilium.europa.eu/media/37059/20181121-co ver-political-declaration.pdf> accessed 26 November 2018. It was supplemented by: European Commission, 'Joint Statement supplementing the Political Declaration setting out the framework for the future relationship between the European Union and the United Kingdom of Great Britain and Northern Ireland' TF50 (2019) 62 – Commission to EU27 (11 March 2019) <https://ec.europa.eu/commission/sites/beta -political/files/joint_statement_.pdf> accessed 15 May 2019.

the evolution of EU citizenship law and free movement rights after Brexit. Under the first model, the rights of EU citizens living or working in the UK, and those of UK nationals in the EU 27, would remain identical to those they had before Brexit. This would be tantamount to 'freezing' those rights at the time of Brexit, and preserving them for the lifetime of their holders. Under the second model, their rights would increase in range and/or strength, pursuant to an agreement (or network of agreements) between the EU 27 and the UK. The WA could also lay down, if it followed this model, more lenient requirements than hitherto for acquiring or preserving the rights enshrined therein. Under the third model, their rights would decrease or otherwise deteriorate in range and/or strength. Such rights could also be subject, under this model, to additional conditions or formalities, or to more stringent requirements, as was the case hitherto.

As will be shown in this chapter, the regulatory technique used in the Joint Report and the draft WA is that the rights of EU and UK nationals resident in one another's territory would build on existing primary and secondary Union law (notably, the Citizens' Rights Directive 2004/38/EC), albeit with some adaptations. Such adaptations give rise to a messy legal reality that evades neat classification in light of the models set out above. It will be shown that, for the largest part, the Joint Report and the draft WA seek to preserve those rights that UK and EU nationals currently enjoy (as per model one). However, this is only true for those that would be resident in one another's territory before the cut-off date. What is more, in some important cases, the draft WA would serve, if concluded, to decrease the rights that EU and UK nationals currently enjoy (as per model three). This is subject to the argument put forward later in this chapter that such rights could be complemented by the provisions of the agreement(s) to be concluded between the EU 27 and the UK on their future relationship (such as a deep and comprehensive Free Trade Agreement), and/or 'topped up' through more favourable domestic provisions. To make things yet more complicated, there are further (limited) cases, where the Joint Report and the draft WA set out more lenient conditions for preserving the rights granted to the persons concerned (as per model two).

The chapter is structured as follows. The discussion begins with the Joint Report on progress during the first phase of the negotiations. The Joint Report provides a neat summary of the key issues with respect to citizens' rights and will set the scene for the discussion to follow. The focus then shifts to the draft WA, as was most recently finalised (the November 2018 draft). The chapter examines four sets of issues with respect to both these documents: their legal effects and methods of interpretation; their personal scope with respect to citizens' rights; administrative procedures for application for status; and the substantive provisions on citizens' rights. Reference to existing UK or EU legislation concerning citizens' rights (broadly conceived) is also made where appropriate. The penultimate section looks at the future mobility framework, which for the time being is mostly a matter for speculation. The chapter concludes with some preliminary reflections on the Joint Report and the draft WA, thereby highlighting the various issues that may arise therefrom.

II. *The Joint Report on progress during the first phase of the negotiations*

The negotiating parties state in the Joint Report that '[t]he overall objective of the Withdrawal Agreement with respect to citizens' rights is to provide reciprocal protection for Union and UK citizens, to enable the effective exercise of rights derived from Union law and based on past life choices, where those citizens have exercised free movement rights by the specified date.'[7] That specified date is, according to the Joint Report, the time of the UK's withdrawal from the EU.[8]

1. *The legal effects and interpretation of the Withdrawal Agreement*

The Joint Report includes a number of provisions which explicate the legal effects of the WA, as well as the methods for its interpretation. These are as follows. 'Both Parties agree that the Withdrawal Agreement should provide for the legal effects of the citizens' rights Part both in the UK and in the Union.'[9] 'The provision in the Agreement should enable citizens to *rely directly* on their rights as set out in the citizens' rights Part of the Agreement and should specify that inconsistent or incompatible rules and provisions will be *disapplied*' (emphasis added).[10]

More specifically, as regards the EU 27, it is stated that '[t]he Withdrawal Agreement will be binding upon the institutions of the Union and on its Member States from its entry into force pursuant to Article 216(2) TFEU.'[11] For its part, the UK Government undertakes to bring forward a Bill, *the Wi-*

---

7 Joint Report, para 6.
8 Ibid para 8.
9 Ibid para 34.
10 Ibid para 35.
11 Ibid para 36.

thdrawal Agreement and Implementation Bill [now known as the *EU (With-drawal Agreement) Bill*],[12] which will fully incorporate the citizens' rights Part into UK law.[13] 'Once this Bill has been adopted, the provisions of the citizens' rights Part will have effect in primary legislation and will prevail over inconsistent or incompatible legislation, unless Parliament expressly repeals this Act in future.'[14] This is in line with parliamentary sovereignty. The reference to express repeal in the Joint Report alludes to the legal status of this future Act as a *constitutional statute*, which could not be subject to implied repeal through a subsequently adopted statute which would be (partially) inconsistent with the Act (unless the result contended for was "irresistible").[15] Moreover, as mentioned above, the provisions on citizens' rights would be backed by the legal remedy of disapplication, which would otherwise not be readily available in the UK after Brexit.[16]

The Joint Report further includes a section on the 'consistent interpretation of the citizens' rights Part', pursuant to which the UK courts shall have 'due regard' to the relevant decisions of the CJEU after Brexit.[17] The Joint Report further foresees a role for the CJEU with respect to citizens' rights: the Agreement shall establish a mechanism enabling a UK court or tribunal to decide, having had due regard to whether relevant case law exists,

---

12 'Government confirms detail on new Bill that will put Withdrawal Agreement into law' (24 July 2018) <https://www.gov.uk/government/news/government-confir ms-detail-on-new-bill-that-will-put-withdrawal-agreement-into-law> accessed 14 December 2018.

13 Joint Report, para 36.

14 Ibid.

15 A constitutional statute is 'one which (a) conditions the legal relationship between citizen and state in some general, overarching manner, or (b) enlarges or diminishes the scope of what we would now regard as fundamental constitutional rights'. *Thoburn v Sunderland City Council* [2002] EWHC 195 (Admin); [2003] Q.B. 151 (DC), paras 62-63. On constitutional statutes, see e.g. Mikołaj Barczentewicz, '"Constitutional Statutes" Still Alive?' (2014) 130 LQR, 557; Paul Craig, 'Constitutionalising Constitutional Law: HS2' (2014) Public Law, 373 (382-387); Farrah Ahmed and Adam Perry, 'Constitutional Statutes' (2017) 37 OJLS, 461.

16 This is with the exception of pre-exit, 'retained' EU law, which would still prevail over domestic legislation adopted prior to Brexit. See section 5(1)-(3) of the EU (Withdrawal) Act 2018. See further Alison Young, 'Benkharbouche and the Future of Disapplication' (24 October 2017) <https://ukconstitutionallaw.org/2017/1 0/24/alison-young-benkharbouche-and-the-future-of-disapplication/> accessed 30 October 2017; Menelaos Markakis, 'Brexit and the EU Charter of Fundamental Rights' (2019) Public Law, 82 (96-98); Catherine Barnard, 'So Long, Farewell, Auf Wiedersehen, Adieu: Brexit and the Charter of Fundamental Rights' (2019) 82 MLR, 350 (363-365).

17 Joint Report, para 38.

to ask the CJEU questions on the interpretation of those rights where they consider that a CJEU ruling on the question is necessary for it to be able to give judgment in a case pending before it. This mechanism should be available for UK courts and tribunals for litigation brought within 8 years from the date of application of the citizens' rights Part.[18] Moreover, there is provision for 'an exchange of case law between the courts and regular judicial dialogue', with a view to supporting and facilitating the consistent interpretation of the citizens' rights Part.[19] It is further envisaged to give the UK Government and the European Commission the right to intervene in relevant cases before the CJEU and before UK courts and tribunals respectively.[20] The implementation and application of the citizens' rights Part will be monitored in the EU 27 by the Commission and in the UK by an independent national authority.[21]

2. The personal scope of the Withdrawal Agreement with respect to citizens' rights

The Joint Report states that the WA shall cover the situation of *Union nationals who legally reside in the UK* and *UK nationals who legally reside in the EU 27*, as well as *their family members* as defined by Directive 2004/38/EC who are legally resident in the host State by the specified date.[22] There is a further provision for family members who were not residing in the host State on the specified date but will nevertheless be entitled to join a Union citizen or UK national right holder after the specified date for the lifetime of the right holder.[23] These family members are, according to Directive 2004/38/EC, Article 2, the spouse, the partner with whom the Union citizen has contracted a registered partnership, the direct descendants who are under the age of 21 or are dependants and those of the spouse or partner, and the dependent direct relatives in the ascending line and those of the spouse or partner. Family members also include, according to the Joint Report, children born, or legally adopted, after the specified date, whether inside or outside the host State.[24] Moreover, '[t]he UK and EU 27 Member

---

18 Ibid.
19 Ibid para 39.
20 Ibid.
21 Ibid para 40.
22 Ibid para 10.
23 Ibid para 12.
24 Ibid para 12.

States will facilitate entry and residence of *partners in a durable relationship* [Article 3(2)(b) of Directive 2004/38/EC] after the UK's withdrawal in accordance with national legislation if the partners did not reside in the host State on the specified date, the relationship existed and was durable on the specified date and continues to exist at the point they wish to join the right holder' (emphasis added).[25] The right to be joined by family members not covered by the above provisions after the specified date will be subject to national law, which may or may not allow for the Union/UK citizen to be joined by such members.[26] The Joint Report further states that the WA will cover the situation of *frontier workers*, who reside in the EU 27 and work in the UK, and vice versa.[27]

3. Administrative procedures for applications for status

The Joint Report gives the green light to the UK and the EU 27 Member States to require that EU and UK nationals respectively apply to obtain a status conferring the rights of residence as provided for by the WA and be issued with a residence document attesting to the existence of that right.[28] The UK and the EU 27 Member States can also continue with the present system under which entitlement of rights under the WA may be attested by any other means of proof than a residence document.[29] Where the host State requires the persons concerned to apply for a status, no status is obtained if no successful application is made.[30] This is subject to the proviso that adequate time of at least two years will be allowed to persons within the scope of the WA to submit their applications.[31] It is further provided that during this period they will continue to enjoy the rights conferred on them in the WA.[32]

The Joint Report provides that administrative procedures for applications for status will be transparent, smooth and streamlined.[33] This part of the Report addresses a deep concern with regard to the treatment that EU

---

25 Ibid para 13.
26 Ibid para 14.
27 Ibid para 15.
28 Ibid para 16.
29 Ibid.
30 Ibid.
31 Ibid para 17e.
32 Ibid.
33 Ibid para 17.

citizens may be subject to by the UK Home Office in the run-up to and after Brexit.[34] More specifically, the WA will specify that the host State cannot require anything more than is strictly necessary and proportionate to determine whether the criteria have been met.[35] The host State will avoid any unnecessary administrative burdens.[36]Application forms will be short, simple, user friendly and adjusted to the context of the WA. The host State will work with the applicants to help them prove their eligibility under the WA and to avoid any errors or omissions that may impact on the application decision. Competent authorities will give applicants the opportunity to furnish supplementary evidence or remedy any deficiencies where it appears a simple omission has taken place. A principle of evidential flexibility will apply, enabling competent authorities to exercise discretion in favour of the applicant where appropriate.[37] A proportionate approach will be taken to those who miss the deadline for application where there is a good reason. Applications made by families at the same time will be considered together.[38]

Decisions taken under the procedure for obtaining status under the WA will be made in accordance with the objective criteria established therein (i.e. no discretion, unless in favour of the applicant). There will be safeguards in the WA for a fair procedure, and decisions will be subject to the redress mechanisms and judicial controls provided in Directive 2004/38/EC.[39] Pending a final decision by the competent authorities on any application made for status under the WA, as well as a final judgment handed down in case of judicial redress sought against any rejection of such application, the citizens' rights Part of the WA will apply to the applicant. The host State may, however, remove applicants who submitted

---

34 Gareth Davies, 'The State of Play on Citizens' Rights and Brexit' (6 February 2018) <https://europeanlawblog.eu/2018/02/06/the-state-of-play-on-citizens-rights-and-br exit/> accessed 9 July 2018 castigates the arcane workings of UK migration controls: 'One of the great problems for those living in the UK has always been its somewhat random approach to administration, veering between nonchalance and mercilessness, so that a migrant is typically not required to do any kind of paperwork in order to get on with their life, but should they for whatever reason actually need to prove that they have been resident for the past years will be faced with inflexible demands that they document every weekend away, every job and home, and almost every pizza that they have ordered.'

35 Joint Report, para 17a.
36 Ibid para 17b.
37 Ibid para 17c.
38 Ibid para 17d.
39 Ibid para 19.

fraudulent or abusive applications from its territory under the conditions set out in Directive 2004/38/EC, in particular Articles 31 and 35, even before a final judgment has been handed down in case of judicial redress sought against any rejection of such application.[40]

4. *The substantive provisions on citizens' rights*

The Joint Report provides that 'any discrimination on grounds of nationality will be prohibited in the host State and the State of work in respect of Union citizens and UK nationals, and their respective family members covered by the Withdrawal Agreement.'[41] However, this is 'without prejudice to any special provisions therein', which may hence allow (or require) treating UK nationals differently from EU citizens and vice versa.[42]

With regard to residence rights, the Joint Report provides that '[t]he conditions for acquiring *the right of residence* under the Withdrawal Agreement are those set out in Articles 6 and 7 of Directive 2004/38/EC, including the right to change status' (emphasis added).[43] It will be recalled that the latter Directive distinguishes between stays for a period of up to three months (Article 6) and stays for a period of longer than three months (Article 7). No conditions or formalities, other than the requirement to hold a valid identity card or passport, are attached to the right of residence for a period of up to three months.[44] As regards the right of residence for more than three months, the Directive provides that:

1. All Union citizens shall have the right of residence on the territory of another Member State for a period of longer than three months if they:
(a) are workers or self-employed persons in the host Member State; or
(b) have sufficient resources for themselves and their family members not to become a burden on the social assistance system of the host

---

40 Ibid para 18. On what constitutes fraud and abuse of rights, see Communication from the Commission to the European Parliament and the Council on guidance for better transposition and application of Directive 2004/38/EC on the rights of citizens of the Union and their family members to move and reside freely within the territory of the Member States COM(2009) 313 final, 15.
41 Joint Report, para 11.
42 Ibid para 11.
43 Ibid para 20.
44 Directive 2004/38/EC, art 6, para 1.

Member State during their period of residence and have comprehensive sickness insurance cover in the host Member State; or

(c)— are enrolled at a private or public establishment, accredited or financed by the host Member State on the basis of its legislation or administrative practice, for the principal purpose of following a course of study, including vocational training; and

— have comprehensive sickness insurance cover in the host Member State and assure the relevant national authority, by means of a declaration or by such equivalent means as they may choose, that they have sufficient resources for themselves and their family members not to become a burden on the social assistance system of the host Member State during their period of residence; or

(d) are family members accompanying or joining a Union citizen who satisfies the conditions referred to in points (a), (b) or (c).[45]

Directive 2004/38/EC extends the same right to 'family members who are not nationals of a Member State, accompanying or joining the Union citizen in the host Member State, provided that such Union citizen satisfies the conditions referred to in paragraph 1(a), (b) or (c).[46] It further lays down the requirements under which a Union citizen who is no longer a worker or self-employed person shall retain the status of worker or self-employed person, which – to simplify things – include a temporal inability to work due to illness or accident, involuntary unemployment, and embarking on vocational training.[47]

With regard to *permanent residence*, the Joint Report provides that '[t]he conditions for acquiring the right of permanent residence under the Withdrawal Agreement are those set out in Articles 16, 17 and 18 of Directive 2004/38/EC, with periods of lawful residence prior to the specified date included in the calculation of the conditions set out in Articles 16 and 17 of Directive 2004/38/EC.[48] It will be recalled that Article 16 of the latter Directive provides that 'Union citizens who have resided legally for a continuous period of five years in the host Member State shall have the right of permanent residence there.[49] The same right is enjoyed by 'family members who are not nationals of a Member State and have legally resided with the Union citizen in the host Member State for a continuous period of five

---

45 Ibid art 7, para 1.
46 Ibid art 7, para 2.
47 Ibid art 7, para 3.
48 Joint Report, para 21.
49 Directive 2004/38/EC, art 16, para 1.

years.'[50] The same provision lays down the requirements under which continuity of residence shall not be affected by temporary absences;[51] and provides that, '[o]nce acquired, the right of permanent residence shall be lost only through absence from the host Member State for a period exceeding two consecutive years.'[52] The Directive further lays down a number of exceptions for persons no longer working in the host State and their family members.[53] It further makes provision for non-EU family members wishing to acquire the right of permanent residence under very special personal or family circumstances (death of the Union citizen, divorce/annulment of marriage, and so on).[54]

The WA will partially deviate from these requirements. The Joint Report states that '[p]ersons who acquired the permanent residence rights in the host State under the Withdrawal Agreement can be absent from its territory *for a period not exceeding five consecutive years* without losing their residence right under the Withdrawal Agreement' (emphasis added).[55] It further provides that '[a]ny restrictions on grounds of public policy or security related to conduct prior to the specified date [i.e., prior to Brexit] of persons covered by the Withdrawal Agreement will be in accordance with Chapter VI of Directive 2004/38/EC.'[56] 'Any restrictions on grounds of public policy or security related to conduct after the specified date [i.e., after Brexit] will be in accordance with national law.'[57]

It should be stressed, however, that, according to the Joint Report, the UK and the EU 27 Member States can apply *more favourable* national provisions in accordance with Directive 2004/38/EC, Article 37.[58] The latter provision does not in and of itself set out any requirements for doing so. EU law referred to in the WA would therefore be a starting point, from which the two parties could unilaterally (or reciprocally) deviate in order to provide for more lax requirements for the acquisition of the right of (permanent) residence in their territory. Whether the same, more favourable provisions would need to be extended to other nationals – non-EU (or even UK) nationals in the case of the UK and other third-country nationals in

---

50 Ibid art 16, para 2.
51 Ibid art 16, para 3.
52 Ibid art 16, para 4.
53 Ibid art 17.
54 Ibid art 18.
55 Joint Report, para 25.
56 Ibid para 26.
57 Ibid para 27.
58 Ibid para 22.

the case of the EU – is a matter governed by UK and EU law (and politics) respectively.

The Joint Report further includes provisions on *the coordination of social security systems* (e.g., on the aggregation of periods of social security insurance with respect to Union and UK citizens who had in the past worked or resided in the UK or an EU Member State).[59] Regulations (EC) No. 883/2004 and (EC) No. 987/2009 will apply, and a mechanism will be established to decide jointly on the incorporation of future amendments to those Regulations in the WA.[60] It further includes *rules on healthcare* (including the European Health Insurance Card).[61] '*Equal treatment* will apply within the limits of Articles 18, 45 and 49 TFEU, Article 24 of Directive 2004/38/EC and Regulation (EU) No. 492/2011 including the rights of workers, self-employed, students and economically inactive citizens with respect to social security, social assistance, healthcare, employment, self-employment and setting up and managing an undertaking, education (including higher education) and training, social and tax advantages' (emphasis added).[62] Further, there is provision for *the recognition of professional qualifications.*[63]

III. The Withdrawal Agreement

This section will focus on the draft WA as agreed at negotiators' level on 14 November 2018. References to the draft published on 19 March 2018 ('the earlier draft'), and comparisons with the latest draft, will also be made where appropriate.[64]

---

59 Ibid para 28.
60 Ibid paras 28, 30.
61 Ibid para 29.
62 Ibid para 31.
63 Ibid para 32.
64 For a comprehensive overview, see also Rebecca Zahn, 'Brexit Deal Series: The Draft Withdrawal Agreement and Citizens' Rights' (20 November 2018) <https://www.scer.scot/database/ident-9045> accessed 25 November 2018; Steve Peers, 'The Brexit Withdrawal Agreement: Overview and First Observations' (22 November 2018) <http://eulawanalysis.blogspot.com/2018/11/the-brexit-withdrawal-agreement.html> accessed 25 November 2018.

1. Foundational issues and methods for interpretation

The WA consists of six parts: common provisions (Articles 1-8); citizens' rights (Articles 9-39); separation provisions (Articles 40-125);[65] transition (Articles 126-132); financial provisions (Articles 133-157); and institutional and final provisions (Articles 158-185). It further includes protocols on Ireland/Northern Ireland; the Sovereign Base Areas of the UK in Cyprus; and Gibraltar. This section chiefly focuses on Part Two of the WA, which concerns citizens' rights.

The provisions of Part Two shall apply as from the end of the transition period.[66] Part Two should be read in the light of the 'methods and principles relating to the effect, the implementation and the application of this Agreement', which are found in Part One of the draft WA. Notably, Article 4, para 1 provides that:

> The provisions of this Agreement and the provisions of Union law made applicable by this Agreement shall produce in respect of and in the United Kingdom the same legal effects as those which they produce within the Union and its Member States.
>
> Accordingly, legal or natural persons shall in particular be able to rely directly on the provisions contained or referred to in this Agreement which meet the conditions for direct effect under Union law.

Article 4, para 2 adds that: 'The United Kingdom shall ensure compliance with paragraph 1, including as regards the required powers of its judicial and administrative authorities to disapply inconsistent or incompatible domestic provisions, through domestic primary legislation.' This is in line with the Joint Report as well as with the earlier draft of the WA.[67]

---

65 This part includes the following titles: goods placed on the market; ongoing customs procedures; ongoing VAT and excise duty matters; intellectual property; ongoing police and judicial cooperation in criminal matters; ongoing judicial cooperation in civil and commercial matters; data and information processed or obtained before the end of the transition period, or on the basis of this agreement; ongoing public procurement and similar procedures; EURATOM related issues; Union judicial and administrative procedures; administrative cooperation procedures between Member States and the United Kingdom; privileges and immunities; and other issues relating to the functioning of the institutions, bodies, offices and agencies of the Union.

66 Draft WA, art 185. This is with the exception of arts 19 (on issuance of residence documents during the transition period) and 34(1) (on administrative cooperation).

67 See art 4, para 1 of the earlier draft WA.

The remainder of Article 4 is also broadly in line with the earlier draft, though at that stage it did not yet reflect an agreement between the negotiating parties. Article 4, para 3 provides that '[t]he provisions of this Agreement referring to Union law or to concepts or provisions thereof shall be interpreted and applied in accordance with the methods and general principles of Union law.' This may seem logical, especially to EU lawyers, but it should be stressed that it would introduce, if agreed upon, duties on the UK courts/tribunals and executive that would extend beyond those currently enshrined in the EU (Withdrawal) Act 2018 – the Act adopted by the UK legislature in preparation for Brexit.[68] Article 4, para 4 adds that '[t]he provisions of this Agreement referring to Union law or to concepts or provisions thereof shall in their implementation and application be interpreted in conformity with the relevant case law of the Court of Justice of the European Union handed down *before* the end of the transition period' (emphasis added). Again, this would expand the duties incumbent upon the UK authorities.[69] As regards the case law handed down by the CJEU *after* the end of the transition period, the UK judicial and administrative authorities 'shall have due regard' to it.[70] This is also in line with the treatment that the post-Brexit CJEU case law on 'retained' EU law receives in the EU (Withdrawal) Act.[71] However, it should be noted that, in contrast to the EU (Withdrawal) Act 2018 which refers to CJEU case law *before exit day*, the draft WA also covers case law handed down *before the end of the transition period*.[72]

---

68 The legal position under the EU (Withdrawal) Act 2018 is that 'retained' general principles of EU law are used to determine the validity, meaning and effect of pre-exit, 'retained' EU law (section 6(3)). The WA is not, technically speaking, retained EU law (section 6(7)). Moreover, there is no provision in the Act on applying the same methods for interpretation as was the case under EU law before exit day.

69 The current position under the EU (Withdrawal) Act 2018 is that pre-exit, 'retained' case law is used, just like 'retained' general principles, in order to determine the validity, meaning and effect of pre-exit, 'retained' EU law (section 6(3)). But the Withdrawal Agreement is clearly not 'retained EU law' within the meaning of the Act (section 6(7)).

70 Draft WA, art 4, para 5.

71 Section 6(2) of the EU (Withdrawal) Act 2018 provides that '…a court or tribunal may have regard to anything done on or after exit day by the European Court, another EU entity or the EU so far as it is relevant to any matter before the court or tribunal.'

72 'Exit day' means, according to EU (Withdrawal) Act 2018, section 20(1), '29 March 2019 at 11p.m.' See however EU (Withdrawal) Act 2018, section 20(2)-(5). Notably, a Minister of the Crown may by regulations amend the meaning of 'exit

The key difference between the draft WA and the EU (Withdrawal) Act 2018 is with respect to CJEU case law handed down *before* Brexit. The EU (Withdrawal) Act does not treat pre-exit EU case law as binding, at least insofar as the UK Supreme Court and the High Court of Justiciary (when there is no appeal to the Supreme Court) are concerned, which may choose to depart from it.[73] However, the draft WA provides that the case law handed down before the end of the transition period would be binding on *all* judicial and administrative authorities. That is the only logical conclusion to be drawn from an Agreement that lays down a legal obligation to interpret EU law provisions/concepts 'in conformity with' relevant pre-exit CJEU case law. The EU (Withdrawal Agreement) Bill would almost certainly have to introduce a further exception to this effect, which would serve to prevent the UK's highest courts from departing from 'retained EU case law' on Part Two citizens' rights delivered before the end of the transition period.

Part One of the draft WA further includes *an obligation of good faith* (Article 5), which enjoins the parties to the Agreement to assist each other, in full mutual respect and in good faith, in carrying out the tasks which flow from the Agreement. 'They shall take all appropriate measures, whether general or particular, to ensure fulfilment of the obligations arising from this Agreement and shall refrain from any measures which could jeopardise the attainment of the objectives of this Agreement.'[74] Judging from the standpoint of the principle of sincere cooperation in EU law (which is also mentioned in Article 5), this obligation of good faith could serve as an aid to the interpretation of other WA provisions and/or as a source of legal obligations, taken together with other provisions of the WA. Article 6, para 1 further provides that '[w]ith the exception of Parts Four [transition] and Five [financial provisions], unless otherwise provided in this Agreement *all references in this Agreement to Union law shall be understood as references to Union law*, including as amended or replaced, as applicable on the last day of the transition period' (emphasis added). Article 6, para 2 adds that: 'Where in this Agreement reference is made to Union acts or provisions thereof, such reference shall, where relevant, be understood to include a reference to Union law or provisions thereof that, although replaced or superseded by the act referred to, continue to apply in accordance with that

---

day', in order to reflect agreement on extending the art 50 period. At the time of writing, the projected exit day is 31 October 2019.
73   EU (Withdrawal) Act 2018, section 6(4). See further Menelaos Markakis (n 16) 92-95.
74   Draft WA, art 5.

act.' It shall also include, according to Article 6, para 3, 'references to the relevant Union acts supplementing or implementing those provisions' – presumably adopted under TFEU, Articles 290-291 or according to other systems for the delegation of such powers to Union bodies, offices or agencies.[75]

Moreover, the draft WA provides that, whenever there is a case that raises a question on the interpretation of Part Two of the WA, the UK courts or tribunals may, if they consider that a decision on that question is necessary to enable them to give judgment in that case, *request the CJEU to give a preliminary ruling.*[76] This is, however, subject to a time limit: the case must have commenced at first instance within 8 years from the end of the transition period.[77] The latter will, according to current plans, end on 31 December 2020. In political terms, preserving the possibility of referral to the CJEU reveals a certain level of distrust from the EU's side with respect to the manner in which the relevant provisions on citizens' rights may be interpreted and applied by the UK authorities. The time limit reflects, on the other hand, a willingness on behalf of the UK Government to limit the CJEU's jurisdiction *ratione temporis*, so that no political 'red lines' appear to turn pink. There is further provision in the draft WA for a UK independent authority that would monitor the implementation and application of Part Two.[78] The latter shall also have the right, following complaints by Union citizens and their family members, to bring a legal action before a UK court or tribunal.[79]

Part Two of the draft WA is structured as follows. Title I consists of *general provisions* (viz., on definitions, the personal scope of Part Two rights, continuity of residence, and non-discrimination). Title II sets out *rights and*

---

75 See Case C-270/12, 22.01.2014, *United Kingdom of Great Britain and Northern Ireland v European Parliament and Council of the European Union*, ECLI:EU:C:2014:18, paras 69-87.
76 Draft WA, art 158, para 1.
77 Ibid. However, art 158, para 1 also provides that 'where the subject matter of the case before the court or tribunal in the United Kingdom is a decision on an application made pursuant to Article 18(1) or (4) [application for new residence status or for issuance of residence document] or pursuant to Article 19 [issuance of residence documents during the transition period], a request for a preliminary ruling may be made only where the case commenced at first instance within a period of 8 years from the date from which Article 19 applies.' Moreover, in the event that the EU and the UK agree under art 132, para 1 to extend the transition period, this period of 8 years shall be extended accordingly (art 158, para 3).
78 Draft WA, art 159, para 1.
79 Ibid.

obligations. It includes chapters on rights related to residence and residence documents; rights of workers and self-employed persons; and professional qualifications. Title III sets out *rules on the coordination of social security systems*. Title IV includes *other provisions* (on disseminating information concerning the rights and obligations of the persons covered by Part Two of the Agreement; the applicability of more favourable provisions to those persons; and the lifelong protection of their rights). In what follows, we will follow the same division in terms of substance.

2. The personal scope of citizens' rights

Article 10 defines the *personal scope* of Part Two of the WA. These provisions are near identical to the earlier draft. More specifically, the WA will cover Union citizens and UK nationals who exercised their right to reside in the UK and the EU respectively in accordance with Union law *before the end of the transition period* and continue to reside there thereafter.[80] It further covers frontier workers.[81] It also covers the family members of UK/EU citizens and frontier workers, and that is so regardless of whether they had joined the UK/EU national before the end of the transition period or not.[82] The draft WA further covers '[p]ersons falling under points (a) and (b) of Article 3(2) of Directive 2004/38/EC whose residence was facilitated by the host State in accordance with its national legislation before the end of the transition period in accordance with Article 3(2) of that Directive', as well as 'persons falling under points (a) and (b) of Article 3(2) of Directive 2004/38/EC who have applied for facilitation of entry and residence before the end of the transition period, and whose residence is being facilitated by the host State in accordance with its national legislation thereafter.'[83] These persons are, according to Article 3(2) of the Directive, the following: '(a) any other family members, irrespective of their nationality, not falling under the definition in point 2 of Article 2 who, in the country from which they have come, are dependants or members of the household of the Union citizen having the primary right of residence, or where serious health grounds strictly require the personal care of the family member by the Union citizen; (b) the partner with whom the Union citizen has a

---

80 Ibid art 10, para 1, subparas a-b.
81 Ibid art 10, para 1, subparas c-d.
82 Ibid art 10, para 1, subpara e. See also ibid art 10, para 1, subpara f.
83 Ibid art 10, paras 2-3.

durable relationship, duly attested.[84] Further, there is provision for the partner with whom the citizen or frontier worker concerned has a durable relationship, duly attested, where that partner resided outside the host State before the end of the transition period.[85]

Article 10 should be read together with Article 17, which concerns *changes of status*. It provides that '[t]he right of Union citizens and United Kingdom nationals, and their respective family members, to rely directly on this Part shall not be affected when they change status, for example between student, worker, self-employed person and economically inactive person.'[86] There is, however, a legal caveat: '[p]ersons who, at the end of the transition period, enjoy a right of residence in their capacity as family members of Union citizens or United Kingdom nationals, cannot become persons referred to in points (a) to (d) of Article 10(1)', i.e. they cannot be protected as Union citizens/UK nationals or frontier workers in their own right.[87] Article 17 further provides that '[t]he rights provided for in this Title for the family members who are dependants of Union citizens or United Kingdom nationals before the end of the transition period, shall be maintained even after they cease to be dependants.'[88]

3. *Rights related to residence*

Article 13 lays down the *residence rights* of Union citizens and UK nationals, as well as of their family members who are either Union citizens/UK nationals or third-country nationals. To simplify things, these persons shall have the right to reside in the host State as set out in Treaty on the Functioning of the European Union (TFEU), Articles 21, 45 or 49 and in Directive 2004/38/EC, Articles 6, 7, 13, 14, 16, 17 or 18, as they pertain to the situation.[89] It is stated in the draft WA that:

> The host State may not impose any limitations or conditions for obtaining, retaining or losing residence rights on the persons referred to in paragraphs 1, 2 and 3, other than those provided for in this Title. There shall be no discretion in applying the limitations and conditions

---

84 Directive 2004/38/EC, art 3, para 2, subparas a-b.
85 Draft WA, art 10, para 4.
86 Ibid art 17, para 1.
87 Ibid.
88 Ibid art 17, para 2.
89 Ibid art 13, paras 1-3.

provided for in this Title, other than in favour of the person concerned.[90]

It should be noted that Article 13 also refers to TFEU, Article 21, which was not mentioned explicitly in the Joint Report.[91] This is a welcome addition, which will serve to grant *a derived right of residence under TFEU, Article 21 to family members* who may otherwise not have been covered by the provisions of Directive 2004/38/EC. Cases such as *Lounes* and *Coman* serve to illustrate the importance of including this Treaty provision. In *Lounes*, the Court ruled that the Algerian husband of a Spanish-UK national was eligible for a derived right of residence in the UK under TFEU, Article 21, para 1, which he could not have otherwise claimed under Directive 2004/38/EC, as the latter was not applicable to the case.[92] This was because the Directive ceased to apply to his wife once she acquired the UK citizenship. However, third-country nationals who are family members of a Union citizen and are not eligible, on the basis of Directive 2004/38/EC, for a derived right of residence in the Member State of which that citizen is a national could be accorded such a right on the basis of TFEU, Article 21, para 1. Furthermore, the Court ruled in *Coman*, a case concerning a US-Romanian national returning to Romania with his American husband, that TFEU, Article 21, para 1 grants a third-country national of the same sex as a Union citizen whose marriage to that citizen was lawfully concluded in another Member State (Belgium) the right to reside in the territory of the Member State of which the Union citizen is a national (Romania) for more than three months.[93] This was so notwithstanding the fact that the Romanian law did not provide for same-sex marriage. The litigants in the main pro-

---

90 Ibid art 13, para 4.
91 See Joint Report, paras 20-21. It was however mentioned in the earlier draft of the WA.
92 Case C-165/16, 19.04.2018, *Toufik Lounes v Secretary of State for the Home Department*, ECLI:EU:C:2017:862. Vincent Réveillère, 'Family rights for naturalized EU citizens: *Lounes*' (2018) 55 CMLR, 1855. For a view on the legal consequences of the draft WA for the *Lounes* case, see Gareth Davies, '*Lounes*, Naturalisation and Brexit' (5 March 2018) <https://europeanlawblog.eu/2018/03/05/lounes-naturalisation-and-brexit/> accessed 10 July 2018.
93 Case C-673/16, 05.06.2018, *Relu Adrian Coman and Others v Inspectoratul General pentru Imigrări and Ministerul Afacerilor Interne*, ECLI:EU:C:2018:385. For a discussion of the case (prior to the judgment being delivered), see generally René Repasi, *Wirkungsweise des unionsrechtlichen Anwendungsvorrangs in autonomen IPR* (2018).

ceedings would have been unable, according to the Court's ruling, to claim such a derived right of residence under Directive 2004/38/EC.[94]

It should be stated, however, that Article 13 does not explicitly refer to TFEU, Article 20. This may leave *third-country nationals who are family members of a Union citizen who has not exercised her/his free movement rights* in a precarious position.[95] The significance of this omission is brought out by cases such as *Rottman* and *Zambrano*.[96] In *Zambrano*, for example, TFEU, Article 20 was used by the Court to preclude a Member State from refusing a third-country national upon whom his minor children, who are Union citizens, were dependent, a right of residence in the Member State of residence and nationality of his children, and from refusing to grant a work permit to that same person, in so far as such decisions deprived those children of the genuine enjoyment of the substance of the rights attached to the status of EU citizen. It is not clear whether this omission means that the principle established in *Zambrano* would not be applicable to the persons falling within the ambit of the draft WA. This is more especially so since there is case law from the CJEU that examines the principle established in *Zambrano* from the standpoint of TFEU, Article 21, which *is* men-

---

94 See also Case C-89/17, 12.07.2018, *Secretary of State for the Home Department v Rozanne Banger*, ECLI:EU:C:2018:570, where the Court said that TFEU, art 21 required the Member State of which a Union citizen is a national to facilitate the provision of a residence authorisation to her/his unregistered partner, who is a third-country national with whom that Union citizen has a durable relationship that is duly attested. This would be so in cases where the Union citizen, having exercised her/his right of freedom of movement to work in a second Member State, returns to her/his home Member State with her/his partner (and is therefore not covered by Directive 2004/38/EC). This ruling is very important for EU citizens returning to their home State with their UK partner after Brexit.

95 See generally Case C-133/15, 10.05.2017, *H.C. Chavez-Vilchez and Others v Raad van bestuur van de Sociale verzekeringsbank and Others*, ECLI:EU:C:2017:354. For a commentary, see Fulvia Staiano, 'Derivative Residence Rights for Parents of Union Citizen Children under Article 20 TFEU: *Chavez-Vilchez*' (2018) 55 CMLR, 225.

96 Case C-135/08, 02.03.2010, *Janko Rottman v Freistaat Bayern*, ECLI:EU:C:2010:104; Case C-34/09, 08.03.2011, *Gerardo Ruiz Zambrano v Office national de l'emploi (ONEm)*, ECLI:EU:C:2011:124. See also Joined Cases C-356/11 and 357/11, 06.12.2012, *O and S v Maahanmuuttovirasto and Maahanmuuttovirasto v L*, ECLI:EU:C:2012:776. See most recently, Hester Kroeze, 'The substance of rights: new pieces of the Ruiz Zambrano puzzle' (2019) 44 ELRev, 238.

tioned in the draft WA,[97] or from the standpoint of both TFEU, Articles 20 and 21.[98]

Going back to the WA, Article 14 grants Union citizens/UK nationals and their families *a right to leave the host State, as well as a right to enter it*, without it being required that they hold an exit or entry visa (or other equivalent formality), provided that they hold a valid document issued in accordance with Articles 18 or 26 of the Agreement.[99] Where the host State requires family members who join the Union citizen or the UK national after the end of the transition period to have an entry visa, the host State shall grant such persons every facility to obtain the necessary visas.[100]

It should be noted at this juncture that there is no right granted to UK nationals in the WA to enter the territory of *Member States other than their host State* ('onward free movement rights'). Accordingly, the concern is that UK nationals living in the continent will be 'landlocked' in their State of residence. Their rights to live and work across the EU will be dependent on national migration laws, as well as EU migration laws (wherever these are applicable). With regard to the latter laws, the Long-term Residents Directive provides that those who have resided legally and continuously for five years in a first Member State have the right to reside in a second Member State, for a period exceeding three months, on three main grounds: exercise of an economic activity in an employed or self-employed capacity; pursuit of studies or vocational training; or other purposes.[101] Moreover, there is provision in the Blue Card Directive for highly-skilled workers to move to another Member State for the purpose of highly-qualified employment.[102] Furthermore, there are provisions on intra-EU mobility in the Intra-Corporate Transfers Directive[103] and the Students and Researchers Directive.[104] Beyond these rather limited exceptions, national migration laws are applicable. The problem discussed here would not arise for Union citizens living in the UK, as they could exercise their free movement rights

---

97 See, e.g., Case C-434/09, 05.05.2011, *Shirley McCarthy v Secretary of State for the Home Department*, ECLI:EU:C:2011:277.

98 See, e.g., Case C-40/11, 08.11.2012, *Yoshikazu Iida v Stadt Ulm*, ECLI:EU:C:2012:691; Case C-86/12, 10.10.2013, *Adzo Domenyo Alokpa and Others v Ministre du Travail, de l'Emploi et de l'Immigration*, ECLI:EU:C:2013:645.

99 Draft WA, art 14, paras 1-2.

100 Ibid art 14, para 3.

101 Council Directive 2003/109/EC, as is currently in force, art 15.

102 Council Directive 2009/50/EC, art 18.

103 Directive 2014/66/EU, arts 20-23.

104 Directive (EU) 2016/801, arts 27-32.

anywhere in the EU 27, provided that this would not result in a loss of their rights of residence in the UK under the WA.

Article 15 of the WA grants *a right of permanent residence* to Union citizens, UK nationals, and their families. It provides that 'Union citizens and United Kingdom nationals, and their respective family members, who have resided legally in the host State in accordance with Union law for a continuous period of 5 years or for the period specified in Article 17 of Directive 2004/38/EC [exemptions for persons no longer working in the host Member State and their family members], shall have the right to reside permanently in the host State under the conditions set out in Articles 16, 17 and 18 of Directive 2004/38/EC.'[105] It further sets out rules on *continuity of residence*, which bring the draft WA in line with Directive 2004/38/EC.[106] Last, it provides that '[o]nce acquired, the right of permanent residence shall be lost only through absence from the host State for a period exceeding *5 consecutive years*' (emphasis added).[107] This provision is clearly more generous than its equivalent in Directive 2004/38/EC, which provides that the right of permanent residence shall be lost through absence from the host Member State for a period exceeding two consecutive years.[108] Nevertheless, there is no 'lifelong right of return' (meaning that one would lose this right after five years of absence).

The draft WA further permits *the accumulation of periods* of legal residence or work. 'Union citizens and United Kingdom nationals, and their respective family members, who before the end of the transition period resided legally in the host State in accordance with the conditions of Article 7 of Directive 2004/38/EC for a period of less than 5 years, shall have the right to acquire the right to reside permanently under the conditions set out in Article 15 of this Agreement once they have completed the necessary periods of residence.'[109] 'Periods of legal residence or work in accordance with Union law before and after the end of the transition period shall be included in the calculation of the qualifying period necessary for acquisition of the right of permanent residence.'[110]

The draft WA also includes provisions on such other matters as 'restrictions of the rights of residence and entry', 'safeguards and right of appeal', 'related rights', and 'equal treatment', which broadly reflect the respective

---

105 Draft WA, art 15, para 1.
106 Ibid art 15, para 2.
107 Ibid art 15, para 3.
108 Directive 2004/38/EC, art 16, para 4.
109 Draft WA, art 16.
110 Ibid.

provisions of the Joint Report and/or Directive 2004/38/EC.[111] Exigencies of space preclude detailed analysis of these provisions. Suffice it to say for present purposes that Article 22 grants *the right to take up employment or self-employment to family members* of a Union citizen or UK national who have the right of residence or the right of permanent residence in the host State or State of work. Moreover, Article 23, para 2 *limits access to benefits* and, accordingly, equal treatment between EU citizens/UK nationals and the nationals of the host State. More specifically, there shall be no obligation for the host State to provide social assistance during the first three months of residence (Directive 2004/38/EC, Article 6) or for longer periods in the case of persons entering the territory of the host State in order to seek employment [Directive 2004/38/EC, Article 14, para 4, subpara (b)]. Nor shall the host State be obliged, prior to the acquisition of the right of permanent residence in accordance with Article 15 of the Agreement, to grant maintenance aid for studies, including vocational training, consisting in student grants or student loans to persons other than workers, self-employed persons, persons who retain such status and members of their families. These provisions reproduce almost verbatim Article 24, para 2 of the Citizens' Rights Directive, and may accordingly be subject to the same criticism as the latter provision.

4. Residence documents

The draft WA further includes detailed provisions on the *issuance of residence documents*, which are near identical to the earlier draft (Articles 17-17a) and largely mirror the relevant provisions of the Joint Report.[112] For this reason, they will not be analysed in detail in this section. For the present it is sufficient to note that Article 18 permits the host State to *require* Union citizens or UK nationals, their respective family members and other persons, residing in its territory in accordance with the conditions set out in Title II of the WA, to apply for a new residence status which confers the rights under this Title and a document evidencing such status,

---

111 Ibid arts 20-23. They are further near identical to the respective provisions of the earlier draft WA (arts 18-21).
112 Ibid arts 18-19. See generally Meghan Benton, Aliyyah Ahad, Michaela Benson, Katherine Collins, Helen McCarthy and Karen O'Reilly, *Next Steps: Implementing a Brexit Deal for UK Citizens Living in the EU-27* (April 2018), Brussels: Migration Policy Institute Europe, esp. 35-41.

which may be in a digital form.[113] It should be stressed that, if the host State opts to require that Union citizens or UK nationals apply for a new residence status, the enjoyment of their rights will hinge on their application being successful. In other words, the issuance of residence documents would be a condition for the enjoyment of their rights in the future. Where the host State has chosen not to require that those persons apply for a new residence status as a condition for legal residence, those persons shall have a right to receive a residence document, which may be in a digital form, that includes a statement that it has been issued in accordance with this Agreement.[114]

With respect to *supporting documentation* that may need to be presented in addition to identity documents, it is submitted that requiring evidence that the persons concerned have sufficient resources for themselves and their family members not to become a burden on the social assistance system of the host State during their period of residence will most likely cause problems for prospective applicants. The methods for the interpretation of the draft WA, which were explicated above, are crucial here. There is an older case law by the CJEU that confirms that the condition concerning the sufficiency of resources is met where the financial resources are provided by a family member or a partner, such that a 'legal link' between the provider and beneficiary of those resources is not required.[115]

The requirement that the persons concerned have comprehensive sickness insurance may also prove hard to meet (as well as to prove).[116] With respect to the UK, it is noted by Steve Peers that:

> The underlying problem here is the UK's insistence that NHS cover does not count as "comprehensive sickness insurance". While the UK has promised to waive this requirement, this is in principle not an enforceable right and there is a risk that the Agreement could be interpreted as meaning that the persons concerned are not covered by it at all.[117]

---

113 Draft WA, art 18, para 1.
114 Ibid art 18, para 4.
115 Case C-200/02, 19.10.2004, *Kunqian Catherine Zhu and Man Lavette Chen v Secretary of State for the Home Department*, ECLI:EU:C:2004:639; Case C-408/03, 23.03.2006, *Commission of the European Communities v Kingdom of Belgium*, ECLI:EU:C:2006:192.
116 See, in this respect, Case C-413/99, 17.09.2002, *Baumbast and R v Secretary of State for the Home Department*, ECLI:EU:C:2002:493.
117 Steve Peers, 'EU27 and UK Citizens' Acquired Rights in the Brexit Withdrawal Agreement: Detailed Analysis and Annotation' (13 March 2018) <http://eulawan

For this reason, he recommends that this condition be satisfied for EU citizens residing in the UK by proof of registration with the NHS.[118]

The UK Government recently revealed its plans with respect to the process for applying for 'settled status.' EU citizens will have to apply by 30 June 2021 the latest. From 1 July 2021, EU citizens and their family members in the UK must hold or have applied for UK immigration status to be in the country legally. Those who have lived in the UK for less than 5 years and are therefore not yet eligible for 'settled status' may apply for 'pre-settled status', which will allow them to stay there for another 5 years. Thereafter, they may apply for 'settled status.' Existing close family members (a spouse, civil partner, unmarried partner, dependent child or grandchild, and dependent parent or grandparent) living in the UK or overseas are also eligible for the scheme.[119] It should be noted, with respect to the requirement for comprehensive sickness insurance that was discussed above, that the currently available information by the UK Government on 'settled' and 'pre-settled status' makes it look like, if anything, access to public services, such as healthcare, will be a *benefit* attached to such status, and not something that should count towards the acquisition of such status.[120]

5. The rights of workers and self-employed persons

The draft WA further includes provisions on the rights of workers and self-employed persons.[121] The regulatory technique is familiar: the relevant provisions in the WA build on primary and secondary Union law, notably TFEU, Articles 45 and 49 and Regulation (EU) 492/2011, whilst taking into account the particular circumstances of Union citizens and UK nationals following the UK's withdrawal from the EU.

With regard to *the rights of workers*, it is provided that, '[s]ubject to the limitations set out in Article 45(3) and (4) TFEU, workers in the host State

---

alysis.blogspot.com/2018/03/eu27-and-uk-citizens-acquired-rights-in.html> accessed 18 June 2018.
118 Ibid. See further Gareth Davies, 'The UK and Sickness Insurance for Mobile Citizens: An Inequitable Mess for Brexit Negotiators to Address' (17 March 2017) <https://europeanlawblog.eu/2017/03/17/the-uk-and-sickness-insurance-for-mobile-citizens-an-inequitable-mess-for-brexit-negotiators-to-address/> accessed 9 July 2018.
119 See further <https://www.gov.uk/guidance/status-of-eu-nationals-in-the-uk-what-you-need-to-know> accessed 26 November 2018.
120 Ibid.
121 Draft WA, arts 24-26.

and frontier workers in the State or States of work shall enjoy the rights guaranteed by Article 45 TFEU and the rights granted by Regulation (EU) No. 492/2011.'[122] These rights include:

(a) the right not to be discriminated against on grounds of nationality as regards employment, remuneration and other conditions of work and employment;

(b) the right to take up and pursue an activity in accordance with the rules applicable to the nationals of the host State or the State of work;

(c) the right to assistance afforded by the employment offices of the host State or the State of work as offered to own nationals;

(d) the right to equal treatment in respect of conditions of employment and work, in particular as regards remuneration, dismissal and in case of unemployment, reinstatement or re-employment;

(e) the right to tax and social advantages;

(f) collective rights;

(g) the rights and benefits accorded to national workers in matters of housing;

(h) the right for their children to be admitted to the general educational, apprenticeship and vocational training courses under the same conditions as the nationals of the host State or the State of work, if such children are residing in the territory where the worker works.[123]

With respect to the *limitations* referred to above, it will be recalled that TFEU, Article 45, para 3 foresees the possibility to restrict free movement of workers on grounds of public policy, public security or public health. In cases of indirect discrimination or where restrictions are placed on market access, one may further rely on judicially-developed mandatory requirements in the public interest. Further, TFEU, Article 45, para 4 provides that free movement of workers shall not apply to employment in the public service. Regulation (EU) 492/2011 also includes restrictions: for example, Article 3, para 1 permits conditions relating to linguistic knowledge required by reason of the nature of the post to be filled. All the limitations adumbrated above should be read in the light of the CJEU's case law before the end of the transition period, as per the draft WA.[124] After the end of the transition period, we have seen that the UK courts and tribunals shall have

---

122 Ibid art 24, para 1.
123 Ibid art 24, para 1.
124 Ibid art 4, para 4.

due regard to the CJEU's case law.[125] Moreover, we have seen that, whenever there is a case that raises a question on the interpretation of Part Two of the WA, the UK courts or tribunals may request the CJEU to give a preliminary ruling.[126] However, as a general rule, the case must have commenced at first instance within 8 years from the end of the transition period.[127]

With regard to *the rights of self-employed persons*, the draft WA provides that, '[s]ubject to the limitations set out in Articles 51 and 52 TFEU, self-employed persons in the host State and self-employed frontier workers in the State or States of work shall enjoy the rights guaranteed by Articles 49 and 55 TFEU.'[128] These rights include, according to the draft WA:

(a) the right to take up and pursue activities as self-employed persons and to set up and manage undertakings under the conditions laid down by the host State for its own nationals, as set out in Article 49 TFEU;
(b) the rights as set out in points (c) to (h) of Article 24(1) of this Agreement.[129]

6. *Other provisions*

Similarly to the Joint Report, the draft WA further includes provisions on *professional qualifications*[130] and *the coordination of social security systems*.[131] It further includes, again in line with the Joint Report, a clause explicating that *more favourable provisions in the host State* (or, in the case of frontier workers, the State of work) shall not be affected by the provisions of Part Two of the WA.[132] This clause does not, however, apply with respect to the rules on the coordination of social security systems (Title III of Part Two).[133] The draft WA further provides for the *lifelong protection of Part Two rights*, unless the persons concerned cease to meet the conditions set out in the relevant Titles of the WA.[134]

---

125 Ibid art 4, para 5.
126 Ibid art 158, para 1.
127 Ibid.
128 Ibid art 25, para 1.
129 Ibid.
130 Ibid arts 27-29.
131 Ibid arts 30-36.
132 Ibid art 38, para 1.
133 Ibid.
134 Ibid art 39.

IV. *The future mobility framework*

The discussion thus far has focused on the Joint Report and the draft WA. Assuming that the latest draft of the WA will largely reflect the final text of the WA, and that Brexit will go forward, UK nationals in the EU 27 and EU citizens' resident in the UK will have the rights adumbrated above. The WA may indeed be amended by the Joint Committee established thereunder, which is granted the power to 'adopt decisions amending this Agreement, provided that such amendments are necessary to correct errors, to address omissions or other deficiencies, or to address situations unforeseen when this Agreement was signed, and provided that such decisions may not amend the essential elements of this Agreement.[135] This power may only be exercised by the end of the fourth year following the end of the transition period.[136] Save for this limited exception, UK/EU nationals will have to live with the rights enshrined in this Agreement, unless and until the EU-UK agreement(s) on their future relationship provide otherwise.

In this connection, the European Council has already expressed a strong preference for including such arrangements in the future partnership:

> The future partnership should include ambitious provisions on movement of natural persons, based on full reciprocity and non-discrimination among Member States, and related areas such as coordination of social security and recognition of professional qualifications. In this context, options for judicial cooperation in matrimonial, parental responsibility and other related matters could be explored, taking into account that the UK will be a third country outside Schengen and that such cooperation would require strong safeguards to ensure full respect of fundamental rights.[137]

Moreover, the political declaration setting out the framework for the future relationship between the EU and the UK, which accompanies the WA, includes provisions on 'mobility'.[138] The mobility arrangements to be established 'will be based on non-discrimination between the Union's Mem-

---

135 Ibid art 164, para 5, subpara d. This is, as provided in ibid, with the exception of Parts One, Four and Six of the Agreement.
136 Ibid.
137 See European Council (Art. 50) (23 March 2018) – Guidelines <http://www.consilium.europa.eu/media/33458/23-euco-art50-guidelines.pdf> accessed 15 June 2018, para 10.
138 Political declaration (n 6) paras 50-59.

ber States and full reciprocity.'[139] 'In this context, the Parties aim to provide, through their domestic laws, for visa-free travel for short-term visits.'[140] 'The Parties agree to consider conditions for entry and stay for purposes such as research, study, training and youth exchanges.'[141] The political declaration further makes provision 'for the temporary entry and stay of natural persons for business purposes in defined areas', thereby catering for the situation of service providers and investors.[142] 'The Parties also agree to consider addressing social security coordination in the light of future movement of persons.'[143] 'In line with their applicable laws, the Parties will explore the possibility to facilitate the crossing of their respective borders for legitimate travel.'[144] Furthermore, '[t]o support mobility, the Parties confirm their commitment to the effective application of the existing international family law instruments to which they are parties.'[145] They will further 'explore options for judicial cooperation in matrimonial, parental responsibility and other related matters.'[146]

V. Some reflections on citizens' rights after Brexit

There will be no attempt to summarise the preceding arguments in their entirety. Instead, we will highlight certain features which are of particular importance. These are of course interrelated.

Thinking in terms of the models or ideal types for the future evolution of the rights of UK and EU nationals, there was, fortunately, no decision by the negotiating parties to remove the rights of UK and EU expats altogether. Their existing rights will nevertheless be affected in multiple ways, in the manner set out in the Joint Report and the draft WA. In some cases, their rights would be clearly diminished. The most immediate consequence is, as we have seen, that EU 27 nationals have to apply to stay in their own homes.[147] To give another powerful example, UK nationals in the EU 27 risk being 'landlocked' after Brexit day, because no 'onward free

---

139 Ibid para 51.
140 Ibid para 52.
141 Ibid para 53.
142 Ibid paras 32, 59.
143 Ibid para 54.
144 Ibid para 55.
145 Ibid para 57.
146 Ibid para 58.
147 The same could be required of UK nationals resident in the continent.

movement rights' were granted to them in the WA. Other rights attached to the status of EU citizenship (such as the right to vote and to stand as a candidate in the elections to the European Parliament or at local elections,[148] and the right to participate in a citizens' initiative)[149] would also be lost for UK nationals after Brexit, as a legal consequence of losing their EU citizenship.[150] As a matter of fact, they will lose these rights already during the transition period.[151] Nor has provision been made, according to the House of Lords' EU Committee, for EU citizens resident in the UK to retain their voting rights in elections for the European Parliament.[152] Furthermore, the diminution of opportunities presented to expat workers and self-employed persons is also important. For example, a researcher based in the UK could lose access to research funding from the EU institutions after Brexit, unless the UK continued to participate in – and contribute to – such EU-funded research programmes.[153] Overall, the life and work opportunities of UK and EU nationals resident in one another's territory are bound to be affected in multiple ways.

We have seen that the regulatory technique used in the Joint Report and the draft WA is to rely on existing provisions of primary and secondary Union law and to use them as a springboard or point of departure for the future rights of the persons concerned. The draft WA largely reflects the

---

148 TFEU, art 20, para 2, subpara b. The UK Government claims that it 'will continue to pursue reciprocal arrangements with Member States to secure the right to stand and vote in local elections for UK nationals in the EU', in both 'deal' and 'no-deal' scenarios: Department for Exiting the European Union, 'Citizens' Rights – EU citizens in the UK and UK nationals in the EU: Policy Paper' (6 December 2018) <https://assets.publishing.service.gov.uk/government/uploads/syste m/uploads/attachment_data/file/762222/Policy_paper_on_citizens__rights_in_th e_event_of_a_no_deal_Brexit.pdf> accessed 14 December 2018, para 30.
149 TEU, art 11, para 4.
150 See European Commission, Task Force for the Preparation and Conduct of the Negotiations with the United Kingdom under Article 50 TEU, 'Internal EU27 Preparatory Discussions on the Framework for the Future Relationship: "Mobility"' (21 February 2018) TF50 (2018) 31 <https://ec.europa.eu/commission/sites/b eta-political/files/mobility-future-relationship_21february2018_en.pdf> accessed 11 July 2018 (Brexit preparedness note), 4.
151 Draft WA, art 127, para 1, subpara b.
152 European Union Committee, *Brexit: the Withdrawal Agreement and Political Declaration* (2017-19, HL 245), para 73. 'This includes Irish citizens resident in Northern Ireland, notwithstanding the prospect, if the "backstop" came into force, that substantial elements of EU law would continue to apply in Northern Ireland' (ibid para 73).
153 On UK participation in Union programmes after Brexit, see generally the political declaration (n 6) paras 11-13.

current position under primary and secondary Union law concerning citizens' rights. As such, any criticism that could be levelled against the relevant EU rules currently in force is equally applicable to the Joint Report and the draft WA. It is well known that those provisions are restrictive in many ways. Those persons that fall through the gaps in the relevant EU law provisions will simply not be protected, unless the Withdrawal (or future) Agreement to be concluded provides to the contrary. Perhaps the most notable example is that persons who are not economically active and are not in possession of comprehensive sickness insurance are not covered by the Citizens' Rights Directive.[154] Moreover, partners will not be covered in all cases. One could think, for example, of a person who only met (or began a 'durable' relationship) with her/his partner after the end of the transition period.[155] One could further think of an EU citizen living with her/his non-EU partner in the UK, whilst the couple does not have 'sufficient resources' under the law. The draft WA also omits key provisions: persons whose status could have been protected under TFEU, Article 20 (such as third-country nationals who are family members of a Union citizen who has not exercised her/his free movement rights) may be left in a precarious position, in the manner explained above.[156]

What is more, the provisions in the WA are to be interpreted and applied in the light of the CJEU's case law prior to end of the transition phase.[157] A glimpse into the relevant case law exposes the limits of the regulatory approach opted for by the negotiating parties. For example, access to benefits is circumscribed by the Court's rulings in cases such as *Brey*,[158] *Dano*,[159] *Alimanovic*,[160] *García-Nieto*,[161] and *Commission v UK*.[162]

---

154 European Union Committee (n 152) para 83.

155 Draft WA, art 10, para 4 requires that 'the relationship was durable before the end of the transition period and continues at the time the partner seeks residence under this Part'.

156 Ibid art 13.

157 Ibid art 4, para 4.

158 Case C-140/12, 19.10.2013, *Pensionsversicherungsanstalt v Peter Brey*, ECLI:EU:C:2013:565.

159 Case C-333/13, 11.11.2014, *Elisabeta Dano and Florin Dano v Jobcenter Leipzig*, ECLI:EU:C:2014:2358.

160 Case C-67/14, 15.09.2015, *Jobcenter Berlin Neukölln v Nazifa Alimanovic and Others*, ECLI:EU:C:2015:597.

161 Case C-299/14, 25.02.2016, *Vestische Arbeit Jobcenter Kreis Recklinghausen v Jovanna García-Nieto and Others*, ECLI:EU:C:2016:114.

162 Case C-308/14, 14.06.2016, *European Commission v United Kingdom of Great Britain and Northern Ireland*, ECLI:EU:C:2016:436.

The key features of these cases may only be telegraphed here. These rulings permit restrictions to access by EU nationals to special non-contributory benefits. They further permit Member States to restrict access by jobseekers from other Member States to benefits whose predominant function is social assistance, without necessarily conducting proportionality tests on a case-by-case basis. The net result is, as argued in the relevant literature, that low-income individuals, working variable hours and experiencing job insecurity, are left in a precarious position.[163] In political terms, it is unrealistic to think that the UK Government may push domestically for more favourable provisions than the ones in the draft WA concerning such persons. Absent any revisions of Regulations (EC) No. 883/2004 and (EC) No. 987/2009 which may be incorporated into the WA in the future,[164] or any future CJEU case law that the UK courts and tribunals may have regard to,[165] there is not much hope of their receiving more favourable treatment.

It should further not be forgotten that those persons covered by the draft WA will have to meet a number of conditions and formalities of an administrative nature, in order to secure the continued enjoyment of their rights. The concern is, as outlined above, that such administrative processes may prove too cumbersome for prospective applicants. Furthermore, one of the key recommendations made by advocacy groups thus far is that the UK Government (and the EU 27 Member States, for that matter) should make sure that everyone who is eligible submits an application. The current position is that the persons concerned are in principle themselves (and themselves alone) responsible to submit an application.

As regards those EU/UK nationals who will not make use of their free movement rights until the end of the transition phase, their situation is less fortunate. It is clear that there is no aspiration to confer rights in the WA on those EU citizens who will move to the UK after the end of the transition phase. Nor will the WA grant any rights to those UK nationals who may wish to move to the EU 27 after the end of the transition period.

---

163 For a view on this, see Charlotte O'Brien, 'Civis Capitalist Sum: Class as the New Guiding Principle of EU Free Movement Rights' (2016) 53 CMLR, 937; Charlotte O'Brien, 'The ECJ Sacrifices EU Citizenship in Vain: *Commission* v. *United Kingdom*' (2017) 54 CMLR, 209. See also Michael Blauberger, Anita Heindlmaier, Dion Kramer, Dorte Sindbjerg Martinsen, Jessica Sampson Thierry, Angelika Schenk and Benjamin Werner, 'ECJ Judges Read the Morning Papers. Explaining the Turnaround of European Citizenship Jurisprudence' [2018] JEPP, https://doi.org/10.1080/13501763.2018.1488880.
164 Draft WA, art 36.
165 Ibid art 4, para 5.

Accordingly, Brexit means Brexit for free movement of persons, unless and until the agreement(s) on the future relationship between the UK and the EU provide otherwise. We have seen that the European Council has already expressed a strong preference in this direction, and that the political declaration which accompanies the WA includes mobility arrangements. Unless and until such arrangements were concluded, the treatment of UK nationals in the EU 27 and of EU nationals in the UK would revert to being a matter for the respective national migration laws which would be applicable to their case. This would be subject to any requirements that would flow from EU migration laws (in the case of UK nationals resident in the EU 27). It would be further subject to any requirements flowing from international human rights instruments.[166] EU migration laws cover, as we have seen, long-term residents, highly-skilled workers, intra-corporate transferees (ICTs), and students and researchers. But there are formidable gaps, whose existence is openly admitted by the EU: 'Other categories *[self-employed, low and medium skilled economic migrants (except seasonal workers), international service providers (except ICTs), jobseekers, family members of non-mobile EU citizens, retired persons …]* will be covered by national law, as well as rules on regularisation.'[167]

What is more, it should be stressed that even those third-country nationals (*in casu*, UK nationals) who are fortunate enough to be covered by existing EU migration laws would be subject to *much less generous family reunification rules*, compared to what was the case for UK nationals living in the continent before Brexit. These are persons who are either not covered by the WA (because they did not exercise their free movement rights prior to the end of the transition period) or persons who would rely on these rules following a 'no-deal' Brexit. More specifically, the Family Reunification Directive only requires that the Member States authorise the entry/residence of the spouse and minor children.[168] Admitting first-degree relatives in the direct ascending line, adult unmarried children, and the unmarried partner is left in the discretion of the Member States.[169] Moreover, the Directive lays down a great number of requirements, exceptions, restrictions and

---

166 See further Jo Shaw, 'EU Citizenship: Still a Fundamental Status?' (March 2018) EUI Working Paper RSCAS 2018/14, 10. See also Virginia Mantouvalou, 'EU Citizens as Bargaining Chips' (14 July 2016) <https://ukconstitutionallaw.org/20 16/07/14/virginia-mantouvalou-eu-citizens-as-bargaining-chips/> accessed 17 July 2018.

167 Brexit preparedness note (n 150) 8.

168 Council Directive 2003/86/EC, art 4, para 1.

169 Ibid art 4, paras 2-3.

derogations, designed to keep out, if needed, yet more people. Member States shall, however, have due regard to the best interests of minor children when examining an application for family reunification.[170] Furthermore, 'Member States shall take due account of the nature and solidity of the person's family relationships and the duration of his residence in the Member State and of the existence of family, cultural and social ties with his/her country of origin where they reject an application, withdraw or refuse to renew a residence permit or decide to order the removal of the sponsor or members of his family.'[171] It should be stressed that these rules should be interpreted and applied in the light of hierarchically superior norms, such as the EU Charter of Fundamental Rights, Articles 7 (respect for private and family life), 24 (the rights of the child) or 25 (the rights of the elderly), as well as the general principles of protection of legitimate expectations, equal treatment, and proportionality. The EU Member States should exercise their discretion (or derogate from these rules, wherever this is permitted) in conformity with EU law. I argue that, in light of the exceptional personal and family circumstances facing UK nationals in the continent, a narrow margin of discretion should be granted to the authorities of the Member States when applying these rules. This is more especially so in the event of a 'no-deal', chaotic Brexit.[172]

In this connection, there is policy debate in the UK and the EU over the future of free movement of persons. In the UK, up until recently it was indeed the case that '...the Government ha[d] given little indication of its preferences for EU immigration controls post-Brexit, or whether it [was] willing to negotiate these as part of discussions on the UK's future relationship with the EU.'[173] A recent statement from the UK Government on the country's negotiating position for the future UK-EU relationship includes reference to '...a mobility framework so that UK and EU citizens can continue to travel to each other's territory, and apply for study and work – sim-

---

170 Ibid art 5, para 5.
171 Ibid art 17.
172 For the treatment of EU citizens in the UK in a 'no deal' scenario, see Department for Exiting the European Union (n 148) paras 7-33; Steve Peers, 'Staring into the Abyss: Citizens' Rights after a No Deal Brexit' (6 December 2018) <http://eulawanalysis.blogspot.com/2018/12/staring-into-abyss-citizens-rights.html> accessed 14 December 2018.
173 'Brexit: New Guidelines on the Framework for Future EU-UK Relations' House of Commons Library Briefing Paper No 8289, 19 April 2018, 44.

ilar to what the UK may offer other close trading partners in the future.[174] The UK Government further elaborates on its plans in a recent White Paper on the future UK-EU relationship, albeit still at a somewhat general level.[175]

Barnard and Fraser-Butlin explain how such a mobility framework could look like. They argue that the UK's new arrangement with the EU could mark a return to the ideas underpinning the Treaty of Rome (1957), whose focus was, according to their argument, on the rights of individuals to move for work and hence was not connected to broader ideas of citizenship and State building.[176] They argue that the current schemes for Bulgarian, Romanian and Croatian nationals, which generally permit persons engaged in (highly skilled) economic activity to remain in the UK, might provide a template as to how this could be operationalised: 'a work permit scheme dependent on having genuine employed or self-employed activity (or sufficient resources for migrants and their families), accompanied by a simplified registration scheme.'[177] Their proposal further includes some limits to equal treatment of workers, notably with respect to access to benefits, which largely build on the CJEU's case law and the ill-fated New Settlement Agreement.[178] There is also provision for an emergency brake to migration, operating at regional level, which builds, according to the argument, on provisions in the Agreement on the European Economic Area, the bilateral agreement with Switzerland on free movement of persons, and the New Settlement Agreement.[179]

There is equally debate in the EU over the future status of UK nationals in the EU 27. Dora Kostakopoulou floats the idea of 'a special EU protect-

---

174 Statement from HM Government (Chequers, 6 July 2018) <https://assets.publish ing.service.gov.uk/government/uploads/system/uploads/attachment_data/file/72 3460/CHEQUERS_STATEMENT_-_FINAL.PDF> accessed 8 July 2018.

175 HM Government, 'The Future Relationship between the United Kingdom and the European Union' (Cm 9593, July 2018), 32-35, paras 72-91.

176 Catherine Barnard and Sarah Fraser-Butlin, 'The Future of Free Movement of Persons in the UK (Part 1)' (19 June 2018) <http://eulawanalysis.blogspot.com/20 18/06/the-future-of-free-movement-of-persons.html> accessed 19 June 2018.

177 Catherine Barnard and Sarah Fraser-Butlin, 'Fair Movement of People: Equal Treatment? (Part Two)' (20 June 2018) <http://eulawanalysis.blogspot.com/2018/ 06/fair-movement-of-people-equal-treatment.html> accessed 8 July 2018.

178 Ibid.

179 Catherine Barnard and Sarah Fraser-Butlin, 'Fair Movement of People: Emergency Brake (Part Three)' (25 June 2018) <http://eulawanalysis.blogspot.com/2018/0 6/fair-movement-of-people-emergency-brake.html> accessed 9 July 2018. See further Catherine Barnard and Sarah Fraser-Butlin, 'Free Movement vs. Fair Movement: Brexit and Managed Migration' (2018) 55 CMLR, 203.

ed citizen status, which '...would ensure that all EU citizens affected by Brexit ... would continue to enjoy their EU citizenship rights and to be subject to the same conditions relating to their residence, employment and family reunification which apply to all other EU citizens.[180] Such status would be gradually phased out, as it would not be automatically trans-ferrable to all those who would become members of their families follow-ing the entry into force of the WA.[181]

Ideas of 'associate citizenship' and the like would be immensely com-plex, legally and politically, to implement within the constraints of the available time.[182] A viable alternative, which is indeed the current ap-proach, is to reciprocally provide for the respective rights of UK and EU nationals in the WA. This Agreement would have to be concluded and im-plemented by both parties before the UK's EU membership lapses. On top of that, EU migration laws could be reformed to provide for more favourable treatment of so-called 'third-country nationals' whenever deemed appropriate.[183] However, if no WA were to be concluded before ex-it day (and no further extension of the TEU, Article 50 period were to be agreed), national migration laws would have to do the hard labour, com-bined with EU migration laws where applicable. In this connection, Steve Peers argues that, in case of 'no-deal' Brexit, EU-wide legislation should be adopted on the basis of TFEU, Article 79 to guarantee the rights of UK na-tionals.[184] Absent such EU-wide legislative initiatives, it should be stressed that national migration laws, even combined with EU law and internation-al human rights instruments, would simply not solve all problems arising from 'no-deal' Brexit.[185] For example, there would be no coordination of social security systems, save for whenever there are pre-existing bilateral

---

180 Dora Kostakopoulou, '*Scala Civium*: Citizenship Templates Post-Brexit and the European Union's Duty to Protect EU Citizens' (2018) 56 JCMS, 854 (863).

181 Ibid 863.

182 This does not mean that they are without merit.

183 On visa policy and travel authorisation, see Steve Peers, 'Brave New World? The New EU Law on Travel Authorisation for Non-EU Citizens' (26 April 2018) <http://eulawanalysis.blogspot.com/2018/04/brave-new-world-new-eu-law-on-tra vel.html> accessed 9 July 2018; Steve Peers, 'Revising EU Visa Policy' (8 July 2018) <http://eulawanalysis.blogspot.com/2018/07/revising-eu-visa-policy.html> accessed 9 July 2018.

184 Steve Peers 'UK Citizens in the EU after Brexit: Securing Unilateral Guarantees after a "No Deal" Brexit' (3 July 2018) <http://eulawanalysis.blogspot.com/2018/ 07/uk-citizens-in-eu-after-brexit-securing.html> accessed 9 July 2018.

185 For the treatment of EU citizens in the UK in a 'no deal' scenario, see Depart-ment for Exiting the European Union (n 148) paras 7-33.

agreements between the countries concerned.[186] However, it is argued that such agreements may be outdated.[187] In the absence of a deal on citizens' rights, only uncertainty would be certain.

The future evolution of the CJEU's case law on citizenship and free movement is also important. Both the EU 27 Member States and the UK would be affected, but the UK would only be affected within the limits set out in the draft WA. This is vividly demonstrated by cases such as *Tjebbes*, which was recently decided by the Court of Justice.[188] The Court was asked whether a national law which leads to automatic loss of citizenship (and therefore of EU citizenship, too) after a 10-year period of residence outside the Union was compatible with EU law or not. It ruled that EU law did not preclude, in principle, that in situations such as those referred in the impugned national legislation, a Member State prescribed for reasons of public interest the loss of its nationality, even if that loss entailed, for the persons concerned, the loss of their EU citizenship.[189] However, it was for the competent national authorities and courts to determine whether the loss of the nationality of the Member State concerned, when it entailed the loss of citizenship of the Union and the rights attaching thereto, had due regard to the principle of proportionality so far as concerns the consequences of that loss for the situation of the person concerned and, if relevant, for that of the members of her/his family.[190] The loss of the nationality of a Member State by operation of law would be inconsistent, said the Court, with the principle of proportionality, if the relevant rules did not permit at any time an individual examination of the consequences of that loss for the persons concerned from the point of view of EU law.[191] The outcome of the *Tjebbes* case is tremendously important for, *in casu*, Dutch

---

186 Brexit preparedness note (n 150) 12.
187 See the discussion in Stefano Giubboni, Feliciano Iudicone, Manuelita Mancini and Michele Faioli, *Coordination of Social Security Systems in Europe* (November 2017) <http://www.europarl.europa.eu/RegData/etudes/STUD/2017/614185/IPO L_STU(2017)614185_EN.pdf> accessed 10 July 2018, 18-21; and Herwig Verschueren, 'Scenarios for Brexit and Social Security' (2017) 24 Maastricht Journal of European and Comparative Law, 367.
188 Case C-221/17, 12.03.2019, *M.G. Tjebbes and Others v Minister van Buitenlandse Zaken*, ECLI:EU:C:2019:189.
189 Ibid para 39.
190 Ibid para 40.
191 Ibid para 41.

nationals staying in the UK after Brexit, and will also affect other Member States with similar laws.[192]

Overall, the 8-year window of opportunity opened up in the draft WA would allow the EU courts to resolve the most pressing legal issues arising from the UK's withdrawal from the EU, provided that the UK courts/ tribunals made use of the opportunity to refer cases to the CJEU. Thereafter, the UK courts/tribunals could only have 'due regard' to the case law of the CJEU concerning citizens' rights. However, where a dispute regarding the interpretation and application of the provisions of the WA 'raises a question of interpretation of a concept of Union law' or 'a question of interpretation of a provision of Union law referred to in this Agreement' the arbitration panel shall request the CJEU to give a ruling on the question.[193] This may allow for citizens' rights cases to reach the CJEU after the end of the 8-year period.

---

192 For a critical look on the case, see Martijn van der Brink, 'Bold, but Without Justification? Tjebbes' (European Papers, European Forum, Insight of 25 April 2019) <http://www.europeanpapers.eu/en/europeanforum/bold-without-justifica tion-tjebbes> accessed 16 May 2019; Dimitry Kochenov, 'The Tjebbes Fail' (European Papers, European Forum, Insight of 25 April 2019) <http://www.europeanp apers.eu/en/europeanforum/the-tjebbes-fail> accessed 16 May 2019.
193 Draft WA, art 174, para 1.

Brexit: Challenges and Regulatory Solutions in the field of Competition Policy and State Aid

Florian Wagner-von Papp[*]

A. Introduction

The main problem which any contribution to the 'Brexit' debate faces is that we still do not know what form Brexit will eventually take, even though we are, at the time of writing, already some two months after the originally planned day of departure (29 March 2019) and some five months away from the second extension date agreed under Article 50(3) TEU ('Exit Day'[1] on 31 October 2019).[2] Theoretically there is a whole panoply of Brexit options to choose from.[3] At the time of the initial sub-

---

[*] The contribution is based on a presentation first presented at the Conference on Trade Relations after Brexit, organised by the EURO- CEFG of the University Leiden and the Mannheim Centre for Competition and Innovation (MaCCI), and subsequently at Waseda University and the Keidanren in Tokyo. I would like to thank the audiences at these venues, Konstanze von Papp, and the editors for their comments. This contribution was initially submitted in the summer of 2018 on the basis of the 'Future Relationship White Paper' (n 4), but has been updated in January 2019 to reflect the Withdrawal Agreement negotiated between the EU and the UK and the Political declaration setting out the framework for the future relationship between the European Union and the United Kingdom, as agreed at negotiators' level and agreed in principle at political level of 22 November 2018 (XT 21095/18), and as endorsed by the European Council on 25 November 2018 (EUCO XT 20015/18), the rejection by the UK Parliament of the Withdrawal Agreement, and the UK preparations for a no deal Brexit, in particular in the Competition (Amendments etc.) (EU Exit) Regulations 2019, Statutory Instruments 2019 Nr. 93. minor amendments at proof stage were made on 20 May 2019.

1 European Union (Withdrawal) Act 2018, *c* 16, s 20(1)–(5).

2 The caption to the Cartoon in the *Financial Times* on 16.07.2018, which depicts a woman presenting a paper entitled 'Brexit Forecasts' to a manager (with a Brexit Countdown showing 256 days left in the background), reads: 'Fred in research says the executive summary of this is: "Haven't the faintest". In this respect, nothing has changed in the ten months that have since gone by.

3 The referendum question was 'Should the United Kingdom remain a member of the European Union or leave the European Union?' There was no definition what leaving the European Union would entail for the future relationship between the UK and the EU. In its softest option, the United Kingdom (UK) could leave the

mission of this chapter, the most current proposals of the UK Government had been made in the 'Future Relationship White Paper' of July 2018, with modifications introduced in the 'Taxation (Cross-border Trade) Act 2018'.[4] Since then, the negotiators for the EU27 and the UK have agreed on a 'Draft Agreement on the withdrawal of the United Kingdom of Great Britain and Northern Ireland from the European Union and the European Atomic Energy Community, as agreed at negotiators' level on 14 November 2018' (the 'Withdrawal Agreement'), and as endorsed by the European Council on 25 November 2018.[5] It was meant to be voted on in the UK Parliament on 11 December 2018, but Prime Minister Theresa May, expecting a defeat, delayed the vote to 15 January 2019. This strategy was only moderately successful, as the margin of defeat of 230 (432 Nos, 202 Ayes) on 15 January 2019 still turned out to be the largest in recorded Parliamentary history. Two further attempts, on 12 March 2019 and 29 March 2019 failed by slightly less extreme but still substantial margins (149 and 58 votes, respectively). At the time of updating this chapter on 20 May 2019, a further vote on an – as yet unpublished – 'new and improved' European Union (Withdrawal Agreement) Bill ('WAB') is planned for the first week of June 2019; chances of success are generally considered to be low. The

---

European Union (EU), but stay in the European Economic Area (EEA) and its Custom Union. It could stay in the EEA, but leave the Customs Union (the 'Norway option'). It could stay in a Customs Union, but leave the Single Market (the 'Turkey option'). It could leave both the Single Market and the Customs Union. In this latter case, this could be on terms of a negotiated 'deep and special' Free Trade Agreement (FTA), which, in turn, could range from the 'Canadian (CETA) option' to the 'Ukraine option' or, in the minds of some, a 'CETA plus, plus, plus option'), or it could be on WTO rules ('WTO Brexit'). See Armstrong, *Brexit Time: Leaving the EU — Why, How and When?* (2017) 139–178.

4 *The Future Relationship Between the United Kingdom and the European Union*, presented to Parliament by the Prime Minister by Command of Her Majesty, Cm 9593 (July 2018) (the 'Future Relationship White Paper', informally referred to as the 'Chequers Proposal'), with the modifications in the Taxation (Cross-border Trade) Bill 2017-19 (HC Bill 128), including the amendments accepted by the Government at Report Stage on 16.07.2018, which partially modified the stance of the Future Relationship White Paper, in particular by requiring the EU to collect UK tariffs at its borders (amendment NC36, clause 54 in HL Bill 125, and now s. 54 of the Taxation (Cross-Border Trade) Act 2018 c. 22), something the Future Relationship White Paper had explicitly excluded (Ch 1 para 17). The Bill has received Royal Assent on 13.09.2018 and has become the Taxation (Cross-Border Trade) Act 2018, c. 22 (the stages of the Bill can be traced at <https://services.parliament.uk/Bills/2017-19/taxationcrossbordertrade.html> (last accessed 20.05.2019)).

5 EUCO XT 20015/18. The Withdrawal Agreement can be accessed at <https://ec.europa.eu/commission/sites/beta-political/files/draft_withdrawal_agreement_0.pdf>.

options under discussion for the future relationship between the UK and the EU are still the ones the UK faced from the start, ranging from a revocation of the Article 50 TEU notice (an option whose existence was confirmed by the Court of Justice in the *Wightman* case[6]) or remaining in the European Economic Area (EEA) and Customs Union, to, at the other end of the spectrum, mere WTO terms.

For the purposes of this contribution on competition law, however, we need not distinguish between all of the possible variants of Brexit. The first and main question is whether the United Kingdom remains in the EEA or not. If it does not, the second question is whether there will be a Free Trade Agreement (FTA) with the EU, in which case the EU insists that the FTA 'must ensure a level playing field, notably in terms of competition and state aid.'[7] A third—separate, but not independent—question is whether there will be a 'crash exit' ('no-deal scenario') on 31 October 2019, whether there will be a further agreed extension of the period of negotiation under Article 50 TEU beyond 31 October 2019, or whether there will be a transition period during which the terms of a negotiated withdrawal agreement apply.[8] The Prime Minister's strategy appears to be to 'run down the clock' in a game of brinkmanship, forcing Parliament to choose eventually between 'her deal' (the Withdrawal Agreement) or 'no deal' with the widely expected chaotic consequences. For competition law, the immediate consequences of a 'no-deal Brexit' are primarily set out in the

---

6 Judgment of the Court (Full Court) of 10.12.2018, Case C-621/18, *Wightman & ors v Secretary of State for Exiting the European Union*, ECLI:EU:C:2018:999, in particular paras 48–75.

7 European Council, *Guidelines following the United Kingdom's notification under Article 50 TEU*, 29.04.2017, EUCO XT 20004/17, para. 20; similarly European Parliament resolution of 14.03.2018 on the framework of the future EU-UK relationship (2018/2573(RSP)), P8_TA(2018)0069, para 4, sixth indent. See now Political Declaration setting out the framework for the future relationship between the European Union and the United Kingdom, as agreed at negotiators' level and agreed in principle at political level of 22 November 2018 (XT 21095/18) at paras 17, 79.

8 The *Agreement on the Withdrawal of the United Kingdom of Great Britain and Northern Ireland from the European Union and the European Atomic Energy Community*, 14.11.2018, would provide for a transition period until 31.12.2020 (Article 126 of the Withdrawal Agreement), which may be extended once (Article 132 of the Withdrawal Agreement). On 24.07.2018, the UK Government had presented (on the basis of the previous draft of the Withdrawal Agreement dated 19.03.2018) a White Paper *Legislating for the Withdrawal Agreement between the United Kingdom and the European Union*, presented to Parliament by the Secretary of State for Exiting the European Union by Command of Her Majesty, Cm 9674 (July 2018) (the 'Withdrawal WP').

'Competition (Amendments etc.) (EU Exit) Regulations 2019', which were made on 22 January 2019, and enter into force on Exit Day.[9]

Unless the 'red lines' in the United Kingdom (UK) negotiating position for the future relationship change, which includes the ending of free movement of workers,[10] the EEA solution is off the table.[11] The House of Lords had adopted an amendment which would have inserted into the European Union (Withdrawal) Act 2018 a clause under which many of the provisions of the Bill would not have come into force 'until it is a negotiating objective of the Government to ensure that an international agreement has been made which enables the United Kingdom to continue to participate in the European Economic Area after exit day'.[12] However, this amendment was defeated in the House of Commons and did not become part of the Act.[13] The Future Relationship White Paper repeated the intention of the UK to leave the Single Market as well as the Customs Union,[14] and the mutually exclusive demands of the UK and the EU in paragraph 4 of the Political Declaration would necessitate this result. For most of this contribution, I will therefore assume that the UK will leave the EEA as well as the EU, although it remains possible that the UK will eventually prefer an EEA solution to a crash exit at the last minute.[15]

---

9 Statutory Instruments 2019 No. 93.

10 See para 50 and the third sentence of para 4 of the Political Declaration, n 7. See already Prime Minister Theresa May's speech on our future economic partnership with the European Union (02.03.2018) (the 'Mansion House Speech').

11 See the second sentence of para. 4 of the Political Declaration, n 7, emphasizing the need to ensure the integrity of the Single Market including the indivisibility of the four freedoms.

12 Clause 24(5) of the European Union (Withdrawal) Bill, after Amendments by the Lords (report stage). The development of the Bill into the Act can be traced at <https://services.parliament.uk/Bills/2017-19/europeanunionwithdrawal/documents.html> (last accessed 20.05.2019).

13 European Union (Withdrawal) Act 2018, *c* 16, which received Royal Assent on 26.06.2018. See also para. 7 of the Explanatory Notes: 'Withdrawing from the EU means the UK will also cease to participate in the European Economic Area (EEA) Agreement [...]'.

14 Future Relationship White Paper, n 4, 7.

15 While some 'Remainers' in the UK continue to hope that the Article 50 TEU notification will be revoked in accordance with the *Wightman* judgment of the Court of Justice (n 6), possibly after yet another Referendum or another General Election, there is currently no majority in Parliament for any of these options, given that both the Conservative and the leader of the Labour Party Jeremy Corbyn want to be seen as abiding strictly by the outcome of the Referendum of June 2016. Even if there were another General Election, any pro-EU party would stand little chance in a first-past-the-post system that has in most constituencies seen

The contribution first discusses the necessary or probable changes in substantive competition law in part B. These will turn out to be relatively modest—with the exception of the area of state aid. The same, however, cannot be said about the changes with regard to, and resource implications of, competition law procedure and international cooperation, which are discussed in part C. In this area, there are major challenges, with regard to both public and private enforcement. The contribution finishes by looking very briefly at transitional arrangements (part D), what would happen if the UK did stay in the EEA after all (part E), and what changes Brexit will bring on the side of the EU (part F). Part G concludes.

B. Substantive Competition Law

I. Antitrust

Currently, antitrust law in the UK is contained in particular in the Competition Act 1998,[16] which includes the so-called 'Chapter I prohibition',[17] which is the domestic equivalent to Article 101 TFEU against horizontal and vertical anticompetitive agreements, and the 'Chapter II prohibition',[18] which is the domestic equivalent to Article 102 TFEU against abuses of dominant positions. Nothing in Brexit requires these provisions to change, and it is not expected that these provisions will be changed, despite their being closely modelled on the European provisions. The UK Government has stated, in response to questions raised by the House of Lords EU Internal Markets Select Committee,[19] that at least for the time being the current

---

Conservative or Labour win in previous elections. While there are increasing calls for a Second Referendum (a 'People's Vote'), the time-frame for getting the primary legislation for such a Second Referendum in place would be very tight even if a majority in Parliament could be found, and it would most likely require a further extension of the Article 50 TEU negotiating period, which requires unanimity under Article 50(3) TEU.

16 Competition Act 1998, *c* 41.
17 Competition Act 1998, s 1.
18 Competition Act 1998, s 18.
19 House of Lords – European Union Committee *Brexit: competition and state aid*, 12th Report of Session 2017-19, HL Paper 67 (02.02.2018) (the 'House of Lords Committee Report Brexit & Competition').

system will continue to be used.[20] The Future Relationship White Paper states that the UK's proposals include 'maintaining current antitrust prohibitions [...] with rigorous UK enforcement of competition law [...]'.[21] If the Withdrawal Agreement should be adopted, the EU antitrust rules continue to be applicable, and the EU institutions continue to be competent for the enforcement of all antitrust proceedings enforcing Articles 101, 102 TFEU under Regulation 1/2003 that were initiated under Article 2(1) of Regulation 773/2004 before the end of the transition period under Article 92(1), (2), (3)(b) of the Withdrawal Agreement. Even if there is a no-deal Brexit, the Competition (Amendments etc.) (EU Exit) Regulations 2019 do not provide for any changes to the Chapter I or Chapter II prohibitions.

1. Block Exemptions

The situation is only slightly more complicated with regard to the practically important Block Exemption Regulations. Currently, EU Block Exemption Regulations (BER) are in the UK incorporated by reference, so as to exempt the agreements permitted in the BER also from domestic competition law.[22] Of course, agreements that are exempt from Article 101(1) TFEU under an EU BER are also automatically exempt from the application of the Chapter I prohibition; this derives directly from the first sentence in Article 3(2) of Regulation 1/2003,[23] but is also explicitly provided in s 10(1) Competition Act. More importantly, agreements that may not affect trade between Member States, but otherwise fulfil the conditions of an EU BER are also exempt from the Chapter I prohibition (until now known as the 'parallel exemption').[24]

After Brexit, the EU block exemptions do not apply to the UK anymore *as EU law*. However, s 3 of the European Union (Withdrawal) Act 2018 transforms the existing EU BERs into domestic law. The Competition

---

20 Department for Business, Energy & Industrial Strategy, Government Response to the House of Lords Committee Report Brexit and Competition, letter to Lord Whitty dated 29.03.2018 (The 'Government Response to the House of Lords Committee Report Brexit and Competition'): 'Beyond the changes necessary to ensure our competition regime remains fully operational when we leave the EU, we do not plan to make fundamental changes to the UK competition framework.'
21 Future Relationship White Paper, n 4, Ch. 1 para. 108 lit b.
22 Competition Act 1998, s 10.
23 Regulation (EC) No 1/2003 of 16.12.2002 on the implementation of the rules on competition laid down in Articles 81 and 82 of the Treaty, [2003] OJ L 1/1.
24 Competition Act 1998, s 10(2), (3).

(Amendments etc.) (EU Exit) Regulations 2019 provide that the 'parallel exemptions' will in the future be called 'retained exemptions' and lists the retained block exemption regulations.[25] A new s 10A to be inserted into the Competition Act 1998 gives power to the Secretary of State to vary or revoke retained block exemption regulations, either on recommendation from the Competition and Markets Authority (CMA) or on his own motion after taking the CMA's comments into account.[26] The continued application of the BERs—including the retained exemptions for agreements that may not affect trade between Member States—should not lead to problems after Brexit.

In the longer term, the question of regulatory divergence arises. Even if the UK does not choose to revoke or vary any of the existing BERs which are transformed into domestic UK law by virtue of the European Union (Withdrawal) Act 2018, the question will arise at the latest when the existing EU BERs expire and are replaced by new ones in the European Union. The UK could, of course, copy paste the new EU BERs voluntarily into a domestic BER,[27] and it seems likely that it will choose to do so on a case by

---

25 Regulation 3, listing in regulation 3(9) the following block exemption regulations, as amended from time to time:

(a) Council Regulation (EC) 169/2009 applying rules of competition to transport by rail, road and inland waterway;

(b) Commission Regulation (EC) 906/2009 on the application of Article 81(3) of the Treaty to certain categories of agreements, decisions and concerted practices between liner shipping companies (consortia);

(c) Commission Regulation (EU) 330/2010 on the application of Article 101(3) of the Treaty on the Functioning of the European Union to categories of vertical agreements and concerted practices;

(d) Commission Regulation (EU) 461/2010 on the application of Article 101(3) of the Treaty on the Functioning of the European Union to categories of vertical agreements and concerted practices in the motor vehicle sector;

(e) Commission Regulation (EU) 1217/2010 on the application of Article 101(3) of the Treaty on the Functioning of the European Union to certain categories of research and development agreements;

(f) Commission Regulation (EU) 1218/2010 on the application of Article 101(3) of the Treaty on the Functioning of the European Union to certain categories of specialisation agreements;

(g) Commission Regulation (EU) 316/2014 on the application of Article 101(3) of the Treaty on the Functioning of the European Union to categories of technology transfer agreements.

26 Regulation 4.

27 Competition Act 1998, s 6.

case basis.[28] However, given the government's insistence that the Referendum was a vote to 'take control of... our laws'[29] it seems very unlikely that the UK will introduce a transformation rule that would automatically adopt new EU BERs,[30] and the Competition (Amendments etc.) (EU Exit) Regulations 2019 do not provide for automatic adoption. It will be for the CMA to recommend alignment in the future (or, less likely, for the Secretary of State to take this up without prompting by the CMA), and the expiry of various of the Block Exemption Regulations in 2020 will show soon to what extent the UK will seek future alignment with the revised Block Exemption Regulations.

2. *Alignment or divergence in the longer run?*

This raises the more general question, to what extent there will be alignment between EU and UK competition law in the future. It is to be expected that for the greatest part, there will continue to be alignment for two reasons:

- First, modern UK competition law has developed and has been shaped under EU law. Competition lawyers will likely aim at continuity with the pre-Brexit practice, and this implies that at least on the broad principles there will continue to be alignment.
- Secondly, EU competition law will continue to be applicable to much conduct within the UK by virtue of its extraterritorial application, especially since the Court of Justice's *Intel* judgment has finally committed

---

28 This is also the position taken by the UK Government in response to the House of Lords' EU Internal Market Sub-Committee's questions (n 20 above): '[W]here a block exemption regulation is enacted by the European Commission after EU exit, the Government will be able to decide, in consultation with the CMA [the Competition and Markets Authority], whether to use its existing powers under section 6 of the Competition Act 1998 to issue a domestic Block Exemption Order to similar effect.'

29 Mansion House Speech, n 10. For a description of the genesis and claims made about the need to 'take back control of our laws' in the Brexit campaign; see *Armstrong, Brexit Time: Leaving the EU — Why, How and When?* (Cambridge University Press 2017) 113–124.

30 *Whish*, 'Brexit and EU competition policy' (2016) 7 *Journal of European Competition Policy & Practice* 297, 298.

the EU to the qualified effects test.[31] If UK competition law were to depart in its assessment from EU law, many undertakings in the UK would have to comply with divergent sets of competition law.[32] Such a duplication would constitute a disadvantage for the UK in regulatory competition, and the UK legislature will likely avoid this unless necessitated by weightier considerations.

It is therefore to be expected that there are strong incentives to keep EU and UK competition law aligned unless there are overwhelming reasons for the UK to depart from the EU position.

Nevertheless, *automatic* alignment is politically unpalatable. This has implications for s 60 of the Competition Act 1998, which currently essentially provides that UK competition law must be interpreted consistently with EU competition law as it is applied by the EU institutions, unless differences are necessitated by the differences in the respective provisions. It always seemed unlikely that this provision would continue to exist in its current form, as the deference it pays to EU law is inconsistent with the 'taking back control' mantra of the UK Government,[33] and the Competition (Amendments etc.) (EU Exit) Regulations 2019 now indeed provide for the omission of s 60.[34] A number of competition experts had suggested a different course, namely to amend section 60 of the Competition Act 1998 so that those applying the Competition Act 1998 should *'have regard to* relevant EU Court judgments and EC decisions.'[35] The House of Lords

---

31 Judgment of the Court (Grand Chamber) of 06.09.2017, Case C-413/14 P, *Intel v Commission*, EU:C:2017:632, para 45. Ironically, it may have been precisely the leaving of the EU by the UK that gave an impetus to the Court finally to come down on the side of the qualified effects test, because it had been the UK that was the strongest opponent. See *Behrens, The extraterritorial reach of EU competition law revisited: The "effects doctrine" before the ECJ*, Discussion Paper No. 3/16, Europa-Kolleg Hamburg, Institute for European Integration, Hamburg, 14.

32 See already *Whish*, 'Brexit and EU competition policy' (2016) 7 *Journal of European Competition Policy & Practice* 297; *Vickers*, 'Consequences of Brexit for competition law and policy' (2017) 33 *Oxford Review of Economic Policy* S70, S71.

33 Ibid.

34 Regulation 22.

35 Brexit Competition Law Working Group, *Conclusions and Recommendations* (July 2017), para 2.8, 2.9('BCLWG'); *Lianos/Mantzari/Wagner-von Papp/Thepot*, 'Brexit and Competition Law', *UCL Centre for Law, Economics & Society (CLES) Policy Paper Series* 2/2017 (the 'CLES House of Lords submission') para 28; *Vickers*, 'Consequences of Brexit for competition law and policy' (2017) 33 *Oxford Review of Economic Policy* 70 (77).

EU Internal Market Sub-Committee had also suggested this approach.[36] The UK Government had appeared to be amenable to introducing such a toned-down version of s 60 Competition Act 1998, although the Government's response mentioned only taking account of CJEU jurisprudence, an approach that would fall far short of the current obligations under s 60 Competition Act 1998, which also includes Commission decisions and guidance.[37]

The Competition (Amendments etc.) (EU Exit) Regulations 2019 instead introduce a new s 60A into the Competition Act 1998.[38, 39] The new s 60A requires courts, tribunals, the CMA, and persons acting for the CMA to avoid inconsistency between the principles they apply and decision they reach on the one hand, and, on the other hand, 'the principles laid down by the Treaty on the Functioning of the European Union and the European Court before exit day, and any relevant decision made by that Court before exit day, so far as applicable immediately before exit day in determining any corresponding question arising in EU law', except where subsections (4) to (7) provide otherwise; the court, tribunals, the CMA, and persons acting for the CMA must also 'have regard to any relevant decision or statement of the European Commission made before exit day and not withdrawn.' The need to avoid inconsistency does not apply, first, where the principle or decision is excluded from the Law of England and Wales, Scotland, and Northern Ireland, or if a principle or decision from these jurisdictions requires the person to act otherwise. Much more problematic is the highly subjective exemption from the requirement to avoid inconsis-

---

36 House of Lords Committee Report Brexit & Competition, n 19, para 82.
37 Government Response to the House of Lords Committee Report Brexit & Competition, n 20, response to Recommendation 2: '[T]he Government understands that consistency might be appropriate in some cases, as our competition regime mirrors the EU's [...]. The Government welcomes the arguments put forward to the Committee on the retention of some form of duty on UK courts to take account of CJEU jurisprudence and will take account of the views in the Committee's account.'
38 Regulation 23.
39 There was a separate debate whether s 6(3) of the European Union (Withdrawal) Act 2018 imposes, independently of s 60 Competition Act 1998, an obligation to interpret the Chapter I and Chapter II prohibitions against anticompetitive agreements and abuses of dominant positions in accordance with the EU case law as it stands on Exit Day. See the discussion in *Grenfell*, 'A View from the CMA', Speech at the Advanced Competition Law Conference, 16.05.2018, part 3. The insertion of s 60A Competition Act 1998 has rendered this discussion moot.

tency in the new s 60A(7) Competition Act 1998, under which this requirement does not apply:

if the person thinks that it is appropriate to act otherwise in the light of one or more of the following—

(a) differences between the provisions of this Part under consideration and the corresponding provisions of EU law as those provisions of EU law had effect immediately before exit day;

(b) differences between markets in the United Kingdom and markets in the European Union;

(c) developments in forms of economic activity since the time when the principle or decision referred to in subsection (2)(b) was laid down or made;

(d) generally accepted principles of competition analysis or the generally accepted application of such principles;

(e) a principle laid down or decision made, by the European Court on or after exit day;

(f) the particular circumstances under consideration.

S 60A(8) Competition Act 1998 clarifies that there is no requirement to avoid inconsistency with EU law principles and decisions established on or after exit day. However, it seems unlikely that even in the long run there will be fundamental divergences in the area of anticompetitive agreements and abuses of dominant positions. This does not preclude, however, deviations on individual aspects. The competition law discourse in the UK has always been influenced more by Chicago School notions than by ordoliberalism and European competition law, and so it does not seem impossible that UK competition law will take a more laissez-faire attitude towards vertical restraints and in the area of abuses of dominant positions.[40] Not being bound any longer by the parallel application rule in Article 3(1) of Regu-

---

40 The Government Response to the House of Lords Committee Report Brexit & Competition, n 20, includes the somewhat cryptic sentence: 'The Government recognises that there may be areas for innovation in the future. These include issues of non-cartel enforcement, particularly in abuse of dominance cases in large online platforms and other fast-paced digital markets.' Given that more demanding domestic provisions were never prohibited by Article 3(2) Regulation (EC) 1/2003 (see its second sentence), this can only mean a more permissive approach — or that the Government has not understood Article 3(2) Regulation (EC) 1/2003. A more permissive approach also seems to be indicated by the oral evidence of Dr Coscelli from the CMA before the House of Lords EU Internal Markets Sub-Committee (<http://data.parliament.uk/writtenevidence/committeeevide

lation 1/2003, or the convergence rule in Article 3(2) of Regulation 1/2003,[41] means that the departure from the stricter European law will become legally possible, because EU competition law will no longer have to be applied in parallel. As we will see below, a laxer approach to verticals and abuses will be quite likely, if only because the CMA will need to prioritise its enforcement resources carefully to be able to deal with the additional workload that Brexit will bring in other areas.

II. Mergers

With regard to mergers, again the substantive test[42] will not necessarily need to change, and the UK Government has announced that it proposes to 'maintain [...] the merger control system [...]'.[43] If the Withdrawal Agreement is ratified by all parties, EU merger control law, including the procedural provisions and the institutions' competences, will continue to apply to all concentrations that have been notified by the end of the transition period (or where the conditions for referral under Article 4(5) or Article 22(3) EUMR were met at that time).[44]

The big change will, of course, be that the one-stop shop principle of Article 21(3) EUMR will, after the end of the transition period (if any), no longer apply. The EU Commission will no longer consider anticompetitive

---

nce.svc/evidencedocument/eu-internal-market-subcommittee/brexit-competition/oral/70457.pdf> (last accessed 20.05.2019), p. 6, indicating that in non-cartel antitrust cases there may be a shift towards the US position). *Vickers*, 'Consequences of Brexit for competition law and policy' (2017) 33 *Oxford Review of Economic Policy*, 70 (77), considers the arguments for and against divergence to be balanced, because 'EU law on abuse of dominance and some kinds of vertical agreement has arguably become more formalistic and less economics-based than is good for competition and consumers'.

41 See regulation 63 with Schedule 3 of the Competition (Amendments etc.) (EU Exit) Regulations 2019.

42 The 'substantial lessening of competition' test, Enterprise Act 2002, *c* 40, ss 22(1)(b), 33(1)(b), 35(1)(b), 36(1)(b).

43 Future Relationship White Paper, n 4, Ch. 1 para 108 lit. b. There is a discussion whether the older 'public interest test' should be revived, but the competition community is strongly against opening up merger control to political considerations, see, eg, *Vickers*, 'Consequences of Brexit for competition law and policy' (2017) 33 *Oxford Review of Economic Policy* S70, S74-75, Lindsay/Berridge, 'Brexit, merger control and potential reforms' (2017) 38 *European Competition Law Review* 435–436.

44 Articles 92(1), (2), (3)(c), 94 of the Withdrawal Agreement.

effects of mergers in the UK as such. Conversely, these mergers will often be notified in the UK as well as in the EU, and the UK can scrutinise these mergers in parallel. In terms of resources, this will be a significant change, because the CMA will now have to deal with a whole new range of complex and often international mergers that had previously been dealt exclusively by the Commission; for the undertakings, the burden of notifications is duplicated.[45]

Again, while there is no necessity to change the substantive merger control law, it is *possible* that the law will change in the longer term. However, for mergers below the Union dimension, the UK has always been able to set and apply the law as it wished, and it is not readily apparent why its preferences should dramatically shift post Brexit. There may, however, be changes with regard to thresholds in order to reduce the workload of the CMA, although such ideas have been opposed by competition law experts.[46] It is also possible that the UK will shift at some point from the voluntary notification of mergers to a mandatory notification system, and that it may move away from the 'share of supply' test to clearer turnover thresholds.[47] It seems likely, however, that the CMA will try to postpone such a major shift until the manifold uncertainties that are connected to Brexit have been resolved.[48]

III. Market Investigations

With regard to market investigations under the Enterprise Act 2002,[49] again there is no need for a change. Currently, the CMA can, in principle, choose between, on the one hand, pursuing a Chapter I or Chapter II prohibition under the Competition Act 1998 and, on the other hand, pursuing a market investigation under the Enterprise Act 2002. However, at least with regard to the Chapter I prohibition, this choice is currently constrained by EU law: where the agreement may affect trade between Member States, the EU antitrust rules have to be applied (Article 3(1) of Regulation 1/2003), so that more lenient domestic law would be irrelevant, and

---

45 *Vickers*, 'Consequences of Brexit for competition law and policy' (2017) 33 *Oxford Review of Economic Policy* S70, 74.
46 BCLWG, n 35, para 8.10, 8.11.
47 See *Lindsay/Berridge*, 'Brexit, merger control and potential reforms' (2017) 38 *European Competition Law Review* 435–436.
48 Ibid, 436.
49 Enterprise Act 2002, c 40, part 4.

domestic law may not prohibit an agreement that is not prohibited under Article 101 TFEU, so that stricter domestic law would also be irrelevant. In such cases, using the domestic market investigation procedure in addition to the EU rules does not make sense.

Given that the UK will no longer have to apply EU law in parallel or abide by the convergence rule of Article 3(2) of Regulation 1/2003,[50] the application of market investigations will be less constrained in the future. This could lead to a shift in enforcement practice, and a rebalancing of market investigations on the one hand and Chapter I or Chapter II investigations on the other hand.[51]

IV. State Aid

One major and immediate difference between the post-Brexit and the current situation is that the UK will no longer be subjected to the European state aid regime (unless, of course, the EEA option is chosen).

One possibility would have been that post Brexit there is no substitute at all for the European state aid regime. It is difficult to say what the result would be of an unconstrained ability to give state aid. There are political forces in two directions. On the one hand, at least in the competition authorities, there is a competition policy focus, and in parts of UK politics there is a strong free-trading, libertarian element that would arguably be averse to distortions of the competitive regime such as the creation of national champions. On the other hand, Brexit has also been driven by protectionist forces, and with the emphasis on industrial strategy there is a recognition that attracting foreign direct investment post Brexit will no longer be a matter course. The reaction to the public procurement process that led to the award of the printing of new blue UK passports to a Franco-Dutch bidder (Gemalto), winning against the British firm De la Rue, shows that even those who proclaim to be working for free markets may, in the end, fall into the protectionist camp.[52] Similarly, the award of a GBP13.8m contract to provide emergency ferry services in the case of a no-

---

50 Regulation 63 with Schedule 3 of the Competition (Amendments etc.) (EU Exit) Regulations 2019.

51 BCLWG, n 35, paras 4.1-4.4; John Vickers, 'Consequences of Brexit for competition law and policy' (2017) 33 *Oxford Review of Economic Policy* S70, S75.

52 Cf *Blitz*, 'Britain's passport blues', *Financial Times*, 22.03.2018 (quoting, among others, the 'avowed free trader' Matt Hancock as saying that '[o]ne of the advantages of leaving the European Union is that we will be able to have more control

deal Brexit to Seaborne, a ferry operator without boats and without any experience of operating a ferry service or, at the time of the award, contracts with either of the two ports of Ramsgate or Ostend, and with terms and conditions copied from a takeaway service, does not inspire much confidence into the firmness of conviction for the importance of competition policy.[53] The government justified the use of the negotiated procedure without prior publication, a procedure which is only available in exceptional circumstances, by relying on 'extreme urgency', even though Article 32(2)(c) of Directive 2014/24/EU specifies that the 'circumstances invoked to justify extreme urgency shall not in any event be attributable to the contracting authority.' The presence of the conditions for the negotiated procedure without prior publication have rightly been called into question.[54]

Accordingly, there are some doubts as to the unwavering commitment to the application of competition policy to State activity. Nevertheless, it had been proposed early in the process that the UK should adopt an equivalent to the EU state aid regime under domestic law,[55] and the Government announced in January 2018 that it would introduce such a domestic state aid regime. The Future Relationship White Paper envisages the CMA taking the role of enforcing rules on state aid, in cooperation with the devolved nations.[56] In its technical notice on state aid published on 23 August 2018, the Government explained that in the case of a no-deal Brexit, the substantive state aid provisions in the Treaty will continue to apply by virtue of s 4 of the European Union (Withdrawal) Act 2018, that the CMA will be the competent authority for receiving notifications and approving state aid (*vel non*), and that the Government intends to pass secondary leg-

---

over our own procurement rules'). For the implications of Brexit on public procurement, see Sanchez-Graells's chapter in this book.

53 See, eg, Rovnick and Blitz, 'Ferry group with no ships jettisons takeaway T&Cs', *Financial Times*, 03.01.2019.

54 See *Sanchez-Graells*, 'Written Evidence to the House of Commons Transport Select Committee in relation to its inquiry "Freight and Brexit"', submitted 02.01.2019, <http://www.bristol.ac.uk/media-library/sites/law/documents/Written%20Evidenc e%20to%20the%20House%20of%20Commons%20Transport%20Committee%20(Jan%202019).pdf>.

55 BCLWG, n 35, para 10.7; House of Lords Committee Report Brexit & Competition, n 19, Chapter 6 (paras 170 *et seq.*) and Recommendation 18; UK Government's response to the House of Lords Committee Report Brexit & Competition, n 20, 14, response to Recommendation 18.

56 Future Relationship White Paper, n 4, Ch. 1 para 110, 111.

islation under the European Union (Withdrawal) Act 2018 in the autumn of 2018.[57]

The Draft State Aid (EU Exit) Regulations 2019 currently in the parliamentary procedure clarify and provide, *inter alia*:

- that the substantive state aid provisions in the Treaty on the Functioning of the European Union continue to apply as domestic law under s 4 of the European Union (Withdrawal) Act 2018 with the modifications set out in draft regulation 3 (primarily to account of the CMA's competence instead of the European Commission's),
- that the various EU Regulations for *de minimis* state aid and Block Exemption Regulations (in particular the General Block Exemption Regulation 651/2014, the Fisheries BER 1388/2014 and the Agricultural BER 702/2014) continue to apply under s 3 of the European Union (Withdrawal) Act 2018,
- that certain Council or Commission decisions, for example, the Commission's decision on Services of General Economic Interest (Decision 2012/21/EU) continue to apply, and
- that the CMA takes on the role that so far the Commission has played in the state aid procedure.[58]

This suggestion of a domestic state aid regime, while well-intentioned, is difficult to conceptualise. The European (EU/EEA) state aid system works precisely because the EU is a multi-level governance regime: Member States are constrained by a higher governance level in a constitutionally guaranteed hierarchy of norms. The envisaged domestic state aid regime may work perfectly fine where a public body other than the central government seeks to give state aid. The problems a purely domestic state aid regime would face, however, are twofold. First, where the central government has the desire to award state aid, the implicit (or potentially explicit) pressure on the CMA to accede to the governmental request would be great, especially given that the CMA's budget is in the government's control. Secondly, a purely domestic state aid control regime with teeth seems impossible in a country, such as the UK, which does not allow for constitu-

---

57 Department for Business, Energy & Industrial Strategy, *Guidance: State Aid if there's* [sic] *no Brexit deal*, published 23.08.2018, <https://www.gov.uk/government/p ublications/state-aid-if-theres-no-brexit-deal/state-aid-if-theres-no-brexit-deal> (last accessed 20.05.2019).

58 The CMA has published a quick overview of its role on 23.01.2019 here: <https:// www.gov.uk/government/publications/the-cmas-state-aid-role-if-theres-no-brexit-d eal/uk-state-aid-if-theres-no-brexit-deal> (last accessed 20.05.2019).

tional constraints on what Lord Hailsham has called an 'elective dictatorship'[59] and Lord Acton has called the 'tyranny of the majority'[60]: if Parliament says that white is black and black is white, then white is black and black is white — and, *mutatis mutandis*, if Parliament says that a particular payment is not state aid or is a permissible state aid, then this would be the end of the story, at least from the perspective of domestic law. The UK's stance towards state aid would depend solely on party politics. The leader of the Labour Party, Jeremy Corbyn, has made clear that one of the main reasons for his anti-EU stance is the existence of the EU competition and state aid rules, which (in his mind) prevent bail-outs of domestic industries.[61] If there were to be a General Election and labour under Jeremy Corbyn were to gain power, it seems likely that any purely domestic state aid regime introduced post Brexit would be watered down or abolished.

Should the United Kingdom not enter into an FTA with the EU ('WTO Brexit'), either without a Withdrawal Agreement on 31 October 2019 ('crash Brexit') or after the transition period, the only external constraint on UK state aid would be the Agreement on Subsidies and Countervailing Measures (SCM Agreement) on the WTO-Level.[62] The SCM Agreement categorises specific[63] subsidies[64] as either 'prohibited' or as 'actionable'. Only export subsidies and local content subsidies are prohibited.[65] Most subsi-

---

59 Lord Hailsham used this phrase repeatedly to describe the British constitution, among others in a lecture Lord Hailsham (then Mr Hogg) gave at a Blackpool meeting of Pressure for Economic and Social Toryism: 'Declaring that Parliament had become an "elective dictatorship", Mr Hogg said: "Its constitutional legislative powers are admittedly unlimited. Its legislation cannot be questioned in any court. Originally conceived as a brake on the executive, these powers are now controlled by the executive in the shape of a monolithic Cabinet". 'Mr Hogg's way to end the tyranny of Whitehall', *The Times*, 12.10.1968, 10.

60 'The one pervading evil of democracy is the tyranny of the majority, or rather of that party, not always the majority, that succeeds, by force or fraud, in carrying elections.' Lord Acton (John Emerich Edward Dalberg, first Baron Acton, 1834–1902, historian), 'Democracy in Europe; a History. By Sir Thomas Erskine May, K.C.B., D.B.L. In 2 volumes, 1877. ' (January 1878) 145 *The Quarterly Review* Issue 289, 112, 140.

61 See *Peretz*, 'Corbyn on state aid: fact-checking', 27.02.2018, <http://www.politics.co .uk/comment-analysis/2018/02/27/corbyn-on-state-aid-fact-checked> (last accessed 20.05.2019).

62 For a brief summary of how the WTO regime would change the position on state aid in a post-Brexit UK, see *Crafts*, 'Brexit and state aid' (2017) 33 *Oxford Review of Economic Policy* 105 (107).

63 Art. 2 SCM Agreement.

64 Art. 1 SCM Agreement.

65 Art. 3 SCM Agreement.

dies are at most 'actionable', in which case the subsidy is not prohibited but only challengeable if the complaining Member State can show adverse trade effects, which is a difficult hurdle to overcome.[66] More specifically, the complaining Member State has to show 'injury' in order to take countervailing action, or 'serious adverse effects' or 'nullification or impairment' of benefits under the 1994 GATT (in particular arising from bound tariffs). In any case, the provisions in the SCM Agreement are restricted to trade in goods (*i.e.*, excluding services), there are special provisions for the agricultural sector in the Agricultural Agreement, and – in contrast to the state aid provisions in the TFEU – the remedies for prohibited or actionable subsidies are purely *state-to-state* consultations and dispute resolutions. In other words, even where there is a prohibited or actionable subsidy for goods under the SCM Agreement, any undertakings that feel disadvantaged need to convince their government that the case is sufficiently substantial to take action; there is no private right of action comparable to the one under the EU state aid provisions.

Should there be an FTA, the situation is slightly different. As mentioned in the introduction, the EU has made clear from the beginning that any FTA 'must ensure a level playing field, notably in terms of competition and state aid'.[67] It is clear that the mere application of the rules in the SCM Agreement would not fulfil this precondition of ensuring a level playing field. The EU would most likely insist on substantive rules equivalent to the state aid rules in the TFEU or the EEA-Agreement, and on an external supervisory mechanism. It is true that existing EU FTAs vary greatly in the intensity of state aid control they require from the other party. Most contain at least substantive prohibitions of state aid that distorts trade between the EU and the third country.[68] The EU-Ukraine Association Agreement additionally requires the Ukraine to create and enforce a domestic state aid

---

66 Part III (Art. 5 *et seq.*) of the SCM Agreement.

67 European Council, *Guidelines following the United Kingdom's notification under Article 50 TEU*, 29.04.2017, EUCO XT 20004/17, para. 20; see also European Parliament resolution of 14.03.2018 on the framework of the future EU-UK relationship (2018/2573(RSP)), P8_TA(2018)0069, para 4, sixth indent, and now para. 79 of the Political Declaration, n 7.

68 See, eg, the Albania Stabilisation and Association Agreement (SAA), art. 71(1)(iii), the fYRoM SAA, article 69(1)(iii), article 73(1)(iii) of the Montenegro and Serbia SAAs, respectively, the Bosnia and Herzegovina SAA, article 71(1)(c), and the Kosovo SAA, art. 75(1)(c).

control regime.[69] The provisions in chapter 7 on subsidies of the Comprehensive Economic and Trade Agreement (CETA) between the EU and Canada, on the other hand, take the SCM Agreement (and the Agricultural Agreement) as a starting point and only tentatively expand its reach, for example, to include a consultation procedure on government support for services that have or may have adverse effects on the other party's interests.[70]

However, given the volume of trade and the close integration of trade both in goods and services between the UK and the EU27, it is obvious that the EU will need to safeguard the internal market against distortions from state aid by a large economy just off its shores. Switzerland cannot serve as a counter-example.[71] Given the strong services sector in the UK, the scope of the state aid regime in an EU-UK FTA would clearly have to be much broader than the SCM Agreement, which is restricted to goods, and deeper than the mere consultation process with government assistance in the area of services contained in Article 7.3 of CETA. In addition, one reason for the relatively abstract level of state aid/subsidy provisions in many of the FTAs with other countries is arguably that these countries do not have an established system of state aid control in place, at least not one beyond the relatively narrow WTO rules on subsidies in the SCM Agree-

---

69 See Association Agreement between the European Union and its Member States, of the one part, and Ukraine, of the other part, [2014] *Official Journal of the European Union* L 161/3 art. 267.

70 See Comprehensive Economic and Trade Agreement (CETA) between Canada, of the one part, and the European Union and its Member States, of the other part [2017] *Official Journal of the European Union* L 11/23 art. 7.3.

71 It has sometimes been said that Switzerland, despite de facto participating in large parts of the Single Market through bilateral agreements, is not subject to EU state aid rules (Written evidence of the Commercial Bar Association to the House of Lords EU Internal Markets subcommittee, CMP0038), but this is based on an incorrect assumption: The Agreement between the European Economic Community and the Swiss Confederation [1972] *Official Journal of the European Communities* L 300/189 provides in art. 23(1) that 'The following are incompatible with the proper functioning of the Agreement in so far as they may affect trade between the Community and Switzerland: [...](iii) any public aid which distorts or threatens to distort competition by favouring certain undertakings or the production of certain goods' (with the remedies provided for in art. 27). This provision has, for example, been invoked to address certain cantonal tax provisions (see Commission, 'EU-Switzerland: State aid decision on company tax regimes', *Press Release* IP/ 07/176 of 13.02.2007). It is also common knowledge that the EU has 'expressed "extreme unhappiness" over its arrangements with Switzerland on State aid' and that therefore it is 'very unlikely that the EU would extend that historical accident to [the UK]' (see House of Lords Committee Report Brexit & Competition, n 19, para 181, quoting George Peretz).

ment. The UK, on the other hand, has had more than four decades to get accustomed to the EU state aid regime. Also, the UK Government itself appears to be content to continue with the substantive state aid rules even in the case of a no-deal Brexit.[72] It is therefore likely that the EU will insist, in the light of the volume and depth of the existing trade relationship between the UK and the EU27, the familiarity of the UK with the EU state aid regime, and the explicit threats made by (former and current) members of the UK Government to pursue a low-tax, low-regulation 'Singapore model of Brexit',[73] that UK will abide by substantive state aid rules equivalent to the rules in the TFEU and the EEA Agreement.

It is also likely that the EU's desire to prevent the UK from distorting competition in the internal market will be reflected in the governance mechanism to control UK state aid. This is particularly so because the current UK Government has already indicated that they want to compete by being a low-tax regime without feeling bound by EU state aid rules[74] and has occasionally threatened to pursue a low-tax, low-regulation 'Singapore model of Brexit',[75] and because the Labour opposition in the UK has stated as well that it intends to pursue policies that may be in conflict with the EU state aid rules.[76] An FTA with the EU will, in other words, likely require the UK to submit to a supra-national institution to control state aid in the UK – be it the EU Commission, the EFTA Surveillance Authority, or a new Joint Committee comprising representation from the UK and the EU. A domestic regime alone will not be sufficient. It is also questionable

---

72 See n 57 and accompanying text.
73 See references in n 75.
74 See the Future Relationship White Paper, n 4,Ch. 1 para 112 (excluding tax from oversight by the EU even under the Common Rulebook approach), and Prime Minister Theresa May's promise to have the lowest corporation tax in the G20, speech at the Conservative Party Conference, 03.10.2018 (transcript available at <https://www.telegraph.co.uk/politics/2018/10/03/theresa-mays-conservative-party-conference-speech-full-transcript/> (last accessed 20.05.2019)).
75 See, eg, 'Hammond threatens EU with aggressive tax changes after Brexit', *Guardian*, 15.01.2017, <https://www.theguardian.com/politics/2017/jan/15/philip-hammond-suggests-uk-outside-single-market-could-become-tax-haven> (last accessed 20.05.2019); Boris Johnson, 'My vision for a bold, thriving Britain enabled by Brexit', *The Daily Telegraph*, 15.09.2017, <https://www.telegraph.co.uk/politics/2017/09/15/boris-johnson-vision-bold-thriving-britain-enabled-brexit/> (last accessed 20.05.2019). For commentary why the Singapore model is unrealistic, see, eg, 'Sling the Singapore model out of the Brexit debate', *Financial Times*, 31.07.2017, <https://www.ft.com/content/08726b32-75f2-11e7-a3e8-60495fe6ca71> (last accessed 20.05.2019).
76 See above the reference to Peretz, n 61.

whether the EU27 would accept a regime that merely builds on a Joint Committee's recommendations and in the event of finding of non-compliance would allow countervailing measures (as is the usual remedy in FTAs); it seems more likely that the EU27 would require the further-reaching consequence of repayment of state aid and/or private rights of action for the undertakings concerned.

The proposal in the Future Relationship White Paper tried to address some of these issues, at least partially, by incorporating the state aid rules in the envisaged 'UK-EU economic partnership' agreement, in which the UK would 'make an upfront commitment to maintain a common rulebook with the EU on state aid, enforced by the CMA.'[77] As mentioned above, it is not unprecedented to include an obligation for a national state aid regime in an EU Association Agreement. In principle, this approach could address some of the concerns mentioned above because it introduces a governance level above the domestic level.[78]

The first question however is, how compliance with the state aid regime would be ensured. Specifically with regard to state aid, the Future Relationship White Paper only mentions enforcement by the CMA, as pointed out above. However, the CMA would face institutional pressures that would make it impossible for the EU to rely on its assessment without external verification. The Future Relationship White Paper seems to suggest in the section on dispute resolution in Chapter 4 that the EU could, where it alleges a misapplication of the state aid rules, refer this issue to 'an independent arbitration panel' or the 'Joint Committee', and that these bodies should have the power to make a preliminary reference to the CJEU.[79]

These proposals raise several issues. The new governance regime is clearly meant to be a classic international agreement, devoid of the supra-national character and direct effect that EU law has. This means that under this structure, private parties that want to challenge a CMA state aid decision (either the state aid beneficiary challenging a negative decision or a complainant challenging the award of state aid) would have to rely on domestic UK law (including the 'common rulebook') and domestic appeals in the UK. As the UK courts are no longer Member State courts, they could not make preliminary references to the CJEU.[80] The only concession made by the Future Relationship White Paper is that the UK Courts would

---

77 Future Relationship White Paper, n 4, Ch. 1 para 111.
78 For the proposed governance structure see Future Relationship White Paper, n 4, Ch. 4.
79 Future Relationship White Paper, n 4, Ch. 4 paras 40-43.
80 This is explicitly stated in Future Relationship White Paper, n 4, Ch. 4 para 35.

have to pay 'due regard to CJEU case law.'[81] The White Paper is of the view that this is unproblematic because '[t]he proposal for a common rulebook relates to areas of EU law where there is already a body of case law stretching back for decades.'[82] This seems to suggest that all questions are *acte clair* or *acte éclairé* anyway.[83] This must be that fabled British humour (and one is tempted to consider the proposal a 'cunning plan' worthy of Blackadder's Baldrick) — unless the UK Government seriously means to suggest that no new legal issues arise under the fundamental freedoms or the competition rules.

An additional problem is that the Future Relationship White Paper carves out tax policy: 'The UK's proposal [...] would not fetter its sovereign discretion on tax [...].'[84] This would allow the UK to use its tax regime as a form of state aid without constraint from the state aid rules in the Common Rulebook. The reference to unfettered sovereign discretion on tax also overlooks that the 'sovereign discretion on tax' is already constrained (if only marginally) by the SCM Agreement.[85] One may well debate under what conditions and to what extent tax law and its application constitutes state aid.[86] It does not make sense, however, to permit (even selective) tax

---

81 Ibid.
82 Ibid.
83 Judgment of the Court, Case 283/81, 06.10.1982, C.I.L.F.I.T v Ministry of Health,EU:C:1982:335,ECR 3415, para 21.
84 Ibid., Ch. 1 para 112.
85 See, eg, art. 1.1.(a)(1)(ii) of the SCM Agreement, under which a subsidy is deemed to exist, inter alia, where 'government revenue that is otherwise due is foregone or not collected (eg, fiscal incentives such as tax credits).'
86 DG Competition, Working Paper on State Aid and Tax Rulings, Background to the High Level Forum on State Aid of 03.06.2016, <http://ec.europa.eu/competiti on/state_aid/legislation/working_paper_tax_rulings.pdf> (last accessed 20.05.2019). See, for example, the pending case T-892/16 (*Apple Sales International and Apple Operations Europe v Commission*), action brought on 19.12.2016, 2017/C 053/46, [2017] *Official Journal of the European Union* C 53/37 (following the Commission's decision in SA.38373 – *Apple*); see also, eg, pending cases: T-516/18 (*Luxembourg v Commission*) (following the Commission's decision in SA.44888 – *Engie*); T-318/18 (*Amazon EU and Amazon.com v Commission*) and T-816/17 (*Luxembourg v Commission*) (following the Commission's decision in SA.38944 – *Amazon*); T-636/16 (*Starbucks and Starbucks Manufacturing EMEA v Commission*) and T-760/15 (*Netherlands v Commission*) (following the Commission's decision in SA.38374 – *Starbucks*); T-755/15 (*Luxembourg v Commission*) and T-759/15 (*Fiat Chrysler Financing Europe v Commission*) (following the Commission's decision in SA.38375 – *Fiat*).

interventions without constraints; this would completely undermine the envisaged state aid regime.[87]

The Withdrawal Agreement (including the Protocol on Ireland/Northern Ireland) and the Political Declaration give an indication of the view the EU27 take on such potential attempts to undermine the effectiveness of the European state aid regime and the level playing field more generally, a view that is likely to be reflected in future negotiations about the future relationship regardless of whether or not the Withdrawal Agreement is eventually ratified by the parties.

The Political Declaration states that ensuring open and fair competition entails, among other things, rules on competition law, state aid, and 'relevant tax matters'; that these rules will build on the provisions of the Withdrawal Agreement; and that '[t]hese commitments should combine appropriate and relevant Union and international standards, adequate mechanisms to ensure effective implementation domestically, enforcement and dispute settlement as part of the future relationship.'[88]

The Withdrawal Agreement, first, deals with ongoing state aid procedures in Articles 92 *et seq.*, and unsurprisingly provides for the continued competence of the EU's institutions to deal with all state aid procedures initiated before the end of the transition period. Article 93 of the Withdrawal Agreement extends this period during which the EU institutions remain competent to initiate new state aid proceedings for four years after the end of the transition period so far as state aid was granted before the end of the transition period, and in these cases, the EU institutions remain competent for the entire duration of the proceedings, that is, even after the

---

87 The European Council 2017 Art 50 Guidelines, n 7, state in para 20: '[Any FTA] must ensure a level playing field, notably in terms of competition and state aid, and in this regard encompass safeguards against unfair competitive advantages through, inter alia, tax [...] measures and practices.' See now also the Political Declaration, n 7, para 22 ('level playing field for open and fair competition' in trade for goods), para 37 ('fair competition' in financial services), and in particular para 79:
'The future relationship must ensure open and fair competition. Provisions to ensure this should cover state aid, competition, [...] and relevant tax matters, building on the level playing field arrangements provided for in the Withdrawal Agreement and commensurate with the overall economic relationship. The Parties should consider the precise nature of commitments in relevant areas, having regard to the scope and depth of the future relationship. These commitments should combine appropriate and relevant Union and international standards, adequate mechanisms to ensure effective implementation domestically, enforcement and dispute settlement as part of the future relationship.'
88 Political Declaration, n 7, para. 79.

expiry of the four-year period. In these cases, the UK will be largely treated as if it were still a Member State of the European Union:

- the European Commission will adopt the state aid decision accordingly [Articles 92(5), 93(1) of the Withdrawal Agreement],
- the procedural state aid provisions apply [Article 94(1)],
- lawyers authorized to practice in the UK shall be treated in all respects as if they were lawyers authorized to practice in a Member State [Article 94(2)], and
- UK representatives may (in derogation from the principle in Article 7 of the Withdrawal Agreement that the UK ceases participation in the bodies, offices and agencies of the Union) upon invitation attend meetings, without voting rights, during the discussion of specific agenda items where 'the discussion concerns individual acts to be addressed during the transition period to the United Kingdom or to natural or legal persons residing or established in the United Kingdom' [Articles 94(3), 128(5) of the Withdrawal Agreement].

Furthermore, the Protocol on Ireland/Northern Ireland provides in Article 12 that measures that affect trade between the Republic of Ireland and Northern Ireland (with the exception of agricultural support up to a specified maximum) remain subject to the state aid provisions. As already predicted in the assessment of the Future Relations White Paper above, the EU is not content with relying on UK institutions in this regard: Article 14(4) of the Protocol provides that EU institutions, bodies, offices and agencies retain the powers conferred upon them by Union law with regard to the United Kingdom and legal and natural persons in the United Kingdom, that the Court of Justice of the European Union retains jurisdiction (with the UK and its lawyers being granted procedural rights as if the UK were still a Member State, Article 14(7) of the Protocol), and that courts in the United Kingdom retain the right and obligation to make preliminary references to the Court of Justice of the European Union under the second and third paragraph of Article 267 TFEU.

The provisions in the Protocol for Ireland/Northern Ireland are not only, and perhaps not even primarily, of interest as and of themselves, but also, and more importantly, because they may foreshadow the position that the EU will take in the upcoming negotiations on the future relationship with the United Kingdom. For the reasons outlined above in the discussion of the Future Relationship White Paper, it seems likely that the EU will insist on provisions for state aid granted by the United Kingdom that are comparable to the ones in the Protocol for Ireland/Northern Ireland, including retaining institutional oversight over the enforcement. In this regard, at least, it seems very likely that the United Kingdom has 'take[n] back control' only to cede it back to the European Union.

C. Procedural Law, Cooperation and Resource Implications

The discussion so far may give the impression that Brexit will not lead to a major upheaval as far as competition law is concerned, with the possible exception of state aid. This impression would be mistaken. Major problems arise on the procedural and resource level.

I. Public enforcement: cooperation in the ECN and the Advisory Committee on concentrations.

Regardless which Brexit option is eventually chosen, the CMA will crash out of the European Competition Network (ECN). Under Regulation 1/2003, the ECN allows, inter alia, for the coordination of investigations, the consultation with the Commission and other NCAs, and an exchange of confidential information.[89] Regulation 1/2003 also allows for facilitated legal assistance, for example, when it comes to inspections in other Member States, and for cooperation between the national courts and the Commission.[90] Once the UK is no longer a Member State, the UK competition authorities and courts will be cut off from these communication channels. Given that in many cases there will now be parallel investigations by the CMA on one side and the Commission or NCAs on the other side, there is a danger of unnecessarily redundant and insufficiently coordinated investigations and duplication of work, on the side of both the authorities and the undertakings. There is currently no agreement between the EU and the UK, or between the UK and the EU27 Member States, that would allow the transmission of confidential information in the absence of a waiver by the parties concerned.

---

89 For the following see in particular art. 11–16 of Regulation (EC) No 1/2003 and Commission Notice on cooperation within the Network of Competition Authorities (the 'Network Notice'), [2004] OJ C 101/43.

90 See art. 20 and 15 of Regulation (EC) No 1/2003, respectively, as well as Commission Notice on the co-operation between the Commission and the courts of the EU Member States in the application of Articles 81 and 82 EC, [2004] OJ C 101/54.

Various competition experts in the UK appeared to be under the impression that they will continue to be able to attend the ECN or to replicate its effects. The Brexit Competition Law Working Group 'strongly recommends' negotiating continued participation in the ECN, or at least, similar to the non-EU Member States of the EEA, the Advisory Committee meetings.[91] Similarly, the CMA has mentioned the hope that they would be able to continue to be members of the ECN,[92] or to have the powers in Regulation 1/2003 'replicated for effective EU-UK cooperation.'[93]

While the UK's desire for remaining in the ECN or replicating its effects is perfectly understandable, it is difficult to see how this desire could realistically be fulfilled. It is true that the negotiation of a close cooperation agreement between the CMA and the ECN is in their mutual interest. Nobody wants to go back to the pre-1973 position with little institutionalised cooperation. The EU will, post Brexit, lose its ability to conduct inspections and other investigatory measures on UK territory because enforcement jurisdiction is strictly territorial. The EU therefore has an interest in facilitated legal assistance with the UK, just as the UK has an interest in the cooperation with the ECN.

However, a post-Brexit UK as a third country has no better claim to staying a member of, or becoming an observer in, the ECN than do the Swiss competition authorities. All that Switzerland has been able to negotiate is a cooperation agreement, albeit a second-generation agreement including the exchange of confidential information.[94] Moreover, it seems politically

---

91 BCLWG, n 35, para 7.5.
92 CMA, Written Evidence (CMP0002), 02.10.2017, para 27: 'While it is *possible* the CMA will no longer be a member of the European Competition Network, or at least not in the same way [...]' (emphasis added). Lord Currie (then Chairman of the CMA) said in his Oral Evidence to the House of Lords EU Internal Market Sub-Committee (<http://data.parliament.uk/writtenevidence/committeeevidence. svc/evidencedocument/eu-internal-market-subcommittee/brexit-competition/oral/ 70457.pdf> (last accessed 20.05.2019)): 'Clearly, we will want to work closely with our European counterparts, *whether we are formally part of the ECN or not*' (emphasis added) and Dr Coscelli (Chief Executive of the CMA) said it would probably be 'very much in the interest of the European Commission and other national authorities for us to remain in the tent as much as possible. Whether this can be delivered through the negotiations we will have to wait and see. From our point of view, we would like to retain the current arrangement with the ECN as much as we can [...]'.
93 CMA, Written Evidence (CMP0002), 02.10.2017, n 92, para. 24.
94 Agreement between the European Union and the Swiss Confederation concerning cooperation on the application of their competition laws, [2014] Official Journal L 347/3.

exceedingly difficult to give the UK greater access to the ECN than to the non-EU Member States of the EEA — and these can only attend ECN meetings with regard to general policy discussions, not with regard to the practically important enforcement actions. Furthermore, the European Council has stated in its Conclusions on 28 March 2018, that 'the Union will preserve its autonomy as regard to its decision-making, which excludes participation of the United Kingdom as a third-country [sic] in the Union Institutions and participation in the decision-making of the Union bodies, offices and agencies.'[95]

Moreover, not letting third countries participate in the close cooperation in the ECN is not an arbitrary choice. The close cooperation within the ECN is built on the basis not only of mutual trust and the duty of sincere cooperation under Article 4(3) TEU, but also on the basis of the guarantee of fundamental rights under Article 6(3) TEU and the Charter on Fundamental Rights (see recital 37 of Regulation 1/2003), as well as on the basis of adjudication of any arising issues by the CJEU as the ultimate arbiter of EU law.

Even if the Withdrawal Agreement should be ratified by the parties, the cooperation between the UK competition authorities and the Commission will be substantially curtailed. The UK competition authorities will only be allowed, upon invitation, to participate without voting rights in those agenda items where 'the discussion concerns individual acts to be addressed during the transition period to the United Kingdom or to natural or legal persons residing or established in the United Kingdom' [Article 128(5)(a) with Article 94(3) of the Withdrawal Agreement] in cases where the proceedings were initiated before the end of the transition period (Article 92 of the Withdrawal Agreement).

The same applies, *mutatis mutandis*, to the participation of UK authorities in the Advisory Committee under Article 19 of the EUMR 139/2004 with regard to concentrations that have been notified (or referred) before the end of the transition period.

It seems likely that the UK will eventually be able to negotiate a second-generation cooperation agreement similar to the Swiss agreement, including the exchange of confidential information. This, however, falls far short of the close cooperation that takes place within the ECN and the Advisory Committee, and, as Richard Whish has pointed out shortly after the Brexit Referendum vote, 'a cooperation agreement would be very different from

---

95 European Council, (Art 50) Guidelines on the framework for the future EU-UK relationship, 23.03.2018, EUCO XT 20001/18, para 7.

being a major player within the current institutional framework of the EU.[96]

II. Public enforcement: cooperation with third countries.

On Brexit, the UK will not only lose the cooperation that takes place within the ECN; it also loses the indirect access to competition cooperation agreements with third countries which the EU has negotiated in previous years.[97] The EU-Switzerland agreement mentioned in the previous paragraph is one of these, but there are many more, including agreements with the US, South Korea, Japan and Canada, as well as Memoranda of Understanding with numerous other States such as with the BRICS States (Brazil, Russia, India, China, South Africa).[98]

Unless the UK agrees to the EEA option, the UK would also lose the indirect benefit of the cooperation between the EU Commission and the EFTA Surveillance Authority, laid down in Protocols 23 and 24 to the EEA Agreement.

These cooperation agreements, be they separate or part of free trade agreements, will have to be renegotiated. The initial plan was to 'roll over' the EU agreements, and with regard to the free trade agreements, the Secretary for International Trade Dr Liam Fox had been certain in 2017 that this would be done by 29 March 2019 for 'up to 40 trade deals;[99] until he found out that the counterparties have to agree to the renegotiated agree-

---

96 *Whish*, 'Brexit and EU competition policy' (2016) 7 *Journal of European Competition Policy & Practice* 297.

97 *Wagner-von Papp*, 'Competition Law in EU Free Trade and Cooperation Agreements (and What the UK Can Expect After Brexit)' (2017) 8 *EYIEL* 301. More generally, the UK will drop out of some 750 to 1250 international agreements (of varying importance) concluded by the EU, unless the various parties to the agreements agree to 'roll over' the agreements. *Fella*, 'UK adoption of The EU's external agreements after Brexit', *House of Commons Library Briefing Paper* No. 8370, 24.07.2018; *McClean*, 'After Brexit: the UK will need to renegotiate at least 759 treaties', *Financial Times*, 30.05.2017; *Barker*, 'Britain faces Brexit dilemma over ties with rest of the world', *Financial Times*, 19.12.2017. With regard to trade agreements, see House of Commons International Trade Committee, *Continuing application of EU trade agreements after Brexit*, HC 520, 07.03.2018.

98 Overview in *Wagner-von Papp*, 'Competition Law in EU Free Trade and Cooperation Agreements (and What the UK Can Expect After Brexit)' (2017) 8 *EYIEL* 301, 324–341.

99 *Blitz, Pickard* and *Parker*, 'UK fails to close global trade deals ahead of Brexit deadline', *Financial Times*, 17.01.2019, <https://on.ft.com/2TSEzRG>.

ments.[100] At the time of writing, the extent of accords ready is unclear – while some 21 agreements have been made and 13 more were said to be imminent, they all appear to be limited in scope (nuclear cooperation and aviation); trade deals that are said to be close to fruition include Switzerland, Chile, the Palestinian Authority and the Faroe Islands.[101]

III. Public enforcement: resource implications

As mentioned above, post Brexit the UK will be confronted with numerous additional tasks.[102] First, given that the one-stop shop in merger control will no longer be available, the CMA will have to scrutinise the larger and more complex mergers that have a Union dimension and were up to now be scrutinised by the Commission, and the Competition Appeal Tribunal (CAT), and potentially the courts, will have to deal with the appeals in these cases. Secondly, the CMA will also have to investigate the UK aspects of those larger and more complex infringements of Articles 101 or 102 TFEU that have until now been scrutinised by the Commission and/or other NCAs, and the CAT, and potentially the courts, will have to deal with the appeals.

While the CMA will gain in independence ('take back control'),[103] it will be challenging, to say the least, for the CMA to take on these new tasks. The CMA, while an excellent competition authority, is stretched for resources. Its deficiencies in enforcement when compared to, for example, the Bundeskartellamt have been remarked upon by the UK's National Audit Office, which noted that the CMA had taken in some '£65 million of competition enforcement fines between 2012 and 2014 (in 2015 prices), compared to almost £1.4 billion of fines imposed by their German coun-

---

100 *Mance*, 'Liam Fox explains failure to replicate EU trade deals', *Financial Times*, 20.01.2019, <https://on.ft.com/2sF2wAp>: '"We're ready and we've put all our proposals forward," Mr Fox told the BBC Andrew Marr Show on Sunday. "A number of countries ... are unwilling to put the preparations in for no deal", while a couple of others were in the process of elections or had "no effective government".

101 *Brunsden*, 'UK letter to EU reveals slow progress on global deals pre-Brexit', *Financial Times*, 30.01.2019, <https://on.ft.com/2CRYklO>.

102 See also the CLES House of Lords submission, n 35, paras 88–96.

103 See, eg, *Grenfell*, Speech, n 39.

terparts.[104] Wouter Wils, in his assessment after 10 years Regulation 1/2003, noted that while the European Commission and the German, French, and Italian NCAs had each notified between 82 and 90 final decisions in the period between 1 May 2004 and 31 December 2012, the UK had notified a mere 16.[105]

The point here is not to talk down the CMA for a lack of initiative. As Bill Kovacic and David Hyman have noted, activity is not the same as effectiveness, and perhaps the CMA has taken a conscious decision 'to invest' rather than 'to consume' by taking enforcement decisions.[106] The CMA is beyond reproach when it comes to research and policy papers. However, it is the case that the CMA is already struggling to increase enforcement efforts with the available resources, although it has made some progress.[107] Piling new and more complex cases on to the already resource-strained CMA will hardly help. And, as described above, the CMA will—in the absence of a negotiated agreement—no longer benefit from the information flow from the ECN, the Member States' national competition authorities or from third-country competition authorities, which is particularly problematic because the new cases will frequently be the larger cases with international aspects, importance, and implications.

There are two mitigating aspects. First, to some extent it may be possible even after Brexit to free ride on enforcement efforts by the EU. In particular in the area of Articles 101 and 102 TFEU, enforcement by the EU Commission may sufficiently deter infringements which would have effects in the UK. There are, however, limits to this free riding. Free riding in this

---

104 National Audit Office, The UK competition regime, HC 737, Session 2015–16, 05.02.2016: '[T]he low case flow we identified in 2010 has continued, with the Office of Fair Trading and the CMA making 24 decisions and the regulators just eight since 2010. The UK competition authorities issued only £65 million of competition enforcement fines between 2012 and 2014 (in 2015 prices), compared to almost £1.4 billion of fines imposed by their German counterparts. The CMA faces significant barriers in increasing its flow of competition cases, although recent activity means it now has 12 ongoing cases.'

105 Wils, 'Ten years Regulation 1/2003 — a retrospective' (2013) 4 *Journal of European Competition Law & Practice* 293, 296.

106 *Kovacic/Hyman*, 'Consume or invest: What do/should agency leaders maximize?' (2016) 91 *Washington Law Review* 295.

107 *Grenfell*, Speech, n 39; Catherine Belton, 'UK's competition watchdog sharpens its teeth ahead of Brexit', *Financial Times*, 03.01.2017 (although one of the record fines mentioned in that article, the £84m fine against Pfizer, has in the meantime been annulled by the CAT because the CMA misapplied the test for excessive pricing; *Flynn Pharma Ltd and Flynn Pharma (Holdings) Ltd v CMA and Pfizer Inc and Pfizer Ltd v CMA* [2018] CAT 11).

context only works where the anticompetitive conduct affects both the EU and the UK, the EU imposes deterrent sanctions, and the conduct cannot be discontinued in the EU without also being discontinued in the UK. Such free riding may also result in under-deterrence, because EU penalties will no longer take into account the UK turnover. Lastly, free riding does not work for mergers, because the tight deadlines in merger control do not lend themselves to a wait-and-see approach whether the decision by the EU sufficiently takes care of any concerns regarding the UK market; in addition, the EU Commission and the UK authorities would scrutinise different relevant markets.[108]

The second mitigating aspect in favour of the UK is that the increased enforcement tasks will also result in higher filing fees for mergers and higher fines for the larger cartel cases that have until now gone into the EU budget.[109] This would allow the UK Government to increase the CMA budget without necessarily being out of pocket. However, as Lord Whitty as the Chairman of the Select Committee noted, this argument 'slightly presum[es] the outcome of [the CMA's] cases',[110] and it is far from certain that the CMA would succeed before the CAT and UK courts as often as the European Commission succeeds before the CJEU.[111] In addition, it has not been the experience of the CMA that the government is willing to give more funding to the CMA as soon as the marginal benefit outweighs the marginal cost. On the contrary, the target for the CMA was originally to provide demonstrable benefits of £5 for every £1 spent, and this has been increased to require £10 benefits for every £1 spent.

The Chancellor allocated additional funds to the CMA in the Spring Budget of 13 March 2018, which amounted to £20.3m, or an increase of the CMA budget of 29%,[112] in order to allow the CMA to prepare for the increased burden in consumer protection, antitrust and merger control. The CMA plans to increase its staff by 39%, that is, 240 full-time equivalent

---

108 *Vickers*, 'Consequences of Brexit for competition law and policy' (2017) 33 *Oxford Review of Economic Policy* S70, S74.

109 Cf. Dr Coscelli, Oral Evidence before the House of Lords EU Internal Market Sub-Committee, n 92, p. 4.

110 Lord Whitty, Oral Evidence before the House of Lords EU Internal Market Sub-Committee, n 92, p. 4.

111 *Demetriou*, 'The future is a foreign country: they do things differently there – the impact of Brexit on the enforcement of competition law' (2018) 39 *European Competition Law Review* 99, 105–106.

112 National Audit Office, Report by the Comptroller and Auditor General, Exiting the EU: Consumer protection, competition and state aid, HC 1384, Session 2017-19, 06.07.2018, para 3.15 ('NAO, Exiting the EU').

staff, 150 of whom are to deal with competition enforcement.[113] The CMA appears to be confident that this is sufficient to deal with the increased workload and that they can recruit in sufficient numbers and quality. The National Audit Office sounds a little more skeptical,[114] which is understandable, given that the CMA itself has stated that it expects the number of cases in merger control to increase by 30-50% and in antitrust cases by 'at least 50%', and that furthermore these will be cases of substantially greater complexity.[115] The Brexit Competition Law Working Group, consisting of experienced enforcers and competition law academics, consider the CMA's estimation of the increase in merger cases to be 'conservative'.[116] Even the CMA admits that it has difficulty competing with private-sector salaries when recruiting experienced enforcers. Also, the increase in the budget is owed to funds being made available for Brexit preparations; whether the budget increase will be lasting, as it would have to sustain the increased workload and workforce, is a different question. In addition to the increased workload at the CMA, it is also likely that the workload at the Competition Appeal Tribunal would increase substantially.[117]

With regard to the new tasks, the CMA would have with regard to state aid, an additional £3.3 million has been allocated to the CMA. Considering that this would have to cover the setting up of a completely new unit working under a completely new regime, this seems ambitious.

IV. Private enforcement

Currently, the UK is one of the three most attractive venues for private competition litigation in the EU.[118] Reasons include specialized courts and tribunals, especially since the Competition Appeal Tribunal was strength-

---

113 NAO, Exiting the EU, n 112, para 3.16.
114 NAO, Exiting the EU, n 112, para 3.18.
115 Lord Currie and Dr Coscelli, Oral Evidence before the House of Lords EU Internal Market Sub-Committee, n 92, 2, 3.
116 BCLWG, n 35, para 8.5.
117 NAO, Exiting the EU, n 112, para. 3.19.
118 See, eg, *Geradin/Grelier*, 'Cartel damages claims in the European Union: Have we only seen the tip of the iceberg?' in *Charbit/Ramundo* (eds) *William E. Kovacic – An Antitrust Tribute: Liber Amicorum Vol. II* (2014), 257, 260–263, mentioning the UK, Germany, and the Netherlands as particularly attractive venues; these three are also mentioned by *Whish*, 'Brexit and EU competition policy' (2016) 7 *Journal of European Competition Policy & Practice* 297, 298, and by *Gamble*, 'The European embrace of private enforcement: this time with feeling', (2014) 35 *European*

ened in the Consumer Rights Act 2015; the well-established practice of access to evidence rules in the disclosure procedure under the Civil Procedure Rules and the CAT Rules; the access to litigation funding; and the possibility of collective litigation and arbitration introduced in the Consumer Rights Act 2015.[119]

1. Recognition and enforcement

The effect of Brexit on the attractiveness of the UK as a litigation venue is not yet clear, given that there may or may not eventually be an agreement on jurisdiction, recognition and enforcement of judgments. If the Withdrawal Agreement should be ratified by the parties, the Brussels I (Recast) Regulation 1215/2012 would continue to apply to the recognition and enforcement of judgments in proceedings instituted before the end of the transition period, 'and to authentic instruments formally drawn up or registered and court settlements approved or concluded before the end of the transition period' (Article 67 of the Withdrawal Agreement). If there is, however, a no-deal Brexit, then the Brussels I (Recast) Regulation 1215/2012 would cease to apply, and unless a judgment by a UK court was already exequatured in the EU27 at the time of the withdrawal, it can no longer be enforced in the EU27 under EU rules, even if it was handed down before the time of withdrawal, and even if enforcement proceedings had already been initiated at that time.[120] In these cases, enforcement would depend on bilateral agreements or on international conventions to which both the UK and the Member State in which the judgment is to be enforced are parties.[121] This means, for example, that the *lis pendens* rule in Article 29 would not apply, so that bringing an action in the UK would not necessarily preclude the parties from bringing another action in an EU

Competition Law Review 469, 478. *Rodger*, 'The Empirical Data Part I' in Barry Rodger (ed), *Competition Law, Comparative Private Enforcement, and Collective Redress across the EU* (2014) 95, includes seven Member States into the category with 'considerable private enforcement experience' (in addition to the three Member States mentioned above, France, Belgium, Italy and Spain).

119   See, eg, *Kreindler/Gilbert/et al.*, 'Impact of Brexit on UK Competition Litigation and Arbitration', (2016) 33 *Journal of International Arbitration* 521, 525–528.

120   See European Commission, 'Revised Notice to stakeholders – withdrawal of the United Kingdom and EU rules in the field of civil justice and private international law', 18.01.2019, <https://ec.europa.eu/info/sites/info/files/notice_to_stakeholders_brexit_civil_justice_rev 1_final.pdf>.

121   Ibid.

Member State (although the MS court *may* stay the proceedings under Articles 33, 34). The judgment's enforcement would not be able to benefit from the abolition of the exequatur in the Brussels I (Recast) Regulation. Instead, the UK would have to fall back on the 1968 Brussels Convention,[122] which arguably revives but is more restrictive in terms of coverage, both geographically and substantively.[123] With regard to enforcement in Denmark, Iceland, Norway and Switzerland, the situation is even more problematic:[124] while the UK was a Contracting Party to the original 1988 Lugano Convention, this Convention was replaced by the 2007 Lugano Convention—and the 2007 Lugano Convention was negotiated, concluded and ratified by the European Community (EC) and only mentions the EC and its Member States, Denmark, Iceland, Norway and Switzerland. The UK has, on 2 January 2019, deposited the notice of accession to the Hague Convention on choice of court agreements of 30 June 2005 in case there is a no-deal Brexit;[125] however, in competition cases this does not provide any relief, because competition matters are excluded from its scope in Article 2(2)(h).

The Future Relationship White Paper envisages the UK joining the 2007 Lugano Convention and seeking a new bilateral agreement with the EU on civil judicial cooperation.[126] The at best unclear status of the enforceability of judgments post Brexit will, to use British understatement, not be a pull factor for future private competition actions in the UK. How problematic of an issue this will eventually be depends largely on whether the Withdrawal Agreement will be ratified, on the accession of the UK to the relevant international conventions and on a successful negotiation of an agreement with the EU after the transition period (if any). As the White Paper recognises, however, none of the existing international conventions have the same scope or depth as the Brussels I (Recast) Regulation.

---

122 1968 Brussels Convention on jurisdiction and the enforcement of judgments in civil and commercial matters, [1972] *Official Journal* L 299/32.

123 *Dickinson*, 'Back to the future: the UK's EU exit and the conflict of laws' (2016) 12 *Journal of Private International Law* 195, 204–206.

124 Ibid., 206–207.

125 <https://treatydatabase.overheid.nl/en/Verdrag/Details/011343/011343_Notificati es_13.pdf>.

126 Future Relationship White Paper, n 4, Ch. 1 para 128 lit. g, paras 145–148.

2. Follow-on actions based on Commission decisions

The even bigger question is whether the claimants in damages actions will, post Brexit, be able to bring follow-on actions based on Commission decisions. Currently, sections 47A and 58A of the Competition Act 1998, allow follow-on actions based on Commission decisions, treating the latter as binding once they have become final. The UK Government had initially declared that for Commission decisions that are 'made' before Exit day this would continue to be the case even in the case of a no-deal Brexit (without making clear whether the relevant date is the date of the decision or the date when the decision becomes final). The, in the longer term, more important question is whether the binding effect will apply to decisions 'made' *after* Exit day. The Brexit Competition Law Working Group advocated continuing with this regime.[127]

For a long time, the position remained unclear. The EU (Withdrawal) Bill in its original form would have prevented Commission decisions from being treated as binding. Clause 6(2) of the Bill originally provided: 'A court or tribunal need not have regard to anything done on or after the exit day by the European Court, another EU entity or the EU but may do so if it considers it appropriate to do so.' This would have removed the binding effect on the court or tribunal that section 58A of the Competition Act 1998 would otherwise establish. However, the wording in s 6(1) of the European Union (Withdrawal) Act was changed to 'A court or tribunal— (a) is not bound by any principles laid down, or any decisions made, on or after exit day by the European Court, and (b) cannot refer any matter to the European Court on or after exit day.' Curiously, this altered version would, in the absence of a competition law specific provision to the contrary, have appeared to prevent giving binding effect to a Commission decision that was modified by the CJEU, but not prevent giving binding effect to Commission decisions that became final without modification from the CJEU. In any case, under the European Union (Withdrawal) Act 2018, it would have been possible for the court or tribunal to 'have regard' to decisions by the CJEU or the Commission,[128] but this falls arguably well short of the certainty required by claimants, because they, to be on the safe side, would have to spend resources on taking evidence on the questions that would otherwise have been settled by the binding effect of a final Commission decision.

---

127 BCLWG, n 35, paras 2.21–2.24.
128 European Union (Withdrawal) Act 2018, s 6(2).

The hope of competition practitioners in the UK had therefore been that specific provisions would clarify that follow-on actions can in the future still be based on infringement decisions by the European Commission. If the Withdrawal Agreement should be ratified, it appears as if this wish was granted for decisions in cases initiated up until the end of the transition period, although the issue does not appear to be entirely free from doubt: Article 94(1) Withdrawal Agreement provides, in combination with Article 92, that the procedural rules of Regulation 1/2003 remain applicable to the administrative procedure. This would seem to make Article 16 of Regulation 1/2003 applicable, according to which national courts may not take decisions running counter to a Commission decision, so that a national court (here, a UK court) could not deviate from the finding of an infringement found in a final Commission decision. The issue turns on the interpretation of Article 94(1) Withdrawal Agreement: its primary aim is to make clear that where the Commission retains competence to investigate in transition cases, it can rely on the provisions in Regulation 1/2003 in the *administrative* procedure, and on a restrictive reading one could confine Article 94(1) to the administrative procedure, to the exclusion of private follow-on actions. Nevertheless, there is a Union interest also in ensuring the scope of the binding effect of Commission decisions on the UK's courts, Article 16 is contained in Regulation 1/2003, and so the quasi-binding effect of Commission decisions on UK courts when deciding private follow-on actions is arguably ensured for cases initiated by the end of the transition period.

If there is, however, no deal, then the position is clear: the UK legislator has, against the advice of practically all competition experts who commented on the issue, excluded Commission decisions under Article 101 or 102 TFEU from the binding effect under the Competition Act 1998 in regulation 16 of the Competition (Amendments etc.) (EU Exit) Regulations 2019. The concerns of competition experts were arguably meant to be addressed by the new s 60A Competition Act 1998, introduced by regulation 23 of the Competition (Amendments etc.) (EU Exit) Regulations 2019 and described in more detail above. Section 60A provides in its subsection (3) that the decision-maker 'must have regard to any relevant decision or statement of the European Commission made before the exit day and not withdrawn', and subsection (9) clarifies that 'references to a decision of the European Court or the European Commission include a decision as to [...] (b) the civil liability of an undertaking for harm caused by its infringement of EU law'. This falls short of what competition had hoped for in several ways. First, it pertains exclusively to decisions 'made before exit day'; decisions after Brexit day would not be captured. If this were the only problem, then private enforcement in the UK could thrive for a long time to come, as private actions usually lag several years behind. However, secondly, the decision-maker only has to 'have regard' to the Commission decision – this falls far short of a binding effect. True, one could argue that a judge in a private enforcement action will likely give greater evidential weight to the Commission decision. And yet, there is a substantial difference for a claimant between being able to rely on a conclusive finding of an infringement in a follow-on action, as is currently the case, and having to prove an infringement in a stand-alone action (even if the action is, in regard to some elements, supported by the evidential weight of a Commission decision). Finally, while paragraph 35 of Schedule 8A to the Competition Act 1998, which implemented the Damages Directive, currently provides that the final decisions of NCAs from other Member States (and of review courts) will be given weight as prima facie evidence in damages actions, regulation 30(6) of the Competition (Amendments etc.) (EU Exit) Regulations 2019 omits paragraph 35 of Schedule 8A.

To the extent follow-on actions can no longer be based on the binding effect of Commission decisions, this will likely severely impact on the attractiveness of the UK as a competition litigation venue. Most damages actions are, for the obvious reasons, follow-on actions (or, even where they are technically stand-alone actions, are based in part on the binding effect of infringement decisions). Additionally, there is an additional procedural question: in the UK, the content of foreign law is treated as a matter of fact, and so proving the content of EU law may in the future require expert witnesses.[129] Even though it seems likely that UK courts would afford considerable evidential weight to the existence of a Commission decision finding an infringement even in the absence of its formally binding effect, there is a substantial difference between such an evidential effect and a binding effect: the parties are allowed to adduce evidence to the contrary (with the attendant effect on costs), and it is quite well possible that English courts apply a more stringent standard of proof than the EU institutions before they find an infringement.[130]

While it is true that at least in some cases there will be a parallel domestic decision, again the CMA may face stricter scrutiny on appeal before the CAT and English courts,[131] and so it seems less likely that the number of

---

129 BCLWG, n 35, para 2.25.
130 On this point, see *Demetriou*, 'The future is a foreign country: they do things differently there – the impact of Brexit on the enforcement of competition law' (2018) 39 *European Competition Law Review* 99, 105–106.
131 Ibid.

final CMA decisions will be able to compete with the number of final Commission decisions.

It is not impossible that the other attractions of the UK as a venue will still outweigh the potential detriment of no longer being able to rely on the binding effect of Commission decisions.[132] It could even be that English courts and tribunals become marginally more attractive in so far as the disclosure rules of English civil procedure and the CAT Rules may, after coming into force of the Competition (Amendments etc.) (EU Exit) Regulations 2019, be used to compel information from the EU Commission's and NCAs' leniency statements and settlement submissions. This is the indirect effect of reducing the definition of 'competition authorities' in paragraph 3(1) of Schedule 8A to the CMA and UK regulators,[133] because this indirectly affects the definitions of cartel leniency programmes and settlement submissions. Whether or not courts and tribunals will consider the protection of a foreign leniency programme a sufficiently weighty consideration to deny disclosure requests under the proportionality principle (which applies to disclosure both under the Civil Procedure Rules and the CAT Rules 2015) remains to be seen.

However, it is more likely that at least on the margin Brexit will make the UK as a litigation forum less attractive for the reasons outlined above.[134] The effects on arbitration are more subtle: while there will no longer be a direct obligation to apply EU competition law, arbitrators will have to bear in mind the enforceability of awards within the EU.[135]

---

132 For a consideration of the pros and cons for post-Brexit competition litigation in the UK see *Kreindler/Gilbert et al.*, 'Impact of Brexit on UK Competition Litigation and Arbitration', (2016) 33 *Journal of International Arbitration* 521, 528–532.

133 Regulation 30(1)(a) and (b) of the Competition (Amendments etc.) (EU Exit) Regulations 2019.

134 *Andreangeli*, 'The consequences of Brexit for competition litigation: an end to a "success story"?' (2017) 38 *European Competition Law Review* 228; CLES House of Lords submission, n 35, paras 29–64.

135 See ibid, 532–539; *Blanke*, 'Brexit and private competition law enforcement under the Arbitration Act 1996: taking stock: Part 2' [2017] *Global Competition Law Review* 1; see also *Ndolo/Liu*, 'Is this the end? The effect of Brexit on the arbitration of EU competition laws in the UK' (2017) 38 *European Competition Law Review* 322.

D. *Transitional arrangements*

A practically important question that has not been touched upon systematically above is what will happen with the cases in that span of time period including Exit Day (whether that is on 31 October 2019 or after a transition period), such as notified mergers, notified state aid, pending investigations into antitrust violations, or commitments and merger remedies that have been imposed under EU law for a period lasting beyond Exit Day. How these transition cases are treated will mostly depend on whether the Withdrawal Agreement will be ratified by both parties. If the Withdrawal Agreement comes into force, then Articles 92 *et seq* largely determine the answers to these questions.

If there is no agreement even on these transitional issues, then, in principle the rules on third countries will apply as of Exit Day. Nevertheless, there are difficult questions to be considered, depending on, inter alia, (1) when the conduct took place, (2) whether the European Commission had started an investigation before Exit Day or not, and (3) whether a remedy or commitment had already been imposed or made binding before Exit Day. It is also not clear that the transition would necessarily be seamless or without overlaps: in other words, it may be that the Commission continues to apply its (substantive) law for ongoing investigations, but that the UK competition authorities are no longer constrained (by article 11(6) Regulation 1/2003) from initiating their own investigation. The Guidance provided by the UK Government in the case of a no-deal Brexit reflects the uncertainty for these transitional cases: 'Businesses subject to an ongoing antitrust investigation should take independent legal advice on how to comply with any ongoing investigation by the European Commission and/or the Competition and Markets Authority (or the relevant UK regulator).'[136] Space constraints prevent an elaboration, but the interested reader may refer to the literature on transition cases,[137] and to the (very limited)

---

136 Department for Business, Energy & Industrial Strategy, *Guidance: Merger review and anti-competitive activity if there's no Brexit deal*, published 13.09.2018, <https://www.gov.uk/government/publications/merger-review-and-anti-competitive-activity-if-theres-no-brexit-deal/merger-review-and-anti-competitive-activity-if-theres-no-brexit-deal> (last accessed 20.05.2019); similarly for mergers notified but not yet cleared, *ibid*.

137 BCLWG, n 35, paras 5.1-6.14; Chapter 4 of the House of Lords Committee Report Brexit & Competition, n 19, paras 86–120.

Guidance the CMA has given for the enforcement of antitrust rules and merger rules in the case of a no-deal Brexit.[138]

E. *What if the UK stayed in the EEA?*

Most of the issues discussed above would be attenuated if the UK chose to stay in the EEA. The competition rules of the EU and the EEA are in large part identical or equivalent. The UK could continue to rely in many cases on enforcement by the EU Commission or the EFTA Surveillance Authority. While the CMA would not remain in the ECN, it would be part of the cooperation between European Competition Authorities (ECA), and could attend general policy discussions of the ECN; it could not, however, exchange information for purposes of enforcement. The UK would be bound by the EFTA state aid regime.

F. *Changes from the perspective of the EU*

From the EU's perspective, Brexit will change things only on the margin. Fines calculated under the Fining Guidelines will often be lower because the UK turnover is no longer a factor, unless the UK stays in the EEA; on the other hand, the fines will arguably less often hit the ceiling of the 10% of global annual turnover cap. Similarly, fewer mergers will exceed the turnover thresholds of art. 1 EUMR. In cases in which a restriction of competition affects trade between the United Kingdom and just one EU Member State, the EU antitrust rules will no longer apply. The UK will, as of Exit Day, be extraterritorial from the EU's perspective, and so the principles of extraterritorial enforcement will have to be applied: while jurisdiction to prescribe will usually be unproblematic under the qualified effects test, jurisdiction to enforce will depend on legal assistance from, and cooperation with, the UK. For the reasons discussed in part C.I., it is likely that there will eventually be a competition cooperation agreement between the EU and the UK, regardless of what form Brexit will take. However, it is not

---

138 CMA, *Guidance: Antitrust enforcement if there's* [sic] *no Brexit deal*, published 30.10.2018, <https://www.gov.uk/government/publications/cmas-role-in-antitrus t-if-theres-no-brexit-deal>; CMA, *Guidance: Merger cases if there's* [sic] *no Brexit deal*, published 30.10.2018, <https://www.gov.uk/government/publications/cmas-role-in-mergers-if-theres-no-brexit-deal>.

impossible that the UK will, conversely, invoke its blocking statute to obstruct investigations, sanctions or damages awards in the future, especially because the UK has a traditional aversion to extraterritorial enforcement on the basis of the effects test.[139] National blocking statutes have occasionally been invoked even between EU Member States (a practice that is, in my view, contrary to EU law).[140] Once the UK is a third country, it may be more likely to make use of its blocking statute vis-à-vis the EU or its Member States.

G. Conclusion

In terms of substantive competition law, Brexit will not change much even in the case of a 'hard Brexit', but the introduction of an effective state aid regime will be a difficult task. The greatest challenges, however, will be the resource implications for the competition authorities in the UK, and the international cooperation with the EU, the EU Member States and with third countries. Over time, competition cooperation agreements will undoubtedly be concluded, and it seems likely that the cooperation agreement with the EU will include the exchange of confidential information; it will, however, inevitably fall far short of the current cooperation in the ECN. The UK will become a less attractive venue for private enforcement; how much less attractive depends on, among other things, into what judicial cooperation agreements the UK will enter with the EEA, and to what extent Commission decisions will be considered binding in follow-on actions.

Life could be much easier if the UK stayed in the EEA, but politically a lot would have to happen until the UK Government is ready for this approach. There is not a lot of time left until Exit Day. But then, a week is a long time in politics, as the turbulent developments in the UK since the Referendum have shown.

---

139 Protection of Trading Interests Act 1980 c. 11.
140 *National Grid v ABB & others* [2011] EWHC 1717 (Ch) (describing Areva's and Alstom's refusal of disclosure on the basis of the French blocking statute).

Bibliography

Books and chapters

Kenneth A Armstrong, *Brexit Time: Leaving the EU — Why, How and When?* (Cambridge University Press, Cambridge, 2017)

Damien Geradin & Laurie-Anne Grelier, 'Cartel damages claims in the European Union: Have we only seen the tip of the iceberg?' in Nicolas Charbit & Elisa Ramundo (eds) *William E. Kovacic – An Antitrust Tribute: Liber Amicorum Vol. II* (Institute of Competition Law, New York, 2014) 257

Barry Rodger, 'The Empirical Data Part I' in Barry Rodger (ed), *Competition Law, Comparative Private Enforcement, and Collective Redress across the EU* (Wolters Kluwer, Alphen aan den Rijn, 2014) 95

Articles, Reports and Working Papers

Lord Acton (John Emerich Edward Dalberg, first Baron Acton), 'Democracy in Europe; a History. By Sir Thomas Erskine May, K.C.B., D.B.L. In 2 volumes, 1877.' (January 1878) 145 *The Quarterly Review*, Issue 289, 112-142

Arianna Andreangeli, 'The consequences of Brexit for competition litigation: an end to a "success story"?' (2017) 38 *European Competition Law Review* 228

Peter Behrens, *The extraterritorial reach of EU competition law revisited: The "effects doctrine" before the ECJ*, Discussion Paper No. 3/16, Europa-Kolleg Hamburg, Institute for European Integration, Hamburg, <http://hdl.handle.net/10419/148068> (last accessed 20.05.2019)

Gordon Blanke, 'Brexit and private competition law enforcement under the Arbitration Act 1996: taking stock: Part 2' [2017] *Global Competition Law Review* 1

Brexit Competition Law Working Group, *Conclusions and Recommendations* (July 2017), <http://www.bclwg.org/activity/bclwg-conclusions>(last accessed 20.05.2019)

Nicholas Crafts, 'Brexit and state aid' (2017) 33 *Oxford Review of Economic Policy* S105

Marie Demetriou, 'The future is a foreign country: they do things differently there – the impact of Brexit on the enforcement of competition law' (2018) 39 *European Competition Law Review* 99

Andrew Dickinson, 'Back to the future: the UK's EU exit and the conflict of laws' (2016) 12 *Journal of Private International Law* 195

Stefano Fella, 'UK adoption of The EU's external agreements after Brexit', *House of Commons Library Briefing Paper* No. 8370, 24.07.2018, <https://researchbriefings.parliament.uk/ResearchBriefing/Summary/CBP-8370#fullreport> (last accessed 20.05.2019)

Roger Gamble, 'The European embrace of private enforcement: this time with feeling', (2014) 35 *European Competition Law Review* 469

William E Kovacic & David A Hyman, 'Consume or invest: What do/should agency leaders maximize?' (2016) 91 *Washington Law Review* 295

Richard H. Kreindler, Paul Gilbert, et al., 'Impact of Brexit on UK Competition Litigation and Arbitration', (2016) 33 *Journal of International Arbitration* 521

Ioannis Lianos, Denis Mantzari, Florian Wagner-von Papp & Florence Thepot, 'Brexit and Competition Law', *UCL Centre for Law, Economics & Society (CLES) Policy Paper Series 2/2017* (the 'CLES House of Lords submission') <https://ssrn.com/abstract=3077221> (last accessed 20.05.2019), <http://data.parliament.uk/writtenevidence/committeeevidence.svc/evidencedocument/eu-internal-market-subcommittee/brexit-competition/written/70279.html> (last accessed 20.05.2019)

Alistair Lindsay & Alison Berridge, 'Brexit, merger control and potential reforms' (2017) 38 *European Competition Law Review* 435

David Mwoni Ndolo & Margaret Liu, 'Is this the end? The effect of Brexit on the arbitration of EU competition laws in the UK' (2017) 38 *European Competition Law Review* 322

Albert Sanchez-Graells, 'Written Evidence to the House of Commons Transport Select Committee in relation to its inquiry "Freight and Brexit"', submitted 02.01.2019, <http://www.bristol.ac.uk/media-library/sites/law/documents/Written%20Evidence%20to%20the%20House%20of%20Commons%20Transport%20-Committee%20 (Jan%202019).pdf> (last accessed 20.05.2019)

John Vickers, 'Consequences of Brexit for competition law and policy' (2017) 33 *Oxford Review of Economic Policy* S70

Florian Wagner-von Papp, 'Competition Law in EU Free Trade and Cooperation Agreements (and What the UK Can Expect After Brexit)' (2017) 8 *European Yearbook of International Economic Law* 301

Richard Whish, 'Brexit and EU competition policy' (2016) 7 *Journal of European Competition Policy & Practice* 297

Wouter PJ Wils, 'Ten years Regulation 1/2003 — a retrospective' (2013) 4 *Journal of European Competition Law & Practice* 293

Official documents, guidance, press releases

Commission, DG Competition, Working Paper on State Aid and Tax Rulings, Background to the High Level Forum on State Aid of 03.06.2016, <http://ec.europa.eu/competition/state_aid/legislation/working_paper_tax_rulings.pdf> (last accessed 20.05.2019)

Commission, 'EU-Switzerland: State aid decision on company tax regimes', Press Release IP/07/176 of 13.02.2007

Competition and Markets Authority (CMA), Written Evidence to the House of Lords EU Internal Markets Sub-Committee Inquiry of the Impact of Brexit on Competition and State Aid (CMP0002), 02.10.2017,<http://data.parliament.uk/writtenevidence/committeeevidence.svc/evidencedocument/eu-internal-market-subcommittee/brexit-competition/written/69571.html≥ (last accessed 20.05.2019)

Competition and Markets Authority (CMA), Guidance: Antitrust enforcement if there's [sic] no Brexit deal, published 30.10.2018, <https://www.gov.uk/government/publications/cmas-role-in-antitrust-if-theres-no-brexit-deal>;

Competition and Markets Authority (CMA), Guidance: Merger cases if there's [sic] no Brexit deal, published 30.10.2018, <https://www.gov.uk/government/publications/cmas-role-in-mergers-if-theres-no-brexit-deal>

Department for Business, Energy & Industrial Strategy, *Government Response to the House of Lords Committee Report Brexit and Competition*, letter to Lord Whitty dated 29.03.2018 (The 'Government Response to the House of Lords Committee Report Brexit and Competition'), <https://www.parliament.uk/documents/lords-committees/eu-internal-market-subcommittee/brexit-competition/290318-Government-Response-to-HoL-EU-Internal-Market-Sub-Committee-competition.pdf≥ (last accessed 20.05.2019)

Department for Business, Energy & Industrial Strategy, *Guidance: Merger review and anti-competitive activity if there's no Brexit deal*, published 13.09.2018, <https://www.gov.uk/government/publications/merger-review-and-anti-competitive-activity-if-theres-no-brexit-deal/merger-review-and-anti-competitive-activity-if-theres-no-brexit-deal> (last accessed 20.05.2019)

Department for Business, Energy & Industrial Strategy, *Guidance: State Aid if there's [sic] no Brexit deal*, published 23.08.2018, <https://www.gov.uk/government/publications/state-aid-if-theres-no-brexit-deal/state-aid-if-theres-no-brexit-deal> (last accessed 20.05.2019).

European Commission, *Revised Notice to stakeholders – withdrawal of the United Kingdom and EU rules in the field of civil justice and private international law*, 18.01.2019, <https://ec.europa.eu/info/sites/info/files/notice_to_stakeholders_brexit_civil_justice_rev 1_final.pdf> (last accessed 20.05.2019)

European Council, *Guidelines following the United Kingdom's notification under Article 50 TEU*, 29.04.2017, EUCO XT 20004/17, <http://www.consilium.europa.eu/media/21763/29-euco-art50-guidelinesen.pdf≥ (last accessed 20.05.2019)

European Council, *(Art 50) Guidelines on the framework for the future EU-UK relationship*, 23.03.2018, EUCO XT 20001/18, <http://www.consilium.europa.eu/media/33458/23-euco-art50-guidelines.pdf≥ (last accessed 20.05.2019)

European Parliament resolution of 14.03.2018 on the framework of the future EU-UK relationship (2018/2573(RSP)), P8_TA (2018) 0069, <http://www.europarl.europa.eu/sides/getDoc.do?type=TA&language=EN&reference=P8-TA-2018-0069> (last accessed 20.05.2019)

The Future Relationship Between the United Kingdom and the European Union, presented to Parliament by the Prime Minister by Command of Her Majesty, Cm 9593 (July 2018) (the 'Future Relationship White Paper'), <https://assets.publishing.service.gov.uk/government/uploads/system/uploads/attachment_data/file/725288/The_future_relationship_between_the_United_Kingdom_and_the_European_Union.pdf≥ (last accessed 20.05.2019)

House of Commons International Trade Committee, *Continuing application of EU trade agreements after Brexit*, HC 520, 07.03.2018, <https://publications.parliament.uk/pa/cm201719/cmselect/cmintrade/520/520.pdf>____(last accessed 20.05.2019)

House of Lords – European Union Committee *Brexit: competition and state aid*, 12th Report of Session 2017-19, HL Paper 67 (02.02.2018) (the 'House of Lords Committee Report Brexit & Competition'), <https://publications.parliament.uk/pa/ld201719/ldselect/ldeucom/67/67.pdf> (last accessed 20.05.2019)

Legislating for the Withdrawal Agreement between the United Kingdom and the European Union, presented to Parliament by the Secretary of State for Exiting the European Union by Command of Her Majesty, Cm 9674 (July 2018) (the 'Withdrawal WP'), <https://assets.publishing.service.gov.uk/government/uploads/system/uploads/attachment_data/file/728757/6.4737_Cm9674_Legislating_for_the_withdrawl_agreement_FINAL_230718_v 3a_WEB_PM.pdf≥ (last accessed 20.05.2019)

National Audit Office, *The UK competition regime*, HC 737, Session 2015–16, 05.02.2016, <https://www.nao.org.uk/wp-content/uploads/2016/02/The-UK-Competition-regime.pdf>(last accessed 20.05.2019)

National Audit Office, *Report by the Comptroller and Auditor General, Exiting the EU: Consumer protection, competition and state aid*, HC 1384, Session 2017-19, 06.07.2018, para 3.15, available at: <https://www.nao.org.uk/report/exiting-the-eu-consumer-protection-competition-and-state-aid/> (last accessed 20.05.2019) (cited as 'NAO, Exiting the EU')

Withdrawal Agreement negotiated between the EU and the UK and the Political declaration setting out the framework for the future relationship between the European Union and the United Kingdom, as agreed at negotiators' level and agreed in principle at political level of 22 November 2018 (XT 21095/18), and as endorsed by the European Council on 25 November 2018 (EUCO XT 20015/18)

Speeches

Michael Grenfell, 'A View from the CMA', Speech at the Advanced Competition Law Conference, 16.05.2018, part 3, <https://www.gov.uk/government/speeches/a-view-from-the-cma-brexit-and-beyond> (last accessed 20.05.2019)

Prime Minister Theresa May's speech on our future economic partnership with the European Union (02.03.2018) (the 'Mansion House Speech'), <https://www.gov.uk/government/speeches/pm-speech-on-our-future-economic-partnership-with-the-european-union> (last accessed 20.05.2019)

Prime Minister May's speech at the Conservative Party Conference 2018 on 03.10.2018, transcript available at <https://www.telegraph.co.uk/politics/2018/10/03/theresa-mays-conservative-party-conference-speech-full-transcript/> (last accessed 20.05.2019).

President Donald Tusk, Remarks after the Salzburg informal summit 519/18, <https://www.consilium.europa.eu/en/press/press-releases/2018/09/20/remarks-by-president-donald-tusk-after-the-salzburg-informal-summit/> (last accessed 20.05.2019).

Newspaper and online articles

Alex Barker, 'Britain faces Brexit dilemma over ties with rest of the world', *Financial Times*, 19.12.2017

Catherine Belton, 'UK's competition watchdog sharpens its teeth ahead of Brexit', *Financial Times*, 03.01.2017

James Blitz, 'Britain's passport blues', *Financial Times*, 22.03.2018

James Blitz, Jim Pickard and George Parker, 'UK fails to close global trade deals ahead of Brexit deadline', *Financial Times*, 17.01.2019, <https://on.ft.com/2TSEzRG> (last accessed 20.05.2019)

Jim Brunsden, 'UK letter to EU reveals slow progress on global deals pre-Brexit', *Financial Times*, 30.01.2019, <https://on.ft.com/2CRYklO>

FT View, 'Sling the Singapore model out of the Brexit debate', *Financial Times*, 31.07.2017, <https://www.ft.com/content/08726b32-75f2-11e7-a3e8-60495fe6-ca71> (last accessed 20.05.2019)

Boris Johnson, 'My vision for a bold, thriving Britain enabled by Brexit', The Daily Telegraph, 15.09.2017, <https://www.telegraph.co.uk/politics/2017/09/15/boris-johnson-vision-bold-thriving-britain-enabled-brexit/> (last accessed 20.05.2019)

Mance, 'Liam Fox explains failure to replicate EU trade deals', Financial Times, 20.01.2019, <https://on.ft.com/2sF2wAp> (last accessed 20.05.2019)

Paul McClean, 'After Brexit: the UK will need to renegotiate at least 759 treaties', *Financial Times*, 30.05.2017

N.A., 'Hammond threatens EU with aggressive tax changes after Brexit', Guardian, 15.01.2017, <https://www.theguardian.com/politics/2017/jan/15/philip-hammond-suggests-uk-outside-single-market-could-become-tax-haven> (last accessed 20.05.2019)

N.A., 'Mr Hogg's way to end the tyranny of Whitehall', *The Times*, 12.10.1968, 10

George Peretz, 'Corbyn on state aid: fact-checking', politics.co.uk, 27.02.2018, http://www.politics.co.uk/comment-analysis/2018/02/27/corbyn-on-state-aid-fact-checked(last accessed 20.05.2019)

Naomi Rovnick and James Blitz, 'Ferry group with no ships jettisons takeaway T&Cs', *Financial Times*, 03.01.2019, <https://on.ft.com/2R4TkE6> (last accessed 20.05.2019)

UK Bills and Legislation

Competition Act 1998, c. 41

Competition (Amendments etc.) (EU Exit) Regulations 2019, Statutory Instruments 2019 Nr. 93

Draft State Aid (EU Exit) Regulations 2019, <http://www.legislation.gov.uk/ukdsi/2019/9780111178768/pdfs/ukdsi_9780111178768_en.pdf>

European Union (Withdrawal) Act 2018, c. 16, with Explanatory Notes, <http://www.legislation.gov.uk/ukpga/2018/16/pdfs/ukpgaen_20180016_en.pdf> (last accessed 20.05.2019)

Protection of Trading Interests Act 1980 c. 11

Taxation (Cross-border Trade) Act 2018 c. 22 (previously: HC Bill 128, HL Bill 125) https://services.parliament.uk/Bills/2017-19/taxationcrossbordertrade.html (last accessed 20.05.2019)

EU Legislation, Agreements and Notices

Agreement between the European Economic Community and the Swiss Confederation [1972] Official Journal L 300/189

Agreement between the European Union and the Swiss Confederation concerning cooperation on the application of their competition laws, [2014] Official Journal L 347/3

Association Agreement between the European Union and its Member States, of the one part, and Ukraine, of the other part, [2014] Official Journal L 161/3

1968 Brussels Convention on jurisdiction and the enforcement of judgments in civil and commercial matters, [1972] Official Journal L 299/32

Commission Notice on cooperation within the Network of Competition Authorities (the 'Network Notice'), [2004] Official Journal C 101/43

Commission Notice on the co-operation between the Commission and the courts of the EU Member States in the application of Articles 81 and 82 EC, [2004] Official Journal C 101/54

Comprehensive Economic and Trade Agreement (CETA) between Canada, of the one part, and the European Union and its Member States, of the other part [2017] Official Journal L 11/23

Council Regulation (EC) No 1/2003 of 16.12.2002 on the implementation of the rules on competition laid down in Articles 81 and 82 of the Treaty, [2003] Official Journal L 1/1

Cases

Flynn Pharma Ltd and Flynn Pharma (Holdings) Ltd v CMA and Pfizer Inc and Pfizer Ltd v CMA [2018] CAT 11

National Grid v ABB & others [2011] EWHC 1717 (Ch)

Judgment of the Court (Grand Chamber) of 06.09.2017, Case C-413/14 P (Intel v Commission) ECLI:EU:C:2017:632

Judgment of the Court of 06.10.1982, Case 283/81 (C.I.L.F.I.T v Ministry of Health) [1982] ECR 3415, ECLI:EU:C:1982:335 [21]

Case T-892/16 (Apple Sales International and Apple Operations Europe v Commission), action brought on 19.12.2016, 2017/C 053/46, [2017] Official Journal of the European Union C 53/37

EU-UK procurement-based trade relations after Brexit: Some thoughts

Dr Albert Sanchez-Graells[1]

ABSTRACT

In this paper, I reflect on the main types of gains derived from the regulation of public procurement in the context of the EU internal market that are at stake post Brexit. Despite the difficulties in identifying and quantifying advantages derived from EU procurement rules, I submit that they can be seen as a major enterprise in (i) dismantling non-tariff barriers to trade in public markets, (ii) fostering administrative cooperation as a trade-facilitation strategy, and (iii) boosting the enforceability of a rules-based system. On this basis, I suggest that a future EU-UK Free Trade Agreement covering public procurement should prioritise collaboration aimed at (i) preventing the reappearance of non-tariff barriers, (ii) fostering continued administrative cooperation, and (iii) retaining the enforceability of the rules of the future EU-UK FTA. I conclude with some thoughts on the peculiar dynamics that can ensue in the negotiation of a future EU-UK FTA.

KEYWORDS

Brexit, Public Procurement, Government Procurement Agreement, GPA, UK, EU, Regulatory Reform, International Trade, Free Trade Agreements, Liberalisation, Convergence, Technical Cooperation.

---

1 Reader in Economic Law at the University of Bristol Law School and former Member of the European Commission Stakeholder Expert Group on Public Procurement (2015/18). Author of the blog howtocrackanut.com. All opinions are of my own and they do not represent those of the institutions to which I am affiliated. This paper offers an updated version of the presentation given at the Joint Conference of EURO-CEFG, MaCCI and the University of Mannheim 'Trade Relations after Brexit: Impetus for the Negotiation Process' held on 25-26 January 2018. I am grateful to participants for lively and thought-provoking discussion. The standard disclaimer applies. Comments welcome: a.sanchez-graells@bristol.ac.uk. Please note that this chapter was last revised on 24 May 2019.

JEL CODES

F13, H57, K23, K42, P45

A. *Introduction*

Since the United Kingdom (UK) served official notice of its intention to leave the European Union (EU) on 29 March 2017 (the 'Brexit notice'),[2] both sides have been engaged in complex negotiations aimed at disentangling the UK from the EU legal order. These negotiations are controlled by the Treaty on European Union (TEU) Article 50, and were initially bound to generate the automatic exit of the UK from the Union two years after the Brexit notice. The protracted domestic political process in the UK has resulted in a long extension to this deadline, which at the time of writing is set to 31 October 2019. Such 'automatic Brexit' would, in the absence of an agreement regulating a future EU-UK relationship,[3] create a cliff edge that could inflict severe and damaging consequences on existing trade relationships, including in public procurement.[4]

Therefore, both the UK and the EU have a clear interest in establishing the parameters of a future trade arrangement that avoids such negative consequences, and this has been driving the negotiations that led tot he adoption of a Draft Withdrawal Agreement. These negotiations were organised

---

2 The notification was given in exercise of the powers created by the *European Union (Notification of Withdrawal) Act 2017*, 2017 c. 9. This followed protracted domestic litigation regarding the 'constitutional requirements' applicable to the notification; see *R (on the application of Miller and another v Secretary of State for Exiting the European Union* [2017] UKSC 5 (24 January 2017). An exploding literature on Brexit provides detailed insights on the background to the UK's EU membership referendum, the potential reasons for the vote to leave the EU, as well as analysis of open questions about the organisation and funding of the political campaigns and other interesting issues. However, the purpose of this paper is to limit the discussion to the field of public procurement and to concentrate on the future EU-UK trade relationship in this area. Therefore, to keep it manageable, I will not include references to more general issues, except where strictly necessary.

3 The consequences in the area of public procurement are clearly spelled out in the brief European Commission Notice to Stakeholders, *Withdrawal of the United Kingdom and EU rules in the field of public procurement*, ec.europa.eu/docsroom/documen ts/27347 (18.01.2018).

4 See UK Parliament House of Commons, European Scrutiny Committee, *Report on Public Procurement*, publications.parliament.uk/pa/cm201719/cmselect/cmeuleg/301 -vii/30108.html (19.12.2017).

in consecutive phases, with phase one dealing with pressing matters linked to the immediate effects of the UK's EU withdrawal,[5] and phase two concentrating on the creation of a transitional period to delay the disconnection until (at least) 31 December 2020.[6] A third phase will have to set the blueprint for a future EU-UK free trade agreement (the 'EU-UK FTA'), which should ideally enter into force on 1 January 2021. Of course, although this does not seem likely at the time of writing—given the uncertainty surrounding the ratification of the Withdrawal Agreement by the UK after repeated negative votes in Parliament—the EU and the UK can still agree on further extensions of the transition period beyond 2020. Any such extensions would delay the entry into force of the future EU-UK FTA. The main purpose of this paper is to offer some thoughts on the priorities that should inform the public procurement chapter of a future EU-UK FTA, regardless of its scheduled entry into force.

Before entering discussion of the future EU-UK FTA, it is worth placing it in the context of the Brexit negotiations in some more detail. During phase two (which has been extended until at least 31 October 2019), the EU and the UK have concentrated on the design of rules applicable to a transition period towards the full effectiveness of the UK's withdrawal from the Union and its loss of the condition of a Member State. The EU had published an early position paper on ongoing procurement procedures in September 2017,[7] which formed the basis for initial discussions during phase two. Public procurement issues were then explicitly addressed in the initial draft transition agreement prepared by the European Commission,[8] triggered further analysis in a position paper by the UK Govern-

---

5 Joint report from the negotiators of the European Union and the United Kingdom Government on progress during phase 1 of negotiations under Article 50 TEU on the United Kingdom's orderly withdrawal from the European Union. TF50 (2017) 19, ec.europa.eu/commission/sites/beta-political/files/joint_report.pdf (08.12.2017).

6 Draft Agreement on the withdrawal of the United Kingdom of Great Britain and Northern Ireland from the European Union and the European Atomic Energy Community highlighting the progress made (coloured version) in the negotiation round with the UK of 16-19 March 2018. TF50 (2018) 35, ec.europa.eu/commissio n/sites/beta-political/files/draft_agreement_coloured.pdf (19.03.2018).

7 Position paper on Ongoing Public Procurement Procedures. TF50 (2017) 12/2, ec.europa.eu/commission/sites/beta-political/files/public_procurement.pdf (20.09.2017).

8 European Commission, Draft Withdrawal Agreement on the withdrawal of the United Kingdom of Great Britain and Northern Ireland from the European Union and the European Atomic Energy Community. TF50 (2018), ec.europa.eu/commiss ion/sites/beta-political/files/draft_withdrawal_agreement.pdf (28.02.2018).

ment,[9] and ultimately featured rather prominently in the draft transition agreement agreed on 19 March 2018[10] and in the final version of the agreement agreed at negotiatiors' level on 14 November2018 (the 'EU-UK DTA').[11] The EU-UK DTA concentrates on ongoing procurement procedures at the time of Brexit and aims for a phased disapplication of EU law to public procurement carried out by the UK authorities after that date, as well as a phased exclusion of UK tenderers from within the pool of beneficiaries of market access under the EU public procurement rules. On the whole, the EU-UK DTA provides a solution based on the assumption that there will be no regulation of trade in procurement between the UK and the EU after 31 December 2020 (or any extension thereof). Thus, it establishes rules for a transition towards completely unregulated procurement. As discussed elsewhere, this could have triggered some complications linked to the repositioning of the EU and the UK within the World Trade Organisation Government Procurement Agreement (WTO GPA),[12] which have now been cleared in principle by the WTO GPA Members' decision to accept the UK's independent membership post-Brexit.[13] In any case, the design oft he EU-UK DTA generates the need to establish a future *transition from the transition* governed by the EU-UK DTA into a future EU-UK FTA, if there is one.[14]

For the purposes of this paper, suffice it to stress that the EU-UK DTA largely manages to preserve the pre-Brexit *status quo*, which allows for the starting point that a future EU-UK FTA could also aim for the same ap-

---

9 HM Government, *Technical Note: Other Separation Issues – Phase 2*, gov.uk/govern ment/uploads/system/uploads/attachment_data/file/685748/Other_Separation_Iss ues_Technical_note_March_2018.pdf.
10 See TITLE VIII – Ongoing Public Procurement and Similar Procedures, Arts. 71-74.
11 European Commission, Draft Agreement on the withdrawal of the United Kingdom of Great Britain and Northern Ireland from the European Union and the European Atomic Energy Community, as agreed at negotiators' level on 14 November 2018. TF50 (2018) 55, ec.europa.eu/commission/sites/beta-political/file s/draft_withdrawal_agreement_0.pdf (24.05.2019). See TITLE VIII – Ongoing Public Procurement and Similar Procedures, Arts. 75-78.
12 Telles/Sanchez-Graells, 'Examining Brexit Through the GPA's Lens: What Next for UK Public Procurement Reform?' (2017) 47(1) Public Contract Law Journal, 1-33.
13 UK Government, Department for International Trade, Press release: WTO agreement secures £1.3 trillion market for British contractors (27 February 2019) gov.uk/government/news/wto-agreement-secures-13-trillion-market-for-british-co ntractors (24.05.2019).
14 Telles/Sanchez-Graells, 'Brexit and Public Procurement: Transitioning into the Void?' (2019) 44(2) European Law Review, 257-279.

proach towards consolidating the gains generated by over 50 years of continued improvement in the regulation of public procurement within the internal market. In this paper, I will reflect on the procurement aspects of a future EU-UK FTA from the perspective of trying to minimise the losses that could ensue from a change of paradigm from the UK's existing membership of the Union towards a bespoke EU-UK FTA. The reader will thus be forgiven for reading this paper as an attempt at ensuring that things change so that everything can stay the same.

The remainder of the paper is organised as follows. Section B provides a succinct account of the achievements to date in the regulation of procurement in the context of the internal market, and thus identifies what gains could potentially be lost in a future EU-UK FTA. Section C then lays out the priorities and challenges in setting up an EU-UK FTA that preserves those gains. Section D concludes by providing some additional reflections on the very peculiar dynamics that can ensue in the negotiation of the future EU-UK FTA.

B. Public procurement regulation in the internal market: what has been gained

Taking stock of the advantages generated by the regulation of public procurement in the context of the EU's internal market is a difficult exercise, for several reasons. First, because of the notorious difficulties in creating a counterfactual scenario to use as a benchmark — *i.e.* should the existing system be compared to a baseline of 'perfectly-regulated' free trade in procurement or rather against a baseline of nationally-closed procurement system? Self-evidently, advantages would be easier to identify in the second setting than in the former, but both are equally unrealistic comparators. Second, due to methodological issues with the estimation of costs and benefits of the existing rules,[15] or even in estimating them by *proxy* by looking at the volume of cross-border trade in procurement.[16] Third, as a result of the incremental approach to the development of EU public procu-

---

15 See *e.g.* Commission Staff Working Paper, *Evaluation Report. Impact and Effectiveness of EU Public Procurement Legislation*, SEC (2011) 853 final; PWC, Ecorys and London Economics, *Public procurement in Europe. Cost and effectiveness*, ukmin.lrv. lt/uploads/ukmin/documents/files/Studija%20d%C4%97l%20kainos%20ir%20efe ktyvumo%20vie%C5%A1uosiuose%20pirkimuose.pdf (March 2011).

16 VVA Consulting, London Economics, JIIP, *Measurement of impact of cross-border penetration in public procurement*, publications.europa.eu/en/publication-detail/-/pub lication/5c148423-39e2-11e7-a08e-01aa75ed71a1/language-en/ (February 2017).

rement law and policy, which tends to be permanently geared towards unlocking *additional gains*,[17] rather than the recognition of the value created by the existing rules. This can be understood in the context of the permanent aspiration towards a further consolidation of the EU's internal market. However, it also tends to create a narrative of imperfection and unfitness, or at least limitation, around EU public procurement rules — which are almost permanently expected to deliver higher volumes of cross-border trade, as well as higher levels of permeation of specific policies.[18] Taking stock of the gains that ensue from those existing rules is also difficult due to the visibility of (perceived) failures of procurement rules and the invisibility of (presumed) successes, which makes the 'ordinary' gains of the existing regulation go largely unnoticed and possibly underappreciated.

That said, in my opinion, the regulation of public procurement in the internal market can be seen as a major enterprise in (i) dismantling non-tariff barriers to trade in public markets, (ii) fostering administrative cooperation as a trade-facilitation strategy, and (iii) boosting the enforceability of a rules-based system. From this perspective, it becomes easier to identify clear advantages derived from the current EU procurement rules, even if their quantification remains elusive or questionable. The purpose of this paper is not to provide a critical assessment of the always perfectible EU mechanisms in these or other areas, but simply to stress that there is significant value in the current rules and enforcement architecture that could be lost if a future EU-UK FTA did not concentrate on specific areas of future collaboration (as discussed below, section C).

I. Dismantling of non-tariff barriers to trade in public markets

The existence of non-tariff barriers to trade in procurement markets is well documented,[19] and their dismantling is the main rationale for the conclusion of procurement chapters in bilateral or multilateral free trade agree-

---

17 See *e.g.* European Commission, *Making Public Procurement work in and for Europe*, COM (2017) 572 final.
18 Most recently, sustainable (i.e. green and social) outcomes. *Cfr* PWC, *Strategic use of public procurement in promoting green, social and innovation policies*, ec.europa.eu/DocsRoom/documents/17261/attachments/1/translations/en/renditions/native (December 2015).
19 *E.g.* OECD, Working Party of the Trade Committee, *Emerging policy issues: taxonomy of measures affecting trade in government procurement processes*, TAD/TC/WP (2016) 10/FINAL.

ments.[20] In the context of the EU,[21] this priority was already established in the 1988 Cecchini Report[22] and it has not lost currency despite intervening developments.[23] The dismantling of non-tariff barriers has largely concentrated on three main issues: (i) the harmonisation of administrative procedures,[24] (ii) the harmonisation of technical norms, and (iii) the mutual recognition of qualifications and experience. Indeed, EU rules have, firstly, ensured a significant degree of convergence in the procedures underpinning public procurement tenders,[25] which reduces the regulatory burden imposed on economic operators willing to compete for public contracts in different Member States, as they are only forced to 'learn one rule book' with relatively minor local adaptations. It also facilitates mutual learning and the exchange of expertise and so-called best practices, which is currently an area of policy concentration for the European Commission.[26] Secondly, EU rules have created a significant number of checks and balances against the use of technical requirements (either directly in the technical

---

20 For a good overview in relation to the WTO GPA, see Anderson/A. C. Müller, 'The Revised WTO Agreement on Government Procurement (GPA): Key Design Features and Significance for Global Trade and Development' (2017) 48 Georgetown Journal of International Law, 949-1008, 956 and ff. See also Mulabdic/Rotunno, 'Trade barriers in public procurement' (2017) working paper, lagv 2017.sciencesconf.org/file/283993.

21 See Carboni/Iossa/Mattera, *Barriers to Public Procurement: A Review and Recent Patterns in the EU* (2017) IEFE Bocconi Working Paper n. 92, ftp.repec.org/opt/ReDIF /RePEc/bcu/papers/iefewp92.pdf.

22 WS Atkins Management Consultants, 'The cost of non-Europe in public sector procurement', in Research on the "Cost of Non-Europe". Basic Findings, Volume 5 Part B (1988).

23 See European Parliament, *The Cost of Non- Europe in the Single Market. 'Cecchini Revisited'. An overview of the potential economic gains from further completion of the European Single Market*, europarl.europa.eu/RegData/etudes/STUD/2014/510981/E PRS_STU%282014%29510981_REV1_EN.pdf (September 2014).For detailed analysis, Europe Economics, *Cost of Non-Europe in the Single Market — vol IV Public Procurement and Concessions*, europarl.europa.eu/EPRS/EPRS_STUDY_536355 _CoNE_Single_Market_IV.pdf (September 2014).

24 Harlow/Rawlings, *Process and Procedure in EU Administration* (2014), 143-169.

25 This has been the case, in particular, since 2004; Arrowsmith, 'The Past and Future Evolution of EC Public Procurement Law: From Framework to Common Code?' (2006) 35(3) Public Contract Law Journal, 337-384.

26 Not without problems, though. See European Commission, *Helping investment through a voluntary ex-ante assessment of the procurement aspects for large infrastructure projects*, COM (2017) 573.

specifications[27] or, indirectly, through *e.g.* the use of labels,[28] test reports, certification and other means of proof of technical conformity,[29] contract award criteria,[30] or contract performance clauses[31]) in a manner that unduly favours or disadvantages certain economic operators – which is now also enshrined as a general principle of EU procurement law.[32] Indeed, EU public procurement law and its interpretation by the Court of Justice of the European Union (CJEU) have been highly supportive not solely of broader efforts of standardisation at EU level,[33] but also of efforts to ban seemingly neutral uses of technical requirements that can create trade barriers.[34] Thirdly, EU public procurement rules also operationalise the principle of non-discrimination in the mutual recognition of qualifications and experience; in the sense that contracting authorities are bound to accept participation in their tenders by economic operators that may not meet local mandatory requirements (provided they meet relevant requirements in their home jurisdiction),[35] and cannot restrict the assessment of relevant experience to the prior execution of contracts with a specific public authority, or even with the public sector of a specific jurisdiction.[36] On the whole, EU procurement rules have significantly reduced non-tariff barriers – and, as discussed below (section B.III), this translates into enforceable rights that tend to boost the effectiveness of these measures.

II. *Administrative cooperation as a trade-facilitation strategy*

Beyond mutual recognition in the sense discussed above, the EU public procurement rules have also pushed for cross-border administrative cooperation as a further tool to facilitate cross-border trade in procurement. A cross-border administrative cooperation of sorts can be identified in the creation of a single focal point for the advertisement of procurement op-

---

27 Directive 2014/24/EU, art. 42, para 2.
28 Directive 2014/24/EU, art. 43.
29 Directive 2014/24/EU, art. 44.
30 Directive 2014/24/EU, art. 67, para 4.
31 Directive 2014/24/EU, art. 70.
32 Directive 2014/24/EU, art. 18, para 1, subpara II.
33 Case C-6/05, 14.06.2007, *Medipac-Kazantzidis*, ECLI:EU:C:2007:337, para 55.
34 Case C-225/98, 26.09.2000, *Commission v France*, ECLI:EU:C:2000:494, para 81.
35 Directive 2014/24/EU, art. 58, para 2.
36 Case T-59/05, 10.09.2008, *Evropaïki Dynamiki v Commission*, ECLI:EU:T:2008:326, para 104.

portunities across the EU in the Tenders Electronic Daily (TED) database,[37] and the Common Procurement Vocabulary (CPV) that underpins its operation.[38] This has created a system of transparency that facilitates cross-border participation in procurement procedures. More clearly, administrative cooperation has concentrated, in particular, in the development of the European Single Procurement Document (ESPD)[39] and the joint database eCertis.[40] These tools aim to support a system of procurement based on self-certification and (partial) electronic verification of documentation bound to reduce the administrative burden imposed on public authorities and economic operators.[41] In addition to this, EU public procurement rules also aim to facilitate the development of common standards in the area of e-procurement[42] and e-invoicing,[43] which can generate additional significant facilitative effects in as much as they harmonise the technical infrastructure underpinning public procurement across the internal market. These may still be early stages of what can be seen as a frustratingly long-winded transition to electronic procurement, but these are also the initial stages of a potential fully integrated digital public procurement market in the EU. Given the difficulties in agreeing standardisation and migration across e-procurement solutions once they are implemented, there seems to be value in ensuring that the commonality of approach and the drive towards standardisation and interoperability of solutions continue to drive efforts in this area.

III. Boosting the enforceability of the rules

A final area worth highlighting concerns the enforceability of the EU public procurement rules, including the general principles of EU procurement law, which comprises both public and private enforcement. Public enforcement of the EU procurement rules, which is subject to the general

---

37 ted.europa.eu/TED/main/HomePage.do.
38 Regulation (EC) No 2195/2002.
39 Directive 2014/24/EU, art. 59. Commission Implementing Regulation (EU) 2016/7.
40 ec.europa.eu/growth/single-market/public-procurement/e-procurement/espd/.
41 For critical discussion, see Telles, 'The European Single Procurement Document' (2017) 1 Procurement Law Journal, 1-21.
42 ec.europa.eu/growth/single-market/public-procurement/e-procurement_en.
43 ec.europa.eu/growth/single-market/public-procurement/e-procurement/e-invoicing_en.

powers of the European Commission as the guardian of the treaties,[44] is however leveraged by the fact that public contracts are usually the conduit for the deployment of EU funds in the beneficiary Member States. This has led to recent initiatives aimed at taking stock of existing administrative capacity at Member State level,[45] as well as the development of tools aimed to support them in the application, oversight and enforcement of EU public procurement law.[46] The relevance of these measures in each of the Member States depends on their internal levels of administrative capacity and strategic decisions on self-organisation. Differently, the promotion of private enforcement of EU public procurement rules offers an arguably more effective mechanism of redress across all jurisdictions,[47] and imposes significant constraints on the way public procurement is conducted in the internal market. The EU rules on procurement remedies are in need of revision to ensure that they continue to support the effectiveness of substantive rules (such as those discussed above, section B.I).[48] However, the CJEU case law is constantly moving in the direction of strengthening the enforceability of procurement rules on the basis of general guarantees linked to the duty of good administration and due process requirements of the Charter of Fundamental Rights of the EU[49] — all of which results in non-negligible mechanisms for the enforcement of trade-facilitating EU public procurement rules.

---

44 Treaty on the Functioning of the European Union (TFEU), arts. 258-260.

45 ec.europa.eu/regional_policy/en/policy/how/improving-investment/public-procur ement/study/.

46 European Commission, *Public procurement guidance for practitioners on the avoidance of the most common errors in projects funded by the European Structural and Investment Funds*, ec.europa.eu/regional_policy/sources/docgener/guides/public_pro curement/2018/guidance_public_procurement_2018_en.pdf (February 2018).

47 However, measuring the effectiveness of the remedies system also raises its own challenges. See *e.g.* European Commission, *Report on the effectiveness of Directive 89/665/EEC and Directive 92/13/EEC, as modified by Directive 2007/66/EC, concerning review procedures in the area of public procurement*, COM(2017) 28 final.

48 Sanchez-Graells, "'If it Ain't Broke, Don't Fix It'? EU Requirements of Administrative Oversight and Judicial Protection for Public Contracts' in Torricelli/Lalliot (eds), *Oversight and Challenges of Public Contracts* (2018), 495-534.

49 Sanchez-Graells, 'Territorial Extension and Case Law of the Court of Justice. Good administration and access to justice in procurement as a case study' (2018) Europe and the World: A Law Review, doi.org/10.14324/111.444.ewlj.2018.04 (24.05.2019).

C. Post-Brexit EU-UK procurement regulation: priorities and challenges in keeping the gains

In view of the gains derived from the construction and consolidation of the EU's internal market for public procurement (above section B), I submit that the priority of a procurement chapter in a future EU-UK FTA should be to preserve them to the maximum possible extent, and to foresee mechanisms to facilitate the generation of additional gains in the future. Mirroring the previous discussion, this section will cover mechanisms aimed at (i) preventing the reappearance of non-tariff barriers to trade in public markets, (ii) fostering continued administrative cooperation as a trade-facilitation strategy, and (iii) retaining the enforceability of the rules of the future EU-UK FTA. Unavoidably, some of those issues are dependent upon the EU's and the UK's future position within the WTO GPA,[50] which will condition the extent to which the content of their future FTA can deviate from current arrangements—in particular in the direction of de-regulation of procurement. However, this section discusses issues on the assumption that they are compatible with the EU's and UK's WTO GPA position because they are included in the context of what could be termed a *GPA plus* agreement that generates no issues of incompatibility with strict WTO GPA obligations.[51]

I. Preventing the re-appearance of non-tariff barriers to trade in public markets

One of the counter-intuitive aspects of discussing a future EU-UK FTA covering procurement concerns the extent to which it will be able to ensure substantive convergence in the regulation of procurement in the EU and

---

50 Telles/Sanchez-Graells, 'Examining Brexit Through the GPA's Lens: What Next for UK Public Procurement Reform?' (2017) 47(1) Public Contract Law Journal, 1-33; Telles/Sanchez-Graells, 'Brexit and Public Procurement: Transitioning into the Void?' (2019) 44(2) European Law Review, 257-279.

51 In that regard, it is important to stress that given the way in which the agreement operates, which does not include a strict most favoured nation obligation (which only exists for developing countries under Article V), the WTO GPA does not oppose more intense bilateral collaboration amongst its signatories. This is clear from the conclusion of recent trade agreements including 'GPA plus' procurement obligations between the EU and Canada, or the EU and Singapore. See EU-Canada Free Trade Agreement, consilium.europa.eu/en/press/press-releases/2016/10/28/eu-canada-trade-agreement/; and EU-Singapore Free Trade Agreement, trade.ec.europa.eu/doclib/press/index.cfm?id=961.

the UK. As is obvious, given the UK's transposition of the 2014 EU public procurement package, the starting point is one of *full harmonisation* and the EU-UK FTA can seemingly only cover two dimensions: (i) ensuring future convergence regarding the regulation of new issues and (ii) limiting regulatory divergence if either of the parties seeks to deviate from the initial fully harmonised standards. This makes the dynamics completely opposite to that of regulatory cooperation and convergence clauses in other FTAs. While in most FTAs regulatory convergence is aspirational and developments in that area tend to generate advantages for both parties, in an EU-UK FTA context, making space for regulatory divergence will tend to create increased costs for relevant parties (most likely, for economic operators) and can result in strict losses of competitiveness of tenderers and efficiency of the procurement function. This is thus something to consider carefully and it would not seem unreasonable to expect a future EU-UK FTA to crystallise the regulatory *status quo* and prevent regulatory divergence except in issues to be regulated afresh — where convergence (and mutual recognition), rather than uniformity may suffice. Or, in other words, it would not be unreasonable for the parties to agree that a future EU-UK FTA requires indefinite continued application of the EU's procurement rules in the UK.

However, this may be a slightly over-simplified view of things. Given the recent major reform of EU public procurement rules through the 2014 package and the scarcity of case law interpreting them that will likely be generated by the end of the transition period initially foreseen in the EU-UK DTA (31 December 2020), what exactly *full initial harmonisation* means may require some further thought. Given the UK's unwillingness to accept a binding obligation to follow the future CJEU case law,[52] and the importance of CJEU case law in shaping public procurement rules and developing new doctrines on the scope of application of the rules,[53] ensuring commonality of the *law in the books*[54] will hardly ensure actual regulatory har-

---

52 See section 6(2) of the *European Union (Withdrawal) Act 2018*, which reads: " *a court or tribunal may have regard to anything done on or after exit day by the European Court, another EU entity or the EU so far as it is relevant to any matter before the court or tribunal.*"

53 Sanchez-Graells/De Koninck, *Shaping EU Public Procurement Law: A Critical Analysis of the CJEU Case Law 2015–2017* (2018).

54 This problem is hardly new. Roscoe Pound, 'Law in Books and Law in Action' (1910) 44 American Law Review,12. For a recent reflection, see Halperin, 'Law in Books and Law in Action: The Problem of Legal Change' (2011) 64 Maine Law Review, 45.

monisation. In that regard, an obligation for the UK to continue following the entirety of the *EU acquis* may be necessary and this may well require continued collaboration between the European Commission and the UK Government in order to ensure a commonality of approach to the reception and application of new developments in the CJEU case law. Finding ways to do so may be difficult, but the need for close collaboration can only be intensified by the recent increased reliance on *soft law* by the European Commission, which has committed to limiting future reforms of EU procurement law and to rather try to maximise the effectiveness of the current rule book through policy interventions.[55] Barring any return to a strategy of developing EU procurement policy and practice through hard law, this approach is bound to result in relevant changes in EU procurement *law in action*, and this is where regulatory convergence may well need to concentrate.

Similar issues around the need to ensure harmonisation, compatibility and mutual recognition arise concerning the use of a common approach to technical standards and specifications. The relevance of neutrality and transparency in the setting of technical specifications in the context of competitive procurement can hardly be overstated.[56] However, it is also clear that this is not an issue of exclusive relevance in the field of public procurement, but rather more generally one of the key issues in ensuring continued 'frictionless trade' due to the importance of standardisation as a mechanism to prevent non-tariff barriers to free trade.[57] Whether a future EU-UK FTA will include significant rules on harmonisation or mutual recognition of technical standards is beyond the scope of this discussion. However, suffice it to stress here that any deviation from the current rules to the effect of allowing for the existence of parallel EU and UK standards can create a significant administrative burden for contracting authorities and tenderers.

---

55 See the European Commission's October 2017 procurement package, europa.eu/r apid/press-release_IP-17-3543_en.htm.

56 For discussion, see Arrowsmith, *The Law of Public and Utilities Procurement. Regulation in the EU and the UK*, vol 1 (3rd Edition, 2014), 648 ff; and Sanchez-Graells, *Public Procurement and the EU Competition Rules*, (2nd Edition, 2015), 327-336.

57 As an indication of the relevance of standardisation for the functioning of the internal market and the threat that Brexit presents, see the recent report by the Swedish standardisation agency SWEDAC, *Brexit and technical regulations for goods*, marknadskontroll.se/wp-content/uploads/2018/02/Brexitrapport-ENG-180201.pdf (01.12.2017).

A final point to mention in relation to the potential reappearance of non-tariff barriers concerns the trade implications of the potential instrumentalization of procurement as a tool of industrial policy, either directly, or as a result of some types of smart procurement strategies (*i.e.* social procurement) with strong elements of local preference. In that regard, the interaction of public procurement and State aid rules is bound to attract significant attention.[58] The current position under EU law is that compliance with EU public procurement rules excludes the existence of State aid,[59] which comes to add to the relevance of ensuring substantive convergence in the regulation of procurement in the UK and the EU post Brexit. This will create a double relationship of interdependence between public procurement and State aid control in any future EU-UK FTA, as it will also have to be coordinated with the potential exclusion of tenderers or tenders that have benefited from State aid in the context of a system to prevent dumping.[60]

II. *Continued administrative cooperation as a trade-facilitation strategy*

As mentioned above (section B.II), one of the areas of particularly intense administrative cooperation concerns the development and continued use of the ESPD and eCertis. The disconnection of the UK from eCertis would affect contracting authorities in the UK and the rest of the EU, as none of them would be able to rely on existing systems and procedures — UK contracting authorities because they would not have access to eCertis and EU authorities because, despite having access to the database, that would not ensure accurate and updated information concerning UK-based tenderers participating in their tender procedures. This would raise the administrative costs of running procurement processes (particularly for UK authorities willing or having to consider tenders from EU economic operators) and potentially disadvantage (and/or discourage) economic operators considering cross-border participation in tenders for public contracts. The importance of a system of self-certification backed up by a common database

---

58 An issue only touched in passing by the House of Lords European Union Committee in its Report on *Brexit: competition and State aid* on the basis of an assumed compliance with EU public procurement rules, publications.parliament.uk/pa/ld2 01719/ldselect/ldeucom/67/67.pdf.

59 European Commission, *Notice on the notion of State aid as referred to in Article 107(1) of the Treaty on the Functioning of the European Union* [2016] OJ C 262/1.

60 *Cfr* Directive 2014/24/EU, art. 69, para 4.

(be it in the current ESPD form, or in a revised manner) is unlikely to diminish in any meaningful way in the future, and a potential opening of eCertis to non-EU States in the context of FTAs[61] or the WTO GPA could only increase it. Therefore, for all its flaws and practical difficulties, continued collaboration in the running and use of eCertis by both the UK and the EU would be beneficial in terms of keeping the costs of red tape associated with procurement as low as possible.

A second important aspect concerns the transparency of procurement opportunities, which goes beyond the relatively simple issue of ensuring on-line publication of contract notices or equivalent future business opportunity notices in a website in a language of common use in international trade (*i.e.* English).[62] Whether the UK will or could have access to the *Official Journal of the European Union* and TED to publish such notices, or the UK's own database (*Contracts Finder*)[63] will remain open access and free to use can be important elements in ensuring continued transparency of procurement opportunities. However, there are more relevant issues of detail that can determine the actual transparency of such notices. The current EU regime is underpinned by the use of the Common Procurement Vocabulary (CPV) that aims to ensure that the procurement opportunities that are publicised can be properly identified by economic operators active in the relevant field. Compliance with the CPV may be far from perfect, but it is actively monitored by the European Commission and economic agents, and lack of compliance can carry relevant legal consequences.[64] Therefore, future collaboration on transparency of procurement opportunities should not only concentrate on the medium for such transparency and other important issues concerning metadata and the facilitation of automated treat-

---

61 On the relevance of eCertis within the context of the EU-Canada FTA (CETA), see *e.g.* Global Affairs Canada, *European Union Government Procurement Guide for Canadian Businesses*, publications.gc.ca/collections/collection_2017/amc-gac/FR5-109-2017-eng.pdf.

62 On the continued relevance of the English language for the operation of the EU, despite the UK withdrawal and the implications this may have for the status of English as an official language of the Union, see 'Britain is leaving the EU, but its language will stay', The Economist, economist.com/news/europe/21721861-despite-jean-claude-junckers-joke-anglophones-should-rest-easy-britain-leaving-eu-its (13.05.2017).

63 gov.uk/contracts-finder.

64 More recently, in the context of the EEA but with references to the relevant CJEU case law, see EFTA Court, Case E-4/17, 21.03.2018, *EFTA Surveillance Authority v Norway (Kristiansand's parking)*, eftacourt.int/uploads/tx_nvcases/4_17_Judgment.pdf.

ment of information, but also include relevant technical aspects ensuring homogeneity of classification and the interconnectedness and interoperability of transparency mechanisms.

Beyond the above, administrative cooperation would also be necessary in the area of technical standardisation,[65] as well as in relation to other mechanisms aimed at reducing red tape in procurement or at facilitating compliance with certain environmental and quality control standards, as well as promoting the use of labels in procurement.[66] Cooperation will be equally relevant in the context of the implementation of current strategic priorities concerning the use of procurement for environmental or social goals, as well as the professionalisation of the procurement task force,[67] or in the development of networks for knowledge exchange *e.g.* in relation to large infrastructure projects.[68] If Brexit were to put a halt to these initiatives, the potential gains derived from ongoing collaboration would likely be lost — at least, largely, to the UK, but would also impoverish the EU given the value of input and expertise coming from the UK. Therefore, seeking ways of maintaining administrative collaboration seems like another area of priority for a future EU-UK FTA covering procurement matters.

Another issue that may deserve careful consideration concerns cross-border cooperation in the context of specific procurement projects, as well as for the cross-border provision of centralised purchasing services or supplies by central purchasing bodies (CPBs).[69] This is a novel area of regulation in the 2014 EU public procurement package that relies on the common regulatory baseline across the EU Member States to allow them to enter into specific arrangements to carry out joint collaborative procurement, either on an *ad hoc* basis or in a more permanent manner. The UK public sector has been a pioneer — in particular in the context of healthcare procure-

---

65 Directive 2014/24/EU, art. 44.

66 Directive 2014/24/EU, art. 43 and art. 62.

67 European Commission, *Recommendation on the professionalisation of public procurement: Building an architecture for the professionalisation of public procurement*, C (2017) 6654 [2017] OJ L 259/28, available at http://eur-lex.europa.eu/legal-content/EN/TXT/?uri=CELEX:32017H1805.

68 European Commission, *Helping investment through a voluntary ex-ante assessment of the procurement aspects for large infrastructure projects*, COM (2017) 573.

69 Directive 2014/24/EU, art. 37 to art. 39. See also Sanchez-Graells, 'Collaborative Cross-Border Procurement in the EU: Future or Utopia?' (2016) 1 Procurement Law Journal, 11-37; and *ibid.*, 'Is Joint Cross-Border Public Procurement Legally Feasible or Simply Commercially Tolerated?: A Critical Assessment of the BBG-SKI JCBPP Feasibility Study' (2017) 12(2) European Procurement & Public Private Partnerships Law Review, 97-111.

ment[70] — so there could be significant potential for cross-border collaboration involving the UK (*e.g.* but not limited to with Ireland) in case regulatory divergence created obstacles in the organisation of collaborative cross-border procurement. Therefore, this is another area of relevance for a future EU-UK FTA covering procurement.

III. Retaining the enforceability of the rules

If the content of the EU-UK DTA[71] is a useful indication of the priorities of the EU and the UK in the regulation of procurement matters, this is another area of high relevance for a future EU-UK FTA covering procurement. However, given that the continued application of the EU remedies rules proved difficult to agree upon, and that the system of remedies has a strong connection with the disputed role of the CJEU post Brexit, this can also constitute a stumbling block for a future agreement. There is not much that can be said at this stage. However, it can be stressed that a WTO GPA-compliant remedies system would not look too different from the existing EU requirements and that any reductions in current procedural guarantees can have detrimental effects for the UK procurement system as a whole.[72] Moreover, it is worth bearing in mind that there is an emerging domestic discussion about the unfitness for purpose of the UK's procurement remedies system and the possible development of a tribunal-based remedy avenue,[73] which could be an important determinant of the UK's position in any future negotiations on this point. Suffice it to stress the relevance of effective remedies in the context of any future EU-UK FTA covering procurement.

---

70 See for example the participation of NHS Commercial Solutions in the HAPPI Project, commercialsolutions-sec.nhs.uk/page.php?pid=1330.

71 See art. 73, which is however only agreed in principle.

72 As previously stressed in Telles/Sanchez-Graells, 'Examining Brexit Through the GPA's Lens: What Next for UK Public Procurement Reform?' (2017) 47(1) Public Contract Law Journal, 29-30.

73 This was the content of an event of the Procurement Lawyers' Association on 17 January 2018, where three potential options were discussed: the creation of a specialised tribunal, the maintenance of the current court-based system, and the restriction of the system to judicial review based on public law grounds only. Participants overwhelmingly favoured the possible creation of a specialised tribunal.

D. Concluding remarks

This paper has stressed some of the areas of clear gains for procurement-related trade that are implicit in the regulation of public procurement in the context of the EU internal market. Self-evidently, my proposal is that a future EU-UK FTA should aim to preserve as many of those gains as possible, while also trying to ensure continued support for cross-border collaboration in areas of common future interest, such as the effective transition to interoperable systems of e-procurement. This should not be too controversial or technically problematic, and there seems to be limited space for either of the parties to oppose to continued cooperation in aspects of mutual benefit. However, this should not lead to the naïve assumption that the conclusion of a procurement chapter in a future EU-UK FTA would be straightforward or without complications.

The UK's rejection of the current role of the CJEU in the interpretation of EU law may become an insurmountable stumbling block for some of the proposals discussed in this paper and, more generally, for any EU-UK FTA based on harmonisation of rules and/or mutual recognition elements in issues such as standardisation, certification and regulation of procurement procedures (in particular, remedies). The EU's position in recent comparable FTAs (such as those with Ukraine, Georgia or Moldova) indicates that this could be a deal breaker for the EU — given the low probability of the CJEU accepting an encroachment on its jurisdiction.

Therefore, the entry into force of a procurement chapter in a future EU-UK FTA seems premised on a prior satisfactory solution of these issues. I would thus not discard a possible extension or chained extensions of the draft transition agreement, in case it enters into force.

Legal protection and legal uniformity: Procedural and institutional rules in European-British trade relations after Brexit

Peter-Christian Müller-Graff

"Legal protection and legal uniformity: Procedural and institutional rules in European-British trade relations after Brexit" – this question, formulated by the organisers of the Mannheim Conference on "Trade Relations after Brexit" is a *vast* topic.[1] Its discussion is all the more challenging since many parts of it have already been addressed in the foregoing contributions. The *justifying* reason for this concluding contribution may be that the discussed parts have not yet been treated in a *cross-sectional systematic* "*rapport de synthèse*"-*analysis* under the general aspects of "legal"– in the sense of *judicial* – protection and legal "uniformity" – in the sense of *common rules*. In the specific context of future trade relations between the European Union (the Union; EU) and the United Kingdom (UK) the issue of judicial protection is in particular relevant, as far as common rules for mutual market access of market participants will be established. Common rules are required for establishing a so called "equal level playing field" without distortions of competition for market actors and without loopholes in the protection of consumers, health and the environment. Judicial protection is required for settling disputes on the interpretation of agreed provisions and for the enforcement of reliable legal standards. A modest attempt of answering the given question can be divided into three parts: first, looking at the scenario of a total lack or severe shortcomings of an agreement on common marketing and competition relevant rules and on judicial protection after Britain 's withdrawal from the Union (A); second pondering on the scenario of establishing common rules for trade relations in a future relationship (B); and third considering the scenario of establishing rules on judicial protection (C).

---

1 Text of the concluding lecture at the Joint Conference of EURO-CEFG, MaCCI and the University of Mannheim on 'Trade Relations after Brexit: Impetus for the Negotiation Process' on 26 January 2018.

A. Scenario of No Agreement on These Topics.

I. Reasons for Specific EU-UK Common Substantive Rules.

The question of common (uniform or at least compatible) marketing and competition relevant rules arise *if* the Union and/or the UK are not satisfied with the existing basic international public legal framework of the WTO (as presented by *Christoph Herrmann*), but see a need for a bilateral free trade agreement after a transitional or interim period, if it ever ends (as cautiously reflected by *Stefaan Van den Bogaert* and *Albert Sanchez-Graells*) – a need that was somewhat scaled down by *Clemens Fuest's* economic estimations. But in the case of a future Free Trade Agreement (FTA) the *main driving factors* for legal alignment (as subtly differentiated in the forms of mutual recognition, equivalence and harmonization by *René Repasi*, exemplified by others and profoundly fanned out for services by *Gavin Barett*) will arise from political, economic and legal continuity reasons.

The main *political* reason is mentioned by par. 49 of the Joint Report of 8 December, 2017 (Joint Report),[2] namely Britain's commitment to its (possibly not fully feasible) guarantee of avoiding a "hard" border on the Irish island, which entails the necessity of uniform mandatory standards of health, safety, consumer protection etc for products imported from Northern Ireland into the Republic of Ireland (as stated by several discussants).

The main *economic* factors concern the interests of enterprises on both sides, namely, in particular, the interest to avoid the necessity to comply with different standards for the marketing of products in different jurisdictions (as knowledgeably outlined by *Friedemann Kainer* and *Elmar Brok*). The reply to *Patrick Minford's* pure free trade recommendation is: Transnational liberalisation requires regulatory cooperation. Zero tariffs don't overcome non-tariff barriers, such as specific marketing requirements for safeguarding health, safety, the consumer, intellectual property etc, but also specific technical standards and restrictions of competition (such as the handling of public procurement and subsidies). This was already the wisdom behind the empowerment of the EEC "for the approximation of such legislative and administrative provisions of the Member States as have direct incidence on the establishment or functioning of the Common Mar-

---

2 Joint report from the negotiators of the European Union and the United Kingdom Government on progress during phase 1 of negotiations under Article 50 TEU on the United Kingdom's orderly withdrawal from the European Union, TF 50 (2017) 19 – Commission to EU 27 (08.12.2017).

ket".[3] The intensity of such regulatory cooperation has to be – as a matter of course – debated in the course of the adoption of every concrete standard. But the necessity of approximation or at least mutual recognition of the relevant different standards as a pre-condition of free trade can not be negated.[4]

Eventually, a certain demand for *legal continuity* appears as a driving force for legal alignment (as substantiated for competition law in the relation between the Union and the UK by *Florian Wagner*).

II. Scenario of No Agreement on Common Substantive Rules

As far as *no agreement* between the EU and the UK is reached on these oftenly very detailed standards as they exist and as they will develop, the UK – with a view to the situation on the Irish island – committed itself in par. 49 Joint Report that it "will maintain full alignment with those rules of the Internal Market and the Customs Union which, now or in the future, support North-South cooperation, the all-island economy and the protection of the 1998 Agreement." However, already two days later, Her Majesty's Brexit Secretary labelled par. 49 of the Joint Report as just "a statement of intent."[5]

Hence, if the total or partial absence of such an agreement occurs, then it seems plausible that the *gravity* of the respective subject relevant territorial markets and the persuasiveness of standards on both sides will urge the legislator of one side into the issue to align with the standards set by the other side. While the quantitative gravity-relation between such markets in the case of the Union and the UK may relatively differ from that of the Union and Switzerland, the experience in the latter relation might nevertheless be of interest. There, the trading interests have created the widely applied Swiss practice of the so called "autonomer Nachvollzug"[6] ("au-

---

3 Former Article 100 EEC-Treaty; today developed into Articles 114 and 115 TFEU.

4 See for the pre-conditions of mutual recognitionMüller-Graff, 'Gegenseitige Anerkennung im Europäischen Unionsrecht', ZVglRWiss 111 (2012), 72.

5 Asthana/O′Carroll, 'David Davis clashes with Ireland over Brexit deal', The Guardian, https://www.theguardian.com/politics/2017/dec/10/david-davis-clashes-with-ireland-over-brexit-deal (10.12.2017).

6 Forstmoser, 'Der autonome Nach-, Mit- und Vorvollzug europäischen Rechts: das Beispiel der Anlagefondsgesetzgebung' in: Forstmoser/von der Crone/R. H. Weber/Zobl (eds.), *Der Einfluss des europäischen Rechts auf die Schweiz*: The Festschrift of Roger Zäch (1999), 523.

tonomous national adaptation to EU-rules"). Well elaborated examples of this technique can be found on the website of the "Schweizerischen Bundeskanzlei".[7] In the British case the EU Withdrawal Bill already demonstrates this method in relation to existing EU law.[8]

III. Lack of Common Rules on Judicial Protection.

In the scenario of the absence of any agreement on *judicial* protection for the market participants after the termination of the jurisdiction of the ECJ for the UK, the situation would be similar to that between the Union and Switzerland. There, legal protection of individuals and enterprises under the manifold bilateral Agreements is in the hand of the rules and the interpreting minds of the respective autonomous jurisdiction of both sides with *no common* judicial authority to overcome discrepancies of interpretation or judicial protection.[9] Hence, the solution of controversial interpretation is left to diplomats as, e.g., in the case of the disputed compatibility of a bail requirement of Basel Land for craftsmen from EU-countries who want to provide plaster work (Kautionspflicht für Gipserarbeiten) with the Agreement on the free movement of persons.[10] As a result, market participants lack legal certainty.

B. Scenario of Establishing Common Rules for Trade Relations

I. Presumptions

The treatment of this scenario depends on several presumptions. Most likely *two presumptions* will prove to be strong. *First* presumption: Even as far as the Union and the UK will seek to establish –in its scope still to be defined – uniform rules, the UK will aim at *avoiding* any *supranational* mechanism

---

7 Schweizerische Bundeskanzlei: Übernahme von EU-Recht: Formale Aspekte, in: https://www.bk.admin.ch/bk/de/home/dokumentation/begleitende-rechtssetzung /uebernahme-von-eu-recht-formale-aspekte.html (Rechtsetzungsmethodik und Redaktion in der Schweiz"; „Typische Übernahmebeispiele").

8 See European Union (Withdrawal) Act 2018: 'Retention of existing EU law', http:/ /www.legislation.gov.uk/ukpga/2018/16/contents/enacted.

9 Tobler/Beglinger, *Brevier zum institutionellen Abkommen Schweiz-EU* (Ausgabe 2018-03.1), 8.

10 OJ EU 2002 L 114/6.

for ensuring legal uniformity. On 17 December 2017 Her Majesty´s Foreign Secretary has uttered "Britain must not become a "vassal state" of the Union by being forced to adopt all its regulations."[11] This view is certainly an understandable position for a former imperial power. However, there is a *second* presumption: The Union will *not be willing* to adapt to British law and, even the less, if an attitude towards the continent similar to a certain language attitude should appear. Hence, in view of the present *gravity realities* of trade in the second decade of the 21st century a possible conundrum is how far the UK might be willing to adapt its law to marketing and competition relevant law of the Union. Under this aspect the adaptation of British law to existing Union law and to future Union law have to be *distinguished*.

II. Uniformity of Existing Law.

Under the mentioned two presumptions alignment to *existing* marketing and competition relevant Union law could best be guaranteed by an agreement that *copies* it for the EU-British relationship into international public law, similar to the Agreement on the European Economic Area between the Union and three of the four EFTA States (EEA-Agreement).[12] This would draw from primary law in particular the basic market freedoms and the competition rules and from secondary law all the provisions which are considered to be trade and competition relevant, similar to the list of secondary law contained in the Annex to the EEA-Agreement, among them also the so called "horizontal provisions relevant for the four freedoms" in Articles 66 to 77 EEA-Agreement which concern social policy, consumer protection, environment, statistics and company law.

If, however – as it is constantly declared by Her Majesty´s Prime Minister[13] (and has been affirmed by *Patrick Minford* in this conference) – the *UK*

---

11 Stewart, 'Boris Johnson breaks ranks with Brexit „vassal state" warning', The Guardian, https://www.theguardian.com/politics/2017/dec/17/boris-johnson-brea ks-ranks-with-brexit-vassal-state-warning (17.12.2017). For the proposals of the British Government see HM Government, The Future Relationship between the United Kingdom and the European Union, presented to Parliament by the Prime Minister by Command of Her Majesty (July 2018).

12 Directive 2014/27/EU, OJ EU 1992 L 1/3.

13 See, e.g., Asthana/Boffey/Perkins, 'Theresa May says Brexit will reduce UK access to single market', The Guardian,https://www.theguardian.com/politics/2018/mar/ 02/theresa-may-says-brexit-will-reduce-uk-access-to-single-market (02.03.2018).

refuses to subscribe to the coherent concept of the internal market, which includes, besides the free movement of goods and capital, as integral part also the free movement of workers, the free establishment of natural persons and the free transnational provision of services,[14] then the Union might be forced by its own normative genetic code and objective, in particular *by Article 1 par. 2 TEU* ("an ever closer union"), to refuse any agreement which jeopardizes the attainment of this substantive and supranational core element of its inner cohesion. Nevertheless, a counter argument in Union law could arise from *Article 8 TEU'*s assignment, that "the Union shall develop a special relationship with neighbouring countries, aiming to establish an area of prosperity and good neighbourliness". The UK is certainly a neighbouring country. However, Article 8 TEU has to be understood to be pursued within the context of respecting the "ever closer union" – principle. This is a so called "fundamental interest" of the Union, which (according to Article 21 TEU) the Union has to safeguard in the cooperation "in all fields of international relations", herein included the common commercial policy (Article 207 par. 1 s. 1 TFEU).[15] It is clear that the Union enjoys a considerable discretionary leeway in defining the way of safeguarding its fundamental interests, but there is an *unalienable core*, an identity, of primary law (a sort of "europäische Verfassungsidentität"), which certainly comprises the basic tasks of the Union as laid down in *Article 3 TEU*,[16] among them prominently the establishment of the internal market (Article 3 par. 2 TEU) as defined in Article 26 par. 2 TFEU and its consequences. While primary law can be amended by the Member States, international Treaties of the Union cannot change it. The reference to the existence of British exceptions and privileges in Union law by *Wolf-Georg Ringe* is not conclusive, since they are rooted in primary law – nor was the reference to crisis measures in point (as rightly emphasized by *Gavin Barett*). Therefore, any envisaged "creative" Agreement with the UK should be brought before the ECJ according to Article 218 par. 11 TFEU for obtaining an opinion as to whether it is compatible with primary law.

Hence, as far as the *radius* of future trade relations between the Union and the UK will be drawn in the negotiations, legal uniformity could, in

---

14 See the definition in Article 26 para.2 TFEU. This concept has been labelled as the "indivisibility" of the internal market; see, e.g. Michel Barnier in his address to the XXVIII Congress of the Fédération Internationale pour le Droit Européen (F.I.D.E.) on 26 May 2018 at Estoril.
15 Explicit reference in Article 205 TFEU to Article 21 TEU.
16 Müller-Graff, in: Frankfurter Kommentar zu EUV, AEUV, GRC (2017), Art. 3 EUV.

principle, be preferably served (in terms of time economy and experience) by using the *proven pattern* of negotiating Accession or Pre-Accession Treaties, Association Agreements, enhanced Free Trade Agreements or New Partnership Agreements of the Union with third States (the labels change). This implies (from the side of the Union) more or less the familiar procedural chapter-technique method[17] – namely *first*, attempting to agree in principle on relevant existing primary and secondary trade relevant market and competition law in a particular subject area as a *starting point* and benchmark in order to enable free trade without distortions of competition, and, *second*, agreeing on those *exemptions* and special rules which are deemed necessary.

III. Uniformity of Future Legislation.

However, such an agreement establishes legal uniformity on the basis of *conventional international law only* at *the time of the conclusion* of the agreement. In view of the *dynamics* of trade, competition and regulatory actions and reactions, the second aspect of legal uniformity concerns the issue of *future* alignment *after* the conclusion of the agreement. In light of the two mentioned presumptions such future legal uniformity could be achieved only by way of later agreements between both sides. If the somewhat bizarre wild growth of consecutive single bilateral agreements as developed between the Union and Switzerland,[18] is to be avoided, the EEA solution[19] could serve as a starting point.

Instead of the necessity of *permanently concluding new agreements* the EEA Agreement contains a *smooth amendment* procedure "in order to guarantee the legal security and homogeneity of the EEA" (Article 102 par. 1 EEA-

---

17 See, e.g., European Commission, European Neighbourhood Policy and Enlargement Negotiations, Chapters of the acquis, https://ec.europa.eu/neighbourhood-e nlargement/policy/conditions-membership/chapters-of-the-acquis_en; European Union Information Centre (EUIC) in Belgrade, Conditions for membership, Negotiation Chapters (2014), https://europa.rs/images/publikacije/07-35_Steps_To ward_EU.pdf.
18 See, e.g., Kaddous, 'Die Zusammenarbeit zwischen der EU und der Schweiz' in Hatje/Müller-Graff (eds.), *Enzyklopädie Europarecht Europäisches Organisations- und Verfassungsrecht* (Vol. 1, 2014), 937ff.
19 See, e.g., Graver, 'Der Europäische Wirtschaftsraum (EWR)' in Hatje/Müller-Graff (eds.), *Enzyklopädie Europarecht Europäisches Organisations- und Verfassungsrecht* (Vol. 1, 2014), 921, 932f.; Fossum/Graver, *Squaring the Circle on Brexit* (2018), 65 et seq.

Agreement) with the purpose "to promote a continuous and balanced strengthening of trade and economic relations between the Contracting Parties with equal conditions of competition, and the respect for the same rules" (Art. 1 EEA- Agreement). To these ends Article 102 EEA-Agreement provides that "the EEA Joint Committee shall take a decision concerning an amendment of an Annex to this Agreement as closely as possible to the adoption by the Community of the corresponding new Community legislation with a view to permitting a simultaneous application of the latter as well as of the Annexes to the Agreement." Although the EFTA States enjoy rights in the shaping of relevant new Union legislation (Articles 99 and 100 EEA-Agreement) and although any of them can block an amendment (Article 102 par. 3 and Art. 93 par. 2 EEA-Agreement), the procedure is obviously *one-sidedly* orientated to the development of Union legislation and its potential parallelism in EEA law. It is *hard to see* that such a device might comfort the British side.[20] *Nevertheless*, it is worthwhile to consider whether a procedure could be provided, which (1.) guarantees the exchange of views in any case, in which new trade relevant legislation is drawn up by either side along the lines of Article 21 of the Comprehensive Economic and Trade Agreement EU-Canada (CETA) with the establishment of a *"Regulatory Cooperation Forum"*(as proposed by *Friedemann Kainer*) and (2.) which enables a Joint Committee to take a unanimous decision of amending the Agreement as closely as possible to the adoption of relevant Union legislation (similar to the EEA).

C. *Scenario for Establishing Rules for Judicial Protection*

I. *Presumptions.*

The treatment of this scenario also depends on presumptions. Here the *main* presumption is again that Britain will aim at *avoiding*, as far as possible, a supranational solution, hence, in particular, the binding jurisdiction of the Court of Justice of the European Union (ECJ) after the transitional period. The wording of *par. 38* of the Joint Report[21] which deals with the

---

20 See OJ EU 2002 L 114/6. As a comparison between the situation of Norway and the UK in this respect see Fossum/Graver, *ibid.*

21 See Joint report from the negotiators of the European Union and the United Kingdom Government on progress during phase 1 of negotiations under Article 50 TEU on the United Kingdom's orderly withdrawal from the European Union, TF 50 (2017) 19 – Commission to EU 27, (08.12.2017).

specific questions of "consistent interpretation" of the citizens rights Part of the projected Withdrawal Agreement underscores already this presumption: first, by calling the ECJ the "ultimate *arbiter* of the interpretation of Union law" in the context of "rights for citizens following on from those established in Union law during the UK's membership of the European Union"; second, by showing the perspective that" UK courts shall therefore have *due regard* to relevant decisions of the CJEU after the specified date" of withdrawal; and third, by envisaging a temporary *question mechanism* of UK courts or tribunals to the ECJ. "Arbiter", "due regard", "question mechanism" – I shall come back to this wording.

A *second* presumption can be drawn (1.) from the Union's increasing *uneasiness* with the lack of a sufficient device for granting market participants judicial protection in issues of market access impediments and for judicially settling disputes on the interpretation in its agreements with Switzerland[22] and (2.) from the new judicial device in the new generation of Association Agreements in the Eastern Partnership (Ukraine, Moldova, Georgia) for certain interpretation issues which involve Union law:[23] namely the presumption that the Union is striving for *reliable judicial dispute settlement mechanisms* and the *involvement of the ECJ* as far as reasonable – and potentially required by the ECJ's jurisprudence. I shall come back to this aspect (see *infra* II 3).

II. Conceivable Models.

Shaping rules for judicial protection leads to the question of *conceivable mechanisms*. Scientists of all disciplines like simple models in order to reduce complexity and to gain clarity and conclusiveness. Legal scholars are no exception. When comparing existing and potential mechanisms of judicial protection of individuals, enterprises and States in the context of transnational law, in particular *four* models can be conceived: an absence model (with full judicial autonomy of both sides), a cooperation model, a common dispute resolution model and an inclusion model.

---

22 As a consequence negotiations between the EU and Switzerland on an institutional framework agreement have been opened; see Tobler/Beglinger, *Brevier zum institutionellen Abkommen Schweiz-EU*, Ausgabe 2018-03.1, 2018, S. 20ff.

23 See Article 322 of the Association Agreement EU-Ukraine (OJ EU 2014 L 161/3); Article 403 of the Association Agreement EU-Moldova (OJ EU 2014 L 260/4); Article 267 of the Association Agreement EU-Georgia (OJ EU 2014 L 261/4).

1. Absence Model (Full Judicial Autonomy of Both Sides).

The first conceivable model can be called an absence model in the sense that the interpretation of ratified provisions and the judicial protection of affected persons is left to the full judicial autonomy of the Parties.

On the Union's side a Withdrawal Agreement and a future Trade Agreement would be an integral part of the Union's legal order with a mezzanine-rank between primary and secondary law (*Haegeman*-jurisprudence).[24] Hence, within the Union both would fall under the full jurisdiction of the ECJ under the available procedures (in particular: annulment procedure[25] and preliminary reference procedure[26]). *Whether* provisions of the Agreements could be *directly applicable* before national courts and whether natural and legal persons could deduce *rights* from them will – in the light of the previous jurisprudence of the ECJ on international treaties of the EU, such as the Turkey-Association[27] and the WTO-Agreements[28] – depend (1.) on the *formulation* of a concrete provision (headwords: clear and unconditional) *and* (2.) on *reciprocity*. Reciprocity would be achieved in the Withdrawal Agreement, if the objective of "reciprocal protection for Union and UK citizens", as envisaged by par. 6 of the Joint Report,[29] will be inserted into it.

Direct applicability will be *underscored*, if par. 35 of the Joint Report becomes part of the Withdrawal Agreement, which states that "the provision in the Agreement should enable citizens to rely directly on their rights set out in the citizens' rights Part of the Agreement and should specify that inconsistent or incompatible rules and provision will be misapplied." Such a provision would substantially be parallel Protocol 35 to the EEA-Agreement and the jurisprudence of the EFTA-Court.[30] It could go further, *if* the direct applicability would flow *directly* from the Agreement and not from the implementation of an obligation into the internal law of the Parties.

---

24 Case 181/73, 30.04.1974, *R.V. Haegeman v Belgian State*, ECLI:EU:C:1974:41.
25 Articles 263 and 264 TFEU.
26 Article 267 TFEU.
27 Case 12/86, 30.09.1987, *Meryem Demirel v Stadt Schwäbisch Gmünd*, ECLI:EU:C:1987:400, para. 14.
28 Case C-149/96, 23.11.1999, *Portugal v. Council of the European Union*, ECLI:EU:C:1999:574 para. 47.
29 Joint report from the negotiators of the European Union and the United Kingdom Government on progress during phase 1 of negotiations under Article 50 TEU on the United Kingdom's orderly withdrawal from the European Union, TF 50 (2017) 19 – Commission to EU 27, (08.12.2017).
30 EFTA Court, Case E-1/94, 16.12.1994, *Restamark*, para. 77.

2. Cooperation Model (Modified Judicial Autonomy).

The second model can be called a cooperation model in the sense that judicial protection is based on the judicial autonomy principle of both sides, but establishes *links* between their judicial systems in order to promote a parallel interpretation. These links can be distinguished according to their legal strength. In view of practiced Treaties´ designs at least five types of links are conceivable.

a. First: A rather *soft* link for supporting and facilitating consistent interpretation is the obligation of *exchanging* relevant judgements between the courts and fostering judicial dialogue on both sides, as it was planned by par. 39 of the Joint Report and has been inserted in Article 163 of the Draft Agreement on the withdrawal of the UK[31] for the citizen rights´ Part of the Withdrawal Agreement. This is practiced within the EEA between the EFTA Court, the ECJ (both the Court and the Tribunal) and the Courts of last instance of the EFTA States and serves the objective "to ensure as uniform an interpretation as possible of this Agreement, in full deference to the independence of courts".[32] It can be supported by establishing an administrative exchange system (as, e.g., in Article 2 and 3 of Protocol 2 to the Lugano Convention) or a common *monitoring* system (as provided for by Article 106 EEA-Agreement[33]) or a common body, as abstractly intended by par. 40 of the Joint Report and inserted in Article 159 of the Draft Agreement on the withdrawal of the UK[34] (Commission and British Authority). The unilateral information on judgments issued after the signing of the Agreement is provided by some of the bilateral Agreements between

---

31 See Draft Agreement on the withdrawal of the United Kingdom of Great Britain and Northern Ireland from the European Union and the European Atomic Energy Community (14 November 2018); see already: Joint report from the negotiators of the European Union and the United Kingdom Government on progress during phase 1 of negotiations under Article 50 TEU on the United Kingdom´s orderly withdrawal from the European Union, TF 50 (2017) 19 – Commission to EU 27, (08.12.2017).
32 Article 106 of the EEA-Agreement.
33 Fredriksen, in: Agreement on the European Economic Area – Commentary (2018), Article 106, notes 1 to 3.
34 See *supra* fn. 33; see already: Joint report from the negotiators of the European Union and the United Kingdom Government on progress during phase 1 of negotiations under Article 50 TEU on the United Kingdom's orderly withdrawal from the European Union, TF 50 (2017) 19 – Commission to EU 27, (08.12.2017).

the Union and Switzerland.[35] This all can be helpful for parallel interpretation, but does not guarantee it, perhaps with the exception of the Schengen Mixed Committee with Norway and Iceland which acts under a guillotine clause, if it fails to settle a dispute within a fixed deadline in the case of a substantial difference in application between the authorities of the Member States concerned and those of Iceland and Norway.[36]

b. Second: *Slightly stronger* worded is the objective "to arrive at as uniform an interpretation as possible" of the agreed provision (as expressed in the Preamble of the Lugano Convention 2007 or in Article 106 of the EEA-Agreement). The EEA-Agreement contains, besides the objective of the uniform interpretation of the Agreement (*internal* homogeneity), the second objective of arriving "at as uniform an interpretation as possible" in view of "the provisions of the Agreement and those provisions of Community legislation which are substantially reproduced in the Agreement"[37] (*external* homogeneity). While this objective "to arrive at as uniform an interpretation as possible" does not seem to have been achieved under the Lugano Convention in relation to Switzerland (as outlined by *Burkhard Hess*[38]), it has worked very well so far in the EEA in both dimensions (according to the assessment of the EFTA Court´s former President *Carl Baudenbacher*[39]), but might encounter specific difficulties in the relation between continental courts and common law courts.[40] It could be made more robust with a restriction for a court or tribunal to deviate from previous interpretations of the ECJ only if justified by mandatory requirements (together with the establishment of a consultative – or even binding – reference procedure of UK courts and tribunals to the ECJ; see *infra*).

---

35 See, e.g., Article 1 para. 2 s. 3 Abkommen der Schweizerischen Eidgenossenschaft und der Europäischen Gemeinschaft über den Luftverkehr v. 21.6.1999.

36 Article 11 of the 'Schengen Association Agreement', OJ EC 1999 L 176/36; similar Article 10 para. 3 of the 'Schengen Association Agreement' with Switzerland, OJ EC 2008 L 53/52.

37 Article 105 para. 1 EEA-Agreement; Fredriksen, in: Agreement on the European Economic Area – Commentary (2018), Article 105, notes 8 to 14; Müller-Graff, in: Agreement on the European Economic Area – Commentary (2018), Article 34 note 5.

38 Hess, *The Unsuitability of the Lugano Convention (2007) to Serve as a Bridge between the UK and the EU after Brexit* (2018),4 et seq.

39 Baudenbacher, 'The Relationship between the EFTA Court and the Court of Justice of the European Union' in Baudenbacher (ed.), *The Handbook of EEA Law* (2016), 179, 192.

40 Hess, The Unsuitability of the Lugano Convention (2007) to Serve as a Bridge between the UK and the EU after Brexit (2018, p. 6 et seq.)

c. Third: A procedural link is established by the device to give both sides the procedural right to *intervene* in relevant cases before a court of the other side, as envisaged by par. 39 of the Joint Report[41] for the UK Government before the ECJ and the Commission before UK courts or tribunals. The Articles 161 and 162 of the Draft Agreement on the withdrawal of the UK state more precisely these possibilities.[42] Good arguments can influence an interpretation, but, as an essential of the rule of law, the judiciary remains independent in its findings.

d. Fourth: *Closer knit* is the device that one Party allows, but does not oblige, its courts *to ask a court of the other Party* for the interpretation of a ratified provision. This is provided for in the EEA for the courts or tribunals of an EFTA State in relation to the ECJ for questions of "interpretation of provisions of the Agreement, which are identical in substance to the provisions of the Treaties establishing the European Communities, as amended or supplemented, or of acts adopted in pursuance thereof"[43]. Such a decision is considered to be binding upon the referring court or tribunal.[44] It has never been used so far.[45] From the *competence side* of primary Union law such a request must be covered by the arbitration power of the ECJ according to Article 272 TFEU (which is the case for the device in the EEA-Agreement).

Concerning the citizens´ rights Part of the potential Withdrawal Agreement, already the mechanism envisaged by par. 38 of the Joint Report[46]

---

41 Joint report from the negotiators of the European Union and the United Kingdom Government on progress during phase 1 of negotiations under Article 50 TEU on the United Kingdom's orderly withdrawal from the European Union, TF 50 (2017) 19 – Commission to EU 27, (08.12.2017).

42 See Draft Agreement on the withdrawal of the United Kingdom of Great Britain and Northern Ireland from the European Union and the European Atomic Energy Community (14 November 2018); see already Commission, Draft Agreement, 19 March 2018 – TF50 (2018) 35 – Commission to EU27.

43 Article 107 EEA Agreement and Article 1 of Protocol 34 to the EEA Agreement; see Fredriksen, in: Agreement on the European Economic Area – Commentary (2018), Article 106, notes 1 to 6.

44 Opinion 1/92, 10.04.1992, *EEA Agreement II*, ECLI:EU:C:1992:189, para. 37; Fredriksen, in: Agreement on the European Economic Area – Commentary (2018), Article 107, note 2.

45 Fredriksen, in: Agreement on the European Economic Area – Commentary (2018), Article 106, note 2.

46 Joint report from the negotiators of the European Union and the United Kingdom Government on progress during phase 1 of negotiations under Article 50 TEU on the United Kingdom's orderly withdrawal from the European Union, TF 50 (2017) 19 – Commission to EU 27, (08.12.2017).

pointed in this direction, but *left open questions*. On the one side it provided – in a certain alliteration to the preliminary reference procedure in Article 267 TFEU – for "enabling UK courts or tribunals to decide, having had due regard to whether relevant case-law exists, to ask the CJEU questions of interpretation of those rights where they consider that a CJEU ruling on the question is necessary for the UK court or tribunal to be able to give judgement in a case before it." "Those rights" were supposed to be those which the Withdrawal Agreement establishes for citizens "following on from those established in Union law during the UK's membership in the … Union." Hence, although "those rights" had to be considered in their legal nature as Agreement rights, they referred in their substance to rights in Union law. Therefore it is conclusive to lay their *interpretation in the hands of the ECJ*. But it remains a strange wording to call the ECJ the "ultimate arbiter of the interpretation of Union law". In relation to Union law the ECJ is not only an arbiter, but the regular ultimate public interpretation authority of the transnational polity. However, in relation to the envisaged *question mechanism*, the ECJ would act on the basis of its arbitration competence (Article 272 TFEU). In view of the *legal force* of its judgements for British courts, par. 38 of the Joint Report spoke only of *"due regard* to relevant decisions of the CJEU" and limited this to decisions "after the specified date". *"Due regard"* is *not identical* with "binding authority" (as documented by *Burkhard Hess* for the Swiss practice of Article 1 of Protocol 2 to the Lugano Convention[47] which reads "that any court applying and interpreting this Convention shall pay due account to the principles laid down by any relevant decision concerning the provision(s) concerned … rendered by the courts of the States bound by this Convention and by the Court of Justice of the European Communities"). *Par. 38* of the Joint Report seemed to echo the "advisory opinion"-procedure on the interpretation of the EEA-Agreement between the courts and tribunals in an EFTA-State and the EFTA Court, which is laid down in Article 34 par. 1 of the Surveillance and Court Agreement between the EFTA States. Now, Article 158 par. 2 of the Draft Agreement on the withdrawal of the UK from the EU[48] provides that the legal effects in the UK of such preliminary rulings "shall be the same as the legal effects of preliminary rulings given pursuant to Article 267 TFEU in the Union and its Member States", hence are bind-

---

47 Hess, *The Unsuitability of the Lugano Convention (2007) to Serve as a Bridge between the UK and the EU after Brexit* (2018), p. 4 et seq.

48 See *supra* fn. 44; see already European Commission, TF50 (2018) 35 – Commission to EU 27 (19.03.2018).

ing on the referring courts or tribunals in the UK. However, the Draft Agreement does not contain an obligation for them to refer such questions to the ECJ, but only a possibility ("may request").

e. Fifth: The strongest linkage in a judiciary cooperation model is the obligation of parallel interpretation. Such a far reaching commitment can be deduced in the EEA-Agreement from its Article 6, which also binds on the courts of the EEA-EFTA-States and the EFTA Court,[49] in conjunction with the principle of loyal cooperation in Article 3 EEA-Agreement. It provides: "Without prejudice to future developments of case law, the provisions of this Agreement, in so far as they are identical in substance to corresponding rules of the (TEEC) and the (TECSC) and to acts adopted in application of these two Treaties, shall, in their implementation and application, be interpreted in conformity with the relevant rulings of the Court of Justice of the European Communities given prior to the date of the signature of this Agreement." This obligation is plausible in the light of the homogeneity objective of the EEA-Agreement. A parallel perspective was opened by par. 38 of the Joint Report[50] which was worded that "the use of Union law concepts in the citizen rights´ Part of the Withdrawal Agreement is to be interpreted in line with the case law of the Court of Justice ... by the specified date." Article 4 par. 3 to 5 of the Draft Agreement on the withdrawal of the UK generalises this orientation in three directions: interpretation and application of the provisions of the Agreement referring to Union law or to concepts or provisions thereof in accordance with the methods and general principles of Union law, implementation and application of such provisions in conformity with the relevant case law of the ECJ handed down before the end of the transition period, due regard of the UK ´s judicial and administrative authorities to relevant case law of the ECJ handed down after the end of the transition period interpretation and application of the Agreement. This device triggers the farer reaching and pivotal political question whether the *conformity-rule* of *Article 6 EEA-Agreement* as the *strongest judiciary cooperation tie* could reasonably serve the objective of uniform interpretation and legal protection in a future EU-UK Trade Agreement, *as far as* its provisions are *identical in substance* to corresponding rules in Union law. It could also help in keeping bridges between

---

49 Wennerås, in: Agreement on the European Economic Area – Commentary (2018), Article 6 note 26.

50 Joint report from the negotiators of the European Union and the United Kingdom Government on progress during phase 1 of negotiations under Article 50 TEU on the United Kingdom´s orderly withdrawal from the European Union, TF 50 (2017) 19 – Commission to EU 27, (08.12.2017).

the European and British legal order – even the more, if dynamically designed for future alignments.

3. Common Dispute Resolution Model.

Agreements on common dispute resolution devices are a standard model in international Treaties, but they usually don't directly serve the legal protection of individuals or enterprises.

a. The ECJ finds, *in principle*, an international agreement of the EU compatible with Union law which provides for an own system of courts "including a court with jurisdiction to settle disputes between the Contracting Parties to the agreement" with binding force on the Union institutions, including the CJEU,[51] inter alia when "the Court of Justice is called upon to rule on the interpretation of the international agreement, in so far as that agreement is an integral part of the Community legal order".[52]

b. *However*, the ECJ sees a *conflict* to its own task of interpretation (today Article 19 TEU) in a case in which an international agreement "takes over an essential part of the rules – including the rules of secondary legislation – which govern economic and trading relations within the Community and which constitute, for the most part, fundamental provisions of the Community legal order".[53] This criterion led to the ECJ's assessment of the incompatibility of the once planned EEA Court with Community law. *Whether* this reasoning applies *only, if and as far* as an objective of securing uniform application and equality of conditions of competition and, hence, of ensuring homogeneity of the interpretation of corresponding rules is intended, is an open question, though, in principle, it might be answered in the affirmative. But a *core of the inner logic* of the *autonomy and coherence of Union law* and the Union appears: The *more* legal uniformity is sought with a third country in trade relations on the basis of internal market and competition relevant Union law provisions, the *less* a common jurisdiction with binding force on the ECJ is compatible with Union law.

c. As a *consequence*, it can be observed that the requirement of the *autonomy of Union law* and the ECJ's task, as emphasized in several opinions of

---

51 Opinion 1/91, ECLI:EU:C:1991:490, para.39; Opinion 2/15, 16.05.2017, *Singapore*, ECLI:EU:C:2017:376, para. 298.
52 Opinion 1/91, ECLI:EU:C:1991:490, para. 39.
53 Opinion 1/91, 14.12.1991, *EEA I*, ECLI:EU:C:1991:490, para.41.

the ECJ,[54] does not seem to be touched by an ancillary dispute settlement system between the Parties on the interpretation and application of substantive provisions of their agreement as envisaged by the *Singapore* – Agreement in form of an *arbitration panel* with the power of adopting rulings binding on the Parties.[55] *But* the more substantive internal EU law is copied or referred to by an international trade agreement of the Union, the more the involvement of the ECJ becomes an issue.

Specific competence issues of Union law are raised in relation to an agreement on an *Investor-State dispute settlement system*. According to the ECJ's opinion, a regime, which provides for removing disputes from the jurisdiction of the courts of the Member States (and, by that, from the preliminary reference procedure of Article 267 TFEU) cannot be established without the Member States' consent.[56] *Pending* before the ECJ are the questions, whether the Investment Court System introduced by Articles 18.8 et seq. of the *CETA* is compatible, in particular, with the exclusive competence of the ECJ to provide the definitive interpretation of Union law, and, furthermore, with the right of access to the courts, with the right to an independent and impartial judiciary and with the general principle of equality and the "practical effect" requirement of Union law.[57] It cannot be excluded that the reasoning of the ECJ on the incompatibility verdict on the Investor-State-dispute settlement system in an intra-EU-bilateral investment Treaty in the *Achmea*-case with the preliminary reference system[58] is transferable to such Treaties between the Union and a third country.

4. The Inclusion Model

The fourth model can be designed as an inclusion model in the sense that a court of one side is entrusted with the binding decision on the interpretation of provisions of the Agreement. Here, two different forms of inclusion can be conceived: an inclusion which requires an *additional* agreement be-

---

54 Opinion 1/91, 14.12.1991, *EEA I*, ECLI:EU:C:1991:490, para.47; Opinion 1/09, 08.03.2011, *Unified patent litigation system*, ECLI:EU:C:2011:123, para. 74; Opinion 2/13, 18.12.2014, *ECHR*, ECLI:EU:C:2014:2454, para 182.
55 Opinion 2/15, 16.05.2017, *Singapore*, ECLI:EU:C:2017:376, para. 276, 303; see also chapter 29 of CETA.
56 Opinion 2/15, 16.05.2017, *Singapore*, ECLI:EU:C:2017:376, para. 292.
57 See: Belgium Request for an Opinion from the European Court of Justice, 8 September 2017.
58 Case C-284/16, 06.03.2018, *Achmea*, ECLI:EU:C:2018:158, para. 58.

tween the Parties in a concrete dispute and the inclusion *without* such an additional agreement.

a. The first form has been inserted in the EEA-Agreement. Article 111 par. 3 of the EEA-Agreement offers the possibility that the Contracting Parties to a dispute on the interpretation of provisions of EEA law "which are identical in substance to corresponding rules" in EU law, "may agree" ("if the dispute has not been settled within three months after it has been brought before the EEA Joint Committee") to request the ECJ "to give a ruling on the interpretation of the relevant rules". This provision does not explicitly address the question of the legal effect of the ruling of the ECJ. However, the procedure would be deprived of its sense if the ruling had no binding effect on the EEA Joint Committee.[59]

b. Even farther goes the inclusion of the ECJ in a dispute resolution system, as it is contained in the new type of an Association Agreement in the Eastern Partnership of the EU for questions of interpretation and application of certain trade and competition related provisions which involve the interpretation of Union law (e.g. Article 322 par. 2 of the EU-Ukraine Association Agreement). There, an arbitration panel, which has to be established on the *unilateral* request of the complaining Party (Article 306 par. 1 of the EU-Ukraine Association Agreement), "the arbitration panel shall not decide the question, but request the Court of Justice to give a ruling on the question" and this ruling "shall be binding on the arbitration panel." This device is also part of the EU-Association Agreements with Moldova and Georgia[60] and discussed in the current negotiations on an institutional framework Agreement EU-Switzerland.[61] In relation to the UK, the Union would be well advised to aim, at least, at generalizing the mentioned "question mechanism" (as conceived by par. 38 Joint Report[62]) for such questions. Such an inclusion model evidently requires the interest of a third country in a particularly intensive connection with the EU, while it

---

59 In the result also ECJ, Opinion 1/92, 10.04.1992, *EEA II*, ECLI:EU:C:1992:189, para.35; Fredriksen, in: Agreement on the European Economic Area – Commentary (2018), Article 111 note 22.

60 See Article 322 of the Association Agreement EU-Ukraine (OJ EU 2014 L 161/3); Article 403 of the Association Agreement EU-Moldova (OJ EU 2014 L 260/4); Article 267 of the Association Agreement EU-Georgia (OJ EU 2014 L 261/4).

61 Tobler/Beglinger, *Brevier zum institutionellen Abkommen Schweiz-EU* (Ausgabe 2018-03.1),27, 30 et seq.

62 Joint report from the negotiators of the European Union and the United Kingdom Government on progress during phase 1 of negotiations under Article 50 TEU on the United Kingdom´s orderly withdrawal from the European Union, TF 50 (2017) 19 – Commission to EU 27, (08.12.2017).

avoids hurdles of Union law for a dispute settlement system as in the case of the failed EEA Court.[63]

D. Conclusion.

As a summarizing impetus for the ongoing negotiations three conclusions may be drawn from this conference: *First*, for the Union, the conclusion that it has to attain the objectives of Article 3 TEU and to realize its mission of Article 1 TEU to promote an ever closer Union (and hence stand firm against seductive songs of pure economic considerations as intoned, e.g., by Her Majesty's former Brexit Secretary in Berlin on 16 November, 2017).[64] In view of the UK's withdrawal from the Union it is no more Britain's task to participate in defining what the Union should be. *Second*, for both sides, the recommendation can be drawn to avoid a wild growth of single bilateral agreements and to avert shortcomings in judiciary protection. And *third*, for both sides, the suggestion can be submitted to keep in mind, as a *fourth scenario*, the potential *return of the UK to the Union* – be it Britain's next generation, be it already the withdrawal from the notification of the withdrawal intention.[65] In the case of a new accession according to Article 49 TEU the granting of special arrangements for the UK in Union law, as it is presently the case, should be reconsidered.

---

63 Opinion 1/91, 14.12.1991, *EEA I*, ECLI:EU:C:1991:490, para.47.

64 Mason/Boffey/Oltermann, 'David Davis warns EU not to put "politics above prosperity" in Brexit talks', The Guardian, https://www.theguardian.com/politics/2017/nov/16/david-davis-warns-eu-not-to-put-politics-above-prosperity-in-brexit-talks (17.11.2017).

65 According to the (disputed) judgment of the ECJ in Case C-621/18, 10.12.2018, *Wightman*, ECLI:EU:C:2018:999 Article 50 TEU allows a Member State "to revoke that notification unilaterally, in an unequivocal and unconditional manner ... after the Member State concerned has taken the revocation decision in accordance with its constitutional requirements." In view of the disruptive potential of this interpretation for the Union's function the Member States should consider to amend Article 50 TEU in the sense of the position of the Council and the Commission as referred in recital 42 of the judgment ("allowing revocation, but only with the unanimous consent of the European Council").